EXPOSITIONAL MODES
AND TEMPORAL ORDERING
IN FICTION

MEIR STERNBERG

EXPOSITIONAL MODES AND TEMPORAL ORDERING IN FICTION

The Johns Hopkins University Press
Baltimore and London

Manufactured in the United States of America

The Johns Hopkins University Press, Baltimore, Maryland 21218
The Johns Hopkins Press Ltd., London

Library of Congress Catalog Card Number 77-18385
ISBN 0-8018-1979-2

Library of Congress Cataloging in Publication data
will be found on the last printed page of this book.

To My Father and My Mother

CONTENTS

ACKNOWLEDGMENTS

The nucleus of this book is my master's thesis (1967) and its basis my doctoral thesis (1971), both submitted to the Hebrew University of Jerusalem. Parts and fragments of the argument have been published over the last ten years in various forms and places, and I wish to thank the editors and publishers involved for their permission to use the material: "The King Through Ironic Eyes: The Narrator's Devices in the Biblical Story of David and Bathsheba and Two Excursuses on the Theory of the Narrative Text" [with Menakhem Perry], *Hasifrut* 1 (1968); "Faulkner's *Light in August* and the Poetics of the Modern Novel," *Hasifrut* 2 (1970); "Delicate Balance in the Story of the Rape of Dinah: Biblical Narrative and the Rhetoric of the Narrative Text," *Hasifrut* 4 (1973); "What Is Exposition? An Essay in Temporal Delimitation," in *The Theory of the Novel: New Essays,* ed. John Halperin (New York: Oxford University Press, 1974); "Retardatory Structure, Narrative Interest, and the Detective Story," *Hasifrut* 5 (1974); "Temporal Ordering, Expositional Distribution, and Three Models of Rhetorical Control in the Narrative Text," *Poetics and Theory of Literature* 1 (1976).

I owe much to the various critics mentioned throughout the book— not least to some whose appearance is less than ideally harmonious or (to certain readers) perhaps even surprising. Since it is nowadays so fashionable to sneer at Aristotle's *Poetics,* or what is hardly better, to disregard it altogether, it becomes almost a duty to say what should have been obvious: to my mind, this is still one of the few perennially seminal and challenging works in the history of critical thought, one which followers of modern "-isms" might do worse than carefully evaluate. It was my grappling with its elliptical dicta, at any rate (though indeed from a viewpoint far from devoutly Aristotelian), that generated my interest in the protean pattern of plot; and this in turn led by a tortuous route to my present concern with one of the most crucial, and least explored, problems of literary art: the relations between the dynamics of the action and the dynamics of presentation. Similarly, but I hope more evidently, in spite of my various disagreements with the work of the Russian Formalists or (to mention a notable work within the English tradition) Wayne Booth's *The Rhetoric of Fiction,* I am gratefully aware that one can sometimes afford to quarrel with them only because so much of their lesson can now be taken for granted.

I recall with special gratitude my long-standing personal debt to two teachers and friends, who have followed and furthered the development

of this study from germinal to terminal form. Professor Dorothea Krook
has given me, among other things, a memorable introduction to Henry
James, the novelist whose crooked corridors (more amply treated elsewhere) have done most to capture and sustain my interest in temporal
structure and the play of hypotheses. Professor H. M. Daleski has closely
read my work draft by draft and sometimes chapter by chapter; his critical acumen and unfailing support, in the face of a recalcitrant subject and
later an equally recalcitrant manuscript, have helped me more than I can
say.

To my colleagues at the Department of Poetics and Comparative
Literature, Tel-Aviv University, I am greatly indebted for many illuminating comments and debates on literature and literary study, often turning
on the controversial issues of text, reader, and reading process. In the late
sixties I particularly benefited from frequent exchanges of ideas with Dr.
Menakhem Perry on matters of textual sequence and narrative technique;
a tangible result of this association is a collaborative early version of the
theory of the literary text as a dynamic system of gaps ("The King Through
Ironic Eyes," 1968), often mentioned in these pages. I should also like to
single out Professor Benjamin Hrushovski, who has long been developing
a notable theory of the literary text; Professor Itamar Even-Zohar, whose
ostensibly different interests more than once proved relevant to mine;
and the late Joseph Haephrati, whose untimely death has deprived literary
studies of an exceptionally gifted reader.

I should like to thank Professor Robert Alter and Professor Malcolm
Bradbury for their interest and encouragement, and Professor Dorrit
Cohn for valuable advice at an important stage. To Tamar Yacobi, in each
of her various roles, I can only take off my hat.

M.S.

EXPOSITIONAL MODES
AND TEMPORAL ORDERING
IN FICTION

CHAPTER ONE

WHAT IS EXPOSITION?
AN ESSAY IN TEMPORAL DELIMITATION

A thing inseparate
Divides more wider than the sky and earth,
And yet the spacious breadth of this division
Admits no orifex for a point as subtle
As Ariachne's broken woof to enter.

Shakespeare, *Troilus and Cressida*

As the whole of anything is never told, the writer of fiction is necessarily confined to presenting his characters in action within the limits of a certain fictive period of time. It is thus unavoidable that he should intersect the lives of his dramatis personae at a given hour. His problem is only to decide which hour it shall be and in what situation they shall be discovered: "There is no more reason why they should not first be discovered lying in a bassinette—having just been deposited for the first time in it— than that the reader should make their acquaintance in despairing middle age, having just been pulled out of a canal."[1] In either case, the reader as a rule has no idea what is going to happen next, nor does he know anything about the characters figuring in the story. Consequently, he is at a loss as to what has driven the poor middle-aged hero to suicide, and must be provided with the necessary information if he is to make anything of the narrative. And even the little cherub has not been born into a vacuum but (as Tristram Shandy complains) into a complex of preexisting circumstances that to some extent determine his future career or ultimate fate.

It is the function of the exposition to introduce the reader into an unfamiliar world, the fictive world of the story, by providing him with the general and specific antecedents indispensable to the understanding of what happens in it. There are some pieces of information, varying in number and nature from one work to another, that the reader cannot do without. He must usually be informed of the time and place of the action; of the nature of the fictive world peculiar to the work or, in other words, of the canons of probability operating in it; of the history, appearance, traits and habitual behavior of the dramatis personae; and of the relations between them.

1

In some instances it may indeed seem (though I shall argue this is not the case) that a certain amount of prior information—about the characters and the fictive world—that is not fully contained in the work itself may be assumed beforehand. In Greek drama, for example, the dramatists, restricted to a well-defined field of material, told and retold myths with which their audience was familiar. Whenever the narrative materials are derived from history, it may likewise seem that the communication of at least part of the expositional information may be dispensed with on the assumption that the author takes for granted his reader's possession of a certain amount of common knowledge. It may then appear that in such cases the author has an easier time of it than most writers of modern times, who, rarely content with re-treating hackneyed material, are accordingly obliged to devote a great deal of space and energy to their expositional duties.

Even a number of modern writers may seem to share the expositional privileges or exemptions of their ancient predecessors. I am referring especially to novelists celebrated for their progressive creation of some private, full-fledged fictive world—Trollope's Barchester, Balzac's nineteenth-century France, or Faulkner's Yoknapatawpha County—repeatedly carrying over not only settings but whole casts of characters and clusters of incidents from one work to another of the same cycle. But the same may be true of any series of works, notably detective stories, in which at least one central character recurs (e.g., Agatha Christie's Hercule Poirot), even though the setting of the fictive world varies.

Many critics work on the implicit (and sometimes even explicit) assumption that in all these cases at least part of the expositional antecedents may indeed by taken as known or obtained by the reader outside the limits of the single work, particularly with reference to different stories of the same cycle, which they regard as a single unit.[2] A close examination of the literary evidence, however, indicates that this assumption is untenable. In their contempt for the fatal futility of Fact, writers usually have no scruples about supplementing, modifying, or even distorting historical evidence or tradition to suit their artistic purposes. Shakespeare is notorious for the free use he made of his sources. In *Julius Caesar,* he drastically both simplifies and complicates the history of the two years between Caesar's triumphant return to Rome and the decisive battle at Philippi. He does not feel the slightest hesitation in telescoping the month between the Lupercalia (February 15) and the Ides of March (March 15) into a single day; nor in collating and freely selecting from different, and even conflicting, traditional conceptions of the main agents in this Roman drama. He turns various historical controversies to artistic account by embodying all the versions in his work and leaving them undecided in order to project the theme of the "conflict of images,"[3] thus reconciling them rhetorically, though not historically. Still more audaciously, a popular historical tradition may be initially embodied in the work only to be demolished or reversed at a later stage, as is the case with the gruesome figure of Richard III in Josephine Tey's *The Daughter of Time.*

When a character or a situation is carried over from one work to another, the writer feels no less free to introduce in them any changes dictated by the distinctive artistic conception of the new work. The Antony of *Julius Caesar,* the libertine turned demagogue, is altogether incompatible with the monumental figure of *Antony and Cleopatra,* and any reader who attempts to reconcile the two will soon find himself in trouble. A totally new expositional presentation of his character is consequently required, and indeed provided, right at the beginning of the later play. Likewise, as Malcolm Cowley himself admits, "as one book leads into another, Faulkner sometimes falls into inconsistencies of detail. . . . Henry Armstid is a likable figure in *As I Lay Dying* and *Light in August;* in *The Hamlet* he is mean and half-demented"; and so on.[4] Trollope's Archdeacon Grantley, on the other hand, is a hard worldling, a bully and something of a hypocrite in *The Warden;* but when he reappears in *Barchester Towers* his weaknesses are softened, and his character, hot-tempered but affectionate, is by no means unattractive. Whether we are to shrug such changes off as "inconsequential errors,"[5] as Cowley does, or, as can easily be established, take them to be deliberate and revealing deviations from previous thematic and structural conceptions,[6] it is evident that they constitute or call for new expositional material. It may even be claimed that in such cases unusually careful expositional measures are required in order to prevent any possible confusions and to effect the factual and normative adjustments that are peculiar to the work.

Moreover, notwithstanding general *ex cathedra* declarations to the contrary, writers as a rule take the necessary precautions to render each of their works as expositionally autonomous as possible, even when the carrying over of characters and fictive world involves no divergence from previous conceptions. In the second chapter of Trollope's *Barchester Towers,* for instance, the narrator informs the reader that "it is hardly necessary that [he] should here give to the public any lengthened biography of Mr. Harding up to the period of the commencement of this tale. The public cannot have forgotten how ill that sensitive gentleman bore the attack that was made on him in the columns of *The Jupiter,* with reference to the income which he received as Warden to Hiram's Hospital, in the city of Barchester. Nor can it yet be forgotten that a lawsuit was instituted against him," and so on. Although Trollope ostensibly professes to assume that Mr. Harding's ordeal, formerly narrated in *The Warden,* must by now be a matter of common knowledge, he in fact cunningly recapitulates the occurrences expositionally relevant to *Bar-*

chester Towers. What was there the core of the action proper is here telescoped into a few passages; and some additional sentences then bring the account up to date and effect the necessary transition to "the commencement of this tale." The same tendency is displayed not only where we have a shift in the focus of interest (as in Trollope) or in narrative technique (as when Huck Finn frees *The Adventures of Huckleberry Finn* from any dependence on Twain's authorially presented *Adventures of Tom Sawyer*) but even in such cases as Robert Graves's *Claudius the God,* a *direct* sequel to his *I, Claudius,* to which it is strongly related by both historic and narrative continuity (the same narrator, Claudius, goes on with his autobiography). Even here Claudius first "reminds" us of his various antecedents, and only then does he proceed to "[pick] up the thread just where [he] dropped it."

Although writers may choose to make use of historical sources or revert again and again to the fictive worlds of their own creation, the works themselves thus reveal the authorial awareness that, in Coleridge's phrase, each work must contain within itself the reason why it is so and not otherwise. Apart from the purely theoretical grounds I mentioned, it is well to remember that novelists are much more realistic people than we sometimes like to think. Trollope, for instance, frankly admits working on the assumption that though *Phineas Finn* (1867) and its sequel, *Phineas Redux* (1873), "are, in fact, but one novel," he "had no right to expect that novel-readers would remember the characters of a story after an interval of six years."[7] Elsewhere he perhaps overstates his case when he claims that he never labored under the illusion that his reader was likely to see such progressively created characters as the Duke of Omnium in the round; their delineation is spread over so wide a canvas that he "cannot expect that any lover of such art should trouble to look at it as a whole," or that his public should retain in memory a series of novels, "each of which will be forgotten by the most zealous reader almost as soon as read."[8]

Furthermore, the cited quotations from Trollope, Twain and Graves imply not only this awareness but also a positive warning to the reader not to drag into a text any associations that are artistically irrelevant to it. In these opening remarks the author seems to caution the reader somewhat as follows: "This is all you need keep in mind for the purposes of the present narrative. If you are possessed of more information than that, all the better, but, in spite of Mr. Harding's recurrence, do not drag the whole conflict to which *The Warden* is devoted into *Barchester Towers* or you will throw the latter novel out of focus." Or, as Percy Lubbock puts it, in any single story by Balzac "such of [the] people as appear by the way, incidentally, must for the time being shed their irrelevant life; if they fail to do so, they disturb the unity of the story and confuse its truth."[9]

In conclusion, these admonitions are perfectly compatible with the dream of such writers to have their work seen as a whole. The limits of a literary unit cannot be fixed *a priori* but are dynamic in that they vary according to the kind of questions the critic poses. When concerned with the description or evaluation of an author's figure in the carpet or his output as a whole, the critic may find it necessary and profitable to trace the evolution of a certain character or situation from work to work, to examine the different traits or aspects selected for intense treatment in each and even the discrepancies between their various presentations. On the other hand, when he is concerned, as I am in the present inquiry, with the problems involved in the analysis of the single work, in all its uniqueness of norms and structure, he cannot but regard all extraneous information about its universe of discourse as external evidence. This evidence may indeed prove useful for the construction of hypotheses about the work or for calling the reader's attention to some of its hidden aspects; and as such it is part of the business of criticism to bring as much as possible of it to bear upon the text. But this evidence is to be regarded as strictly external unless adequately corroborated by internal evidence and thus established as relevant to the particular work. Exposition, therefore, can never be dispensed with with impunity; and the peculiar problems it raises must be confronted and solved by every writer, in every work afresh.

THE LOCATION OF EXPOSITION

So far I have discussed the distinctive function of the exposition. The question arises, however, whether, bearing in mind this function, we can point to any specific part or parts of a narrative work (or any literary text subsuming a narrative sequence) that can be called "the exposition." What is the location of the expositional sections or elements? Is it fixed or variable? And finally, how are the expositional sections or elements to be distinguished from the nonexpositional?

The most detailed and widely accepted theory of exposition is the time-honored view first proposed by Gustav Freytag, whose scheme of dramatic structure includes exposition as an integral part: "The drama possesses . . . a pyramidal structure. It arises from the *introduction* with the entrance of the exciting forces to the *climax,* and falls from there to the *catastrophe.* Between these three parts lie (the parts of) the *rise* and the *fall.*"[10] An important dramatic effect called the exciting moment or force "stands between the introduction and the rise": "the beginning of the excited action (or complication) occurs at a point where, in the soul of the hero, there arises a feeling or volition which becomes the occasion of what follows; or where the counterplay resolves to use its lever to set the hero in motion. . . . In *Julius Caesar* this impelling force is the thought of killing Caesar, which, by the conversation with Cassius, gradually becomes fixed in the soul of Brutus" (pp. 115, 121). Accordingly, in terms of what has come to be called Freytag's pyramid,

the "introduction" or "exposition"—with Freytag, the latter concept is sometimes synonymous with and sometimes subsumed by the former, but their limits are invariably identical[11]—is marked off from the rest of the play by the "exciting force," which "always forms the transition from the introduction to the ascending action" (p. 124).

Freytag's conception of exposition, however, plausible and tidy-looking as it is, seems to me untenable. Its fatal weakness consists not so much in its limited range of applicability as in its internal inconsistency and its failure to stand up to the facts even when tested against works that are constructed "pyramidally." If the function of the exposition is, in Freytag's own words, "to explain the place and time of the action, the nationality and life relations of the hero" (pp. 117–18), it is hardly possible to prescribe or to determine *a priori* that all authors must invariably choose to locate the expositional information within the first act or before the "rising action." And indeed, writers seldom impose on themselves any limitations of this kind. In Ibsen's *Ghosts,* for instance, the exposition is distributed throughout, and new vital facts concerning the past of the agents keep cropping up as late as the last act. But the fallacy can be demonstrated even with reference to the plays. Freytag himself cites in illustration of his theory. In *Julius Caesar,* he maintains, the exciting force "is the thought of killing Caesar, which, by the conversation with Cassius [act 1, scene 2], gradually becomes fixed in the soul of Brutus" (p. 121). In fact, the exposition is not concentrated within the limits of the first act, and only a small part of it precedes the impelling moment. Most of the expositional material is widely distributed: one important aspect of Brutus's expositional "life relations," his relations with his wife Portia, is "explained" only in act 2, scene 1, after Brutus has already assumed the leadership of the conspiracy; Caesar's "life relations" with Calpurnia are dramatically conveyed even later, in act 2, scene 2; while the full disclosure of Antony's relations with Caesar is delayed until his famous soliloquy in act 3, scene 1. These various antecedents ("life relations"), all of them indisputably expositional according to Freytag's definition of the *function* of exposition, turn out to be as indisputably nonexpositional according to his description of its location; and as Freytag's definition of the function of exposition is basically sound, we must conclude that his prescriptive view of its location must be wrong.

In view of its patent weaknesses, it is surprising to discover what a tremendous influence this theory has had on criticism for the last hundred years; one finds it applied time and again not only to plays[12] but to narrative as well. In a fairly recent article, Robin H. Farquhar starts by arguing that Hemingway has patterned his novels upon what is "generally accepted as a schematic model of tragic structure in drama. This is the five-part inverted 'V' which represents the movement from an introduction 'up' through rising action to a climax, and thence 'down' through falling action to a catastrophe, or dénouement." And having applied this scheme to *The Sun Also Rises, A Farewell to Arms, For Whom the Bell Tolls,* and *The Old Man and the Sea,* he concludes that they "all conform to its basic requirements, structural and functional."[13] But Farquhar's account, too, is vitiated by his conception of exposition as invariably preliminary ("The introduction typically provides any necessary exposition and establishes the setting, tone, main plot, and chief characters").[14] In *The Sun Also Rises,* where according to Farquhar the introduction is confined to book 1, the second, middle book not only presents as many major characters as the first (Bill Gorton, Mike Campbell and Pedro Romero) but also conveys previously withheld information about the others—Jake's deep interest in bullfighting, his religious struggles, literary ambitions, etc. And in *The Old Man and the Sea,* which is interspersed almost to the end with reminiscential anecdotes or dreams evoking the old fisherman's past exploits, the distribution of exposition beyond what Farquhar considers the introductory stage is even more conspicuous.

It would be unprofitable, I believe, to go on illustrating the invalidity of this thesis. It applies neither to works, dramatic or narrative, whose general structure is not "dramatic" or "pyramidal" (and to which, indeed, it does not purport to apply), nor to those which plunge *in medias res,* nor even to those in which, though indeed containing some exposition in the first act or chapters, the author temporarily keeps back a certain number of expositional cards. The weakness of Freytag's theory of exposition stems, in fact, from a major flaw in his general model of structure. Freytag purports to describe the structure of the action as a movement in time, in a definite direction and through definite stages—in the temporal order in which the reader or audience learns of the developments of the action. But what he really describes is not the movement of the action but the structure of the conflict. He divorces this from the actual temporal movement of the action, presenting a structure that is viewed by the reader only when he retrospectively looks back on the action and rear-ranges or reassembles it chronologically in his mind. What Freytag and his followers fail to take into account is that the chronological order in which events happen need not necessarily coincide with the order in which they are imparted to the reader. Consequently, the "absolute," chronological order of occurrence (in which exposition is indeed preliminary in point of time) does not necessarily correspond with the actual temporal movement or order of presentation of the same events in an actual work, in which expositional information may even be deferred to the last scene or chap-ter, as it is in Gogol's *Dead Souls* or in the detective story.

In short, as innumerable literary works where the exposition or part of it is either delayed or distributed cannot be fitted into Freytag's Procrustean scheme, his claims about the fixed and static location of ex-position must be rejected. The only acceptable theory of exposition will be one flexible enough to hold good equally for all kinds of structure and to cut across the boundaries of genre.

EXPOSITION, FABULA AND SUJET, STORY AND PLOT

It seems to me possible to define exposition satisfactorily only in terms of fabula, sujet, and scenic norm. The important distinction between fabula and sujet, first proposed by the Russian Formalists,[15] is still amenable to further discrimination and development. A narrative work is composed of myriads of motifs, that is, basic and contextually irreducible narrative units.[16] Examples of such motifs in *The Ambassadors* would be "Strether reached the hotel at Chester," "He found himself facing a lady in the hall," or "Waymarsh made a sudden dash into a shop." The *fabula* of the work is the chronological or chronological-causal sequence into which the reader, progressively and retrospectively, reassembles these motifs; it may thus be viewed as the second-degree "raw material" (postselected and straightforwardly combined narrative) that the artist compositionally "de-forms" and thus re-contextualizes in constructing his work (mainly by way of temporal displacements, manifold linkage, and perspectival manipula-tions). The *sujet,* in contrast, is the actual disposition and articulation of these narrative motifs in the particular finished product, as their order and interrelation, shaping and coloring, was finally decided on by the author. To put it as simply as possible, the *fabula* involves what happens in the work as (re)arranged in the "objective" order of occurrence, while the *sujet* involves what happens in the order, angle, and patterns of presentation actually encountered by the reader.

Suppose an author wishes to compose a narrative which is to consist of three motifs: a_1, a_2, a_3. These motifs, arranged in an order in which a_2 follows a_1 in time and a_3 follows a_2, will form his fabula. He can mold them, however, into any of the six following sujet sequences:

1. a_1, a_2, a_3
2. a_1, a_3, a_2
3. a_2, a_1, a_3
4. a_2, a_3, a_1
5. a_3, a_2, a_1
6. a_3, a_1, a_2

Apart from this—to repair a pronounced bias of the Formalists'—one must also take into account that the fabula is equally amenable to manipulations of point of view, a form of artistic deformation and re-contextualization that frequently coincides with and sometimes even accounts for temporal displacements. The author can postulate an omniscient narrator, or compose an epistolary story, or employ any of the characters as the narrator, or record the action as it passes through the consciousness of any or all of them; in each case the temporal order of the motifs, their combination, significance, weight, and coloring will vary. Henry James used to say that there are five million ways of telling a story. He meant, of course, that out of a given, basically similar fabula, five million sujets can be molded, each with its own temporal structure and narrative strategy and consequently with its own peculiar effect on the reader. James's own Notebooks afford some fascinating examples of strategic deliberation. In his first entry on "The Friends of the Friends," we find him soliloquizing as follows: "There would be various ways of doing it, and it comes to me that the thing might be related by the 3d person, according to my wont when I want something—as I always do want it—intensely objective. . . . Or if I don't have the 3d person narrator, what effect would one get from the impersonal form—what peculiar and characteristic, what compensating, effect *might* one get from it? . . . I might 'impersonally' include the 3d person and his (or her) feelings—tell the thing even so from his, or her, point of view."[17] In *The Ambassadors,* while similarly drawing on the same fundamental aggregate of motifs, James could have postulated Strether as the narrator of his own adventure,[18] or he might have refracted the action through Chad Newsome, or Madame de Vionnet, or Maria Gostrey. And even with Strether as the center of consciousness, James could have started the novel—only it would not have been the same novel —with Strether still in America or already in Paris. In *The Ambassadors* as James actually composed it, the beginning of the fabula is the earliest event in Strether's history that we learn about in the course of the novel (namely, his marriage); while the beginning of the sujet coincides, of course, with the beginning of the first chapter (Strether's arrival at Chester).

Lemon and Reis, in their English translation of Boris Tomashevsky's essay, have given currency to the rendering of the Russian terms *fabula* and *sujet* as "story" and "plot," thus clearly suggesting that the former distinction is identical with that proposed by E. M. Forster in *Aspects of the Novel*. At first glance it may indeed appear that the two pairs of concepts (particularly "story" and "fabula") overlap. The chronological factor, for instance, is conspicuous in Forster's definitions too. "Story" is "a narrative of events arranged in their time sequence—dinner coming after breakfast, Tuesday after Monday, decay after death and so on. Qua story, it can have only one merit: that of making the audience want to know what happens next"; while "plot" is "also a narrative of events, the emphasis falling on causality. 'The king died and then the queen died' is a story. 'The king died and then the queen died of grief,' is a plot."[19] A closer look at Forster's influential account will, however, reveal that these sets of concepts should be sharply distinguished.

The first radical disparity between the pairs of structural principles relates to what may be called their mode of existence. While the sujet is the finished artifact before us, the text as actually molded by the artist, the fabula is essentially both an abstraction and a reconstitution. It is an abstractive pattern in that it does not contain all the elements, groupings and dimensions that make up the sujet—neither such atemporal authorial interpolations as the prefatory chapters in *Tom Jones;* nor the perspectival refractions that distort and ambiguate, or at least weight, the impersonal chronologue; nor such equally omnipresent structural modes as analogy that mainly turn on spatial rather than linear development and integration; nor, finally, the text's concrete verbal art, which not only necessarily embodies and not only shapes and reinforces the large preverbal compositional constructs (e.g., by way of verbal clues, ambiguity, or suprasequential links) but may even be informed by a logic of manipulation "microcosmically" corresponding to theirs. And the fabula is also reconstitutive in that it results from the reader's reconstruction of sujet components according to a preconceived, "natural," logical-chronological frame of reference, the deviations from which in the sujet highlight the modes of presentation chosen by the work. But there is no corresponding difference between story and plot. Both are primarily abstractions—the story is also a reconstitution—denoting different organizing principles that may coexist in isolation from each other in a single work (or sujet). It is precisely in this that Forster's observations on narrative sequences differ from Aristotle's, whom he curiously fails to mention. The distinction between temporally and causally propelled sequences clearly originates in the *Poetics:* "It makes all the difference whether any given event is a case of *propter hoc* or *post hoc.*"[20] But while Aristotle's application of this insight is confined to the differentiation between episodic chronicles and properly artistic wholes, Forster acutely realizes that both story and plot may well coexist as distinct "aspects" of the same work—the more so (one may add) since every causal sequence necessarily subsumes a chronological dimension.

This leads us to another difference in mode of existence. A narrative must necessarily have a story as its compositional backbone; but it can do without a plot or make do with scattered causal elements (as in most picaresque novels). No narrative, on the other hand, can fail to have both a fabula and a sujet of its own.

Second, Forster is not primarily interested in the possibilities of deforming and reforming a given aggregate of motifs through different orders of presentation, not to speak of differently refractive points of view. His chief concern is with two different modes of concatenation or kinds of linkages, distinguishing the temporally additive linkage ("and then?") that characterizes the story from the tighter causal linkage ("why?") peculiar to the plot. In Forster's first two illustrations, cited above, the plot combination remains identical with that of the story in the order and angle of presentation of the motifs: the distinction is made exclusively in terms of mode of linkage. As Forster himself comments on the plot example, "the time sequence is preserved, but the sense of causality overshadows it" (pp. 93-94). And if plot is, like sujet, a high artistic form, this is not because of its "deformity" but because of its superior tightness in comparison with the atavistic principle informing the story.

Let us now proceed to Forster's third, and more complicated, illustrative combination of the two motifs: "'The Queen died, no one knew why, until it was discovered that it was through grief at the death of the king.' This is a plot with a mystery in it. . . . It suspends the time-sequence, it moves as far away from the story as its limitations will allow" (p. 94). In the light of this example it might seem that plot is after all equivalent to sujet, for it may involve "suspensions" of time-sequence too. But this plausible conclusion would be wrong, because according to Forster it is not the deformation of chronology that turns this combination of motifs into a plot but again the *sine qua non* causal linkage, the "logical intellectual aspect" (p. 103). Given the causal concatenation, any complex of motifs is a plot, whether it involves a suspension of the time-sequence or not; but a suspended time-sequence by itself, lacking this linkage, is definitely not a plot, though it may form an important element in some plots. Thus, the sentence "The queen died twenty years after the king had died," though involving an inverted time sequence, would not qualify with Forster as a plot;[21] but on the other hand it is beyond doubt a sujet, an arrangement of motifs in a deformed order. In short, as Forster himself concludes with reference to the death of the queen: "If it is in a story we say 'and then?' If it is in a plot we ask 'why?' That is the fundamental difference between these two aspects of the novel" (p. 94). But that is not the fundamental difference between fabula and sujet. Plot cannot then be equated with sujet in this respect either, for in a plot, given the distinctive causal sequence, everything else (including temporal displacement) is dispensable; whereas in a sujet, given the artistic deformation of the fabula —and the more deformed it is the more of a sujet it is—everything else (including causal sequence) is dispensable.

Nor can story be equated with fabula, though both presuppose an abstraction and a chronological reconstitution of events. For the second defining property of story is its purely additive sequence, while fabula may, and often does, involve causal concatenation. As Tomashevsky explicitly states, "il faut souligner que la fable exige non seulement un indice temporel, mais aussi l'indice de causalité."[22] From this viewpoint, then, fabula is frequently identical not with story but with plot. The differences between the quartet of terms are summarized on page 13.

To conclude, the concepts analyzed are not interchangeable but complementary, and to translate "fabula versus sujet" into "story versus plot" is not only to mislead the reader but to blur a set of very useful theoretical distinctions. For if the properties of each of the four are strictly distinguished, the critic may find their complementary nature of great help. When we wish, for instance, to refer to a narrative work that is actually arranged in an essentially temporal-additive sequence (say, the episodic sequence of some picaresque novels), we may call it a "story-type sujet." But when this sequence does not exist as an actually ordered pattern but has been reconstituted by us during the reading-process—as is often the case with stream-of-consciousness novels—we had better designate it as a "story-type fabula." On the other hand, we should refer to a deformed causal disposition of motifs as a "plot-type sujet" (Aristotle's ideal *mythos,* as devised in *Oedipus Rex,* for example), thus distinguishing it from the "plot-type fabula"—the same aggregate of motifs, reassembled in a chronological-causal sequence and considered from the viewpoint of its amenability to various dynamic dislocations. The adoption of these terms will make for greater precision and intelligibility. In a critical discussion of a "story," for instance, we shall no longer be at a loss to determine (as we sometimes are with Forster) whether the speaker is referring to an actual arrangement of motifs or merely to one aspect of the work, the purely chronological sequence, as abstracted and divorced from the temporal-

	story	fabula	plot	sujet
mode of existence	abstractive and reconstitutive	abstractive and reconstitutive	abstractive	actual (and object of abstraction and reconstitution)
	indispensable	indispensable	dispensable	indispensable
order of presentation	chronological	chronological	chronological or deformed	highly variable, essentially anti-chronological
mode of linkage	additive	additive and/or causal	causal	additive and/or causal and/or spatial and/or other
point of view	irrelevant factor	objective (i.e., impersonal)	irrelevant factor	highly variable, usually different from that of fabula
conclusion no. 1: possible correspondence with other concepts	with fabula	with story and plot, rarely with sujet	with fabula	rarely with fabula
conclusion no. 2: necessary correspondence with other concepts	——	——	——	——

causal sequence. The critic can make his meaning absolutely unambiguous by designating the former as "story-type sujet" and the latter simply as "story."[23] Some of the benefits of having eight terms instead of two or even four will emerge in passing in the course of this study.

Of the two pairs of terms, at any rate, only one is by definition related to the order of presentation of motifs. And it is accordingly in terms of the distinction between fabula and sujet that I can now redefine my main objection to Freytag's theory—its failure to differentiate the absolute dynamics of the causally propelled action from the variable dynamics of the reading-process. To assert that the first act of any play (or the first few chapters of a novel) contains the exposition is to confuse the beginning of the sujet and that of the fabula. The exposition always constitutes the beginning of the fabula, the first part of the chronologically ordered sequence of motifs as reconstructed by the reader; but it is not necessarily located at the beginning of the sujet. The two beginnings coincide and overlap only when the author presents his tale in a straight chronological sequence (as happens, more or less, in the Book of Job, or in the *Laxdaela Saga,* or in James's *Washington Square*). The author, however, may as legitimately choose to plunge *in medias res* or to distribute the expositional material throughout the work; and in these cases, though the exposition is still located at the beginning of the fabula, its position in the order actually devised to present the motifs to the reader radically varies.

REPRESENTED TIME AND REPRESENTATIONAL TIME: THE QUANTITATIVE INDICATOR

So far I have defined exposition as the "beginning" or "first part" of the fabula. This definition, however, though it firmly establishes the expositional *terminus a quo* and though it flexibly covers the innumerable possibilities of combining and ordering a given number of motifs, may still be regarded as seriously incomplete unless we can determine exactly up to what point in the fabula the motifs are expositional. To discover this elusive line of demarcation, we must first consider more of the time values of fiction (time as a dimension, object and indicator of artistic selection as well as of combination and ordering) and the important role they play in guiding the reader's interpretation of the work.

Narrative presents characters in action during a certain fictive period of time. As a rule, however, one finds that the author has not treated the whole of the fictive period in the life of the characters with the same degree of attention. This period falls naturally or is artificially divided into different subperiods, stages, or time-sections. Some of these are rendered at great length, some galloped through or rapidly summarized, some dismissed with a perfunctory sentence or two, while others are even passed over unmentioned. Even within the framework of a single work, therefore, we generally discover different ratios of *represented time* (i.e., the duration of a projected period in the life of the characters) to *representational time* (i.e., the time that it takes the reader, by the clock, to peruse that part of the text projecting this fictive period).[24]

The question of the amount of representational time (manifested, of course, in terms of textual space) to be allotted to each of the different time-sections of which the total span or represented time consists is indeed, in James's words, "always there and always formidable." Most writers have dealt with this central aspect of the general problem of selection in an essentially intuitive fashion. Others, almost obsessed by it, have grappled with it boldly and have left behind them valuable hints as to the principles that guided them in their selective procedure. Fielding, for instance, belongs to the second category:

> We intend in [our work] rather to pursue the method of those writers who profess to disclose the revolutions of countries than to imitate the painful and voluminous historian, who, to preserve the regularity of his series, thinks himself obliged to fill up as much paper with the detail of months and years in which nothing remarkable happened as he employs upon those notable eras when the greatest scenes have been transacted on the human stage. . . .
>
> Now, it is our purpose in the ensuing pages to pursue a contrary method. When any extraordinary scene presents itself (as we trust will often be the case), we shall spare no pains nor paper to open it at large to our reader; but if whole years should pass without producing any-thing worthy his notice, we shall not be afraid of a chasm in our history, but shall hasten on to matters of consequence and leave such periods of time totally unobserved.
>
> These are indeed to be considered as blanks in the grand lottery of time. . . .
>
> My reader, then, is not to be surprised if in the course of this work he shall find some chapters very short, and others altogether as long; some that contain only the time of a single day, and others that com-prise years; in a word, if my history sometimes seems to stand still and sometimes to fly. (*Tom Jones*, bk. 2, chap. 1)

Fielding indeed adheres to this principle in all his novels, taking his cue from the historian tracing the revolutions of countries and from the ingenious traveler, "who always proportions his stay at any place to the beauties, elegancies, and curiosities which it affords," rather than from the painful and voluminous chronicler or the various offspring of wealth and dullness, who jog on "with equal pace through the verdant meadows or over the barren heath" (*Tom Jones*, 11. 9). His contemptuous disdain for keeping even pace with time is most conspicuously flaunted in *Tom Jones*, where sixteen out of the eighteen book-headings contain nothing but information concerning the represented time-span that is to be covered by the book. And the striking disparity in treatment that this procedure involves will be duly appreciated if we compare, for instance, the time-ratio of book 3 with that of book 9. The representational time (in my edition, about thirty pages—say, about an hour of reading time) allotted to each of these books is approximately identical; but since the repre-sented time of the former book (five years) is no less than 3,650 times as long as that of the latter (twelve hours), it is no wonder that in one the action should comparatively seem to fly and in the other to stand still.

The differentiation between what I call representational and represented time dates back, in fact, to the Renaissance and the Neo-Classical age, during which it was exclusively employed as a normative tool for checking the adherence of dramatists to the so-called Aristotelian unity of time. Castelvetro, for example, distinguishes "perceptible time" from "intellectual time";[25] and Dryden denounces the practice of "mak[ing] too great a disproportion betwixt the imaginary time of the play, and the real time of its representation."[26] The concern with time-ratios has, moreover, been revived in modern criticism. Various German scholars distinguish *"erzählte Zeit"* from *"erzählzeit"*;[27] and A. A. Mendilow elaborates a similar distinction between "the chronological duration of the novel" and "the chronological duration of the reading."[28] I believe, however, that these various pairs of terms have not been sufficiently exploited. They have traditionally been used mainly to indicate the ratio between the representational and the represented time of the work *as a whole*— "the time it takes to read a novel" as against "the length of the time covered by the content of the novel"[29]—and also the disparities between different works in this regard, but less often to investigate the variations in time-ratios within a single work. And even when such variations have been pointed out, this has usually been done in order to discuss their implications for the work's tempo or its narrative rhythm. I certainly agree that a comparison of the time-ratios in different works may yield highly significant results, some of which will be referred to below. (The reversion of many modern novelists to the ancient unity of time is, for example, a striking feature of their revolt against their predecessors, and is intimately correlated with their new conception of life and consequently with some of their dominant compositional principles.) It is, however, at least equally important to trace the variations in time-ratio within the limits of a single work as well; for these variations not only lead the reader to various "formal" conclusions (as to tempo) but at the same time play a central role in the interpretation of the text.

The reader is always confronted and frequently baffled by such questions as, Who is the protagonist or center of interest in the work? What is the relative importance of the various characters, incidents and themes? And how do they combine with the center? He is obliged to pose and answer dozens of questions of this sort if he is to construct, or reconstruct, the work's structure and hierarchy of meaning and to compose a fully integrated picture of its art. However, these questions are never settled explicitly and satisfactorily by the text itself, even when overt rhetoric is employed—not even when the author refers to one of the characters as "my hero" or openly calls the reader's attention to the role played by a certain incident or agent. The reader is therefore forced to follow the multifarious implications of the text (its dramatized rhetoric) as to its peculiar principles of selection and combination in order to work out adequate answers. The *quantitative indicator,* revealing the principles of selection operating in the text, forms one of the reader's indispensable guides in the process of interpretation in that it helps him to determine the text's general tendency ("intention") and its particular structure of meaning. For owing to the selectivity of art, there is a logical correlation between the amount of space devoted to an element and the degree of its aesthetic relevance or centrality, so that there is a good prima facie case for inferring the latter from the former.[30]

As the variations in time-ratios form one manifestation of the quantitative indicator, it can be determined that, *mutatis mutandis,* the time-ratio of a narrative time-span or event generally stands in direct proportion to its contextual relevance: one whose representational time approximates its represented time is implied to be more central to the work in question than another in which these two time factors are incommensurate. I have said "implied" because even in Fielding's novels, which abound in comments on this indicator more than the work of any other novelist I know, only few of the references to it are explicit. The explicit references only serve to heighten the reader's consciousness of the temporal manipulations, impressing on him the necessity of studying them whenever he comes up against interpretative problems related to the novel's structure of meaning: "Bestir thyself, therefore . . . for though we will always lend thee proper assistance in difficult places, as we do not, like some others, expect thee to use the arts of divination to discover our meaning, yet we shall not indulge thy laziness where nothing but thy own attention is required" (*Tom Jones,* 11. 9).

Illuminating as Fielding's critical asides are, they may be misleading in one important respect. They often seem to suggest that materials possess an intrinsic, objective and universally prevalent interest or import, and that the author stands still or flies according to the varying degrees of interest inherent in the different episodes. The implication is, for instance, that the author will invariably render at length any fictive time-section containing "revolutions of countries" or "extraordinary scenes," all of which are intrinsically "matters of true importance" or "great prizes"; while, on the other hand, he will as invariably dismiss cursorily all humdrum domestic occurrences as not "worthy a place in this history" or beneath "the reader's notice": "As the tea-table conversation, though extremely delightful to those who are engaged in it, may probably appear somewhat dull to the reader, we will here put an end to the chapter" (*Amelia,* 9. 3).

A conclusion of this sort is utterly unwarrantable. The question whether any material is "worthy of notice" or "of no consequence," whether it belongs to the class of "beauties, elegancies, curiosities" or is a "barren and gloomy heath," can never be determined *a priori* because the conception of its aesthetic relevance may vary not only from one century or from one author to another, but even from one work to another. This conception varies according to writers' different goals, which dictate different principles of selection. Henry James, holding that "it sounds almost puerile to say that some incidents are intrinsically more important than others," rightly refuses (sometimes) to prejudge the degrees of interest adhering to different incidents, "for this will depend on the skill [and, we might add, the poetics] of the painter"; though his own ideal is to demonstrate that the seemingly mild adventures of "inward life" can be converted "into the stuff of drama or . . . of 'story.' "[31] His delight in Stevenson's *Treasure Island,* with its "murders, mysteries, islands of dreadful renown, hairbreadth escapes, miraculous coincidences and buried doubloons," is therefore perfectly compatible with his singling out as the best thing in *Portrait of a Lady* Isabel Archer's minutely evoked meditative vigil, when "she sits up by her dying fire, far into the night, under the spell of recognitions on which she finds the last sharpness suddenly wait . . . motionlessly *seeing.*" Given the particular line of interest, this quiet vigil of searching criticism, "though it all goes on without her being approached by another person and without her leaving her chair," does indeed "throw the action forward more than twenty 'incidents' might have done" and is doubtless "as 'interesting' as the surprise of a caravan or the identification of a pirate."[32]

It is quite understandable that different writers, each with his own conception of life and poetics of art, should differ as to what fields of material merit (thorough) treatment. But the reader finds himself in an altogether different situation. Qua reader, he has no private artistic axe to grind. His only business is to endeavor to grasp the nature and functions of the compositional principles operating in the text, so that he may comprehend as fully as possible its structure of meaning. Having this in view, he cannot apply to the work any scale of intrinsic interest (including his own), because there is not a single one that is universally valid. He must, therefore, measure the value of narrative elements in terms of contextual significance, largely suggested by the quantitative indicator.[33] And the more revolutionary a work is in its conception of the scale of significance, the more does it depend on the operation of the sharply enclosed, value-determining context of the whole work. For in such revolutionary works it is mainly the quantitative indicator that draws the reader's attention to the modification or even inversion of the conventional hierarchy; it is these works that most fully exploit the fact that what is conventionally regarded as trivial can be contextually endowed with artistic significance. Laurence Sterne, for example, demonstrates his acute awareness of the functionality of his seemingly bizarre selective procedure when he claims that "the happiness of the Cervantic humour arises from this very thing—of describing silly and trifling Events, with the Circumstantial Pomp of great Ones."

Fielding himself was, in fact, well aware of the value-determining aspect of the temporal variations, though in his polemical impetus against what seemed to him Richardson's petty psychological preoccupations he at times tended to overstate his plea to the contrary. Regardless of the overt motivation of his selective decisions, they are actually based not on the ostensible criterion of intrinsic interest versus dullness but on that of artistic relevance versus irrelevance, as he himself is driven to admit openly immediately after the muff incident in *Tom Jones:*

> Though this incident will probably appear of little consequence to many of our readers, yet trifling as it was, it had so violent an effect on poor Jones that we thought it our duty to relate it. In reality, there are many little circumstances too often omitted by injudicious historians, from which events of the utmost importance arise. The world may indeed be considered as a vast machine in which the great wheels are originally set in motion by those which are very minute and almost imperceptible to any but the strongest eyes.
>
> Thus, not all the charms of the incomparable Sophia, not all the dazzling brightness and languishing softness of her eyes, the harmony of her voice and of her person; not all her wit, good humour, greatness of mind or sweetness of disposition had been able so absolutely to conquer and enslave the heart of poor Jones as this little incident of the muff. (5. 4)

QUANTITATIVE INDICATOR, SCENIC NORM, AND FICTIVE PRESENT

The quantitative indicator is also an indispensable factor in the delimitation of the exposition, especially in determining the precise temporal point in the fabula which marks the end of the exposition.

As argued above, the literary artist exploits the possibilities of varying the time-ratios in order to throw the contextual centrality of certain fictive periods into high relief against the background of other periods belonging to the total span of the sujet. It is thus the approximation of representational to represented time that draws the reader's attention to some subperiods constituting "discriminated occasions" in the fullest sense of the word.[34] And vice versa: the very disparity between the different time-ratios (and the greater it is the more conspicuously significant it becomes) suggests that the cursorily treated time-sections are non-discriminated because they are meant to occupy but a relatively minor position in the particular structure of meaning established by the work.

Moreover, in most fictional (and dramatic) works we find not only variations but also a basic similarity between the time-ratios of the various scenes or discriminated occasions. Every narrative establishes a certain scenic time-norm of its own. This norm may, of course, vary from one writer, and even from one work, to another. And even within a single work certain scenes may turn out to deviate from the basic time-norm established by the majority of the discriminated occasions. But such deviations (say, a ratio of 2:3 or even 1:5 where the norm is 1:2), which may indeed appear considerable when examined in isolation, generally prove insignificant when considered, as they must be, in the context of the whole work—in the light of the nonscenic as well as the scenic time-ratios. As the nonscenic time-ratio of the same narrative is usually something like 1:10.000 or 1:50.000 or even 1:500.000, the enormous disparity between the scenic and the nonscenic clearly points out the comparative slightness of the occasional divergence (e.g., in climactic episodes) from the basic norm.

Furthermore, this scenic discrimination reveals the structural and semantic priorities of the particular sujet, not of the underlying fabula, which consists of irreducible and variously composible motifs rather than composite units. Scenic disposition, therefore, which synthesizes chronologically heterogeneous, discontinuous motifs by means of such framing devices as reminiscential dialogue or process of association, is highly suggestive as the resultant of temporal and perspectival choices.

Since every work does establish a scenic norm and since the scenic treatment accorded to a fictive time-section underscores its high aesthetic importance, the first scene in every work naturally assumes a special conspicuousness and significance. The author's finding it to be the first time-section that is "of consequence enough" to deserve full scenic treatment turns it, implicitly but clearly, into a conspicuous signpost, signifying that this is precisely the point in time that the author has decided, for whatever reason, to make the reader regard as the beginning of the action proper. That is, the text suggests, why this "occasion" is the first to have been so "discriminated." Sometimes, this implicit indication is even both accounted for and further reinforced by overt references to the extraordinary contextual significance of the first scene. Towards the end of the preliminary exposition in James's *Washington Square,* for instance, the narrator prefaces the representation of the party at which Catherine Sloper is to meet Morris Townsend with the comment that this occasion "was the beginning of something very important"; and he later intrudes upon the scene itself in order to reemphasize that the present "entertainment was the beginning of something important to Catherine" (chaps. 3, 4). If, therefore, the first discriminated occasion is the beginning of what Trollope happily calls "the real kernel of [the] story,"[35] it follows that any motif that antedates it in time (i.e., precedes it in the fabula) is expositional—irrespective of its position in the sujet.

The expositional material, always antedating the first scene, may correspondingly precede it in point of its actual position in the sujet. In this case, the large disparity between the time-ratio of the expositional part and that of the opening scene (a disparity concomitant with several other indicators, to be discussed) lays bare the preparatory nature of whatever precedes the temporal signpost. The communication of the expositional material, however, may also be delayed, so that it will succeed the first discriminated occasion in its actual ordering. In this case, the expositional information will retrospectively throw light on it, that is, enrich, modify or even drastically change the reader's understanding of it; for, within the sharply circumscribed, enclosed world of the literary text, almost every motif or occurrence antedating another tends to illuminate it in some way, no matter what their order of presentation in the sujet. The point marking the end of the exposition in the fabula thus coincides with that point in time which marks the beginning of the *fictive present* in the sujet—the beginning of the first time-section that the work considers important enough to be worthy of such full treatment as will involve, according to the contextual scenic norm, a close approximation or correspondence between its representational time and the clock-marked time we employ in everyday life.

It will be noticed that I dissociate my use of the term *fictive present* from any dependence on dramatic or fictive illusion, with which it is usually thought to be interchangeable. The prevalent view of the fictive present as identical with the illusion of presentness has been ably put forward by A. A. Mendilow:

> There is as a rule one point of time in the story which serves as the point of reference. From this point the fictive present may be considered as beginning. In other words, the reader if he is engrossed in his reading translates all that happens from this moment of time onward into an imaginative present of his own and yields to the illusion that he is himself participating in the action or situation, or at least is witnessing it as happening, not merely as having happened. Everything that antedates this point, as for instance exposition, is felt as a fictive past, while all that succeeds it, as for instance those premonitions and anticipatory hints that novelists find so useful for directing the attention forward to the climax or evoking a feeling of suspense, are felt as future.[36]

Mendilow's view is by no means Freytagean. He does not deal with Freytag's theory, but his passing comments mark a considerable advance over it by reflecting an awareness that the location of the expositional material is not fixed, but variable. And for this he must be given full credit. What basically vitiates Mendilow's references to the problem, however, and ultimately reduces them to little more than a series of shrewd insights, is the lack of some indispensable theoretical tools and the inefficacy of those used in their stead. The absence in his account of a distinction comparable to that between fabula and sujet might perhaps prove less fatal if the concept he proposes as a delimiting temporal signpost, namely the "fictive present," were not so vague as to become useless as a critical tool. The similarity between Mendilow's conception of the fictive present and mine is primarily terminological: his approach, as implicit in this passage, and that which I have so far outlined necessarily differ since the term we both use denotes in each case radically divergent concepts or textual phenomena.[37] While I certainly maintain that the beginning of the fictive present is an important point of reference, I strongly doubt whether "any imaginative shift of the reader from his own chronological present to the fictional past in which novels are written" (pp. 63–64) takes place at all; whether the reader really identifies himself with the hero and even *is* the hero in imagination (p. 96); whether the reader is ever "cheated" of his reason (pp. 109–10), forgetting his own present and by an imaginative effort projecting himself into the tale's fictive present, so that his "actual present, his own time-locus, [is] absorbed into the fictive present of the action" (pp. 97–98). I for one hold that Dr. Johnson's view that "the spectators are always in their senses, and know, from the first act to the last, that the stage is only a stage and that the players are only players" is far closer to the truth. The point, however, is that both views, the illusionist as well as the anti-illusionist, are not only equally undemonstrated but undemonstrable by literary critics *qua* literary critics. This psychological crux, therefore, should be relegated to the discipline of psychology, where it properly belongs.

But even if we assume for the sake of argument that the illusion of presentness does operate, the question immediately arises, What are the objective features or factors in the text itself that bring about this psychological transfer and establish the point of reference? This crucial question has never been satisfactorily answered by the pro-illusionists.

It is here that my definition of the fictive present may come in useful even for the purposes of the illusionist view. If we grasp "fictive present" as a descriptive metaphor denoting an indisputably objective ratio between representational time and represented time, a ratio that involves an approximation of the two times; and if this approximation is interpreted as aiming to achieve (to adopt Mendilow's own phrase in another context) a "closer correspondence between the pace of living . . . and [the] depiction of it" (p. 73), then we shall be able to account for the possibility that a temporal transfer takes place at such a point by referring to the objective compositional elements that may produce it.

THE TEXTURE OF EXPOSITION, SCENIC TEXTURE, AND MODES OF PRESENTATION

A closer analysis of particular works will, I believe, not only confirm the conclusions reached so far but also throw light on expositional versus scenic texture, a most important problem that I have not hitherto treated. Let us consider first the case of preliminary and concentrated exposition by examining some narratives that actually start with a continuous block of antecedents—the Book of Job, for instance:

1. There was a man in the land of Uz, whose name *was* Job; and the man was perfect and upright, and one that feared God, and eschewed evil. 2. And there were born unto him seven sons and three daughters. 3. His substance also was seven thousand sheep, and three thousand camels, and five hundred yoke of oxen, and five hundred she asses, and a very great household; so that this man was the greatest of all the men of the east. 4. And his sons went and feasted *in their* houses, every one his day; and sent and called for their three sisters to eat and to drink with them. 5. And it was so, when the days of *their* feasting were gone about, that Job sent and sanctified them, and rose up early in the morning, and offered burnt offerings *according* to the number of them all; for Job said, It may be that my sons have sinned, and cursed God in their hearts. Thus did Job continually. 6. Now there was a day when the sons of God came to present themselves before the Lord, and Satan came also among them. 7. And the Lord said unto Satan, Whence comest thou? Then Satan answered the Lord, and said, From going to and fro in the earth, and from walking up and down in it. 8. And the Lord said unto Satan, Hast thou considered my servant Job, that *there is* none like him in the earth, a perfect and an upright man, one that feareth God, and escheweth evil? 9. Then Satan answered the Lord, and said, Doth Job fear God for nought? 10. Hast not thou made an hedge about him, and about his house, and about all that he hath on every side? thou hast blessed the work of his hands, and his substance is increased in the land. 11. But put forth thine hand now and touch all that he hath, and he will curse thee to thy face. 12. And the Lord said unto Satan, Behold, all that he hath *is* in thy power; only upon himself put not forth thine hand. So Satan went forth from the presence of the Lord. (1: 1–12)

Every reader will instinctively feel that this chronologically ordered sequence of motifs "falls naturally" into two parts (verses 1–5 and 6–12), the first of which serves to "prepare" us for the second and more "essential" part. But is it possible to isolate and point out objectively the particular devices employed by the text in order so to segment the sequence and give rise to this "feeling" about the different roles of the two component parts?

To say that the difference between verses 1–5 and 6–12 corresponds to that between "summary" and "action" is merely to beg the question; for what, in fact, is summary and what is action? The best manner of accounting for the disparity in effects is to start with the different time-ratios to be found in the two parts. The parts are of about equal textual length; but whereas the first swiftly flies over several decades in the history of Job and his family, the second focuses on a very brief time-section containing the colloquy between God and Satan. It is the striking disparity between the two represented time-sections,[38] and consequently between the two time-ratios, that indicates that the two passages occupy very different positions and fulfil different functions within the context of this particular narrative. The quantitative indicator implies that the discriminated occasion marking the beginning of the fictive present also constitutes the beginning of this particular story about Job; while the preceding passage, which antedates it in the fabula, is intended to communicate to the reader the expositional antecedents indispensable to the comprehension of the action proper. Any doubts the reader may entertain as to the possibility of such a short passage constituting a full-fledged discriminated occasion are soon dispelled by the series of discriminated occasions immediately following it, all of them conforming to, and thereby confirming, the basic scenic norm established in the first scene.[39]

Moreover, this disparity between time-ratios involves or logically correlates with no less salient differences in texture between the two segments—texture being defined here in terms of "specificity," "concreteness," and "actional dynamics." Such a very short passage as the first, with its meager quantity of representational time in relation to a very long represented span, can only touch briefly upon some of the occurrences referred to and/or summarize some of their habitual, recurrent features. The texture of such a passage cannot, first, be *specific:* the narrator cannot afford to go into the details of whatever existed or took place in the course of the represented time, but is compelled to resort to very broad, generalized strokes of summary. Nor can the texture be *concrete,* that is, the narrator cannot restrict himself to incidents that existed only once in time and space: having to telescope a long fictive period into a confined space, he is constantly forced to summarize the fixed or recurrent traits of characters, events, or situations.

And verses 1–5 do indeed concentrate only on the broadest and most typical or habitual features of the character, life, and conduct of Job and his household. The nonspecificity of this passage, its generalized texture as regards the filling in or realization of both spatial arena and especially temporal vista, is very marked: the names of Job's children are not mentioned; about Job's environment the reader can only infer that it is rural rather than urban; his livestock is listed in round numbers; and even the portrait of the hero himself consists of such generalized character traits as "perfect," "upright," or "the greatest of all the men of the east." The texture, moreover, lacks concreteness as well as specificity, being composed not only of drastically foreshortened facts but also of habitual occurrences, tendencies, or features, as the grammar of the passage indicates: the feasts of Job's sons, for example, and their father's offerings are evidently not concrete but customary and recurrent events of their lives. And the narrator himself explicitly points this out, when looking back over the whole passage: "Thus did Job continually."

The texture of verses 6-12 is quite different. In this discriminated occasion, with its brief represented span, the role of summary is minimized. First of all, here the narrator no longer chooses to ignore the many multifarious details of which every event is composed, or at most telescope them into a generalized epithet or a broad statement, but goes into a relatively minute showing of what took place on the occasion, quoting the speeches made by the two characters in all their specificity of wording.

This specifically treated scene is, moreover, also composed of concrete incidents or motifs. This is not a situation with fixed, habitual features that manifest themselves again and again during a long period, but one that existed only once in time and space, one that took place on a particular day, at a particular place, and is never to recur. In the narrator's own words, the difference in concreteness between the two parts precisely corresponds to that between "Thus did Job continually" and "Now there was a day."

The reader is thus led to conclude that verses 1-5 are expositional by a combination of three complementary indicators—two textural and one chronological. The pronounced quantitative difference in specificity, produced by the manipulation of time-ratios, draws the reader's attention to the secondary position occupied by the opening part within the context of Job's story. And so at the same time does the qualitative difference in concreteness, since the "real kernel" of a narrative must necessarily consist of a concrete action, while the deconcretized opening might equally have paved the way for any number of stories about Job. Given these indications, the fact that this opening also chronologically antedates the first scenic occasion leaves no doubt in our minds that its function is preparatory or expositional.

We must, finally, take into account another factor that is closely related to, indeed based on, the opposition in concreteness. In the first segment the narrator portrays a state of affairs that is essentially static or stable—being mainly composed of static and recurrent motifs. By itself, therefore, the initial situation can lead to nothing but a repetition of the same habitual events. The scene that follows it, on the other hand, is not only concrete but also essentially dynamic or developmental, introducing into the once-stable state of affairs the first disturbing, destabilizing element (Satan's challenge and God's response) which causally leads, by necessary or probable sequence, to the next stages of the action. The sequence of concrete discriminated occasions, all of them composed of (increasingly) dynamic and developmental motifs, is closely unified by a causal chain into a network of cause and effect which forms the particular story of Job and which qualitatively distinguishes them from the first static group of motifs. The only way in which the reader can integrate these static motifs into the tale's structure of meaning is to grasp them as what Balzac called "les prémisses à une proposition, " that is, as expositional elements that introduce us into the fictive world, establish its canons of probability, and serve as the groundwork on which the particular narrative edifice is to be erected.

It is these objective variables and resultant features of the text that unambiguously mark off the preliminary exposition from the non- or post-expositional parts and establish the point in time at which the action proper starts. This point in time in the fabula demonstrably coincides with the beginning of the first scene in the sujet. And once this temporal signpost is established, the reader has no difficulty in determining what motifs are expositional, no matter what their position in the sujet. Thus, the circumstance that Job has a number of friends, though its disclosure is subsequent to the beginning of the fictive present, turns out to be as unmistakably expositional as the motifs contained in the first segment, for its location in the fabula precedes the scenic point of reference.

All preliminary expositions in fiction and drama are marked off from the action proper in an essentially similar fashion. Jane Austen's *Emma,* for example, opens by telescoping into a few pages the twenty one years Emma has lived "in the world with very little to distress or to vex her." The disparity in time-ratios between this introductory section (twenty one years of represented time to which the author allots about five minutes of representational time) and the following scene (covering a small part of a single evening in about fifteen minutes of representational time) immediately strikes the reader. This disparity again involves marked differences in texture. The discriminated occasion is both specific (minutely reporting Emma's thoughts and the conversation between Emma, her father and Mr. Knightley during that evening) and concrete, temporally and spatially. In contrast, the opening account is both highly generalized (consisting of a summary of Emma's history, her traits of character and those of her father, their general situation, etc.), and deconcretized. Moreover, the reader perceives that the first scene has not been chosen at random. It coincides with that point in time when the static, peaceful situation at Hartfield has just been destabilized: "Miss Taylor married . . . it was on the wedding day of this beloved friend that Emma first sat in mournful thought of any continuance. The wedding over, and the bride-people gone, her father and herself were left to dine together, with no prospect of a third to cheer a long evening." This change thus marks a crucial turning-point—no less than the beginning of a new era in Emma's history. It is during this scene, when Emma has just been thrown for the first time on her own resources, that she announces her matchmaking plans, which are strongly objected to by Mr. Knightley but lead to the first stage of her humiliating ordeal. The strongly developmental nature of the chain of events, all of them causally connected, that is set into motion by these destabilizing elements, is again contrasted with the static nature of the opening section, which can be integrated with them only as exposition. The same features of the preliminary exposition (its priority in point of time; its reduced time-ratio, which involves a generalized and deconcretized texture; and the static nature of its motifs) as opposed to those of the first discriminated occasion again clearly establish the coincidence of the beginning of the first scene in the sujet with that temporal point marking the end of the expositional section in the fabula.

The point at which the preliminary exposition ends and the action starts is sometimes noted explicitly by the narrator himself. In Balzac's *La Cousine Bette,* after a lengthy account of the family of Baron Hulot d'Ervy and the baron's meeting with the fatal Madame Marneffe, the narrator observes that "ici se termine en quelque sorte l'introduction de cette histoire. Ce récit est au drame qui le complète, ce que sont les prémisses à une proposition, ce qu'est toute exposition à toute tragédie classique."[40] More apologetically but also more cogently, in the fourth chapter of *The Eustace Diamonds* Trollope informs the reader that "dramatists, when they write their plays, have a delightful privilege of prefixing a list of their personages; and the dramatists of old used to tell us who was in love with whom, and what were the blood relationships of all the persons. In such a narrative as this, any proceeding of that kind would be unusual, and therefore the poor narrator has been driven to expend his four first chapters in the mere task of introducing his characters. He regrets the length of these introductions, and will now begin at once the action of his story." These narrators thus mark the *terminus ad quem* of the exposition both in terms of the continuum of the text (e.g., the end of the fourth chapter) and that of events. In some cases, the narrator does not point out explicitly the end of the exposition in the sujet, but only the temporal signpost in the fabula at which the action proper starts. In Charles Reade's *It Is Never Too Late to Mend*, the time of the first discriminated occasion is referred to as "the morning of our tale"; in Trollope's *Barchester Towers*, as "the time at which this history is supposed to commence."[41] In other cases, the preliminary exposition is delimited by the narrator's emphasizing the point of transition from it to the first scene in terms of concreteness, prefixing to the latter such tell-tale opening phrases as "one day" in order to distinguish it from the preceding deconcretized events. In Isaac Bashevis Singer's *Short Friday and Other Stories*, for instance, the first discriminated occasion in "Taibele and Her Demon" opens with the words "one moonless summer evening"; in "Blood," with "One morning"; and in "Big and Little," with "Now listen to this. One day . . ."[42] And in still other cases, the first scene is overtly indicated to destabilize or to have destabilized a hitherto static state of affairs. The second and third chapters of Balzac's *Eugénie Grandet* abound in commentary on Eugénie's transformation from the moment she meets her cousin: "More ideas had poured into her mind in a quarter of an hour than had ever before occurred to her in her whole life"; or "Desiring for the first time in her life to look her best, she felt the satisfaction of having a new dress." The temporal point which "revealed to Eugénie the meaning of things here below" is thus powerfully established.

In most narratives, however, the reader is not explicitly alerted to the point of demarcation but left to discover it by himself, with the aid of the set of indicators, quantitative and qualitative, formal and semantic. Even when a signpost is overtly provided, the reader had better check whether the textual evidence bears out the authorial statement;[43] but elsewhere the careful application of these criteria is evidently imperative.

Nor will a perfunctory or partial application of these criteria do, because the author often complicates our task of delimiting the preliminary exposition by considerably varying the expositional time-ratio (usually towards the end of the opening) so as to make it approximate the scenic norm of the tale. The author may choose to do this for a number of reasons. After a highly generalized summary of the initial state of affairs, he may wish to focus more sharply on a number of expositional points— events, character traits, probabilities—which are more directly or immediately relevant to the sequel. He may wish to vivify or reemphasize dramatically some of the antecedents merely mentioned before. He may at the same time also wish to avoid an abrupt shift to the fictive present, preferring a more gradual and therefore less discernible transition from purely stated or "told" exposition to fully dramatized scene or "showing." He may thus increase the expositional time-ratio towards the end in order to dissimulate the stark referential nature of his leading section. In all these cases, an awareness of all the *differentia specifica* of scene versus concentrated exposition is particularly necessary.

A case in point is the two last verses (4–5) of the opening of the Book of Job, which raise the knotty problem of the illustrative scene. As far as the ratio of representational to represented time is concerned, the feasts projected in these lines are accorded a treatment conspicuously different from that of the other motifs. The time-ratio of this brief complex of incidents, to which about half of the introductory section is devoted, sufficiently diverges from the preceding ratio of three verses to four decades and sufficiently approximates that of the first scenic occasion to prove troublesome to a reader who attempts to determine whether it is expositional or not by the blind application of the quantitative criterion by itself. But if the reader brings the whole set of indicators to bear on the occurrence, he will soon conclude that these verses form an integral part of the exposition. For, though from the viewpoint of degree of specificity this incident indeed approaches the scenic norm in question, it qualitatively differs from it in concreteness, being as habitual and recurrent in the life of Job's family as the other opening motifs. This recurrent incident will then be viewed as no more than a final semidramatic highlighting of the central expositional feature, Job's perfect piety, which has been merely "stated" before but which it is so essential to impress on the reader (in order to set up the tale's internal structure of probabilities) that it is retreated, enlarged on, and exemplified by way of "showing." Furthermore, just like the other expositional motifs, the incident is in no way dynamic or developmental in terms of the action. Once the reader perceives the deconcretized, habitual or illustrative nature of the incident, he also understands that its increased specificity is illusory. In view of its *recurrent* nature, the nominal duration (the few days of the feast) should clearly be multiplied by a hundred or a thousand so as to cover as much represented time as the other expositional motifs. When this is done, the illustrative complex may still be regarded as more specifically treated than the other antecedents, but the disparity vis-à-vis the scenic norm is more than enough to prevent this semidramatized event from being confused with a full-fledged discriminated occasion.

In other instances of thoroughly treated occurrences that are intercalated into the preliminary exposition or round it off, we similarly discover that while the application of the quantitative indicator by itself may mislead us, the criteria of concreteness and actional dynamics lay bare the illustrative, preparatory nature of these pseudo-scenes. The operation of the criterion of concreteness may, however, vary, since there is more than one way of deconcretizing a scene. At the start of part 1, chapter 4 of Dostoyevsky's *The Devils,* the narrator, having presented different aspects of the relationship between Verkhovensky and Mrs. Stavrogin, stops the flow of exposition in order to enact two incidents. One is concerned with Mrs. Stavrogin's anger at Verkhovensky's enthusiastic response to the emancipation of the serfs; the other, with the abrupt way she put an end to their romantic meetings in the summer-house. Each of these events not only is much more specific than the preceding expositional blocks but, unlike verses 4–5 in Job, appears to be fully concrete as well—the first opening with the tell-tale "One day" and the second with "It took place in 1855, in springtime, in the month of May."

Each of these scenes may accordingly seem to sound in turn the gong of first discriminated occasion. But they are nevertheless purely expositional. Though when torn out of context they may pass for concrete, this concreteness is only illusory. What deconcretizes these occasions is neither their tenor nor their "grammar" but the wider narrative framework in which they are set. For the narrator has prefaced them with the revealing comment that in return for her patronage Mrs. Stavrogin "demanded a great deal from him, sometimes even the obedience of a slave. And it was incredible how unforgiving she was. I may as well tell you two stories about that." The context thus leaves no doubt that the two scenes have been interpolated merely as dramatic illustrations of a central character-trait of the lady's and of the nature of her attitude to her protégé. The stories are even linked to the authorial generalization that they exemplify, and to each other, by the fact that in spite of their wholly different tenor they both terminate in an identical whisper hissed by Mrs. Stavrogin: " 'I shall never forgive you for this!' " Consequently, though these anecdotes are concrete in themselves whereas the corresponding incident in Job is not, all three scenes are equally deconcretized in that each ultimately serves to illuminate an habitual state of affairs characterizing the expositional period or to drive home an engrained trait. From the viewpoint of development, moreover, these two scenes are even more starkly expositional, if possible, than the feasts in Job, since they have no sequel and lead us nowhere. Once the narrator has done with them, he resumes his expositional summary: "She even designed the clothes he wore all his life herself," etc.

To conclude, the various indicators that combine to form the set of criteria by which the reader can mark off the preliminary exposition from the action proper are usually concomitant and interdependent. It may sometimes be convenient to start with the quantitative criterion and sometimes with the more qualitative criteria; but any attempt to judge by any of them without reference to the others may lead to serious confusions between summary and scene in general[44] and between preliminary exposition and scenic launch in particular.

On the other hand, the systematic application of this set of factors confirms our conclusion about the temporal boundaries of the exposition and the materials that compose it. We simply have to compare the presentation of motifs in the two sequences and note the temporal point in the fabula at which the action is scenically dynamized in the sujet. All the motifs from the beginning of the fabula up to this *terminus ad quem* are expositional. We have already examined the case of works in which the temporal ordering in the sujet is identical with or at least similar to that in the fabula. In such narratives—and in plays with a prologue—the exposition or part of it both antedates (in point of time) and precedes (in point of actual arrangement) the first discriminated event, while the rest of the work follows it both chronologically and presentationally.

Whenever the author decides (for any of a variety of reasons to be analyzed in the following chapters) to refrain from starting his work with a block of antecedents, he considerably reduces the difficulty of pinpointing the end of the expositional period in the fabula. For in this case the work generally plunges into a full-fledged scene, thus indicating the temporal point of reference to the reader right at the beginning while delaying the communication of the expositional material that will explain what is happening at the present moment and why it is happening. In this case, then, the author prefers a retrospective to a preliminary or anticipatory illumination of the events taking place from the first scene on. And the divergence from the natural sequence strikingly activates and throws into relief the bi-directionality inherent in the reading process—forcing the reader, during his progression along the continuum of the text, to regress in order to relate the material gradually disclosed to earlier stages in the action and/or the reading, to link and re-link past, present and future, and constantly to reinterpret what has gone before. But the problem of reconstructing the fabulaic sequence by spotting and integrating the expositional motifs, as they unfold in the deformed order of presentation, is here solved in essentially the same manner.

In *Vanity Fair,* for example, which opens "on one sunshiny morning in June" with the memorable scene representing the departure of Amelia and Becky from Miss Pinkerton's academy, the flow of the fictive present is stopped twice, right after the beginning. This happens first in chapter 1, in order to impart to the reader some information about Amelia (her appearance, character, circumstances, and relations with various people), which retrospectively throws light on the concrete events that we have just witnessed: "But as we are to see a great deal of Amelia, there is no harm in saying, at the outset of our acquaintance, that she was a dear little creature," etc. After this doubling back into the expositional past, the novel proceeds with the events of the previously established scene, but stops again, soon after Becky's sacrilegious rejection of the precious dictionary, in order to devote about half of the second chapter to a thorough retrospective account of Becky's personality and past history.

Both blocks of information are as expositional as those opening the Book of Job or *Emma* from the viewpoint of their basic function (accounting as they do for the diametrically opposed behaviour of the two girls in the first scene), their chronological anteriority, their time-ratios and texture, and their mode of integration with the scenically rendered and dynamic elements. They differ only in their location in the sujet: these segments of summary have been placed so as to follow the point of reference, whereas the others precede as well as antedate it. But all of them belong at the beginning of their respective fabulas, before the temporal point at which the action proper starts in their respective sujets.

In other cases the text similarly plunges into the fictive present, thus immediately establishing the scenic signpost, but prefers to impart the necessary antecedents to the reader in a radically different mode, namely, by weaving them into the action proper itself. The author may choose, for instance, to break up what is, in the fabula, a continuous as well as preliminary expositional segment into a large number of small units or isolated motifs, which are made to crop up at different points in the sequel—to emerge naturally out of scenes that are themselves essentially nonexpositional. These discontinuous expositional elements, unobtrusively located in standard scenes, consequently do not form separate narrative blocks exclusively concerned with the past, with an individual texture of their own that is perceptibly different from the scenic. They are made to constitute, on the contrary, an integral part of these discriminated occasions themselves and may even be made to fulfill important actional functions in them. Thus, the meetings between Strether and Miss Gostrey at the beginning of *The Ambassadors* form concrete and specific events, which are part and parcel of the novel's action, theme and line of interest: Strether's adventure in Europe. In the course of these (thematically and temporally digressive) conversations, however, many relevant details concerning Strether's past naturally come up, and are thereby indirectly communicated to the reader. So the expositional picture slowly unfolds without the author's stopping the flow of the fictive present even for a moment. While in *Vanity Fair* the communication of the expositional blocks —within the dynamics of the reading-process—necessitates a pause in the dynamics of the fictive action, here the communication of the discontinuous expositional motifs propels the action forward.

All the same, these motifs in *The Ambassadors* essentially fulfil the same distinctive function as the blocks in *Vanity Fair*. They too are all anterior to the first discriminated occasion in the sujet (Strether's arrival at Chester); and this occasion is again indicated to be of extreme importance in that it destabilizes a hitherto static state of affairs, giving Strether "a deep taste of change" and making his "introduction to things." Accordingly, though in one novel the antecedents are concentrated while in the other they are distributed, though in one novel they are presented explicitly as immutable past while in the other they are dissimulatively worked into the present, though in one novel they retard the flow of action while in the other they feed this flow—despite all these differences, the motifs making up the first part of the fabula retrospectively illuminate and account for the dynamic chain of events that starts with the first scene, and are therefore equally expositional.

To sum up, when we call expositions preliminary or delayed, concentrated or distributed, we are referring in fact to their order or mode of presentation in the sujet, for in the fabula the exposition is always wholly concentrated at the beginning. No normative value can be automatically ascribed either to the location of the exposition in the sujet or to its form and texture (just as there are no grounds for the categorically dismissive attitude to exposition, as if it were necessarily limited in quantity and functionality alike). But I shall argue that the various aspects of exposition are always worth inquiring into because they are highly indicative of and integral to the structure and compositional principles of the work as a whole. It is always instructive to inquire why an author has chosen to make the beginning of the sujet coincide with that of the fabula, or why he has decided to make temporal shifts, why he presents the expositional material (or parts of it) in independent solid blocks of fictive past or why he weaves it into the scenic present. For instance, as the straight chronological order of presentation is the most logical and hence natural arrangement, any deviation from it is clearly an indication of artistic purpose—such as an endeavor to move away from a concern with exposition as such and to make the expositional motifs serve functions apart from the merely referential.

All this may be put in a more general way. A literary text is the result of a vast number of selective and combinational decisions that determine its particular structure, both as regards its formal and semantic patterns and its rhetoric, the complex of devices and strategies which bring the meaning of the work home to the reader and manipulate his reactions. I have suggested that the reconstruction of the selective procedures embodied in the work can provide us with important clues to its artistic intentions. The combinational procedures, however, are no less significant, and can often be reconstructed and accounted for in as precise a manner as the selective. I shall argue that the broad combinational principles actually operating in narrative, though their variations in particular narratives are infinite, fall into a number of recognizable structural patterns and definable strategies, each with its own functions and effects, related either to the aims of the particular work or to more general conceptions of fiction and literature. In this study I shall attempt to substantiate this claim through an examination of that part of the narrative text that I have delimited as the exposition. Since the location and form of exposition are fixed in the reconstitutive fabula but highly variable in the finished sujet, the study of the variety of expositional strategies and their functional interrelations with other patterns and levels of the work (whether linguistic, perspectival, spatial, or even generic) may give us some idea of the principles of combination, distribution, and ordering in the narrative text as a whole.

I shall, finally, try to show that these strategies and interrelations, however diverse, have one important thing in common. They derive from an acute consciousness on the part of writers that literature is a time-art, in which the continuum of the text is apprehended by the reader in a continuum of time and in which elements are necessarily communicated and patterns unfolded not simultaneously but successively, and from their realization that these conditions may be exploited and manipulated in order to produce various effects on the reader. The temporal potentialities of literary art as a whole have particularly complex and potent manifestations in texts with a narrative backbone. For here the textual dynamics deriving from the sequential nature of the verbal medium as a continuum of signs necessarily combines and interacts (as it does not do in music or descriptive poetry) with the dynamics of at least two other sequences or processes, informed by a largely extraverbal logic that relates to the semantic referents of those signs: the twofold development of the action, as it objectively and straightforwardly progresses in the fictive world from beginning to end (within the fabula) and as it is deformed and patterned into progressing in our mind during the reading-process (within the sujet). And being in this triple sense a time-problem *par excellence,* expositional communication, far from a limited technical chore, can serve as a paradigm for structural dynamics.

CHAPTER TWO

EXPOSITION AND ORDER OF PRESENTATION: SOME PRELIMINARY NOTES

"Well, where shall I begin, where end, my tale?"
. . . .
Begin it, goddess, at whatever point you will.
  Homer, *Odyssey*

Most epic poets plunge "in medias res"
. . . .
My way is to begin with the beginning.
  Byron, *Don Juan*

I love to dash into the middle
. . . .
There is a comfort on reflection
To think you've done with the beginning.
  J. H. Moore, "The Duke of Benevento"

Consequently, if we begin with my lady, we are
pretty sure of beginning far enough back. And
that, let me tell you, when you have such a job
as mine in hand, is a real comfort on starting.
  Wilkie Collins, *The Moonstone*

"Begin wherever you please, dear madam," cries
Amelia; "but I beg you will consider my im-
patience."
  Henry Fielding, *Amelia*

SOME PRELIMINARY DISTINCTIONS: *IN MEDIAS RES*

As argued in the previous chapter, the location of expositional material in the sujet is variable—in some cases it is preliminary (as in the Book
of Job), while in others (as in *Vanity Fair*) delayed. Regardless of its sujet
position, however, expositional information may be communicated to the
reader in a single continuous block or be broken up into smaller, discontinuous units. The form in which it is presented may thus be either

concentrated (as are both Job's preliminary and Becky's delayed portrayal) or distributed (as is the evocation of Strether's antecedents, spread over the two opening books of *The Ambassadors*). In the latter case, at least part of the exposition is necessarily delayed as well.

These distinctions, *qua* abstract theoretical definitions, are fairly simple. Theoretically, they are clearly exhaustive as far as the two aspects of expositional presentation to which they relate—location and what, for want of a better term, I shall call form—are concerned; although, as will be discovered later, several qualifications and additional discriminations are required in order to cover the wide variety and the intricate combinations of expositional devices actually employed by novelists and dramatists.

The term *in medias res*—which will be used in this study to denote a third aspect of expositional presentation—is much more tricky. First, because the original concept has undergone a significant metamorphosis since the term was coined; and second, because even the modern designation of this popular watchword is not satisfactorily delimited. I accordingly intend to start by briefly indicating the original meaning of *in medias res* and then to proceed to establish what seems to me the proper use of the term in modern times.

In his *Epistle to the Pisos* (or *Ars Poetica*) Horace praises Homer for not having opened "the story of the Trojan War with the twin egg [*ab ovo*, i.e., with Helen's birth]. Always he pushes on toward the outcome, and he rushes his audience into the midst of things [*in medias res*] as though they were already well known."[1] Since the Renaissance, this statement has as a rule been interpreted as a recommendation, addressed to epic poets, to plunge straight into the middle of the fabula and to defer the communication of the events anterior to the starting-point (i.e., of what is, according to my definition, expositional material) to later stages in the sujet. The following pronouncement, in a recent study of epic structure, is representative:

> To point to both the *Iliad* and the *Odyssey* as examples of poems beginning *in medias res* is to misunderstand the essential meaning of the term by confusing the total occasion of an epic with its actual narrative boundaries. The *total* setting of the *Iliad* can be considered to be the Trojan War, which began with Paris's abduction of Helen and ended with the sack of Troy. When the reader keeps this *terminus a quo* and *terminus ad quem* in mind, and he remembers that the first book of the *Iliad* begins with the disastrous quarrel between Achilles and Agamemnon, he assumes that the poet has plunged *in medias res* by beginning his story late in the war. The actual *terminus a quo* and *terminus ad quem* of the *Iliad,* the setting dictated by the plot of the narrative itself, is much more limited however. Although the reader may interpret the

quarrel, in the larger context of the war, as coming *in medias res,* he must recognize that in the limited context of the poem the quarrel occurs precisely at the beginning. What the reader and careless critic have done, therefore, is to confuse the term *in medias res* with *in media belli.* The two terms are certainly not synonymous. . . . If one were to label temporally the order of incidents in the *Iliad,* he would discover a perfectly untampered chronology proceeding from the beginning—the quarrel—to the end—Hector's funeral.

The *terminus a quo* of the *Odyssey*—Ulysses's departure from Troy—does not, however, come at the actual beginning. The departure itself is not spoken of until Book III in Nestor's story, and its details are not explored until Book IX where Ulysses begins his great narration. The epic begins, in terms of *narrated* beginning, where Telemachus decides to make search for his father. . . . The interim details from the *terminus a quo* of the poem to the narrated beginning of the poem thus are supplied later by one major and two minor characters.[2]

As this clearly suggests, Delasanta takes *in medias res* to denote a deviation from the chronological order of presentation, in the form of a plunge into the midst of the fabula (the "actual narrative boundaries"). The context of Horace's dictum reveals, however, that when recommending the *in medias res* opening he had in mind something quite different from a distinction between two possible orders of presentation. In fact, the "careless" critic would be right to persist in equating *in medias res* with *in media belli,* for the two terms *are* synonymous as far as the *Ars Poetica* is concerned.

The whole context is devoted to the problem of the re-handling of ancient myths. Horace ridicules the empty boast of the "Cyclic author" that he is going to trace the whole development of the Trojan War; and he contrasts this foolishly impracticable undertaking with Homer's sensible plan, modestly expressed in the invocation of the *Odyssey,* of restricting himself to a single complex of events—a "single action," in Aristotelian parlance—which he has deftly detached from the overall story of the war.

It is in the light of this preliminary comment that the famous dictum, immediately following it, should be interpreted: Homer is praised for "rush[ing] his audience into the midst of" the ancient myth of the Trojan War (or "the total setting of the *Iliad*"), for plunging at once into his main theme: "Sing, goddess, of the wrath of Peleus's son Achilles." Homer's plunge *in medias res*—both in the *Odyssey* and in the *Iliad*—thus consists in his having selected from the long history of the war a single action that hangs together, omitting whatever is irrelevant to his main concern. As Horace himself goes on to add, in a crucial but usually overlooked statement: "He leaves out what on trial he has despaired of making shine."[3]

Horace does indeed refer to what we have been designating the middle of the fabula too. But this occurs much later, when he points out that it is due to this selective procedure that Homer can achieve unity by other, essentially combinational, means as well: "And he so coins his fables, so mixes the fictitious with the true, that the middle of the story is not incongruous with the first, nor the end with the middle." It is only here, when he comes to deal with the handling of the "fable" or plot, that Horace mentions the actual "middle of the story" and its concatenation with the other parts. So this "middle" is not to be confused with the middle of the whole myth discussed above: it is the former alone that constitutes the middle of the particular complex of incidents actually selected for epic treatment, while the latter may coincide with its beginning.[4]

The claim that when Horace singles out for praise Homer's plunging *in medias res* he is dealing with the "actual narrative boundaries" of the work is thus unfounded. At that stage he is not at all concerned with the order of presentation of an already given aggregate of motifs but with the problem of judicious primary selection with an eye to unity. The "middle" referred to in the dictum, therefore, is not necessarily to be equated with the middle of the fabula sequence but may as well denote its beginning.

During the Renaissance, however—a period whose methodological chaos particularly manifests itself in the free interpretation of ancient critical texts—the original designation of *in medias res* underwent a radical shift in that the term was usually taken to embody not a principle of selection but of combination and ordering. And the grounds for this misconception should be fairly evident (e.g., the inviting vagueness of the word *res,* or the fact that both the *Iliad* and the *Odyssey* can be said to plunge *in medias res* in both senses of the term). It is, at any rate, this reading of the dictum that still prevails in modern criticism; and this designation being incontestably more serviceable for critical purposes (at least in an age when the problem of the adaptation of ancient legends is no longer pressing) than the original Horatian meaning, there is perhaps no reason to dislodge it from the honorable position it occupies, even if it were possible to do so. It is, therefore, in this sense that *in medias res* will be used in the following pages. I believe, however, that it is necessary to clarify the modern meaning of the term as well since, as Delasanta's use of it reveals, it is still seriously mishandled.

Delasanta, like a host of Neo-Classical and contemporary critics before him,[5] maintains that the *Odyssey* does indeed plunge *in medias res* but that to say the same of the *Iliad* is to "misunderstand the essential meaning of the term." But if plunging *in medias res* is taken to mean—as it in effect is by Delasanta—plunging into some point between the beginning and the end of the fabula, thus temporarily delaying the communication of anterior material, there is no sense of the term in which the *Odyssey* may be said to dash into the middle while the *Iliad* may not. To declare that "if one were to label temporally the order of incidents in the *Iliad*, he would discover a perfectly untampered chronology," or that "in the limited context of the poem the quarrel occurs precisely at the [chronological] beginning," is to press critical amnesia a bit too far. The *Iliad* does indeed open with the disastrous quarrel, towards the end of the war. Its fabula, however, starts long before this. And throughout the epic the author distributes a large variety of contextually important antecedents. The enormous Catalogue of Ships in book 2, introducing most of the principal warriors of both armies, is no doubt the best example of delayed exposition in the *Iliad*, constituting as it does a deferred formal opening or playbill, a "natural" beginning for the whole epic. But it is by no means the only example. Nestor's reminiscences, the stories narrated by other leaders during the councils, or the character-sketches, interspersed throughout, in which champions are presented either before or after a combat—all these contain innumerable motifs and clusters of motifs that are temporally anterior to the actual starting-point. Is this varied expositional material essentially different from that composing the tales narrated to Telemachus by Nestor or Helen, or from Odysseus's account of his adventures?

It might possibly be argued that the amount of delayed exposition is larger in the *Odyssey* than in the *Iliad*. Even so, the difference postulated will be one of degree, not of kind; and the possibility of differences of degree between various works plunging *in medias res* is allowed for by the very designation of the term. For while the chronological beginning and end are fixed points in any fabula, the middle—as Aristotle's definition of it already implies—is variable in that it may coincide with any point between the two definite temporal signposts. The feature common to all works using this device is that, whatever the extent of the temporal section that ranges from the beginning of the fabula to that of the sujet, they all involve a deformed order of presentation that consists in the delay of some of the earliest antecedents—usually to a point following the scenic start of the action proper. True, in certain extreme cases a quantitative difference may, for all practical purposes, amount to a qualitative one. It would clearly be absurd to regard a work as opening *in medias res* on the strength of several trivial motifs that are delayed in the way I have indicated. But this is not the case in the *Iliad*, where a great deal of expositional material retrospectively illuminates events to which it is chronologically anterior but presentationally posterior.

Nor does an *in medias res* beginning necessarily correlate with a plunge into a discriminated occasion. Such a beginning is perfectly compatible with preliminary exposition, though it necessarily involves the delayed communication of the earliest expositional material. In *The Idiot* or *The*

Ambassadors or *Ulysses*, the plunge *in medias res* coincides with the initial representation of a full-fledged scene. On the other hand, the *Odyssey*, for example, though dashing into the middle of the fabula, opens with a preliminary account of Odysseus's plight in the tenth year of his wanderings. Most of the anterior expositional information about him is, however, delayed and distributed throughout the epic.

Moreover, though a plunge *in medias res* entails the temporary suppression of a certain amount of exposition, it is well to remember that the opposite is not necessarily true; we may have delayed exposition even with an *ab ovo* beginning. A convenient case in point is again the Book of Job, which opens *ab ovo* with an introductory account of Job and his household but unfolds certain expositional data only later on in the sujet.

Furthermore: Delasanta's insistent claims that after an *in medias res* opening the delayed material must necessarily and exclusively be introduced by way of dramatized occasions on which one character narrates his story to another does not stand up to the facts.[6] This framing device is no doubt common, but, again, far from necessary or exclusive. In the *Iliad*, for example, a considerable amount of exposition (notably the bulky Catalogue) is addressed by the omniscient narrator himself straight to the reader; in the *Odyssey*, which Delasanta regards as the quintessential epic, more of the exposition is conveyed dramatically, but even here we encounter numerous instances of direct authorial summary (the preliminary exposition and the story of Odysseus's scar, to cite one example from the beginning of the work and another from the end). And needless to say, this statement does not apply to the practice of such intrusive modern novelists as Fielding or Dickens.

In conclusion, the term *in medias res* logically denotes no more than a certain deformation of the chronological sequence. Though it often coincides with a plunge into a scenic occasion and the delay of most of the antecedents, it necessarily involves only the preclusion of identical starting-points for fabula and sujet. By itself, it can tell us little about the extent of the chronological deformation, about the specific ordering of the expositional material (in relation to the non- or post-expositional), or about the mode in which it is conveyed. For an adequate description of these aspects of temporal placement and displacement one must resort to the complementary terms defined at the beginning of this section.

The following chapters will accordingly center round three distinct though closely related aspects of the overall problem of the principles of expositional communication in particular and temporal strategy in general: location, form, and order of presentation. The opening set of questions (to be gradually sharpened and enlarged) with which I shall deal can now be roughly formulated as follows: Why do some works choose to start with exposition and others to delay it, some to concentrate and others to distribute it, some to open at the chronological beginning and others to plunge *in medias res?*

TWO ORDERS OF PRESENTATION:
PRELIMINARY AND DELAYED EXPOSITION

Previous to the twentieth century it was in the Renaissance and Neo-Classical periods that criticism was most preoccupied by the time problems of fiction. Some of our basic ideas and prejudices—ultimately challenged, as I shall indicate in a later chapter, by modern novelistic theory and practice—concerning the disposition of events in narrative date back to these eras. It was then commonly held, for instance, that the arrangement of events according to their chronological order of occurrence is more "natural" than the "deformed" disposition that an *in medias res* beginning involves. This view is reflected in the very terms chosen to denote the two different orders: the former was called the "natural" as opposed to the latter, "artificial" order.[7]

Beyond the promulgation of some sloganlike terms and concepts, the results yielded by the critical effort of these ages are nevertheless disappointing as far as the problem of temporal structure is concerned. The distinctions made are usually not only dogmatic but crude; the theoretical assumptions underlying them are left unexamined and unquestioned, for the most part owing to their time-honoured prestige; issues are not pursued to their logical conclusions; and the time features peculiar to particular works are submerged in the darkness of theory or lopped off to fit one Procrustean bed or another. In line with the practice prevalent in these ages of appropriating and freezing the statements of classical critics (or rather the contemporary interpretations of these statements) into frigid dogma,[8] Horace's dictum was erected into a strict injunction, universally binding on all epic poets. The "artificial" order came to be regarded as one of the defining properties of the epic poem as distinguished from the historical treatise, which starts *ab ovo* and follows the "natural" order. Spenser's letter to Raleigh concerning *The Faerie Queene* is representative of this widespread normative approach:

> But because the beginning of the whole work seemeth abrupte and as depending on other antecedents, it needs that ye know . . . [that] the Methode of a Poet historical is not such, as of an Historiographer. For an Historiographer discourses of affayres orderly as they were donne, accounting as well the times as the actions, but a Poet thrusteth into the middest, even where it most concerneth him, and there recoursing to the things forepaste, and divining of things to come, maketh a pleasing analysis of all. The beginning therefore of my history, if it

were to be told by an Historiographer, should be the twelfth booke, which is the last.[9]

The distinction between historical and literary narrative in these terms was considered so inherent in the respective natures of the two arts that the "natural" order, the arrangement of events "orderly as they were donne," was sometimes referred to interchangeably as the "historical," as opposed to the "poetic" order, which artificially "thrusteth into the middest."[10]

As time went on, the almost inevitable opposition with history was gradually dropped; but the avoidance of the fabula sequence has continued to manifest itself to this day. The distaste for preliminaries as such is vividly expressed (to cite an eighteenth-century example) by Sir John Henry Moore, who starts his poem "The Duke of Benevento" by declaring:

> I hate the prologue to a story
> Worse than the tuning of a fiddle,
> Squeaking and dinning;
> Hang order and connection,
> I love to dash into the middle;
> Exclusive of the fame and glory,
> There is a comfort on reflection
> To think you've done with the beginning.
>
> And so at supper, one fine night,
> Hearing a cry of Alla, Alla,
> The prince was damnably confounded,
> And in a fright,
> But more so when he saw himself surrounded
> By fifty Turks; and at their head the fierce Abdalla.[11]

And in a twentieth-century novel, J. D. Salinger's *The Catcher in the Rye,* the narrator, Holden Caulfield, is no less determined on jumping straight into the middle:

> If you really want to hear about it, the first thing you'll probably want to know is where I was born, and what my lousy childhood was like, and how my parents were occupied and all before they had me, and all that David Copperfield kind of crap,[12] but I don't feel like going into it. In the first place, that stuff bores me, and in the second place, my parents would have about two haemorrhages apiece if I told anything pretty personal about them. They're quite touchy about anything like that, especially my father. They're *nice* and all—I'm not saying that— but they're also touchy as hell. Besides, I'm not going to tell you my

whole goddam autobiography or anything. I'll just tell you about this madman stuff that happened to me around last Christmas before I got pretty run-down and had to come out here and take it easy. . . . Where I want to start telling is the day I left Pency Prep.[13]

The question accordingly arises why the "artificially" deformed order has been preferred to the "natural" in so many narrative works of different ages and by different writers, from Homer to Joyce.

Spenser and Moore offer no reasonable explanations of their temporal procedures beyond the postulation of what were considered the universally valid *differentia specifica* of epic poetry as opposed to history in the one case, and the expression of a personal, largely iconoclastic preference in the other. Some of their more sophisticated contemporaries perceived, however, that "no Dictate of Reason . . . restrains the free Choice of the Poet."[14] We see them groping toward the conclusion, never clearly formulated, that the different orders of presentation in the two cognate arts are related to the different effects each aims at producing. Goldsmith-Newbery, for instance, maintains that "it is not necessary that the beginning of the poem should begin the action; for there is an artificial order as well as a natural one, and, by making choice of the former, the poet cuts off all languid and unentertaining incidents, passes over the time that is void of action, transports the reader into the middle of the subject, and yet preserves the continuity of his story: this, among other things, distinguishes the epic poem from history."[15]

The categorical distinction between literary and historical narrative in terms of inherent properties is of course far from universally valid, in view of the multiplicity of literary works that refrain from plunging *in medias res*. And yet I believe that it is worth starting an analysis of temporal ordering and expositional modes with an attempt to account for this partly justified distinction in terms of the different overall aims of the two kinds of narrative. We shall ultimately discover that an inquiry along these functional lines will throw some light on the grounds for the variations in presentational strategy between different *literary* narratives as well.

As the historian is bent, first and foremost, upon reconstructing the truth, he necessarily endeavors not only to base his research on well-authenticated facts but also to (re)arrange these facts in the most methodical fashion. It stands to reason, therefore, that whenever he is concerned with tracing a sequence of events he should automatically resort to a strictly chronological presentation. For him the arrangement of events according to their order of occurrence is indeed "natural," particularly since it is the one most compatible with the scientific progression from cause to effect, which necessarily subsumes this temporal dimension.

It is thus the need to portray events accurately that determines the historian's principles of combination and ordering as well as selection. Qua historian, on the other hand, his prime aim cannot be to interest, let alone to amuse, his reader; and he certainly cannot afford to do so at the expense of historical truth or scientific methodology. He will usually adhere, therefore, to the "natural" order, however dull this may prove.

This nonrhetorical orientation (sometimes largely a pose serving the rhetoric of authenticity) is openly manifested by Thucydides in his harsh attack on the prose chroniclers who, emulating the lying poets, "are less interested in telling the truth than in catching the attention of their public, whose authorities cannot be checked, and whose subject-matter . . . is mostly lost in the unreliable streams of mythology."[16] Thucydides does not explicitly note that his professedly scientific orientation has dictated his own order of presentation as well as his selective procedure. But it is surely no surprise that he should choose to start his narrative at its chronological beginning. The idea that "the beginning" is totally or even temporarily dispensable—and "Hang order and connection"—would be utterly inconceivable to him. On the contrary, true to the historian's belief in the paramount value of the systematic progression from cause to effect, he devotes the first book to a thorough analysis of the origins of the conflict between Athens and Sparta: "I propose first to give an account of the causes of complaint which they had against each other and of the specific instances where their interests clashed: this is in order that there should be no doubt in anyone's mind about what led to this great war falling upon the Hellenes."[17]

Similar doctrines are preached and practiced in innumerable historical works.[18] Some historians even go so far as to denounce temporal manipulations in general, in literary as well as historical narrative. Edward Gibbon, for example, does so in the name of the sweeping generalization that "in every operation of the mind there is a much higher delight in descending from the cause to the effect, than in ascending from the effect to the cause."[19] And the same view is amusingly pressed to an extreme by another "historian"—a fictive one this time—the Emperor Claudius, who serves as narrator in two of Graves's historical novels, *I, Claudius* and *Claudius the God.* In a disparaging allusion to Horace's dictum, this imperial historian declares that "like all honest Roman histories this is written 'from egg to apple': I prefer the thorough Roman method, which misses nothing, to that of Homer and the Greeks generally, who love to jump into the middle of things and then work backwards or forwards as they feel inclined. Yes, I have often had the notion of re-writing the story of Troy in Latin prose . . . beginning from the egg from which Helen was hatched [*ab ovo*] and continuing chapter by chapter, to the apples eaten for dessert at the great feast in celebration of Ulysses's home-coming and victory over his wife's suitors."[20]

Claudius indeed conscientiously practices what he preaches. Convinced of the superiority, in scientific thoroughness, of the "historical" to the "artificial" order, he announces in the first passages of this autobiography his intention of "starting from my earliest childhood and continuing year by year until I reach the fateful point of change . . . at the age of fifty-one." To give his story the maximum of intelligibility, moreover, Claudius finds it necessary to go as far back as his grandmother Livia. Though conscious that introductory "genealogies and family histories are tedious," he, like Thucydides, has no doubt that his duty as historian must prevail over his solicitude for the reader. He may feel the need to apologize for dwelling in such detail on the antecedents before proceeding to the effects, but (he repeatedly explains) this procedure is "unavoidable."[21]

Claudius even goes so far as to claim that such aesthetic effects as may possibly arise from his management of the narrative are wholly unintentional. They are to be regarded not only as chance by-products but as positive defects deriving from deplorable errors of judgment on his part. He thus opens *Claudius the God* with an apology for having ended *I, Claudius* at a "dramatic point" (his unexpected acclamation as emperor by the Palace Guard). To indulge in a closure of this kind, he confesses, "was a most injudicious thing for a professional historian like myself to do. A historian has no business to break off at a moment of suspense."[22]

Like many actual members of his fraternity, however, Claudius, while staunchly upholding the cause of the historian, is less than fair to the poet. In his derogatory comments on the sloppy order of presentation used by Homer, he fails to take into account the radical differences in nature, functions and aims between historical and literary narrative. For the artist evidently owes no allegiance to scientific standards; he is fettered neither by the historian's facts nor by his methodology. These he may adopt or discard at will, out of purely artistic considerations.

In this chapter I shall start by dealing with one of the primary aims of fiction—the creation and manipulation of narrative interest. The artist's position as regards this effect sharply diverges from the historian's: whatever his goals, whether purely aesthetic or extraaesthetic, he has no chance of achieving them unless he succeeds in securing and maintaining the reader's interest by the intrinsic merits of the work. As Dr. Johnson magisterially observes, "Works of imagination excel by their allurement and delight; by their power of attracting and detaining the attention. That book is good in vain, which the reader throws away."[23] The literary writer's orientation is, in other words, essentially rhetorical in that he cannot but have the reader's interest and possible reactions constantly in mind.

This consideration has, among other things, a close bearing on the storyteller's ordering and distributive strategy. Thucydides's goals may impel him to place his long account of the causes that led to the Peloponnesian War right at the outset of the narrative. Many authors, however, prefer to take their cue from Homer, who in similar circumstances refrains from opening his story of the Trojan War at the "natural" beginning, with an analysis of the causes of the conflict, but chooses to start it towards the end of his fabula, with one of the late consequences. One of the purely artistic reasons that induces them to effect such temporal displacements is that in order to seize the reader's attention from the very beginning—a crucial stage in more than one respect—it may be advisable to abstain from greeting him with a solid block of exposition, a segment that often proves to be the most boring part of the whole narrative. They consider it preferable to delay its presentation to a point where it may be communicated with more telling effect.

Most writers, like most readers, are inclined to regard exposition as a necessary evil: qua exposition it constitutes no integral part of the particular action they wish to unfold but merely an account of the antecedents required for its comprehension. As some of them impatiently exclaim, "this narrative is averse to retrospect," or "I hate the prologue to a story," or "that stuff bores me." Others frankly declare that if it were only possible they would with great pleasure do without exposition altogether: "I would that it were possible," Trollope wistfully confesses in the first chapter of *Is He Popenjoy?* "so to tell a story that a reader should beforehand know every detail of it up to a certain point." This wish being manifestly futile, however, storytellers of all ages have been compelled to make the best of this inevitable bad business. Yet, though faced by essentially the same problem, the solutions they have devised vary, at times radically, not only according to their different degrees of artistry but also, I shall argue, owing to differences in their general poetics or particular rhetorical aims. Some authors have simply contented themselves with searching for techniques by which the discharge of their expositional duties should be as summary as possible or should cause the least annoyance to the reader. Others have been inspired by the expositional difficulty to evolve brilliant strategies for yoking the communication of exposition to the service of their overall purposes. At any rate, in the quest for ways of turning the expositional burden to narrative account, many writers have reached the conclusion that the strict adherence to the chronological order is, though indeed "natural," the worst solution possible, precisely because it involves the concentration of the expositional material at the very start of the reading-process.

Even a cursory glance at works by novelists notoriously addicted to the use of lengthy preliminary expositions (Scott, Balzac, Trollope) should reveal why the drawbacks usually attendant upon this mode of presentation have often been considered so dangerous, from the viewpoint of creating narrative interest, as to frighten other authors away. In Trollope's *The Eustace Diamonds,* for example, each of the four opening chapters bears the name of one of the dramatis personae ("Lizzie Greystock," "Lady Eustace," "Lucy Morris," and "Frank Greystock") and is mainly devoted to a portrayal of the eponymous character. It would be tedious to recapitulate these highly condensed introductions. Suffice it to note that each consists of a fairly exhaustive account of the title-character's history up to the temporal point at which the action starts; of a block-characterization interspersed with the narrator's clear-cut evaluative comments; and of a full evocation of this figure's "person and habits, such as they were at the period in which our story is supposed to have its commencement." It is only after this procedure has repeated itself several times that the panting and exasperated reader, having grunted his way through forty close-packed pages of continuous exposition, finally reaches the first discriminated occasion, the starting-point of the "kernel" proper.

Even the mere perusal of this formidable expositional block—not to speak of its retention in memory—cannot but prove an arduous and dull business. This mass of heterogeneous information has every appearance of being thrust down the reader's throat for no other reason than to enable him to follow the future developments of the action. As is indicated by the concentration of drastically generalized or deconcretized motifs, it has little intrinsic value; and this is even admitted openly at last. If one takes into account the merely referential function of this opening, its comparative lack of action and the generalized or deconcretized nature of the action it does contain, and the flimsy, primarily additive integration of the heterogeneous expositional blocks, one can amply account for the tedium produced by most expositions of this kind.

This expositional exordium, moreover, stands in danger of failing to hold the reader's attention not only because of its concentrated form and its texture but also (unlike interscenic summary) because of its preliminary location. For this mass has been presented at a point where we are still far from convinced that the tremendous effort required to master all these innumerable details is worth making. Very little, if anything, has been done to stimulate our imagination so as to reconcile us to noting, absorbing, and retaining the endless procession of expositional items. The situation depicted is essentially static, and it has not yet been demonstrated that the future developments to which it is amenable will be of any interest; similarly, the characters, most of whom have not yet been presented in action, still have to make good their exorbitant expositional claim to our notice. So the "poor narrator's" regretful apology for having expended "his first four chapters in the mere task of introducing his characters" as well as for "the length of his introductions," though it is definitely in place, affords no more than cold comfort. It can hardly compensate for the narrative disadvantages that preliminary exposition usually incurs and that at times, when the dullness of the prefatory section is so unmitigated as to impel the reader to skip parts of it, result in downright artistic failure.

As I shall argue in Chapter 7, preliminary exposition may indeed have its artistic justifications and may also be enlivened in a variety of ways. But the point with which I am now concerned is that as most narratives following the "natural" order suffer, in varying degrees, from similar drawbacks, it is no wonder that some narrators and even authors, who commit the common error of equating preliminary exposition with exposition in general, should wish to dispense with this stumbling-block altogether. Holden Caulfield, for instance, whose interest is limited to narrating a particular complex of recent events, all of them turning round "this madman stuff that happened to [him] around last Christmas," sees no reason why he should bore himself by providing the reader with ancient history. After all, he has not undertaken to tell us his "whole goddamn autobiography or anything." He therefore naively believes that, if where he wants "to start telling" is "the day [he] left Pencey Prep.," he can not only actually start there but also do away altogether with the tedious account of "where [he] was born, and what [his] lousy childhood was like." Unlike more sophisticated writers (including his own creator), this narrator is not aware that exposition is unavoidable as well as indispensable, though it may take a variety of forms. Nor is he aware that his own story is no exception to the rule. In the course of his narration he unconsciously imparts to the reader enough expositional material to give him a clear picture of "all that David Copperfield kind of crap"—though most of it is delayed and distributed. (The disparity between what he intends to do and what he actually does corresponds exactly, then, to that between the Horatian and the later meanings of *in medias res*.) One of the funniest points in the opening passage itself is Holden's explanation that he must not tell the reader anything "personal" about his parents, because they are "touchy as hell."

Moreover, while in this novel the dramatized narrator's lack of sophistication is merely Salinger's cunning device for solving his expositional problems, in "The Duke of Benevento" it is the author himself who seems to believe that exposition is dispensable. And his delight at having "done with the beginning" ultimately proves of course equally unfounded.

More experienced storytellers than either Holden or Moore, however, no less aware of the indispensability of exposition than of the disadvantages of the fabulaic order, have consciously sought for other solutions. In fact, they mostly introduce by the front door what Salinger smuggles in by the backstairs. In practice if not in theory they have put their finger on what is, from the viewpoint of narrative interest, the weakest spot of the standard preliminary exposition: its manifold failure to stimulate the reader's expectations, his suspense and curiosity, with regard to the expositional material. Not a few authors (Henry James, for example) have regarded this artistic fault as so fatal that they were determined to rectify it even at great cost, by deliberate chronological manipulation.

Unfortunately, many critics still suffer from what C. S. Lewis has happily diagnosed as literary Puritanism.[24] They turn up their noses, or at least profess to do so, at what they condescendingly describe as the "lowbrow" liking for curiosity or suspense, preferring to concern themselves with more respectable or "spiritual" aspects of literature, such as theme, world view, or psychology.[25] Such overfastidious readers often seem to have no idea of the extent to which the compositional choices made even by the most solid "highbrow" authors are, as I shall constantly argue, determined by the necessity to arouse and maintain a wide variety of interests, among which the dynamics of expectation occupies an honorable position. On the other hand, Dr. Johnson manifests his critical acumen in his unhesitating denunciation of Prior's *Solomon* for want of "that [excellency] without which all others are of small avail, the power of engaging attention and alluring curiosity"; and in his warm commendation of Shakespeare for excelling "all but *Homer* in securing the first purpose of a writer, by exciting restless and unquenchable curiosity, and compelling him that reads his work to read it through."[26] For curiosity and suspense—with the variety of forms they may assume or objects to which they may adhere (action, psychology, structure, etc.)—are not only perfectly legitimate literary interests; they constitute besides perhaps the most powerful propulsive forces a storyteller can rely on. By playing on them he can, therefore, secure the reader's attention and thus ensure the realization of his other aims as well. From the critical standpoint, moreover, it would be reprehensible to ignore these interests, since it often happens that it is only by bringing them into the open and giving them due weight in the consideration of narrative technique that we can satisfactorily account for otherwise inexplicable literary phenomena.

In the "love of 'a story as a story' . . . the vital flame at the heart of any sincere attempt to lay a scene and launch a drama,"[27] a novel by James or Conrad or Faulkner does not essentially differ from a thriller or an adventure story. In each case the storyteller, qua storyteller, exploits the "strange passion planted in the heart of man for his benefit, a mysterious provision made for him in the scheme of nature,"[28] trying to propel our attention forward by manipulating our curiosity and/or suspense. And what is typologically significant is not the presence or absence of narrative interest but its compositional and functional variables. The notable differences in genre or quality between such novels and thrillers can be explained largely by the degree to which the stimulation of these interests determines the overall narrative strategy, by the objects of these interests (e.g., purely actional as opposed to a rich integration of actional, psychological, and thematic curiosity or suspense), by the uses to which they are put, and by the means devised to arouse and sustain expectation.

This particularly applies to the stimulation of interest in the exposition, a task that is frequently as arduous as it is imperative. Here the author does not confront the relatively easy job of heightening our interest in the intrinsically exciting (because intrinsically developmental) material of the action proper, but the necessity of creating interest in condensed informational blocks that in themselves, in their natural form and location in the fabula, are far from alluring. And at least one basic device has seemed to many writers, of all ages, kinds and literary genres, to be essential for achieving the desired effect—the exploitation of the flexibility of their medium in order to violate or deform the "natural" order of presentation. Since Homer this device has been resorted to time and again with a view to exciting interest through the opening and manipulation of what I propose to call expositional gaps.

The literary text may be conceived of as a dynamic system of gaps. A reader who wishes to actualize the field of reality that is represented in a work, to construct (or rather reconstruct) the fictive world and action it projects, is necessarily compelled to pose and answer, throughout the reading-process, such questions as, What is happening or has happened, and why? What is the connection between this event and the previous ones? What is the motivation of this or that character? To what extent does the logic of cause and effect correspond to that of everyday life? and so on. Most of the answers to these questions, however, are not provided explicitly, fully and authoritatively (let alone immediately) by the text, but must be worked out by the reader himself on the basis of the implicit guidance it affords. In fact, every literary work opens a number of gaps that have to be filled in by the reader through the construction of hypotheses, in the light of which the various components of the work are accounted for, linked, and brought into pattern. Different gaps or systems of gaps may, however, vary in several important respects: some can, for instance, be filled in almost automatically, while others require conscious and laborious consideration; some can be filled in fully and definitely, others only partially and tentatively; some by a single, others by several (different, conflicting, or even mutually exclusive), hypotheses.[29]

The highly complex problems and factors that the construction, clash, unfolding and validation of hypotheses involve will be dealt with and illustrated in the following chapters. At this point I wish to go on to suggest in outline an additional distinction, between temporary and permanent gaps. The latter give rise to questions or sets of questions to which no single, fully explicit and authoritative answer is made by the text from beginning to end. What are Iago's motives, or Raskolnikov's? Is Becky

Sharp "guilty" or "innocent" in her relations with Lord Steyne? Are the ghosts purely hallucinations of the governess's disordered mind? What really happened in the Marabar caves? All these questions point to permanent gaps in the respective works. No reader can afford to disregard them, but he will look in vain for pat explicit answers. Only through a close analysis of the text can he evolve an hypothesis or a set of hypotheses by which these gaps can be filled in with some degree of probability.

A temporary gap, on the other hand, is one that the work opens at some point upon the continuum of the text only to fill it in explicitly and satisfactorily itself—or at least to enable the reader to do so with ease—at a subsequent stage. Who are Tom Jones's parents? Why does Chichikov buy dead souls? What was written in the note Osborne slipped into Becky's hand on the eve of Waterloo? Where did Thomas Sutpen spring from? Is there any truth in Wickham's allegations about Darcy? Who is the narrator of *Pnin,* and who the addressee of "My Last Duchess"? Each of these questions indicates a gap that is kept open only temporarily, so as to arouse the reader's curiosity or surprise and encourage inferential activity; such a gap may, I shall show, serve many other functions as well, but it always serves the dynamics of expectation. The extent to which this kind of gap is manipulated may of course vary from work to work, from author to author, and from genre to genre, according to general aims or particular needs. Temporary gaps are, for example, both fewer in number and less central in position in a novel of manners or a picaresque tale than in a detective story, which stands or falls by the author's skill in handling them.

At this stage in the argument I want to stress three essential, related points. First, both the opening of a gap of either kind and the explicit filling in of a temporary gap necessarily involve a deformation of the chronological order of presentation. Instead of communicating a certain piece of referential information—an incident, a motive, a situational or psychological datum, a general canon of probability—at its "natural," logically and chronologically determined place, the author chooses to withhold it for some time (thus creating the gap), to draw at will the reader's attention to its absence by holding the gap open (thus stressing the original violation of the fabula order), and finally to divulge it at an opportune moment (thus closing the gap in a way that again deforms the chronological sequence). Second, permanent gaps are located both in the fabula and the sujet, whereas temporary gaps belong to the sujet alone—being "artificially" created and sustained through temporal manipulations of some perfectly straightforward and coherent segment or segments of the fabula. The former gap results already from the process of selection that produces the fabula; the latter, from the process of combination and displacement that produces the sujet.

Third, modern criticism has notoriously been concerned with "ambiguity," "plurisignation," "multivalence," or "paradox" on the verbal level of the text as well as on the level of general conceptual meaning. Multiple meaning has come to be generally regarded as a (if not *the*) distinctive feature of literary language. Surprisingly, however, even the ambiguity-hunters shy at ambiguity on the level of action and fictive world, of the field of reality represented in the literary text. Far from being considered an honorific distinctive feature, these equally prevalent *referential* ambiguities—effected and developed through gap-producing dislocations, relating to such large semantic and compositional components as character, event, plot, or situation—are as a rule either dismissed as deplorable obscurities or forcibly resolved one way or the other. It is this flattening tendency, for instance, that has given rise to the interminable controversy about Henry James's *The Turn of the Screw,* which is in fact deliberately constructed round a permanent gap making it impossible for the reader to determine the reality of the ghosts. Neither the Apparitionist nor the Nonapparitionist hypothesis can be legitimately accepted by itself—we must, "illogically," accept both.[30] And the same applies to the dynamics of complementary (e.g., the nature of Iago's motives) as well as mutually exclusive hypotheses, to temporary as well as permanent tensions between hypotheses (e.g., the ultimately removed necessity of viewing each suspect in the detective story as both guilty and innocent at once), and to contextually minor (e.g., the physical appearance of Homer's Helen of Troy) as well as major gaps. The processes of referential ambiguation and disambiguation —their semantic objects, structural modes and varieties, interplay of rhetorical and actional dynamics, and functional interrelation with other levels of the text (e.g., the verbal, thematic, and generic)—will be a central concern of our inquiry into temporal strategy.

This brings me to my last, and primarily methodological, point. The piece of information that is thus wrenched out of its "natural" position and temporarily or permanently withheld from the reader may originally have been located at any point along the fabula, as is indicated by the above examples; and the gap may be opened and filled in at any point along the sujet. In this study, however, I shall be particularly concerned with a special kind of gap, namely, that which is produced by the suppression of expositional material. The disparity between this and other kinds of gap is positional rather than functional: the expositional gap merely relates to that definite part of the fabula delimited in the previous chapter. I have chosen to devote most of my argument to the handling and functions of expositional gaps because they are not only the most common, problematic, and instructively variable, but also the most crucial. The fact that exposition (especially when preliminary) is often a bore must not blind us to its crucial role as complex of premises: like many other things that are slighted or taken for granted, we begin to appreciate it in its absence. Precisely because the fabula material whose suppression gives rise to the expositional gap is largely nonconcrete (habitual, recurrent, etc.), its range of implications for the reading-process may be proportionally wider and more basic than that of the materials of the action proper, and its distribution and ambiguation by way of gaps may, temporarily or even permanently, affect the reader's view not simply of details but of the whole character, situation, or general fictive framework in question. And this is as true of drama and of poetry with some actional development as it is of narrative proper. But I shall constantly try to substantiate the claims made in the concluding remarks of the first chapter by showing that the manipulation of expositional gaps does not differ in essence from that of the postexpositional, but forms part and parcel of the dynamic principles of ordering, distribution and hypothesis-construction that inform each work as a whole.

It is now possible, at any rate, to describe more precisely the principal device resorted to by writers who have endeavored to avoid the drawbacks of preliminary exposition; they exploit the flexibility of their medium—notably the possibility of constructing an innumerable number of sujets out of the same fabula—to open expositional gaps by artificially deforming the chronological sequence. An *in medias res* beginning—the most prevalent form of large-scale chronological dislocation—affords a good chance of stimulating interest in the expositional material, since it entails the creation of an expositional gap that extends temporally from the beginning of the fabula to that of the sujet. In fact, however, the reader's attention is not drawn immediately to this single large gap as a whole but rather to a series or system of smaller, successively opened gaps subsumed by it. And the operation of these gaps is best explained in the wider context of the complex of advantages yielded, even from the viewpoint of narrative interest alone, by the plunge *in medias res*.

First of all, the author's chances of securing our attention from the very start are considerably improved since we are at once hurled into the heart of the matter—in most cases, right into a crucial scene. Once the reader's attention has been captured, the work has already gone a long way towards preparing him for the assimilation of exposition. The opening scenes constitute, temporally and spatially, a sort of concrete frame or scaffold into which the reader can fit the expositional material that is to come and thus effectively integrate it. The construction of this frame, moreover, serves to draw the reader's notice to the existence of various gaps—small and large, crucial and merely intriguing, isolated and closely concentrated or interdependent. For as soon as the initially propelled situation and the characters figuring in it have caught his attention, the reader becomes aware—and this awareness can easily be heightened by a suitable manipulation of gaps—that he will not understand them fully or at all as long as he lacks certain information about the period preceding the beginning of the sujet. The expositional information that is distributed—most of it implicitly—throughout the first scenes is usually too meager and too disconnected to enable the reader to construct satisfactory hypotheses as to how the various expositional gaps, concerning factual antecedent or psychological motive, should be filled in. On the contrary, the very sketchiness of the information thus unfolded renders these gaps even more prominent and proportionately stimulates his curiosity even further. Furthermore, the reader is eager to have this withheld material not only in order to disambiguate and reconstitute the narrative past or even the present state of affairs per se but also to acquire the premises necessary for forming warrantable expectations as to the probable developments of the action in the narrative future. If the action proper is intrinsically interesting due to its natural (quasi-mimetically propelled) dynamics, the antecedents can be artificially rendered interesting, in close reference to these developments, through the rhetorical dynamics of displacement, ambiguity, and consequent bi-directional expectation.

However, the degree to which the reader's desire to have the expositional gaps closed is heightened by an *in medias res* start depends on a number of closely connected, variable factors. It is proportionate, I shall argue, to the interest created by the initially dramatized situation; to the author's skill in opening the gaps and in maintaining the reader's curiosity about them; to the importance of the suppressed information; and to the extent to which the reader is made conscious that he has been plunged into the midst of a causal sequence (or plot-type fabula), where past is ineluctably linked to present and future. But whatever the degree of interest evoked, the reader can as a rule be manipulated to some extent into positively wishing for the disclosure of this "intrinsically dull" narrative material if he is made sufficiently aware that the text has temporarily dispensed with its logical-chronological beginning.[31] It is for this reason that, from the viewpoint of narrative interest, the artfully deformed order, involving a retrospective illumination of the concrete and dynamic action proper, is preferable to the "natural," in which the exposition is anticipatory and its significance must be taken on trust.

After the reader's curiosity has been excited through this delay, it is up to the author to decide how he wishes to exploit it. The way in which the expositional gaps are handled—the duration of the author's abstention from closing them, the uses they are put to, and the technique of filling them in—turns, as I shall argue, not only on the author's skill but to a decisive degree on his overall goals as well. In some rare instances the plunge into the middle is of so brief a duration as to leave little scope for the manipulation of gaps; and it is indeed designed merely to tie a knot in time. In Conrad's *The Secret Agent,* for example, no sooner has the narrator managed to finish his first sentence ("Mr. Verloc, going out in the morning, left his shop nominally in charge of his brother-in-law") than he doubles back to give us an account of Verloc's shop, customers and family. And having thus provided us with some of the necessary antecedents, he reverts at the beginning of the second chapter to the previously postulated temporal point, resuming the representation of the opening scene just where he left it off: "Such was the house, the household, and the business Mr. Verloc left behind him on his way westward at the hour of half past ten in the morning."

In other works, the gaps are kept open only for the shortest time the author thinks necessary to prepare the reader for a willing assimilation of the exposition. In *Vanity Fair,* Thackeray thus appears to have calculated that the gaps opened in the first scene—Becky's strange exit from Miss Pinkerton's academy—have aroused our curiosity enough to justify his introducing immediately into the next chapter the concentrated block of antecedents that retrospectively accounts for Becky's character and conduct.

Still other writers, however, are not content with such brief delays but push the advantages of the plunge *in medias res* much further. They are in no hurry to allay the reader's curiosity. On the contrary, they play on it in different ways (e.g., by a piecemeal distribution of some intriguing complex of expositional motifs, by highlighting the significance of the withheld or ambiguated information, or by constant frustrations of the reader's desire to have the gaps filled in and the clash of hypotheses about past, present and future resolved); and exploit both the reader's expectations and the prolonged openness of the gaps for a variety of ends.

At this point, I believe, it would be advisable to elaborate and illustrate the introductory comments made in this chapter and to pave the way for the future development of the argument by considering a work in which most of the rhetorical potentialities of "deformed" chronology, and the dynamic potentialities deriving from the temporal nature of literary art in general, are brilliantly realized.

CHAPTER THREE

DELAYED AND DISTRIBUTED EXPOSITION IN THE *ODYSSEY:* THE DYNAMICS OF NARRATIVE INTEREST

A Poet thrusteth into the middest, even where
it most concerneth him, and there recoursing to
the things forepaste, and divining of things to
come, maketh a pleasing analysis of all.
  Edmund Spenser, letter to Raleigh

The way Homer's epics begin in the middle and
do not finish at the end is a reflexion of the
truly epic mentality's total indifference to any
form of architectural construction.
  Georg Lukacs, *The Theory of the Novel*

If Homer bores his audience he will not be
invited to dinner again.
  W. H. D. Rouse, Preface to the *Odyssey*

The *Odyssey,* one of the most historically influential *in medias res* narratives, does not start at the beginning of its fabula (say, with Odysseus's exploits at Troy) but at a temporal point about ten years later. The reader (or rather the listener, but I shall use the former as a generic term) is possessed of the most essential expositional data only at the end of book 12, when he is already halfway through the epic.[1] From this point on the narrative proceeds more or less chronologically. In the following analysis I shall accordingly concentrate on the logic of the distribution of narrative elements—expositional and nonexpositional—in the first half of the work. To describe this logic is to answer the following crucial questions:

1. Why does the work choose to delay the communication of the bulk of the expositional information?

2. Why is this information not only delayed but also distributed throughout the first twelve books?

3. Is there any method in the (strikingly nonchronological) order in

56

which the expositional motifs are presented? Is there any reason for the particular location of each of these motifs, and for their location and un-folding vis-à-vis one another, or could they fulfil the same functions irrespective of their position in the overall order of presentation?

4. What are the interrelationships between the principles of exposi-tional presentation and the movement, patterning, and goals of the text as a whole? And what between the dynamics of communication and the dynamics of the action itself? In short, what functions does the material thus manipulated serve apart from the purely referential or informational?

I

After the invocation to the Muse, the omniscient narrator informs us that of all the Greek champions who survived the Trojan War Odysseus alone was prevented from returning home. At present he is being kept prisoner by the nymph Calypso, who wishes him to marry her. The gods, feeling pity for Odysseus, finally take advantage of the absence of Poseidon, his mighty enemy, to assemble in Zeus's palace and discuss the situation (p. 19).

In this opening we already encounter some devices that characterize Homer's expositional strategy throughout. Though plunging *in medias res,* the *Odyssey* starts with a very short preliminary exposition (consisting of the invocation and a generalized report) before rendering the first dis-criminated occasion—the divine assembly. Unlike many preliminary expo-sitions, however, this one not only refrains from opening at the beginning of the fabula and then proceeding chronologically, but also does its best to impress this abstention upon the reader's mind. The fact that most of the exposition is at this point withheld does not emerge only later on, when we retrospectively realize how little of the indispensable data has been imparted in this preliminary account, but immediately leaps to the eye when we compare the meagerness of the information actually com-municated here with the lavish expositional promises made by the invoca-tion itself:

> The hero of the tale which I beg the Muse to help me tell is that resourceful man who roamed the wide world after he had sacked the holy citadel of Troy. He saw the cities of many peoples and he learnt their ways. He suffered many hardships on the high seas in his struggles to preserve his life and bring his comrades home. . . ." (P. 19)

The work, then, insistently draws the reader's notice to the suppression of exposition that the plunge *in medias res* involves by establishing right at the outset of the sujet a chronological *terminus a quo* (Odysseus's departure from Troy) and alluding to some of the expositional events that intervened between this date and the actual starting point, ten years later.

Unlike the standard preliminary exposition, where the introductory account is fairly exhaustive—and at times exhausting—the opening here thus makes no pretence of being more than barely sufficient to enable the reader to understand what happens in the immediately following scenes; and it is certainly far from adequate for the comprehension of the hero's character or even the reasons for his long-drawn struggles.

There are, however, no grounds for the complaint that "this is not a very accurate or systematic introduction to the poem."[2] For this preliminary account is designed rather to open expositional gaps than to fill them in. The paucity and sketchiness of the information it conveys, the cursory or obscure references to past "hardships" or "struggles" in general and to particular adventures, such as the disastrous slaughter of Hyperion's oxen, Calypso's love or Poseidon's enmity—all these are devices that stimulate the reader's curiosity by calling his attention to specific gaps: What are the extraordinary adventures that the hero has undergone since the end of the war? How has he—and he alone of all his comrades—managed to survive? Who is this man who has been singled out for misfortune? Why is he so relentlessly persecuted by Poseidon? What makes him so outstanding that even goddesses fall in love with him? It is the hope of having these gaps closed that forcefully impels the reader's attention forward to the scene of the Olympian assembly.

He soon discovers, however, that this discriminated occasion, like the expositional block that precedes it, provides only partial or fragmentary answers to these questions. It not only refrains from satisfying his curiosity but at some points even proceeds to stimulate it further. We now gather, for instance, that during his wanderings Odysseus somehow overcame the gigantic Cyclops and has had to struggle against Poseidon's malice ever since; and we learn something further of his relations with Calypso, "who is keeping the unhappy man from home in spite of all his tears. Day after day she does her best to banish Ithaca from his memory with false and flattering words; and Odysseus, who would give anything for the sight of the smoke rising up from his own land, can only yearn for death" (p. 20). But again, the skillful distribution of a few intriguing, allusive, disconnected expositional motifs rather whets than allays our appetite for Odysseus's past adventures, for it only makes the specific informational gaps (as well as the large temporal blank that subsumes them) more glaring than before.

This scene, moreover, not only draws our attention to existing gaps but also opens a totally new, major set, namely, the situation at Ithaca. The seemingly casual reference to a hitherto unsuspected aspect of the expositional situation ("a mob of suitors who spend their time in the wholesale slaughter of [Telemachus's] sheep and fatted cattle"; p. 21) raises a host of fresh questions as to the identity and conduct of the Suitors, the attitude of the wife and the son towards them, and the manner in which this newly revealed factor may affect the fortunes of the absent hero.

And this effect links up at once with another expositional function of the assembly scene—the sketching out of Odysseus's figure. As we retrospectively realize, the impression this scene gives us of his personality is radically different from the rounded portrait we carry away when we have perused the whole epic. The expositional unfolding of Odysseus's traits is in fact far from accidental or impartial. In order to create in the reader the maximal sympathetic response to the hero and consequent involvement in his plight, Homer has cunningly restricted himself here to dwelling only on the most engaging of Odysseus's qualities; and in order to leave no doubt about the normative validity of the initial characterization, he does not delegate it to some fallible human being but invests it with the full authority of unanimous divine attestation.[3] Zeus is thus made to characterize Odysseus as "pious," "admirable," "most generous," "the wisest man alive" (p. 20), and Athene to harp on his fidelity to home and family; the bravery he displayed in the encounter with Polyphemus adds another favourable touch. On the other hand, there is no hint even of the seamy side of his complex character—his cunning, his egotism, or his almost morbid suspiciousness. Whatever de-idealization or qualification of character that is to be done can be accomplished later. At this point, the narrator's chief concern is to ensure our sympathetic involvement in the hero's fortunes—past, present, and future. As we soon discover, one reason for this manipulation of the reader's attitude through the tendentious distribution and ordering of expositional material is that unless his sympathies and expectations are directed in the desired way, he may not react properly to the complicated alternations of hope and fear that lie ahead.

Furthermore, the opening scene not only harks back to various aspects of the expositional past but also marks the first stage of the forward-moving action, directing our attention towards the narrative future. The essentially static state of affairs (static though composed of tensions or conflicting pulls, for the tensions are static too: Calypso's love versus Odysseus's homesickness, Poseidon's enmity versus Athene's affection) has finally been destabilized due to the introduction of two strongly developmental motifs: Athene's initiative and the gods' consequent resolution to get the unhappy king home. In its interrelation of past, present and future, this scene affords the first instance of Homer's economical procedure of working backwards and forwards—in terms of both presentational and actional dynamics—at the same time and through the same narrative elements. Thus, when Zeus is accused by Athene of callous indifference to Odysseus's sufferings and is driven to defend himself by the explanation that it is Poseidon alone who is implacable towards her favorite, he is not informing any of the gods, including Athene, of anything they did not know before. The gods have been aware all along of the reasons for Odysseus's prolonged exile and for Poseidon's enmity, it being precisely this awareness that has induced them to assemble in Poseidon's absence. It is only the reader who gains some indispensable information from Zeus's retort. The whole exchange, however, serves more than this purely expositional function. Athene's intention in pretending ignorance is to drive Zeus into a corner, to compel him to state his position unambiguously and publicly, and thus to pass a resolution in Odysseus's favor; and it is the success of her tactics that shatters the long-standing expositional stalemate and sets the action going. That some important antecedents are thereby communicated at the same time, is an additional clear profit of Homer's artistry.

How the various features of this multifunctional scene hang together is fully to emerge only in the next book. But we have already seen enough of Homer's strategy of delaying and distributing the expositional premises to view it as typical that in the immediately following scenes he should provide very little of the expected information about Odysseus. Instead, he concentrates on disambiguating the most recently opened complex of expositional gaps—that concerning the situation at Ithaca.

Some of this information is vividly dramatized through the conduct of the Suitors, who come swaggering in, help themselves to meat and wine, uproariously amuse themselves with music and dancing, and broadly hint at their ambition to ascend the throne (to which Telemachus is heir-apparent) by marrying the queen (pp. 21-28). Athene's generalized reference to the Suitors in the previous scene stamps this scandalous behavior as habitual; so even though this scene is rendered in the fictive present it is in part expositionally illustrative (and proportionally condemnatory).

The scene as a whole would be as illustrative as verses 4-5 in the first chapter of the Book of Job were it not for the introduction of a new factor in the form of the disguised Athene. Her appearance, first of all, serves to convey additional exposition to the reader. As a "stranger," it is perfectly natural that she should give vent to amazement "at the sight of such unseemly behavior" by asking her host questions that deeply interest us: "What is the meaning of this banquet? Who are all these people? And what is your concern in the affair?" (p. 24). And it is as natural that Telemachus should explain to his friendly guest that "of all the island-chieftains in Dulichium, in Same, in wooded Zacynthus, or in rocky Ithaca, there isn't one that isn't courting my mother and wasting my property. As for her, she neither refuses, though she hates the idea of remarrying, nor can she bring herself to take the final step. Meanwhile they are eating me out of house and home. And I shouldn't be surprised if they finished me my-self" (p. 24). The information given in his answers is of course indis-pensable to the reader, not to the omniscient goddess, whose motivated pretense of ignorance enables Homer for the second time to work back-wards and forwards at the same time—propelling the actional dynamics of the fictive world together with the presentational dynamics of the reading process. Athene's real object is again to set the action going by destabilizing a tensely static expositional situation—this time on earth—so as to benefit her favorite. Accordingly, having tested and roused Tele-machus by her questions, she proceeds to instill some spirit into him by maintaining that his father is still alive somewhere, "probably in the hands of enemies," and will soon manage to return and clear his house of the intruders. The hitherto largely illustrative scene is rendered concrete—and the habitual state of affairs is galvanized into life—from the moment Athene persuades the youth to take the initiative by calling the people to assembly, giving the Suitors formal notice to quit the palace, and setting sail for Pylos and Sparta on the chance that he may pick up some stray rumors concerning Odysseus's fate.

The assembly that follows further clarifies the situation at Ithaca, especially the position of the Suitors. It emerges from this showdown that neither entreaties nor threats can budge them from their resolution that one of them shall marry Penelope. They will to go on wasting Telemachus's property "so long as Penelope keeps [them] kicking [their] heels" (p. 35) as a means of pressuring her into a speedy decision; and they give the assembly to understand that they are ready to resort to violence should anybody—Telemachus, the people, even Odysseus himself—attempt to thwart their plans. As Eurymachus announces, they "are afraid of no-one at all—certainly not of Telemachus, for all his rhetoric" (p. 34). Further light is also thrown on another significant aspect of the expositional state of affairs, namely, Penelope's rather ambivalent attitude to her Suitors, the description of her ingenious dilatory stratagems arising in a most natural manner when Antinous pleads not guilty to the blame laid on the gang by Telemachus (p. 32).

In and through the presentation of the Suitors, moreover, the palace and assembly scenes serve still another vital function—the intensification of our sympathetic involvement in Odysseus's fortunes. This is again ac-complished through a highly selective disclosure of expositional material. But while the opening has manipulated our attitude to Odysseus by im-pressing on our attention his sad plight abroad and only those of his traits that are sure to arouse our admiration, during the present scenes the same effect is produced mainly through the application of the opposite proce-dure to the characterization of the Suitors.[4]

How is it possible to claim, as one critic does, that the Suitors "are given sympathetic portraits early on" and that "the logic of most of the second book is kept conveniently vague so as to allow our sympathies to fall to both parties in the conflict"?[5] This misreading of the second book also overlooks the significance of the overall expositional order in which the Suitors' traits as well as the hero's are presented in the sujet. It is only toward the end that Homer somewhat complicates our response to the Suitors by revealing some of the more engaging traits possessed by part of them. The disclosure of these characteristics, however, has been deliberately delayed.[6] And at the present stage they are so rigorously suppressed that they are not even remotely implied. On the contrary, to ensure the polarization of our response to the two camps, Homer presents the Suitors upon their first introduction in the most condemnatory light possible by selecting for intense treatment—out of their overall complex of characteristics in the fabula—none but antipathetic traits. Their cocksureness, rapacity, disregard for the rights of the absent king and his family, and contempt for the voice of public opinion are vividly represented throughout the first two books. But Homer is not content with the normative implications conveyed by the dramatized events themselves. He reinforces them by bringing the whole force of his authorial authority to bear upon the manipulation of the reader's reactions through his repeated explicit references to the Suitors as "insolent," "ill-mannered," or "ruffianly." And he again invests these valuations with the imprimatur of divine testimony. As Athene authoritatively concludes, "Any decent man would be disgusted at the sight of such unseemly behaviour" (p. 24).

Very significantly, moreover, the rhetorical manipulation of judgment through diametrically opposed orders of expositional presentation and the stimulation of interest in the expositional past are related not only to each other but to the movement of the whole action towards the narrative future. In other words, Homer's principles of expositional delay, distribution and ordering are inseparable from his overall suspense strategy.

The assembly scene dramatizes the extent to which the situation is getting desperate. The note of urgency is struck again and again. Time is running out. The Suitors are no longer to be fooled by dilatory tricks and press for an immediate decision: "Send your mother away and make her marry the man whom her father chooses and whom she prefers. She must beware of trying our young men's patience much further" (p. 32). A violent conflict is impending and the Suitors are bound to emerge victorious, for Telemachus, despite the change Athene has effected in him, is hardly qualified to cope with them. And the people of Ithaca, whom nothing can stir out of their abject silence, are revealed to be equally helpless. In this respect the expositional deadlock of tensions has not changed in the least in spite of Telemachus's efforts.

It is in this way that Homer ensures that the gradual unfolding of the situation at Ithaca should increasingly direct our attention not towards Telemachus, who ostensibly figures as the central character in the clash with the Suitors, but towards the absent Odysseus—the only person who has some chance of setting things to rights. As Telemachus regretfully admits, "the truth is that there is no-one like Odysseus in charge to purge the house. . . . We are not equipped like him for the task, and . . . the attempt would serve only to expose our miserable weakness" (p. 31). This indirect centering of our hopes on Odysseus, and Odysseus alone, at a point when we already know that he is destined to return, inevitably generates suspense as to the outcome of the future conflict; and once we start calculating his chances of victory, we are far from reassured. The overwhelming numerical advantage of the Suitors' party is a most disturbing factor; Telemachus later on voices explicitly our present fears for Odysseus when, on first meeting his father, he maintains that "I have heard of your great reputation as a soldier who could use his brains as well as his hands. But this time you have overreached yourself. You appal me! Two men couldn't possibly take on so many, and such good fighters into the bargain. There are not a mere dozen Suitors, nor a couple of dozen, but many times more than that. . . . I am afraid it may be you who pay a cruel and ghastly price for the crimes you have come to avenge" (p. 214). This consideration appears even more weighty when we recall that Athene's patronage of Odysseus is canceled out by Poseidon's enmity; and what is even more, that the gods have not decreed that the hero should destroy his enemies while remaining alive himself, but only that he should be allowed to reach Ithaca.[7]

The text does not bear out, moreover, the oft-made claim that from the very beginning there is no doubt in the reader's mind that Odysseus will prevail since Athene predicts his victory: "If only he could show himself at this moment at the palace gates, with his helmet, his shield and his two spears . . . there'd be a quick death and a sorry wedding for them all" (pp. 24-25).[8] Not only is this prediction significantly qualified at once ("But such matters, of course, lie on the knees of the gods"), but its force is more than counterbalanced by the portent of the two eagles, sent by none other than the omnipotent Zeus ("of the crooked ways"):

> Zeus, who was watching [the assembly scene] from afar, urged two eagles into flight from the mountain-top. For a while they sailed down the wind with outstretched pinions, wing to wing. But as soon as they were directly over the meeting-place, where the sound of voices filled the air, they began to flap their wings and wheel about, glancing down at the faces of the crowd with looks foreboding death. They then fell to work with their talons, ripping each other's cheeks and neck on either side, and so swooped eastward over the house-tops of the busy

town. The people stared at the birds in amazement as this scene was enacted before their eyes, and asked themselves what was to become of such a portent. (P. 33)

Haliserthes, a soothsayer who participates in the assembly, interprets the omen as a foreshadowing of Odysseus's impending return and "a bloody doom for the Suitors one and all" (p. 34). His optimistic reading ultimately proves, of course, to be right; but this must not blind us to its wrong-headedness. At this point in the narrative, when we examine it in the light of the expositional information communicated so far and of the plain meaning of the symbol itself, we are, alas, compelled to question its validity or even to dismiss it as wishful thinking. Not only does the numerical superiority of the (one hundred and eight) Suitors point the other way, but the symbol itself clearly suggests that the two camps will be at best equally matched in power. And the mutual ripping of cheeks and neck added to the "looks foreboding death" are not particularly reassuring: the Suitors' party can afford to lose some men, while Odysseus's obviously cannot.

That the omen should be viewed as portentous rather than reassuring can also be demonstrated by reference to the work's internal norms of foreshadowing. For the omen is to recur several times, with revealing variations, at different stages in the narrative where its meaning can be established beyond doubt. When Telemachus takes leave of Menelaus, "a bird came flying to the right. It was an eagle, carrying in its talons a great white goose, a tame bird from the yard" (pp. 199–200). Later, on reaching Ithaca, he is greeted by "a bird flying to the right. It was a hawk, Apollo's winged herald, folding a dove in its talons, which it plucked so that the feathers fluttered down to earth" (p. 208; see also p. 264). In each instance the youth is exhilarated by an optimistic interpretation (offered by Helen and the soothsayer Theoclymenus, respectively), whose validity is undoubted. This is indicated, first, by the particular terms of the omens, which are convincingly accounted for; second, by explicit authorial commentary (note the "happy omen" of p. 208); third, and most important, by the presentation of both omens at points where the reader has already been authoritatively assured that Odysseus is bound to emerge victorious— so the eagle or hawk can denote nobody but him. And if these optimistic readings are correct, Haliserthes's must be ill-founded, since his omen differs from the subsequent ones at the most essential point: here we have not a formidable bird of prey effortlessly devouring a domestic bird but two matched eagles clawing at each other.

But the portent most appropriately opposed to that of book 2 comes on the very eve of the struggle, when Penelope dreams of a great eagle swooping down from the hills and killing her whole flock of geese with its crooked beak (p. 257; cf. p. 285). Each member of the sequence of omens operates as an objective correlative of the reader's expectations *at the moment;* and the radical differences between the first and the last, which projects the eagle-Odysseus's victory in face of the "numerical advantage" of the flock of geese, structurally correspond to the radical shift in the reader's expectations that has taken place in the meantime.

The suspense Homer now generates by suggesting that Odysseus's fate hangs in the balance is directly related to the curiosity aroused by his suppression of the bulk of the exposition. Both suspense and curiosity are emotions or states of mind characterized by expectant restlessness and tentative hypothcscs that derive from a lack of information; both thus draw the reader's attention forward in the hope that the information that will resolve or allay them lies ahead. They differ, however, in that suspense derives from a lack of desired information concerning the outcome of a conflict that is to take place in the narrative future, a lack that involves a clash of hope and fear; whereas curiosity is produced by a lack of information that relates to the narrative past, a time when struggles have already been resolved, and as such it often involves an interest in the information for its own sake. Suspense thus essentially relates to the dynamics of the ongoing action; curiosity, to the dynamics of temporal deformation. These working-definitions being postulated, it can be demonstrated that from this point on in the epic one can trace two major, theoretically distinct, lines of narrative interest. The first is the line of curiosity, generated and developed mainly by the author's subtle technique of delaying, ambiguating and distributing the expositional material. The second is the line of suspense, sustained by the clash of our intermittently aroused hopes and fears (both being emotively and/or ethically colored hypotheses) about the outcome of the future confrontation.

The psychological tug of war that the tension between these two lines of narrative interest involves sometimes results in artistic failure. As I shall argue in Chapter 6, this usually happens when an author has failed to stimulate the reader's curiosity sufficiently to compel him to dwell on some lengthy expositional account that stands between him and the anxiously awaited conflict or resolution. In this case, when suspense so evidently has the upper hand, the reader can hardly be blamed for impatiently skipping the retardation and dashing forward. One of Homer's notable achievements in the *Odyssey,* however, is his manifold interrelation of these clashing lines of interest. His favorite, and most complex, device of playing them off against each other consists in his skillful distribution of parts of the expositional material in a way that alternately arouses the two components of suspense—hope and fear—and that consequently creates in turn a need for further exposition to resolve the newly generated suspense; and then the same dynamic play recurs all over again.

Homer's manipulation of the reader's expectations throughout books 1 and 2 already illustrates how far literary art can move away from a concern with exposition as such. By initially distributing only such antecedents as cannot fail to heighten our pity for the admirable protagonist and our indignation at his antagonists, he has succeeded in enlisting our sympathies on the right side. The suspense thus aroused concerning Odysseus's fate is consequently more acute than in the case of divided sympathies or of "A plague o' both your houses!" Homer has, moreover, increased this suspense by dramatically revealing that Odysseus will have to bear the brunt of the battle, in view of the impotence or cowardice of his potential followers; and he has intensified our fears even further through the symbol of the two eagles. The reader has by these means been manipulated into a state of mind characterized by a tension between the wish of having Odysseus immediately return to take revenge on his enemies and the fear lest they should prove too much for him. When perched on the horns of this emotional or psychological dilemma, the reader's natural reaction is to demand some additional information about the hero's nature, abilities and past achievements so as to be able to determine whether he is qualified for the accomplishment of the task that threateningly lies ahead. Therefore, the suspense generated in these books, far from rendering us impatient at the communication of exposition, which usually only retards the natural flow of the forward-moving action, actively stimulates our interest in it.

One measure of Homer's art, then, is that at this tense phase of the narrative the reader has been manoeuvred into positively desiring all the information the author can give him about Odysseus. The opening books thus afford us, among other things, an excellent example of the artistic gains that the deformation of a plot-type fabula may yield: the reader has been forced to curb his impatience and satisfy his curiosity at the price of the consequent prolongation of his suspense, for he has been made aware that his expectations and hypotheses as to the narrative future inextricably depend on as full a knowledge as possible of the hidden expositional past.

In the light of all this, we can also explain Homer's decision to refrain from proceeding immediately after the first scene with the disclosure of exposition concerning Odysseus, and instead to clarify first the situation at home. As we realize in retrospect, the amount of exposition relating to Odysseus himself, to his complex character and multifarious adventures, is so large (compared with that required to comprehend the state of affairs at Ithaca) and so important, that its communication had to be led up to carefully. So Homer whets our appetite for this information in two ways. Throughout the opening of book 1 he accomplishes this effect by a skillful manipulation of expositional gaps; that is, by playing directly upon the reader's curiosity. From Athene's arrival at Ithaca to Telemachus's departure for Pylos, however, this device is seldom resorted to.[9] On the contrary, this part draws our attention to the meagerness of our knowledge about the protagonist and heightens our interest in his antecedents not by opening new gaps but rather by filling in some of the old ones—those concerning the Ithacan characters; not by turning the reader's mind back to the narrative past and trying to interest him in the exposition as such, but by impelling it forward to the narrative future and casually relating future to past in a structure of probabilities. Homer's decision to delay the further portrayal of Odysseus has thus enabled him not only to proceed in the manipulation of the reader's response to the situation and to lay the foundations for present and future suspense but also economically to vary the techniques by which he paves the way for the ultimate emergence of the bulk of exposition.

Consequently, when Telemachus sets out on what may be viewed as a voyage in quest of exposition, the reader is as anxious for his success as the lad himself, though for a different reason. Telemachus is above all intent on discovering whether his father is still alive. But the reader, already freed from this doubt by the far-sighted author, is able to look further ahead. He is rather eager to find out the stuff Odysseus is made of.

II

Homer first takes care to sharpen the normative polarization on which his whole suspense strategy rests. When at the beginning of book 3 Telemachus and his crew reach Pylos, they find the people of the city at a feast, just as they do at the beginning of book 4, on their arrival at Sparta. The descriptions of the rites and the hospitality may seem excessively circumstantial if judged by their contribution to the propulsion of the plot ("The poet used far more concrete details than is either customary, or really necessary."[10]) They further, however, an expositional and rhetorical purpose that is at this stage at least as vital; namely, the concrete establishment of internal norms or moral register by which the reader should judge the situation that has prevailed at Ithaca for years.

Our first view of the people in both places is at a ceremony, with the rightful kings (Nestor and Menelaus) at their head (pp. 41, 54). In both places the strangers are cordially received. In Pylos, "as soon as they caught sight of the strangers they all made a move in their direction, waving their hands in welcome" (pp. 41-42); in Sparta, Menelaus has them bathed, dressed, and "seated on high chairs at his own side" (pp. 54-55). These archetypal touchstones of order thus successively offer an eloquent dramatic comment on the anarchy that has been rife in Ithaca ever since the Suitors seized power, being tightly linked and contrasted with the (equally dramatized and illustrative) banquet scene of book 1 and the assembly scene of book 2. Pylos and Sparta are characterized by social and political stability, due reverence paid to the king and elders, piety, and hospitality. Whereas at Ithaca the Suitors have upset all values and norms; none of the customary sacrifices and libations is offered to the gods; the king's property is robbed, his palace turned into a scene of riotous uproar, his family persecuted, and his authority challenged; and all the established political institutions are paralyzed. Old age counts for nothing; the arrival of guests passes unnoticed; and the prince, who alone welcomes the disguised Athene—present in Pylos too—is reduced to entertaining the visitor in a corner of the hall.

This structured and strategically placed clarification of the Suitors' criminality maximizes the normative polarization of the reader's sympathies. Their destruction is to be desired because it will mean not only the reinstatement of the sympathetic protagonist in his personal rights but also the reestablishment of moral, social and political order in his kingdom.

The reader's expectations, however, of receiving through Nestor a full characterization of Odysseus and an account of his travels are sadly frustrated. The only reassuring trait of the hero's that emerges from the old man's rambling, long-winded reminiscences is Odysseus's military resourcefulness: according to the testimony of this great Greek strategist, in the whole course of the Trojan War "there was not a man that dared to match his wits against the admirable Odysseus, who in every kind of strategy proved himself supreme" (pp. 43–44). Neither the reader nor Telemachus, moreover, fares any better as regards the eliciting of information concerning Odysseus's adventures. Nestor indeed starts reminiscing from the point that has already been established as the expositional *terminus a quo* in the fabula—Odysseus's exploits and the departure of the Greeks from Troy. But in spite of his promising beginning, he actually adds nothing to our knowledge of the hero's fabulous adventures beyond the explanation that after the quarrel between the Greek leaders he himself joined Menelaus's fleet, while Odysseus finally stayed behind out of loyalty to Agamemnon, the commander-in-chief. So the sense of mystery shrouding Odysseus's wanderings is this time intensified by quasi-mimetic means: Nestor simply knows nothing from personal experience, and not even a single rumor about his comrade has reached him ever since they parted.

While able, however, to provide his guest only with a meager amount of information about his father, Nestor proceeds to narrate, at great length, the story of Agamemnon's murder by Clytaemnestra and Aegisthus and of the bloody revenge taken by Orestes on the adulterers (pp. 45–48). At first sight the intercalation of this retrospect may seem to be no more than another of Homer's dilatory devices designed to stimulate the reader's curiosity by withholding from him the desired expositional material directly relating to Odysseus while loading him with unnecessarily detailed expositional accounts of various characters who seem at the present stage to have little to do with the main action.[11] It certainly fulfils this function, but there is much more to it than that. In fact, Homer's misunderstood art of digression and amplification is not just a central feature of his own strategy. It also affords an impressive illustration of the multifunctional use to which a seeming waste of expositional materials may be put, and of the variety of devices, patterns and indirections (some of them undreamt of in popular literature) by which literary art may effect the dynamics of narrative interest, notably through the sequential manipulation and development of suprasequential ("spatial") structures.

This is not the first time that Odysseus's fate has been juxtaposed or coupled with Agamemnon's. When we trace Homer's manner of distributing the Agamemnon exposition throughout the first three books, we discover a steady progression toward an increasingly specified emphasis on the points that link his story with Odysseus's present plight. As early as the first scene, Zeus opens the divine assembly with an harangue on the adulterous relations between Clytaemnestra and Aegisthus, Agamemnon's murder and Orestes's ultimate revenge, until Athene brushes this affair aside, declaring that it is rather for the blameless Odysseus that her heart is wrung (pp. 19–20). This implicit juxtaposition of the two affairs, at a point where the reader knows nothing of the situation at Ithaca, is soon followed by an explicit linkage, made with the conduct of the Suitors in full view—namely, Athene's authoritative exhortation to Telemachus to win a fame comparable to Orestes's (p. 25). In book 3 these affairs are then juxtaposed for the third time. Here, moreover, they are repeatedly linked —first by Nestor, who, in words that echo Athene's exhortation, encourages Telemachus to be as brave as Orestes (p. 45), and then by Telemachus himself, who directly relates the comparison to the desperate situation at home: "Ah, if the gods would only give me strength like his, to cope with the insufferable insolence of my mother's suitors" (p. 46).

The problem is only that while the employment of such elaborate distributive devices with regard to Odysseus's own narrative past (e.g., the Cyclops episode) may be accounted for in terms of curiosity or suspense, their application to Agamemnon's history appears pointless. For of what use can this expositional material be to the reader?

However, the progressive coupling, the considerable space ("time") allotted to the actionally irrelevant Agamemnon episode, and the reader's being given this expositional account just when he expects a similar account of Odysseus—all these indicators draw our attention to the contextual importance of Agamemnon's tragedy and ultimately to the striking similarity between the two stories. We realize that the work has taken strong measures to establish firmly the analogical relations between them: in both we have a famous warrior-king returning (or about to return) from Troy; a suitor (or suitors) greatly inferior to the husband but nevertheless intent on marrying the queen, usurping the kingdom, and doing away with the husband or son or both; and a loyal son eager to support his father's cause. They both turn, then, on analogical husband-wife-suitor-son relationships. So though in actional terms, pure and simple, Agamemnon's wholly expositional fate is not directly related to Odysseus's ordeal until book 11 (the Underworld episode), the two are already integrated at this stage in essentially spatial terms.

But what is the function of this analogy? Scholars are in the habit of regarding the two stories as variations on the theme of the Return (honored with a special Greek name, *Nostos*).[12] According to them, these stories form what I would call a contrasted analogy: one component, in which the homecoming king is treacherously murdered by his unfaithful wife and her lover, ironically counterpoints the other, in which a mob of suitors is slaughtered by a more successful warrior. It seems to me, however, that to limit the function of the analogy to ironic parallelism is to misinterpret the whole integrated movement of the epic up to this point and to disregard the complex of expectations this movement has set up in the reader. This *hindsight misreading*, which results in the impoverishment both of the analogy itself and of the narrative as a whole, derives, in fact, from the too common failure to understand the nature and potentialities of the literary work as a time-art.

Qua time-art, the continuum of the literary text is necessarily grasped in a continuum of time in that its verbal signs (and hence also the denoted semantic referents and their patternings) are communicated not simultaneously but successively. It is true that the reader can comprehend the full meaning of the work only when he has turned the last page; but this does not mean that he remains inactive till then. On the contrary, at every point along the continuum of the text he cannot (if he is to make any sense of it, even in the simplest terms) but construct numerous tentative patterns and form tentative conclusions in the light of the information conveyed to him so far. At subsequent stages in the reading-*process* he may of course have to modify these hypotheses or even to reject them altogether under the pressure of new factual and compositional information. But even ultimately rejected hypotheses form an integral part of the meaning, structure, and whole reading experience of the work if it can be demonstrated, as it very often can, that the reader was meant to reach a certain erroneous hypothesis at this or that point. The meaning of a literary work, on all its levels, is not confined to the fully warrantable conclusions we reach at the terminus, but is made up of the sum-total of expectations and effects, trial and error included, produced throughout the eventful, tortuous journey.

One of the main concerns of the following chapters is to show how often the literary text take pains actively to mislead the reader or lay traps for him at certain points by luring him into what Henry James memorably called the crooked corridor; how often, that is, the text resorts to a calculated distribution, ordering, and patterning of elements, so as to induce the reader, for a variety of purposes, to form links and jump at conclusions that retrospectively turn out to be partly or wholly invalid. Let us now concentrate on the present case in point.

My quarrel with scholars such as those mentioned above (and not with Homerists alone) is that they fail to take into account that in literature even the construction of spatial patterns cannot be divorced from the linear movement of the text. Due to the temporal nature of the work, the reader is required to follow the play of analogy and consider its implications and functions not only retrospectively, when he looks back upon the work as a finished and reconstituted whole, but also at every point along the actual continuum of the *Odyssey* as it slowly unfolds in time. In retrospect, when Odysseus's as well as Agamemnon's story has already been played out to its end, the reader can and should dwell on the thematic counterpointing accomplished through this analogical collocation. In book 3, however, when Agamemnon's drama alone is over and done with while Odysseus's has barely started, how can the reader possibly regard their juxtaposition as ironic? To do so he must foreknow the happy outcome of Odysseus's struggle; but he neither is nor can possibly be certain of such an outcome. On the contrary, this is precisely the issue that most troubles him at this early stage. Nowhere has the reader been assured, definitely and authoritatively, that the protagonist will finally purge his house of the Suitors *and* remain alive to enjoy the fruits of his victory; and what is more, the work has done its utmost to generate acute suspense about his fate. To claim, therefore, that at this stage in the narrative sequence the stories are ironically juxtaposed, is to miss the whole point; far from being contrasted, the stories are deliberately made to appear too disturbingly similar.

This conclusion is further reinforced by the two explicit linkages of the expositional past with the narrative present. When urging Telemachus to plan the destruction of the Suitors, Athene addresses him as follows:

"Have you not heard what a name Prince Orestes made for himself in the world when he killed the traitor Aegisthus for murdering his noble father? You, my friend—and what a tall and splendid fellow you have grown!—must be as brave as Orestes. Then future generations will sing your praises." (P. 25)

And Nestor follows suit:

> "Even you must have heard now [Agamemnon] had no sooner got back than he fell a wretched victim to Aegisthus's plot. And a grim reckoning there was for Aegisthus! Which shows what a good thing it is, when a man dies, for a son to survive him, as Orestes survived to pay the murderer out and kill that snake in the grass, Aegisthus, who had killed his noble father. You, my friend—and what a tall and splendid fellow you have grown!—must be as brave as Orestes. Then future generations will sing your praises." (P. 45)

Considering these speeches in the light of the analogy so far revealed, the reader cannot help asking why in both cases the youth is not simply exhorted to be as brave as Orestes but must first be reminded of the well-known tragic circumstances in which his analogue displayed his courage. And Nestor's exhortation is, moreover, even more ominous than Athene's, for his linking of past, present, and future is prefaced by a general reflection on the services a surviving son (e.g., Orestes) can perform for his dead father, a reflection that is immediately followed not only by the inevitable "You, my friend . . . must be as brave as Orestes" but also by Telemachus's comparison of his powers and plight with those of Orestes.

Can these stressed collocations be satisfactorily accounted for as signifying no more than "You must be brave"? Or do they constitute an implicit ironic foreshadowing on the part of the author (ironic because accomplished behind the backs, as it were, though through the mouths of the unsuspecting speakers), suggesting "You must indeed be as brave as Orestes because you will soon find your father murdered and have the same terrible task on your hands"? At the present point in the reading-process, the compositional evidence suggests that the second hypothesis is much the more probable of the two.

Thus, though Agamemnon's history does not immediately affect the actual course or dynamics of events—the two are to be directly related only when Odysseus himself hears the tale from the lips of the murdered man, who warns him against a similar fate—the spatial integration of the two cases has a direct bearing on the dynamics of reader's expectations about the linear development of the action. At this point, the main function of the analogy is neither to pad out the work nor even to counterpoint a theme but to heighten the reader's suspense about the outcome of Odysseus's future confrontation with the Suitors by emphatically linking it with an analogous struggle in the past. The expositional material is exploited in order to establish concretely an internal canon of probability peculiar to the world of the *Odyssey;* and in view of the striking similarities between this precedent and Odysseus's present situation the reader is led to fear lest, according to the "logic" of literary analogy, the symmetry may prove to extend to the outcome of the two conflicts too. The analogical precedent—like the postexpositional portent of the two eagles—operates, then, as an implicit, objectified confirmation of the reader's previous fears, which are consequently redoubled.

Moreover, the insertion of this seemingly superfluous expositional tale is shown to be part and parcel of Homer's overall narrative strategy not only in its interrelation of past, present, and future into a (patterned and developing) structure of probabilities but also in its arousal of suspense that in turn creates a need for more exposition about the hero. The fact that Agamemnon in similar circumstances had indeed met such a fate as we have already feared to be destined for Odysseus clearly intensifies our interest in finding out whether the Ithacan is better qualified than his friend was to cope with such dangers and stay alive.

The masterly interaction of suspense and curiosity generated through this expositional analogy is further stimulated by another of its components. Penelope has been handed down to posterity as a paragon of fidelity and is also described in criticism as "the heroically faithful" wife to whom the treacherous Clytaemnestra serves as a foil. This common view, even though it may accord with our final verdict on Penelope's character, again misses the colorful play of analogy and compositionally controlled hypotheses about past, present, and future all along the continuum of the text. The evidence the reader actually possesses at this point shows Penelope in a strikingly ambiguous light; the expositional gap has thus far been left open. True, she plays for time and she mourns for her husband; but, on the other hand, Telemachus maintains that she wavers between two decisions: "She neither refuses [he tells Athene], though she hates the idea of remarrying, nor can she bring herself to take the final step" (pp. 26-27, 24). In this she resembles Clytaemnestra herself, who (Nestor reveals) first sensibly "turned a deaf ear to [Aegisthus's] dishonourable schemes," till she finally succumbed to the traitor's "seductive talk" (p. 47).

Having previously paved the way for Penelope's surprising analogical collocation with Agamemnon's consort by conveying to the reader conflicting expositional clues and hypotheses concerning her, Homer now exploits the sinister implications of the similarities in situation and conduct between the two queens in order to draw our attention to the possibility that Penelope may follow in the footsteps of her notorious analogue. He thereby creates a second line of suspense by means of the same analogy. The strong implication that Penelope will not hold out against the increasing pressure of the Suitors till Odysseus's return not only squares with the logic of the analogy but is borne out by the dramatization of the state of affairs in Ithaca. Having itself been evoked through the communication of expositional material, this subsidiary line of suspense, like the central one, creates in turn a need for more exposition that will resolve, one way or another, both our fears about the narrative future and our doubts about the past; and, again like the central line of suspense, it is to be reactivated and developed as the narrative progresses.

III

The reader's hopes of finally closing some of the informational gaps during the sojourn at Sparta are strongly raised. Unlike Nestor, Menelaus had wandered for years before managing to return "from a region so remote that one might well give up all hope of return" (p. 48). Therefore (as Nestor himself points out), he may well know something about Odysseus.

The beginning of the visit is indeed promising. Once they identify the son of the man who "of all the Achaeans who toiled at Troy . . . toiled the hardest and undertook the most" (p. 56), the host and hostess naturally recall some of the "daring feats that stand to the credit of the dauntless Odysseus" (p. 59). Helen describes his infiltration into the besieged Trojan citadel, in a beggar's disguise: "By flogging his body till it showed all the marks of ill-usage he made himself look like a slave, and with a filthy rag across his back he slunk into the enemy city and explored its streets." As nobody but herself could penetrate his disguise, he effectively carried out his intelligence mission, and "after killing a number of Trojans with his long sword, he did get back to his friends with a host of information." And Menelaus, who bluntly states that in the whole course of his extensive travels he has never "set eyes on a man of such daring as the indomitable Odysseus," cites his friend's self-control during the crucial moments in the Wooden Horse, when he saved the pick of the Greek army from perdition, in frank contrast to his own impetuous behavior (pp. 59–60).

The next morning, when Telemachus asks his host point-blank if he can tell him any news of his father, Menelaus passes on to him the information he himself has elicited "from the infallible lips of the Old Man of the sea" concerning Odysseus's detention on Calypso's island. This highly circumstantial report (pp. 62–67) contains most welcome news for Telemachus, who has at long last succeeded in establishing his father's survival. But from the reader's point of view, this account seems much less satisfactory, indeed almost pointless. The reminiscential vein of the night before has afforded us such interesting food for thought about the hero that we were naturally led to look forward to more of the same relevant disclosures on the next day. But our expectations are frustrated again. Even the stories of the previous night relate not at all to the period in Odysseus's life we are most interested in—starting with the *terminus a quo* established as early as the invocation and extending to Odysseus's fall into Calypso's clutches—but refer to an earlier date. They consequently fill in few of the expositional gaps to which our attention has repeatedly been drawn before. And to crown our disappointment, Menelaus's newly imparted retrospect appears to thrust upon our attention a host of distracting episodes out of his own expositional adventures and those undergone by other marginal characters, such as Agamemnon and Aias. It includes, on the other hand, no more than a single expositional detail that is directly relevant to the main line of action—the fact of Odysseus's survival—but even of this the reader has already been authoritatively apprised right at the start.

If we take into account, however, the whole tortuous movement of the narrative so far, especially as regards the manipulation of the reader's hypotheses, we can account for these seemingly strange expositional techniques in terms more satisfactory than merely the frustration of expectation and the continued dramatization of the mystery enshrouding Odysseus's adventures. We recall, for example, that book 3 also introduced some ostensibly superfluous expositional information whose selection and placing turned out to be richly functional. I wish to argue that the tales distributed throughout book 4 form another integral part of Homer's complex narrative strategy; this book alternately counteracts and heightens the disturbing effects of the suspense factors worked into the previous books so as to leave the reader in a state of suspense in which fear and hope are more evenly and intricately balanced.

To counterbalance the sinister foreshadowing implications of books 1–3 Homer resorts to three main devices, each turning in its own way on the expositional material communicated. The first concerns the anecdotes about Odysseus himself. The Reconnaissance and Wooden Horse episodes indeed appear to have been chosen at random by their narrators (who propose telling tales as a pleasant pastime); but, in fact, they show the author's functionally selective procedure. Apart from increasing our sympathy for the loyal soldier and devoted friend, what these expositional exploits do more than anything else is to buttress our shaken confidence in Odysseus's ability to grapple with the disturbances at home. Their primary function is to counteract the apprehension generated so far by dramatically projecting, in the most impressive and unambiguous manner, Odysseus's manifold heroic nature: his great physical strength and powers of endurance, his fearlessness and nerve, his resolution, self-control, and resourcefulness—in short, the rare complex of qualities that enabled him in the past to cope single-handed with the most dangerous situations, time and again and against great odds, and to emerge victorious and unscathed.

But the effect of these illustrative reminiscences is not limited to their local countermanipulation of the reader's expectations. They at the same time serve a related expositional (structural and persuasive) function by rendering Odysseus's eventual victory credible within the context of this work. Longinus, holding that the distinctive token of old age is the love of marvellous tales, claims that the prevalence of the fabulous over the realistic elements in the *Odyssey* proves that it was composed in Homer's declining years. And as an instance of the late Homeric "absurdities," he cites "the incredible narrative of the slaughter of the Suitors."[13] In effect, Longinus agrees with the Suitors themselves that according to the laws of probablity Odysseus should "come to an ugly end, if he faced [such] odds" (p. 36). Aristotle, however, demonstrates his superior insight into the art of narrative when he maintains, in reference to the admissibility of the marvellous element in epic, that "it is Homer who has chiefly taught other poets the art of telling lies skilfully. The secret of it lies in a fallacy. For, assuming that one thing is or becomes, a second is or becomes, men imagine that, if the second is, the first likewise is or becomes. But this is a false inference. Hence, where the first thing is untrue, it is quite unnecessary, provided the second is true, to add that the first is or has become. For the mind, knowing the second to be true, falsely infers the truth of the first."[14] The validity of the causal concatenation devised in fiction is not to be automatically judged, then, by "natural" or "realistic" canons of probability—by reference outside the text to the operations of nature or to conventional, generally accepted views of probability. A narrative is perfectly free to deviate from these extratextual laws at will, substituting for them its own internal premises, laws and models of probability, which function according to the process of paralogism. For example: if B, Odysseus's amazing victory over the Suitors, will rest on premise A, his extraordinary abilities, the causal sequence will be quite logical according to the internally established norms of the *Odyssey*. Its perfect validity will, moreover, induce the reader to accept—quite naturally though erroneously— not only the consequent B but even the antecedent A itself.

It is in and through these reassuring reminiscences that Homer also concretely establishes some internal canons of probability that will operate in his epic, using the expositional material to construct his probability-register just as he uses the illustrative banquet scenes to construct his moral register. He particularly counterbalances the disturbing effect of the Suitors' quantitative superiority by highlighting Odysseus's overwhelming qualitative superiority to most men. As we retrospectively perceive, moreover, some typically Odyssean stratagems that are unfolded here recur in the sequel. Just as Odysseus infiltrated into the Trojan citadel disguised as a beggar, he later adopts the same disguise to penetrate undetected into his own palace, which has become the Suitors' headquarters; and just as, at the critical moment in the Wooden Horse, Odysseus calmly saved the Greek army by "[clapping] his great hands relentlessly on [Anticlus's] mouth" (p. 60), thus preventing him from crying out, he later, at a no less critical moment of his private war, grips the throat of old Eurycleia, who has just recognized him by his scar, to ensure her silence (pp. 225–26).

Second, Menelaus further reinforces the reader's confidence in the protagonist's powers and his readiness to accept the internal laws of probability by directly relating Odysseus's heroic qualities to the ordeal awaiting him at Ithaca. When he learns of the Suitors' scandalous conduct, he has no doubt whatever about the outcome of the future confrontation:

> "It's just as if a deer had put her little unweaned fawns to sleep in a mighty lion's den. . . . Back comes the lion to his lair, and hideous carnage falls upon them all. But no worse than Odysseus will deal out to that gang. Once . . . I saw him stand up to Philomeleides in a wrestling-match and bring him down with a terrific throw that delighted all his friends. . . . That's the Odysseus I should like to see these Suitors meet. A swift death and a sorry wedding there would be for all!" (Pp. 61–62)

This whole exhilarating speech—based on what is to the reader Menelaus's expositional knowledge of his friend and rounded off by another illustrative anecdote—operates as a control center at which different suspense signals (originally located in books 1, 2, and 3) meet, to be either counteracted or reinforced. The primary function of the lion-and-fawns simile is thus to act as a specific counterweight to book 2's portent of the two eagles (though its optimism is admittedly less authoritative than the ominous suggestions of the portent sent by the omniscient and omnipotent Zeus himself).[15] It clearly projects a radically different view of Odysseus's chances and implies, in addition, that the numerical advantage of the "fawns" is of little account. Moreover, this speech—whose conclusion reassuringly echoes the words of Athene in book 1[16]—also tends to buttress the doubtful effect of Nestor's hesitant statement in book 3: "Who knows whether some day Odysseus may not come back, alone perhaps, or with his following intact, and pay these Suitors out for all their violence?" (p. 46). The Spartan's expert opinion is reliable and his unshakable confidence in his comrade infectious.

The third counterbalancing measure lies in the conspicuously abundant and ostensibly redundant exposition that refers to Menelaus himself. Its primary function is specifically to counteract the sinister implications of another seemingly digressive retrospect—about Agamemnon, Menelaus's brother, and Clytaemnestra, Helen's sister. For Menelaus's case is also analogical to Odysseus's, all three of them turning on husband-wife-suitor triangles. The Trojan War, we recall, broke out owing to the scandalous behaviour of Paris, who, while a guest in Menelaus's palace, wooed and eloped with Helen during his host's absence. Helen herself is twice made to go out of her way to remind us of this shameful incident (pp. 57, 60); and Menelaus does not miss the opportunity of having a dig at his wife during his narrative of the Wooden Horse crisis. The analogy is established even more firmly by the introduction of various points of similarity between the adventures of the two husbands after their respective departures from Troy. Thus, we gather from Menelaus's tales that, having incurred the wrath of the gods, he was for some time cooped up on an island, till freed through the intervention of a friendly goddess who forced her father's hand (pp. 62-63)—a series of events strongly reminiscent of Odysseus's situation, past, present, and future.

The main function the new analogy fulfills at this stage (again, apart from its development of the Return theme) is to counteract the sinister effect produced by the Agamemnon-Odysseus analogy. The point is, of course, that Menelaus destroyed Paris, regained his wife, and is now living peacefully in his palace. This analogical precedent does not dispel the suggestions of the previous one, but implicitly opposes to it another relevant possibility. If the initially developed analogy, a dramatization of the reader's worst fears for the protagonist, foreshadows one result of the future conflict, the second analogy, a dramatization of the reader's best hopes for Odysseus, points the other way. In line with the two other "reassurance signals," it encourages the reader to hope that just as Menelaus emerged victorious in the tenth year of the national war, so may Odysseus win his private war in the tenth year of his struggles.

The subtle counterbalancing functions of book 4—achieved primarily through the patterning of the exposition distributed in it—is summed up by the following diagram of the major hypotheses and their textual grounds:

suspense

fear (books 1–3)	hope (book 4)
the Suitors' quantitative superiority	Odysseus's qualitative superiority
the portent of the two eagles	the simile of the lion and the fawns
the Agamemnon analogy: the suitor's victory	the Menelaus analogy: the husband's victory

As for the recent question mark concerning Penelope's continued resistance, it will be noticed that while the new pattern counteracts the fearful hypotheses of the first line of suspense, it does no such thing with regard to the second. On the contrary, the Helen-Penelope component of the overall analogy tends to confirm, and thus to reinforce, the probability of the Clytaemnestra-Penelope collocation. Again Homer closely knits the analogical relations between this new couple by providing additional points of contact between the two queens. If Helen is pointedly presented as no less clever than beautiful (e.g., p. 57), we have the testimony of the Suitors that "of all the Achaean beauties of former times, there is not one, not Tyro, nor Alcmene, nor Mycene . . . who had at her command such wits" as Penelope, "that incomparable schemer" (pp. 32–33). And on Helen's first appearance it is her work-basket "full of fine-span yarn, and the spindle with its deep blue wool" that is conspicuously selected for minute depiction (p. 57), the stress laid upon it forming another link with Penelope's weaving (p. 32).

The united, mutually confirmatory implications projected by the linkage of (the still-ambiguated) Penelope with the two adulterous sisters powerfully induce the reader to fear that she too will fall—the unanimity of the two (otherwise conflicting) analogies on this point suggesting that this is destined to happen irrespective of the husband's fate. As the elaborately balanced structure of these books could lead one to predict, however, Homer soon takes care to throw into doubt the probability of this surrender; the suggestions of both analogies are counterbalanced by the moving scene, towards the end of book 4, of Penelope's mourning for her absent husband. So the reader's mind is kept busy again.

IV

Though Homer has variously established a balance of hope and fear about the fate of Odysseus, he goes on to devise, in the same book, a new sequence of effective countermeasures to preclude any possibility of a total neutralization of our suspense. Through another cunning distribution and linkage of ostensibly redundant antecedents, he now tips the scales of expectation on the side of fear.

First of all, book 4 harps on the Agamemnon theme so as to prevent the reader's repressing or freeing himself from the unpleasant associations of this memento mori. Menelaus himself first refers to his brother's assassination at the outset of the meeting (p. 56). But the most skillful case of analogical re-collocation predictably occurs later, following the book's "hope phase," when he reports the Old Man of the Sea's stories concerning the fate of three of his comrades. Proteus chose to start with Aias's death at Poseidon's hands (p. 65); went on to describe the trap Aegisthus had set for Agamemnon on his return home (pp. 65–66); and ended with an account of Odysseus's state of captivity on Calypso's island. The juxtaposition of the fates of these three Returners carries more ominous implications than ever before. For the first time in the epic Orestes' terrible revenge is glossed over, whereas the murder itself is vividly described. Moreover, the similarity between the two kings is at the same time driven home here even more insistently than at any previous phase of the analogy. A small but specific example: as soon as Agamemnon reaches his native land (with Here's divine help; to return is not necessarily to prevail), "The warm tears rolled down his cheeks"; and several lines later we hear about Odysseus sitting disconsolate on Calypso's shore "with the big tears rolling down his cheeks" (p. 66).

Furthermore, the reader's anxiety is now intensified (just as it was before allayed) by the insinuation of a new expositional analogy. Locrian Aias, we discover, was killed as a punishment for having thoughtlessly defied the Lord of the Sea by a foolish boast. So the question immediately arises whether Poseidon is likely to prove less implacable towards Odysseus, who blinded his favorite son. The newly inserted precedent dramatically heightens, then, another aspect of the danger that is sure to confront the hero by harping on Poseidon's power and malice, factors we might have forgotten by now. The evocation of this famous warrior's fate is also designed to undermine to some extent our recently awakened confidence in Odysseus's powers; Aias's story demonstrates the helplessness of any human being, however heroic, when striving against the wrath of a god. And even if Poseidon has enough respect for the decision of the gods to refrain from killing Odysseus on his way home, he is sure to lead him a pretty dance. But what is most startling about this new collocation is its unobtrusive disclosure of two additional points of contact between the analogues. First, that they have shared the very same divine patron and divine enemy, only with the roles reversed; second, that before being suddenly provoked by Aias, Poseidon had saved his life and brought him safely to land "in spite of Athene's enmity." The links are so specific that we are forced to confront the possibility that Odysseus may similarly fall victim not to his old enemy but to a newly antagonized patroness.

The combined force of the two contiguously placed analogies bodes no good for the third person on this list of casualties, whose fate still hangs in the balance. For Odysseus, "though still alive" (p. 65), will have to contend, with double-edged divine help, against greater odds than both of his comrades put together. The specific spatiotemporal patterning of the countermeasures is again rhetorically potent as well as compositionally gratifying in itself.

The last, and most complex, set of suspense-heightening devices is located towards the end of book 4 (pp. 68–73), which, though rendering

the new development at Ithaca, derives its true significance from the exposition so far conveyed. As soon as it transpires that Telemachus has stolen
away, the Suitors—"seething with black passion"—decide that they must
"clip his wings" at once. Antinous picks his men, and at nightfall they set
sail for the straits between Ithaca and the coast of Samos, where they lay
an ambush "with murder for Telemachus in their hearts."

So far Homer has alternately aroused and relaxed the reader's suspense
by way of distributed expositional precedents. And so far the reader has
welcomed the communication of exposition because most of the answers
to his questions inextricably depend both on the hero's qualifications as
displayed in the past and the internal canons of probability manifesting
themselves in similar ordeals undergone by other characters of the same
fictive world. These constant plunges into the narrative past, however,
though invariably pointing to the present and the future, involve what
amounts to a standstill in the action itself, which an epic in particular cannot afford for long. Homer, therefore, makes a virtue of this necessity
by propelling the action forward in such a way as to dovetail this progression too into his overall suspense dynamics.

The introduction of this countermove, first of all, gives the last touch
to the disambiguation of the Suitors' position—straightforwardly revealing
the extent to which they mean business and are united, despite the
rivalry among themselves, in their determination to do away with their
common enemies. If so far they have not gone beyond threats and insults,
the reader is now shown that they will not stick even at murder. Not even
a shred of hope is left for a peaceful solution.

But the revelation of the general danger confronting the royal house
is effected through a very particular threat—the ambush. And I believe
scholars have missed a great deal of the beauty of Homer's compositional
strategy by failing to note that though the ambush is ostensibly set for
Telemachus, the work variously combines presentational and actional
dynamics so as to direct our attention to the contingency that the Suitors'
ship may finally come across, not Telemachus, but the unforewarned
Odysseus himself!

It is with fascinating skill that Homer interweaves narrative past,
present, and future in relating Agamemnon's expositional tragedy to this
recent plot of the Suitors'. Menelaus has just reported the circumstances
of Agamemnon's murder; on the king's arrival, Aegisthus, "his heart full
of ugly thoughts," laid "a clever trap. He selected twenty of the best
soldiers from the town, left them in ambush . . . Agamemnon, never
guessing that he was going to his doom, came up with him from the coast,
and Aegisthus feasted and killed him as a man might fell an ox at its
manger" (p. 66). If up to this point Homer has driven home the broad
similarities (the husband-wife-suitor-son relationships) between the two

components of the analogy, he now focuses the whole force of the analogy, already ominous enough in its general outline, on this concrete plan of the Suitors' by showing it to correspond even in several minute details to Aegisthus's successful regicide. Common to both plots are even the ugly thoughts of the murderer (or the would-be murderers) and the treacherous setting of an ambush, with the manning of the ambush by twenty hand-picked warriors serving as the crowning analogical clue: Antinous "picked the twenty best men" (pp. 72, 69) just as Aegisthus had "selected twenty of the best soldiers" (p. 66).[17] The analogy thus forces the reluctant reader to doubt whether, in view of the inescapable symmetry of the two ambushes, he can even hope for a different result in Odysseus's case from that foreshadowed by the historical precedent. The expositional material, then, illuminates not only the (tangential) past but mainly the present and future:

expositional past *Agamemnon's case*	present and future *Odysseus's case*
king returning from Troy	king returning from Troy
ambitious, unscrupulous suitor	ambitious, unscrupulous Suitors
ambush	ambush
twenty picked soldiers	twenty picked soldiers
murder	?

The fear lest the Suitors should inadvertently catch a bigger fish than they expect is further aroused by the curious (this time, postexpositional) fact that, though the ambush is ostensibly set for Telemachus, Homer goes out of his way to reassure the reader that the boy himself will come to no harm. In the last scene of the book, Athene decides to relieve the anxiety of Penelope, who is lying in her room "fasting . . . and wondering whether her innocent son would escape death." Athene fashions a phantom in the shape of Penelope's sister, who assures the sleeping queen (a dramatic substitute for the reader) that the gods have "settled that [her] son should come home safe. They have no quarrel with the lad whatever." She pointedly refuses, on the other hand, to give the worried questioner any account of her husband's fate (pp. 72-73).

In the light of the overall narrative strategy, the function of this scene —notably its use of perspectival discrepancies—clearly emerges. There was one snag in Homer's plan of propelling the action forward in such a way as to canalize the suspense consistently aroused hitherto by the distributed antecedents into the movement towards the narrative future. As the Suitors are not aware of Odysseus's impending return, they can hardly be made to lay an ambush for him. So Homer is forced to have it devised for Telemachus. But how is he to accomplish his purposes and at the same time prevent the scattering or diversion of attention that this turning of the limelight on Telemachus may involve? This requires a series of complex manoeuvres. He takes care earlier in the book to focus our attention on Odysseus and his analogues by selectively playing down Orestes' role while magnifying those of Agamemnon and Aegisthus; having sent the Suitors to waylay Telemachus, he cleverly suggests that it is really Odysseus who is in danger; and he finally brings the whole force of the analogy to bear on the two ambushes, thereby linking narrative past, present, and future in the tightest and most sinister manner.

The dynamics of expositional distribution is thus brilliantly and instructively interrelated with the general strategy in books 3 and 4 of the *Odyssey*. Almost every detail of the "irrelevant" antecedents selected proves to be highly functional in various ways, some of which emerge only later on. And the different functions combine and mutually reinforce one another to such an extent that only in analysis can they be broadly isolated as, for instance, rhetorical (the manipulation of interest, gap, ambiguity, hypothesis, or emotive response), structural or integrative (sequential and spatial linkage, simultaneous progressive-regressive movement, or the construction of internal probabilities), perspectival (e.g., the denial or granting of antecedents and foreknowledge to the reader, especially vis-à-vis the agents on the one hand and the narrator on the other, by way of compositional indirections), or thematic. Thus the constant retelling of Agamemnon's tragedy is far from "repetitious," as some critics complain. It would be strange indeed to find Homer less accomplished an artist than his own hero, who declares that "it goes against the grain with me to repeat a tale already plainly told" (p. 171). Nor is the different emphasis given by each retelling intended only to avert boredom, as others contend. In fact, there are good artistic reasons not only for the incorporation of the various expositional motifs that make up this tale but equally for their order of presentation and particular location. The author's choice to refrain from concentrating the whole of Agamemnon's ordeal in book 3 but to distribute it so as to delay the most gruesome part to book 4 yields a number of gains. First, the report of the murder is indispensable for the restoration of the proper ratio of hope and fear aimed at in this book, where the murder gains additional power from its collocation with the killing of Aias. As it forms, moreover, the cornerstone of the implicit linkage of past, present, and future, it is best placed as near as possible to the Suitors' plot, too, so that even the minute but clinching points of similarity should not pass unnoticed. The continuous presentation of this expositional block in book 3 would consequently have involved a waste of narrative possibilities.

This brings us to the related question concerning the suitability of the location of the Suitors' countermove. It has been argued that "the plot against Telemachos could more easily have been planned as the boy sails out of Ithaca at the end of the second book."[18] If, however, we take into account the dynamic play of analogy all along and particularly the way the reader is alerted to the possibility that it is the father, not the son, that will fall victim to the ambush, we shall realize that this scenic push—like the expositional material that interprets it—could not be placed more effectively than it actually is. Its presentation at the very end of book 4 focuses on it the multifarious implications of all the preceding spatial patterns; and, precisely before the hero's introduction into the action, fixes the state of affairs in our minds and ends the alternations of hope and fear on a powerfully complicated note of suspense.

I trust that the foregoing illustrative analysis of expositional logic in relation to the overall movement of the work has also sufficiently demonstrated the groundlessness of such prevalent claims as Erich Auerbach's that "the element of suspense is very slight in the Homeric poems; nothing in their entire style is calculated to keep the reader or hearer breathless. The digressions [e.g., the account of Odysseus's scar, or for that matter Menelaus's reminiscences] are not meant to keep the reader in suspense, but rather to relax the tension." No more tenable is the oft-repeated supporting argument that such effects as curiosity or suspense are inconceivable here since Homeric narrative recognizes neither past nor future but only a local present that is absolute: "Any subjectivistic-perspectivistic procedure, creating a foreground and a background, resulting in the present lying open to the depths of the past, is entirely foreign to the Homeric style; the Homeric style knows only a foreground, only a uniformly illuminated, uniformly objective present."[19] Undemonstrated pronouncements of this kind, however attractive, are shown to possess little value when confronted by the hard textual facts. In view of the centrality of the brilliantly handled expositional gaps it can hardly be laid down that in the *Odyssey* "never is there a form kept fragmentary or half-illuminated, never a lacuna, never a gap, never a glimpse of unplumbed depths."[20] The evidence offered by the remarkable multiplicity of temporal and spatial devices that combine to effect the seesaw alternations of hope and fear in the reader's mind similarly quashes the claim that the element of suspense is negligible here. If we consider in addition the tight interrelation of curiosity and suspense throughout these books—i.e., the interrelation of different time-sections and temporal directions—it is difficult to grasp how the reader could manage, even if he wished it, to suspend (or even "forget") narrative past and future at every point along the continuum of the text and immerse himself exclusively in what is narrated at the moment. This nullification of the temporal properties of narrative, in the name of the affective statics of epic, is therefore no more acceptable than the more common one underlying the substitution of the hindsight of retrospection for the trial-and-error dynamics of unfolding.

Even the point Auerbach himself so perceptively makes about Homer's leisurely mode of narration, with its orderly, well-articulated "descriptions of implements, ministrations and gestures," rather complements our understanding of Homer's suspense strategy than establishes its non-existence. The tranquil pace of the narrative, far from corresponding to the reader's allegedly relaxed state of mind or even reinforcing it, in fact actively heightens his tension; it not only forms a contrast with the incessant clash of his expectations but also retards, time and again, the eagerly awaited issue of events. This tonal understatement compels the reader to dwell upon the succession of narrative presents while his mind busily revolves different hypotheses as to the narrative past and future.

In the eternal, though essentially pointless, crusade waged against "criticism" under the slogan of "historical scholarship," the stick of the "modern" reader's interpretative waywardness is liberally and somewhat indiscriminately applied. Auerbach energetically brandishes this stick in warning against the modern reader's anachronistically reading into this ancient text what is not there to be read. In this case, however, I need not even fall back upon the argument that the mark of great works is not only their appeal to various orders of mind but also their accumulation of meaning through the ages; their organization is so complex as to preclude the possibility of their contemporary audience's exhausting their manifold aspects or layers of meaning. I am prepared to go further. We are wholly ignorant, in fact, of the "theory of literature" prevalent in Homer's days or of the actual reactions of his contemporary audience. On the other hand, human nature being what it is, there is every reason to believe that people have always evinced curiosity when some desired information was withheld from them and felt suspense when somebody they liked was in mortal danger; and the tense excitement that characterizes the dramatized reactions of the Phaeacian audience to Odysseus's account of his adventures strongly confirms this claim. There is similarly every reason to believe, and a great deal of evidence to support this belief, that Homer, like other storytellers ancient and modern, exploited and manipulated these primary narrative interests. The onus of proof to the contrary, therefore, obviously rests with the so-called historicists.

V

The manipulation of narrative interest, however, whose compositional dynamics has afforded us (I believe) some major and widely applicable theoretical lessons, is by no means Homer's exclusive concern. Nor is it the *Odyssey*'s only claim to theoretically oriented analysis with a view to bringing out the temporal potentialities of literary art. On the contrary, it is, I shall argue, in terms of Homer's wish to pursue other, and equally central, goals that the notable shift in narrative strategy marked by book 5 is to be accounted for. If throughout the "Telemachia" it has been suggested that Odysseus's chances of surviving the future struggle are no better than even, from book 5 on our suspense as to his victory is increasingly allayed.

This shift is reflected in the subtle disparity between the two Olympian assembly scenes, located at the outset of books 1 and 5. The two scenes may well constitute complementary parts of one and the same occasion;[21] in both Athene addresses the gods on Odysseus's behalf, Zeus responds favourably to her appeal, and Hermes is sent to arrange the captive's return. Each scene is followed by a different line of the action branching out from this single assembly: the first, by Athene's arrival at Ithaca and Telemachus's journey; the second, by Hermes's departure for Calypso's island and Odysseus's release. But in accordance with the conventions of Homeric epic, these two contemporaneous strands of the action are not only narrated in succession but are even made to appear as if they had actually occurred successively—as if the action itself were continuous throughout.

If the two assembly scenes are indeed parts of a single fictive event, then the shift of emphasis in the second is even more revealing than it would otherwise be. While in book 1 Zeus's response to Athene's plea is strictly confined to a promise to ensure Odysseus's return, in book 5 Homer makes the omnipotent god counter her remonstrance with a much more reassuring answer: "My child . . . I never thought to hear such words from you. Did you not plan the whole affair yourself? Was it not your idea that Odysseus should return and settle accounts with these men?" (p. 74). Even here Zeus makes no formally binding promise to ensure Odysseus's victory. Having put his words not in the form of a statement but of a question that attributes the plan to Athene, all he is committed to, explicitly and irrevocably, is again no more than that Odysseus "shall reach his native land and there step under the high roof of his house and see his friends once more" (p. 75). However, since there is no hint that Zeus bears any grudge against the hero; since he has not bound himself to any other course; and since he refers to the issue to which he stands committed in the same breath and in the same ambiguous form as to that hitherto left open—the implied promise, though perhaps not so conclusive as the reader would like it to be, carries considerable weight.

This careful distribution of foreshadowing elements retrospectively supports my description of the logic informing the "Telemachia"; and (like the "unnatural" placing of the Suitors' countermove or the sequential shifts in the eagle omens) shows that such a dynamic logic may apply to the materials of the action proper no less than to their expositional antecedents. A crucial part of Zeus's original promise has been temporarily suppressed from the account of the first scene because its disclosure would have severely limited the scope of the play of mutually exclusive expectations and hypotheses designed for the opening books; and it is deliberately introduced at a point which marks a major shift in the general narrative strategy and the manipulation of suspense in particular.[22] The variations between the two scenes correspond, in fact, to the difference in the expectations engendered by each of their sequels as a whole. From this stage on the ominous anticipatory hints are not only rare but, unlike the Agamemnon analogy, ambiguous as well. On the other hand, we constantly find Odysseus's ultimate victory both overtly prophesied and strongly foreshadowed by implication. The infallible seer Tiresias predicts that Odysseus "will pay out these men for their misdeeds . . . by stratagem or in a straight fight" and that he will die "worn out after an easy old age" (pp. 147-48); while the latter kind of reassurance is again accomplished through actionally digressive expositional material, which on examination proves to carry significant analogical import. I refer, for example, to the story of Hephaestus, Ares, and Aphrodite, sung by Demodocus on the occasion of the Phaeacian games (pp. 109-11). It is evidently far from accidental that our fourth encounter with the husband-wife-suitor triangle— on the divine level for a change—is concerned with the success of the husband, the lame Hephaestus, in ingeniously trapping his stronger rival and putting him to shame.

In view of the regular seesaw shift of probabilities concerning Odysseus's survival—balance (books 1 and 2) → fear (book 3) → hope (book 4, first part) → fear (book 4, second part)—the present tipping of the scales on the side of hope is predictable. What is surprising is that this time the tipping is done for good. This does not mean that suspense is nullified but that our interest in the narrative future is largely shifted from the question of survival to the circumstances of the conflict. And the latter, as the gods themselves foretell, promise to be nerve-racking enough. Zeus lays down that "on the journey he shall have neither gods nor men to help him. He shall make it in hardship" (p. 74); Calypso then warns Odysseus that if he had any inkling of the misery he was bound to endure, he would not budge from her island (p. 78); and Poseidon, infuriated by the gods' change of mind, naturally undertakes "to let him have his bellyful of trouble yet" (p. 80). We soon receive a sample of the intensity of this kind of suspense in book 5 itself, which traces some of Odysseus's hair-breadth escapes during his sea adventures.

Moreover, Homer has long ago provided his bow of suspense with more than one string. So now, having chosen to decrease our fear for Odysseus himself, he keeps up our suspense by increasingly foregrounding and developing the second, and as yet wholly undecided, issue at stake—the question of Penelope. The fact that Zeus refrains from referring to this problem even in passing would not be so disturbing in itself were it not accompanied by an implicit validation of the Odysseus-Menelaus analogy. This collocation is made to appear the correct one, not only with regard to the main issue but to some of the subsidiaries as well, by Zeus's decree that Odysseus shall return possessed of "copper, gold and woven materials in such quantities as he could never have won for himself from Troy" (p. 75)—just like Menelaus (pp. 55–56). Its reinforcement in one important respect—Odysseus's fate—increases the probability of its proving right in the other as well. And our doubts about Penelope's future are even more pointedly raised by the confirmatory implications of a subsequent expositional analogy—that between Odysseus and Haphaestus—which further strengthens the probability of Odysseus's victory over the Suitors being preceded, like that of the lame god as well as Menelaus, by the loss of his wife.

These far-reaching changes in narrative strategy are accounted for in terms of Homer's expositional exigencies and foresight, as related to the overall aims of the work. As we retrospectively realize, the following part of the epic (books 5–12) is designed to impart a very large amount of expositional information, notably the continuous report of Odysseus's fabulous adventures; and the reader's proper assimilation of this complex material is essential. For though the endeavor to manipulate curiosity and suspense plays a central role in Homer's compositional decisions, he has no intention to subordinate everything to these effects and restrict himself to producing a succession of thrills, however subtle. In the mystery genre or the "adventure story" pure and simple,[23] narrative interest is the be-all and the end-all. The *Odyssey*, in contrast, besides greatly excelling most of these in the sophistication and efficacy of the means by which curiosity and suspense are created and sustained, aims at a much wider variety of interests. Homer is at least equally concerned, for instance, with the delineation of character—above all, with that of his hero, whose unusually complicated personality is gradually made to emerge in the course of these books. A thoroughgoing exploration of character, however, is hardly compatible with a strict adherence to a strategy that irresistibly impels attention forward, to the final resolution of events. For a powerful suspense generated about the sympathetic hero's very survival would naturally enough be liable to render the reader impatient or even resentful of any attempt at subtle psychological penetration. His mind is not free to dwell on the present moment but is riveted to some distant point in the narrative future. When in this state of mind, the reader wishes for additional information about Odysseus—he will welcome, for instance, any expositional material that will firmly establish the hero's prowess—but only of a kind that is straightforwardly communicated and directly related to the future conflict.

On the other hand, the double shift—both in the kind and the main object of suspense—effected in books 5-12 result in milder suspense tactics that are not only perfectly compatible with the whole variety of Homer's aims, but even positively serve them. By increasingly relieving the reader of the much acuter of his two anxieties for Odysseus, the work manages to divert his attention away from the "what" to the "how" hypotheses—from the outcome of the ordeal to the unfolding of the stages leading to it. It is on these stages that our attention is now centered, for that is where dangers and hardships are promised to await Odysseus. As any decisive *deus ex machina* intervention, moreover, whether favorable or fatal, has been forbidden by Zeus, whose will "no god can evade or thwart" (p. 77), our attention is focused more firmly than ever on Odysseus himself and his personal qualifications for coping with the dangers that lie ahead; in fact, this divine decree is introduced as a motivation for Homer's design to render Odysseus's struggles mainly in human, as opposed to supernatural, terms. It is accordingly his character rather than his fate that has become of paramount interest; and the remaining suspense about the final outcome only heightens our expectations for Homer's further expositional presentation of it.

The *Odyssey,* then, aims to produce at every point the maximal degree of narrative interest that is compatible with the variety of its artistic goals. Suspense is intermittently heightened and decreased according to the needs of the overall strategy. At the present stage it has accordingly not been dissipated but diminished sufficiently to enable Homer to coordinate his most complicated and ambitious expositional tasks, each of them forming one facet of the general strategy of rhetorical control. He can now, I shall argue, proceed at the leisurely pace required in order to complete and deepen the presentation of Odysseus's fascinating character; to manipulate the reader's response to it; to further unfold and round out some spatial structures; to develop some major thematic patterns and induce assent to his problematic normative register; and similarly to establish the internal laws of probability according to which the protagonist will be shown to be qualified to cope with the dangers at Ithaca in essentially human terms.[24]

ORDER OF PRESENTATION, DELAYED AND DISTRIBUTED EXPOSITION, AND STRATEGIES OF RHETORICAL CONTROL

> Now you know the beginning is always the chief thing in every process.
>
> Plato, *The Republic*

> "The poor creature's lost.
> "Lost?
> "Since on the first impression, as we said, so much depends. The first impression's made—oh made! I defy her now ever to unmake it."
>
> Henry James, "The Two Faces"

The expositional unfolding of Odysseus's personality does not, of course, start with book 5; it has been one of the author's main concerns from the very beginning. As already shown, a variety of means have been devised to direct our attention all along to the protagonist's figure and to ensure our assimilation of every detail that illuminates his character. Up to this point, however, Odysseus has been presented indirectly. We have merely caught glimpses of his character through the successive windows of other people's views of him—the gods, the Ithacans, Nestor, Menelaus, and Helen. It is only from book 5 on that we are offered a direct view and can make our own estimate.

When one closely compares, however, the indirect expositional accounts of Odysseus's personality with the subsequent, direct presentation of it, one is brought up short. The Odysseus we now encounter seems at times to be so different from the earlier figure as to make us wonder whether he is the same person. If throughout the "Telemachia" Odysseus has been consistently portrayed as a paragon of virtue and heroism—honorable, pious, resourceful, brave, and loyal—from book 5 on his moral integrity often appears questionable and he is mostly shown to live up to his literary reputation as the supreme man of wile in classical lore.

The striking disparity between the portrayal of Odysseus in the *Iliad* and in the *Odyssey* has not escaped the notice of Homeric scholars. In the *Iliad*, Odysseus's notorious craftiness is often mentioned—and unfavorably commented on by his comrades—but his actual conduct is, though intelligent and resourceful, scrupulously straightforward. As W. B. Stanford observes, "If the *Iliad* were the only early record of Odysseus's career one would find it hard to understand how he had got his notoriety as a man of extreme wiliness. In contrast, the *Odyssey* is a compendium of Ulyssean . . . cunning."[1]

Actually, however, the treatment of Odysseus's character in the *Odyssey* itself is far more complicated than is usually thought. And the failure of critics to appreciate this complexity of presentation—to be distinguished from the concurrent complexity of character—stems again from their disregard of the temporal properties of literary art. It is true that if we indiscriminately abstract from Homer's epic a number of different episodes and string them together, it may indeed appear that the *Odyssey* as a whole is a compendium of Ulyssean wile. But this procedure involves a nullification of the sequential nature of the literary work. If, on the other hand, we follow—as we must—the continuum of the text so as to trace the gradual unfolding of Odysseus's character in and through the order of presentation actually devised, we cannot but be struck by a curious discovery. The character of Odysseus as delineated in the first four books of the *Odyssey* is essentially identical with that of the straightforwardly heroic Odysseus we encounter in the *Iliad*. The disparity in characterization that may justify Stanford's comment is first noticeable in book 5. The problem of accounting for this shift—within the *Odyssey* itself—accordingly becomes even more intriguing than before.

This ostensible inconsistency can by no means be explained in terms of any development undergone by Odysseus in the ten years that have elapsed since Nestor and Menelaus saw him last. For not only do we gather from the *Iliad* that his notoriety as trickster had already dogged his footsteps to the very battlefields of Troy, but, according to the reconstituted chronology of the *Odyssey* itself, he pulls off some of his most memorable ruses while on his journey homewards, immediately after his departure from Troy. Odysseus has not changed, nor does he change in the course of the following ordeal.[2] Consequently, as always with static characters, whatever traits of his that emerge in this epic are all equally expositional, irrespective of the order and mode of their presentation— whether communicated right at the beginning or delayed, whether overtly formulated by the narrator (or for that matter by one of the dramatis personae) or dramatically evoked in and through the action itself.

Odysseus's changelessness, however, does not justify the statement made by Robert Scholes and Robert Kellog:

Characters in primitive stories are invariably 'flat,' 'static,' and quite 'opaque.' The very recurring epithets of formulaic narrative are signs of flatness in characterisation. Odysseus is the man never at a loss—always, whenever we see him. In incident after incident, among gods, men, and monsters, he demonstrates this quality to us. Whatever the situation requires—strength, guile, politeness, generosity—he does the right thing. . . . He does not change, he does not age, except to play a role and fool his enemies. He is never tongue-tied, or clumsy, or even ordinary. Like Achilles, he is a monolith, though perhaps a less massive one.[3]

The generalization about the invariable flatness as well as changelessness of characters in so-called primitive stories is too sweeping. Even in the *Odyssey* itself we discover one dynamic character, Telemachus, whose development from the awkwardness of adolescence to the beginning of maturity is finely traced, as a minor interest; and another, Odysseus himself, who, though indeed static, can take his place in the first row of the roundest characters in fiction.

To claim that Odysseus is "simply conceived" in that he is presented exclusively in terms of one facet ("the man never at a loss") is drastically to oversimplify his presentation. First, though the presence of mind Odysseus usually displays is indeed remarkable, Homer occasionally shows it to be badly shaken. Odysseus is more than once near despair during the hazardous voyage to Phaeacia (pp. 81, 83); and, as he himself admits, he was almost driven to suicide on perceiving that his men had undone the Aeolian bag of winds (p. 132). He is not flatly conceived, then, even in this respect. Second, and more general, his rare presence of mind is not so much an attribute as a consequence of the multifariousness of talents and traits with which he is endowed. And the complexity of his character as a whole consists and manifests itself in the heterogeneity of features composing it. He is both king and rogue, hero and trickster, gentleman and knave, family man and wanderer, faithful husband and roving lover; he is egotistic and considerate, ruthless and tender, prudent and foolhardy. What more can be required to suggest that a character is not flat beyond this constant tension and clash of opposed traits?

In the following sections I shall argue that it is precisely this complexity of conception, or to be more precise still, the necessity to manipulate and control the reader's response to some of the less savory facets of Odysseus's personality—that determines Homer's recourse to what is on the face of it, and on the face of it alone, an inconsistent mode of characterization. Homer aims on the one hand to ensure and maintain our essentially sympathetic attitude towards the protagonist, and on the other hand to explore his character in all its complexity. It is largely in terms of the reconciliation of these mutually exclusive aims that the expositional order and modes of presentation of the *Odyssey* in general and Odysseus's characteristics and antecedents in particular are to be accounted for.

II

Psychologists have recently rediscovered and scientifically investigated several laws of human perception that have from time immemorial been intuited by intelligent people. One of these laws concerns the proverbial tenacity and enduring influence of first impressions.

In a collection of interrelated studies entitled *The Order of Presentation in Persuasion*,[4] a number of psychologists explore the effects that alternative organizations of a given verbal message have upon determining the opinions and attitudes of an audience. The central problem investigated is the relative impact or persuasive potency of the opening part of a message as opposed to that of the subsequently presented, concluding part; or, in their own suggestive terminology, of "primacy" versus "recency" effect.

In the chapter called "Primacy-Recency in Impression Formation," Abraham S. Luchins describes a series of experiments designed to discover "the effect of various kinds and sequences of information communicated about an individual on the impressions formed concerning that person's personality and nature" (p. 33). He prepared two blocks of information reporting the activities of a fictitious person ("Jim") during a single day. The two blocks portray two behavior patterns that are opposed to the point of incompatibility: one represents Jim as a consistently friendly, gregarious extrovert, while the other dramatizes, as emphatically and homogeneously, a complex of introvert traits such as unfriendliness or shyness. The two contradictory blocks of information were presented to some subjects in extrovert-introvert order and to others in the opposite sequence—but in both cases the text was continuous, even without a paragraph indention. The subjects were then asked to select epithets indicative of Jim's traits, to compose a brief character-sketch of him, and to predict his behavior in given situations.

The incompatibility of the two blocks composing each message enabled Luchins to ascertain whether the resultant conception of Jim's personality was influenced equally by both halves of the communication or was determined to a greater extent by the leading half (the primacy effect) or the concluding half (the recency effect). The results are highly significant, especially since the experiment happens to approximate in some respects to the generic features and perceptual conditions of narrative. Although the sum total of the information communicated to the different groups of subjects was identical at all points, and although the subjects were explicitly instructed to respond to the person described in terms of the message as a whole, the conclusions about Jim's character were decisively determined by the order of presentation employed in each case. He was as a rule pronounced to be extrovert or introvert, friendly or standoffish, according to the block of information that was presented first. In both cases primacy effect decidedly prevailed over that of recency: "The first impression [was] made—oh made!"

Equally significant, however, is the light this study throws on the manner in which the two conflicting blocks were integrated. Strange as it may at first appear, the overwhelming majority of subjects did not even notice the glaring incompatibility of the information contained in the two successive segments. And this oversight is not to be attributed to careless reading. Given the laws of human perception, it is really no oversight at all, as further questioning of the subjects indeed revealed. Everything in the pseudo-narrative communication—the continuity of the "text," the identity of the "hero" throughout, and the quick succession of his actions—strongly suggested the need for integration, for a unified conception of character; and the forceful primacy effect did the rest of the work by persuasively impelling the readers to the particular mode in which the reconciliation of the conflicting information was to be accomplished in each case. Due to the successive order of presentation, the first block was read with an open mind, while the interpretation of the second—in itself as weighty—was decisively conditioned and colored by the anterior, homogeneous primacy effect; the leading block established a perceptual set, serving as a frame of reference to which subsequent information was subordinated as far as possible.

In each case, accordingly, the leading block was taken to represent the "real" Jim, the "essential nature" of Jim, while the second was taken to describe exceptional behavior, which is to be explained away in terms of temporary variations in mood or circumstance—in short, as a mere qualification of the previously established conception of character. Thus, when the subjects induced by the primacy effect to view Jim as an extrovert were challenged to account for the abundant evidence of unfriendliness on his part, they found no difficulty in reconciling it with the dominant frame of reference in the following ways (none explicitly indicated in the text): "Jim is essentially a friendly person and when he appeared to act in an unfriendly manner it was because he was tired, or because he had an unhappy day. . . . The girl was a bore . . . Jim is very selective in making friends. . . . There are times when he needs solitude. . . . He is an adolescent," etc. (p. 47). When the opening block represented Jim as an introvert, the same psychological process is to be seen at work—in the opposite direction. In neither case, however, was equal weight given to both segments, a procedure that would inevitably have led to the conclusion that Jim's personality was dual or split. The human tendency to subordinate recency to primacy effects drastically reduced the subjects' awareness of conflict—a reduction institutionalized in language and radicalized in literature through the figure of "blindness"—enabling them to construct and maintain in each case an integrated, unified view of character in face of the objective evidence to the contrary.

These conclusions have a variety of practical and theoretical implications for all areas of communication, from propaganda and judicial procedure to literature and literary research (and the temporal arts in general). To relate such concepts to literary interpretation and theory is definitely not to offer another "psychologistic approach" to literature, one of such questionable validity as the explication of the work in terms of the artist's supposed creative process or the subjective psychology of a particular reader. These researches simply clarify and establish scientifically some of the fundamental and widely intuited laws of human perception, laws to which the reader is, qua human being, bound for better or worse. As such, they form an integral component of literary communication; the work can safely presuppose and exploit them for its rhetorical ends, the more so since it does not by any means operate under laboratory conditions as regards either the general frame of mind in which the text is approached, the demands of scientific fairness (e.g., equally weighty "blocks"), or the sophistication of the distributive, dissimulatory, and persuasive devices. Or, to view the problem from the standpoint of literary study, since the relation of these laws to certain phenomena in the text is frequently the only way of satisfactorily accounting for the effects produced, they constitute an integral part of the description and interpretation of the literary work.

Moreover, what is true of verbal and literary communication in general is, due to a set of important generic and perceptual variables, particularly true of narrative and drama (or, to mention another temporal but syncretic rather than purely verbal art, the cinema). First, because their frame of fictionality ensures that the reader's first impressions shall be those freely devised by the text rather than rigidly derived (as in some of the other experiments in the collection, whose use of discursive, political or ideological material indeed yields different results) from the receiver's extratextual subjective experience and doctrinal preconceptions. Second, because the very duration of their reading-process makes it possible, for instance, to effect both a more durable or settled primacy effect and a more gradual recency effect than in corresponding cases of (say) lyrical poetry. Third, because their objects of manipulation—characters in action—naturally call forth strong emotive and normative response. And fourth, as

I shall soon argue in more detail, because of the superior rhetorical resources afforded by their manifold (actional as well as presentational) dynamics.

Indeed, since Homer and Biblical narrative[5] these laws of perception have variously been exploited for the purpose of directing the reader's response to character, event, theme, or universe of discourse. In literature, as in life, we tend to judge people by the first impression they make on us; but there is in this respect a basic difference between the two. Life, as Virginia Woolf maintains in a different context, is not a series of gig lamps symmetrically arranged. The impressions we receive in life come in an essentially unplanned, accidental, and sporadic manner. We happen to catch a glimpse of one person while he is at his best and of another at his worst, and conclude that the first is a good fellow and the second a fool or a brute. The question, moreover, whether our valuations of them will undergo a change or not is also decided by chance. In the literary work, on the other hand, the sequential manipulation of the reader's attitudes and sympathies, norms and hypotheses, is meaningful because it is, above all, highly controlled.

Due to the properties of the verbal medium—the discreteness of its units, and their successive and irreversible progression—the literary artist holds all the cards in his hands from beginning to end and can trump his aces in any way he chooses. He can break up his fabula into as many parts as he pleases, shuffle and reshuffle them as much as he likes, and arrange their actual emergence in the order that will suit his purposes best. Being in full command of his materials, he can manoeuvre his reader into regarding the same character either as a good fellow with some human frailties or as an ugly customer surprisingly possessed of a few attractive or redeeming traits by doing little more than presenting a given aggregate of motifs in different sequences.[6] Generally, he combines temporal structure with the other principles of deformation, development, and shaping that (according to my definition in Chapter 1) distinguish the sujet from the fabula—such as point of view, analogical juxtaposition, verbal patterning, or direct address to the reader on behalf or in condemnation of his character. And these intricate patterns of semantic and rhetorical interaction (undreamt of in the portrayal of experimental "Jims") will be closely traced in the following chapters. Order of presentation, however, often does the trick by itself. Since during his progress along the continuum of the text the reader knows nothing of present, past, or future beyond what his omnipotent mentor chooses to divulge from moment to moment, he can easily be prevented from suspecting, for the time judged necessary for the primacy effect to take a strong hold of his mind, that conflicting information lies ahead. And when this temporarily suppressed material is finally communicated, it is taken care of by the primacy effect in the way described (and a few others still to be described). Even if the reader retrospectively realizes that he has been tricked, it is usually too late for him to get out of the psychological trap.

In literature, unlike life, it is therefore not only profitable but necessary to pose such questions as: Why has this complex of events been presented first and that delayed? Why has this facet of a character been portrayed before that? Why has this piece of (verbal, actional, structural, or even generic) information been conveyed—or on the contrary, suppressed and ambiguated—at precisely this point? And it is especially imperative to investigate these questions whenever the distribution and ordering of information involve a deviation from a conventional or previously postulated pattern of organization, such as chronological sequence.

The tendentious delay, distribution, and ordering of information can thus be exploited not only for creating and sustaining narrative interest but also for the equally dynamic control of distance, response, and judgment as well as a variety of less emotively or ethically colored hypotheses. In fact, there is no element or pattern in the literary text, down to the meaning of a single word or the spatial relations between analogues, that is not amenable to such temporal twists and reversals. The particular strategy by which these are controlled may, however, vary. It varies, first of all, according to broad generic features and configurations of features. In a piece of discursive or quasi-discursive writing (e.g., Keats's "On the Sonnet") or purely descriptive poetry (e.g., Shakespeare's Sonnet 130, "My mistress' eyes are nothing like the sun"), any sequential change in the reader's attitude is exclusively due to the dynamics of presentation inherent in the verbal medium as a sequence of signs. Since here the represented object itself, existing at a fixed temporal point (as in Shakespeare's poem) or even outside time altogether (as in Keats's) rather than along a temporal continuum, does not develop by definition, the only development possible is within the rhetorical rather than the fictive framework. And this development in the reader's knowledge of and response to the object of manipulation purely derives, therefore, from the textual unfolding and distribution of its constituent parts (words and their meanings, descriptive bits, propositions, themes, etc., and their various linkages). Narrative and drama, however—and in varying degrees, poetry tracing some fictive change—have greater rhetorical resources in that they by definition represent a temporal process rather than a fixed object or state of mind. Consequently, since not only their medium but also their semantic referents necessarily have a sequential and developmental structure, with its own logic of progression and hence its own possibilities of blocking and displacement, this gives them an additional, extraverbal pair of sequences to play with, play up, or play off against each other. They may, that is, reinforce the general literary potentialities of temporal ordering by chronological or chronological-causal deformation, thus promoting the bi-directional processing of information (the play of expectation and hypothesis, retrospective revision of patterns, shifts of ambiguity, and progressive reconstitution in general) along the referential continuum of events as well as the signifying continuum of words. Equally important, the rhetorical strategy may exploit not only this manifold dynamics of presentation—notably by way of expositional distribution—but also the dynamics of the action quasi-mimetically progressing within the fictive world. Even with such a static character as Odysseus—not to speak of the developing Elizabeth Bennet (see Chap. 5) or Rastignac (see Chap. 7)—the shifts and twists in the reader's response are partly due, as they cannot be with Shakespeare's equally static mistress, to the changing conditions and ordeals through which the hero is passed.

Second, regardless of generic potentialities, the control strategy also varies according to the relations actually devised for the reading-process between the successively constructed impressions or hypotheses—between primacy and recency effect. To show this, we shall proceed, as usual, with the particularly complex case of narrative, where expositional unfolding plays a crucial part. The "natural" manner of presenting an expositional object (a character, a state of affairs, a fictive world or framework with all its distinctive properties and probabilities) is of course to *concentrate* all the relevant information the fabula contains about it at the beginning of the sujet, or at least at the point where the need for it as a whole first arises. This straightforward procedure, often flaunted by Trollope for instance, also has its artistic grounds and rhetorical effects. But the point is that it by definition involves no dynamic informational manipulation— no deformed temporal ordering; no temporary suppression and partial or gradual disclosure of such expositional material as potentially antipathetic character traits; no shock of retrospective illumination; and no need to abandon, modify, or even significantly qualify previously formed attitudes and conclusions. Therefore, since this procedure follows in effect the fabula sequence, it is best regarded here as the basic norm from which the three other models of control I shall propose, all of them strongly characterized by conflict or tension between primacy and recency effect, diverge in different ways and degrees and for different rhetorical ends.

These models will be described and illustrated in action first in the two following chapters and then, with reference to more comprehensive objects of manipulation and markedly different presentational modes, in Chapter 7. But before we start to examine in detail the various possibilities of effecting and directing the dynamics of response it may be well to observe that the three narrative strategies may be arranged on a scale according to their distance from the basic norm of straightforward (chronological, preliminary, and concentrated) communication. If this norm is located at one pole, then the strategy located at the opposite pole is naturally one where both the initial suppression of relevant expositional material and the change in attitude consequent upon its ultimate disclosure are most drastic. It may be designated as "the rise and fall of first impressions" in that it involves a homogeneous primacy effect which is sooner or later demolished by subsequent revelations surprisingly establishing the contrary, or is at least reduced by this recency effect to the position of a qualifying factor. In between the poles are located two rhetorical strategies where the dynamics of response is, relatively and progressively, less violently manipulated. In both, the clash between primacy and recency effect is to some extent moderated. In one, because the primacy effect is one-sided rather than downright fallacious and the recency effect is designed to complicate, modify, or qualify rather than demolish the reader's first impressions; in the other—that closest to though still far from identical with, the fabulaic norm—because the primacy effect itself is not homogeneous but interspersed with warning-signals and anticipatory cautions pointing the other way, so that the subsequent disclosures are less surprising to the reader. This gradated range of temporal possibilities—though it accomodates, as we shall see, still finer gradations and subclassifications according to the manner and object of control—is clearly exhaustive.

The first model, exemplified by Faulkner's *Light in August,* consists in a certain primacy effect being produced only to be shattered and ousted by subsequently disclosed exposition. The first impression the reader receives of the hero, Joe Christmas, cannot but engender a response that is far from sympathetic. Joe is first presented in and through the retrospective reflections of the honest Byron Bunch, starting from his sudden arrival at the Jefferson mill three years before. His appearance is sinister:

> He did not look like a professional hobo in his professional rags, but there was something definitely rootless about him, as though no town nor city was his, no street, no walls, no square of earth his home. And that he carried his knowledge with him always as though it were a banner, with a quality ruthless, lonely, and almost proud. . . . He was young. And Byron watched him standing there and looking at the men in sweat-stained overalls, with a cigarette in one side of his mouth and his face darkly and contemptuously still. . . . After a while he spat the cigarette without touching his hand to it and turned and went on to the mill office while the men in faded and worksoiled overalls looked at his back with a sort of baffled outrage. "We ought to run him through the planer," the foreman said. "Maybe that will take that look off his face."[7]

The stranger, "with his dark, insufferable face and his whole air of cold and quiet contempt" (p. 26), seems to his fellow-workers to carry with him "his own inescapable warning, like a flower its scent or a rattlesnake its rattle" (p. 27). Bunch recalls that Christmas's behaviour did not change in the least as the years went by. He proceeded in contemptuously ignoring all of them; and he harshly rebuffed Bunch himself ("keep your muck"), who kindly offered him some of his food when he noticed that the newcomer had brought no lunch with him. Even after several years at the mill nobody knew so much about him as where he slept at night. Later, he left his job without warning and went into bootlegging on a small scale, taking for a partner another stranger, a contemptible creature named Brown. And then we suddenly learn in chapter 4, from Bunch's conversation with Hightower, that the day before Christmas murdered a white woman, Joanna Burden, by neatly cutting off her head; that the woman— it has just been discovered—had not only permitted him to lodge in the cabin adjoining her house but had also been his mistress for years; that it has just come to light that he is part negro; and that the whole Southern town is feverishly hunting for the nigger, with murder in its heart.

A character can hardly appear more repulsive than Christmas at the end of chapter 4. But this chapter not only gives the finishing touch to the antipathetic primacy effect. It also seems to indicate to the reader the terms in which the puzzling motivelessness of Joe's malignity should be explained. As no clue to this disturbing causal gap has so far been suggested, the reader pounces on the new piece of exposition as if it were a godsend: Joe is a nigger! In default of any other explanation, the traditional conception of the blackamoor—by his color associated with the devil—as a natural villain comes to the fore. Christmas's brutality, his ingratitude to his benefactress and to Bunch, his criminality past and present—the reader is led to think—are all to be accounted for in terms of his race, of the notorious animality of the negro. Christmas is simply another Aaron, who, in Shakespeare's *Titus Andronicus,* constantly shocks us by his acts of gratuitous villainy.

This is precisely, we soon realize, the primacy effect Faulkner wished to generate at this stage of the sujet. From the beginning of chapter 5, however, he systematically proceeds to demolish it. He abruptly switches from an outside to an inside view of Christmas, and devotes the heart of the novel (a large narrative block composed of chapters 5-12, pp. 78-215) to a representation of the hero's development from childhood to the time of the murder. The unexpected retrospective illumination of Christmas's character and history, as well as the considerable increase of sympathy consequent upon the drastic shift in narrative perspective, compel the reader to retract or modify his adverse hypotheses and judgments one by one. He learns from this expositional flashback that in fact nobody—not even Christmas himself—knows whether he is part negro or not. It is probable (though this gap is permanently ambiguated) that he is wholly white. But—and this comes as an even profounder shock—irrespective of his race, he is hardly to blame for what he has become, let alone for his crime. We are shown time and again how he has been ruthlessly driven into becoming what he is; it is society, we discover—the people at the orphanage, the McEacherns, Max and Bobbie the waitress—that should shoulder the bulk of the guilt, not he. Society has persistently stifled or perverted every normal instinct in the child, and has turned the man into a rootless, haunted, tortured phantom, who is continually at war with himself and can find peace only in death. Faulkner explores with special care the complex, morbid relations between Joe and his counterpart Joanna, demonstrating that the violent outcome was inevitable. We are jolted again, finally, by the discovery that Joe killed the mad spinster in self-defence, in more than one sense.

The primacy effect of chapters 2-4 has no chance whatever of withstanding the sustained force of the eight subsequent chapters. Not only are the two "blocks" far from equally weighty; much of the information contained in the first turns out to be partly or wholly wrong as well. In this representative instance, therefore, it is the shocking recency effect (to the brilliance of which I have not even begun to do justice) that prevails, while the primacy effect is relegated to the position of a qualifying factor. But it is due to the tenacity of first impressions that Faulkner signally succeeds in driving home his thematic point—the crippling effect that the pressure of society and abstract or preconceived ideas has upon the individual. For the uprooting of the primacy effect is so drastic that the reader cannot but perceive and deplore the terrible mistake he has (or might have) made. The author has, in fact, deliberately lured us into a trap baited with stereotypes that invite stock-responses: the sinister Stranger and his brutality, the Bootlegger and his shady activities, and above all, the lecherous, ungrateful, homicidal Negro. He has thus brought to life some of the most primitive and contemptible instincts and prejudices that lie dormant within us, particularly the racial ones; and the trap has been so elaborately devised that it is difficult to avoid falling into it. Once the reader has swallowed the alluring bait, however, the sequel bursts upon him like an unexpected slap in the face. The recency effect not only blows to pieces the Myth of the Murderous, Black-hearted Nigger, but also opens our incredulous eyes to the bitter discovery that in essence there is little to choose between us and the mob of lynchers who are out for Christmas's blood.[8]

The strategy by which primacy effect is taken advantage of in the *Odyssey*—roughly corresponding to the experiment described at the start—is in some crucial respects different from, and in others similar to, that in *Light in August.* As it retrospectively emerges, Homer's problem of control was twofold in that he had to manipulate the reader's response to two distinct, though related, facets of the protagonist's personality. First, though Odysseus's military exploits indisputably stamp him as an heroic figure, by any standards, he is at the same time endowed with certain qualities—such as inveterate guile—that have been considered, from his days to our own, to be incompatible with the truly heroic. [9] "As I detest the doorways of Death, I detest that man, who hides one thing in the depths of his heart and speaks forth another": this is the note of Achilles, significantly sounded in response to the diplomatic offers made by Odysseus in the *Iliad*'s embassy scene. Homer conceived of Odysseus as a unique character who can be fitted into no conventional mold—neither that of the Hero nor that of the Trickster—because he is so complex that he defies and transcends these ready-made labels. But since many of Odysseus's victories (over the Cyclops, for example) are brought about by cunning and deceit rather than conventional military prowess, the reader is liable to dismiss him as a contemptible trickster. The presentation of this aspect of his character accordingly requires wary handling and a tight control over the audience's reactions, the more so in view of its significant thematic implications. As in *Light in August,* characterization here involves an exploration and to a large extent a demolition of a myth—in this case that of the heroic figure; and though Homer's attack is in the main more obliquely conducted than Faulkner's favorite shock-tactics, the dramatized conclusions are no less iconoclastic.

Second, the work wishes to highlight the whole complex of traits, pulls, and motives, some of them far from engaging in themselves, that make up what may be called the moral aspect of Odysseus's personality, and yet to generate an essentially sympathetic, though clear-eyed, attitude towards him. So this facet too requires great care, otherwise the portrayal of his egotism, guile, and suspiciousness may irretrievably turn us against him. It will be seen even from this brief formulation of the problem that some of the main qualities that are liable to diminish Odysseus's heroic stature—for example, his trickery—overlap with those that may be thought to undermine his moral fiber.

III

Homer brilliantly reconciles the seemingly incompatible tasks of thoroughgoing characterization, on the one hand, and retention of sympathy and respect on the other, through a far-sighted distribution, ordering, and patterning of the expositional material. He devises a strategy of presentation that involves first a homogeneously idealized portrayal and then a gradual and subtle complication of the primacy effect.

As I have already argued, the narrative strategy of the first four books ensures the reader's unqualified sympathy for Odysseus and his cause. Out of the static—and hence purely and uniformly expositional—complex of heterogeneous traits that constitute Odysseus's character, Homer has restricted himself to rendering only those qualities which we cannot but wholeheartedly admire, carefully suppressing for the time being the less engaging ones. On the one hand, his war exploits characterize him as the quintessential heroic figure—physically powerful, daring, resourceful, and cool-headed even in the tightest corners. On the other hand, he is revealed to be no less perfect as a moral and social being—a just king, a devoted husband, a loyal friend, and a pious worshiper of the gods. Moreover, in order to leave no doubt in the reader's mind as to the validity of this initial characterization, the author stamps it both with divine imprimatur and expert evidence: the gods themselves are made to testify to his moral perfection and wisdom; old Nestor, the great strategist, to his military genius; and Menelaus, the redoubtable warrior, to his soldiership.

This sympathetic attitude has been heightened by the insistent depiction both of his plight abroad and of the situation at home. The rapacious Suitors are used in more than one way to intensify our involvement in the fortunes of the absent king. The polar contrast with their antipathetic, and divinely denounced, collective character effectively highlights the attractiveness of his; and their plots arouse our indignation, thus clinching our identification with the sufferer and his house.

In retrospect it also emerges that the multifarious suspense effects of books 1-4 form not only an independent artistic end but at the same time a means for increasing the potency of the primacy effect. The suspense strategy first ensures that the favorable traits of Odysseus that abundantly emerge should be appreciated and retained in the memory on account of their decisive actional value. Second, the constant alternations of hope and fear prevent our sympathy from remaining inert (as it generally is when only a preliminary character-sketch is given) but activate it by continually bringing it into play as each threatening or reassuring signal crops up, thus fixing our attitude more firmly with each new emotional commitment. The functional dovetailing of the dynamics of suspense with the dynamics of normative manipulation is indeed remarkable; what was previously the end has now become the means, and vice versa.

Homer thus manages to inculcate in the mind of the unsuspecting reader a primacy effect that is as extreme in its sympathy as our initial response to Christmas is extreme in its antipathy. Unlike Faulkner, however—and this is the distinctive feature of the second as opposed to the first model of control—Homer has no intention of subsequently shattering his elaborately contrived primacy effect, but only of richly complicating and balancing it in a way that will involve a minimal increase of distance. In *Light in August* the first impression is later revealed as a false and deliberately misleading hypothesis; in the *Odyssey,* it is revealed as misleading indeed but still true as far as it goes—it just does not go far enough. The transitional stage, at which the epic starts the process of rounding out the hitherto somewhat schematic and overidealized portrait of the Ithacan king, is book 5—a point that is rendered especially convenient, as I have already explained, for embarking upon this delicate job.

The very homogeneity of Odysseus's sympathetic presentation throughout the "Telemachia" raises, as early as the beginning of the countermovement in book 5, a set of three formidable problems (which no author using any of the three models can afford to ignore): (1) How to account for the disparity in characterization between the initial and the subsequent parts, and for the delayed communication (or previous systematic suppression) of whole areas of relevant expositional material, all of them suspiciously relating to the less attractive facets of Odysseus's changeless personality? Or, to put it bluntly, how to avoid incurring the reader's indignation at having been cheated? (2) How to prevent Odysseus's character from splitting apart as the result of the sudden introduction of a host of unsympathetic expositional traits? That is, how is the reader's sense of the unity of character to be maintained? And, of course: (3) How to accomplish in these circumstances the full exploration of this complex character not only without forfeiting altogether the reader's liking and respect for the protagonist but with the minimal increase of distance?

The first problem is solved by a shift in both point of view and situational context. Like Faulkner, who started by rendering Christmas's reflection in the consciousness of Bunch and only later reinforced the abrupt shift in sympathy by a corresponding shift in narrative perspective, Homer first presents Odysseus indirectly—mainly through the eyes of his friends—and only later, from book 5 on, begins to dramatize him directly (books 5–8) or delegate to him the task of narration (books 9–12). Moreover, the expositional information concerning Odysseus that is conveyed through the reminiscences of his friends derives solely from their acquaintance with him during the Trojan War; whereas the subsequently presented exposition (that gained both from our direct observation of the protagonist in action and from his own account of his past adventures) relates to totally different situational contexts: Calypso's island, Phaeacia, and the wanderings on sea and land.

The shifts in perspective and environment form two complementary realistic motivations for the initial suppression and the deferred disclosure of the various antecedents sunk into books 5–12. Nestor, Menelaus, and Helen base their portrayals of Odysseus on his conduct in Troy, where he not only lived among open friends and open enemies but was also bound by a rigid code of heroic etiquette. Our subsequent acquaintance with him suggests that the prudent and adaptable Odysseus was quite capable of repressing his Autolycan propensities—his craftiness, above all—in order to conform to the code of honor jealously adhered to by his aristocratic comrades. In view of his unsavory reputation for wiliness and his dubious ancestry it is no wonder that he should have done so—the foremost Greek champions of the *Iliad* were inclined to suspect him of overcleverness anyway.[10] On the other hand, on Calypso's island, in Phaeacia, or in the wilderness he is on his own—away from an heroic environment, away from the watchful eyes of his fellow-warriors, and fighting for survival. In these circumstances, he has no reason to impose on himself the restraints required by the code; indeed, it would be madness to do so. So now he can give rein to the whole gamut of his talents, Autolycan as well as heroic.

Homer can therefore afford to let Odysseus's friends tell all they know about him without having to report so much as a single reprehensible or socially unacceptable feature of his hero (just as Byron Bunch can be made to divulge all he knows about Christmas without coming up with a single attractive trait or redeeming fact). They can tell us only what they know from direct observation, and they know only what Odysseus chose to display. The whole truth emerges only later, in other circumstances. If the reader feels cheated, he can at most blame the obtuseness of the informants, who have taken the image for the man and the part for the whole, not the unfairness of their creator, who has scrupulously recorded everything they said. Homer thus manages to account for his artistic necessity—control of distance, dictating a tendentious distribution of expositional information throughout the first half of the epic—in convincingly quasi-mimetic terms.

To the impressive array of (equally representative) techniques by which Homer solves the two other problems, and to showing that not even a single one of them can be divorced from the sequential unfolding and twisting of the information, the rest of this chapter will be devoted. For theoretical purposes, however, it may be well at this point to formulate, in general terms, the central control devices composing Homer's strategy, notably the overall principles of expositional distribution:

1. The three stages in and through which the exposition is unfolded: initial—books 1-4; transitional—books 5-8; and final—books 9-12. This multiform tripartite movement (considerably subtler in effect and richer in possibilities of dynamic shift and integration than the simple, dichotomous, and pivotless, Primacy-Recency sequence) may sometimes be viewed as thesis, antithesis, and synthesis.

2. Exploitation and constant reinforcement of the prolonged primacy effect.

3. & 4. Introduction of unfavourable expositional facts as either veri-similar qualifications or more radical redefinitions of the primacy effect.

5. Balance and counterbalance: the equally delayed communication of favourable expositional facts as a counterweight.

6. Nicely graded emergence of potentially antipathetic features.

7. Relation of antipathetic (or negative) to sympathetic (or positive) traits with a view to complicating or extenuating adverse judgment.

8. Recurrence of contextually, cumulatively charged materials (or "control centers") at strategic points.

9. Quantitative, selectional shifts of emphasis (including scene vs. summary, progressive foregrounding, and apparently redundant but significantly variant repetitions).

10. Circumstantial extenuation (including geographical patterning and sequential manipulation of space).

11. Verbal dynamics (notably gradual shifts of contextually revitalized formulaic epithets, in line with the general compositional movement).

12. Shift of point of view (including architechtonic as well as local shifts).

13. Discrepancies in awareness (especially between reader and characters as well as between reader and narrator).

14. Authoritative (not necessarily authorial) commentary.

15. Shift of normative basis.

16. Analogical collocation: straight, contrasted, mixed, and dynamic.

17. Interaction of presentational contiguity and suprasequential similarity (e.g., in the form of structural framing or sandwiching of tricky material).

18. Manipulation of (initially perceptible or camouflaged) gaps and ambiguities.

19. Intensification of suspense.

20. Interrelation of presentational and actional dynamics.

This list can in itself hardly do justice to the subtlety of Homer's procedure or to the ways in which the different indirections combine to produce the desired effects; though it does perhaps give us an idea of the variety of devices repeatedly interacting in literary persuasion, and will hopefully serve as a corrective to the fairly widespread fallacy that rhetoric is mainly a function of point of view and figurative language. I shall proceed, therefore, to an analysis of the rhetorical strategy of the transitional books 5-8.

Let us take the treatment accorded to one of the most moving factors in Odysseus's predicament—his captivity on Calypso's island where, as was eloquently described in book 1 (pp. 19, 20), he has long been yearning for home and family and resisting the allurements of the goddess. In books

5-8 Homer first takes care to intensify the personal sympathy generated by these circumstances, and by the laudable traits they bring out, through a full scenic dramatization of Odysseus's previously stated homesickness and of his withstanding a series of temptations to stay abroad. As was the case with Athene's descent to Ithaca, the facts now dramatized in and through the progression of the action are often explicitly indicated to be expositionally illustrative, i.e., to reflect an habitual or recurrent state of affairs.

Thus, on his first appearance in book 5 (and in the epic as a whole) Odysseus is shown sitting on the shore "in his accustomed place," looking out across the sea, his eyes "wet with weeping, as they always were. Life with its sweetness was ebbing away in the tears he shed for his lost home" (pp. 76, 77). He is, moreover, so eager to regain his rocky Ithaca that he unhesitatingly rejects the beautiful Calypso's proposal to take on immortality as her lawful consort and share her home, a spot—the narrator pointedly comments—"where even an immortal visitor [like Hermes] might pause to gaze in wonder and delight" (p. 75). The circumstantial foregrounding strongly reinforces the "primary" effect of this recurrent expositional feature of Odysseus's life with Calypso. And our sympathy is soon redoubled owing to the reproduction of this temptation on the human level—in the analogical advances of Nausicaa, a princess young, rich, and "tall and beautiful as a goddess" (p. 86).

What might, however, be regarded so far as a sentimentalized portrayal of an overheroic resistance is now persuasively rendered credible by a series of realistic or ironic touches, consisting mainly of hitherto suppressed features of Odysseus's relations with the goddess. Their relationship, we suddenly gather, has been far from Platonic all along—even after her promise to release him has been given, "the two retired to a recess in the cavern and there in each other's arms they spent a night of love" (p. 79). Homer not only makes it perfectly clear that this has been an habitual feature of their life together but, more interesting still, he at the same time throws some retrospective light on Odysseus's motives for turning down the goddess's tempting offers. It is now revealed for the first time that the captive has been able to show such resistance not only on account of his genuine homesickness; an additional, and more realistic reason, is now unobtrusively slipped in: "For the Nymph had long ceased to please. At nights . . . he had to sleep with her under the roof of the cavern, cold lover with an ardent dame" (p. 77). In the past she did please him, then, but now that he is tired of her he is doubly glad to take the first opportunity to be off. The reader is somewhat surprised, moreover, that the desperately homesick Odysseus fails to jump at Calypso's promise to set him free but thinks of his personal safety first. Even at such a moment, he has his wits sufficiently about him to suspect the goddess of treachery and to extort from her a solemn oath that she will hatch no plots against him (p. 78).

The ironic undertones of these disclosures form the first welcome antidote to the previously idealized portrait of the hero as a moral paragon. And yet, this initial throwing of a more verisimilar, complicating light on Odysseus involves no disintegration of character and only a very slight loss of sympathy. His behavior is, under the circumstances, human and understandable; and the traits that it reveals him to have possessed all along do not, in spite of their unexpected emergence, directly clash with our conception of his character but qualify and enrich it. Moreover, the implications as to his mixed motives and suspicious nature are not only subordinated to the forceful primacy effect but are also counterbalanced afresh[11] by the vivid dramatization of his sufferings and the attractiveness of the rejected temptations.[12]

Furthermore, the work proceeds to counteract or compensate for any loss of sympathy that the disclosure of these less attractive features involves by opposing to them some undeniably engaging facets, the revelation of which has likewise been deliberately deferred to this point. Odysseus's courtesy and tact are, for instance, highlighted time and again. Having extorted from his captress the desired oath, he placates the jealous Calypso by pronouncing her unfading beauty to be incomparably superior to Penelope's mortal charms (p. 79). And his conduct towards Nausicaa— from the exchange on their first encounter, through the gentlemanly lie by which he saves her from her father's displeasure, to his graceful rejection of her implied proposal of marriage—is similarly a masterpiece of civilized manners, which cannot wholly be attributed either to the necessity of securing her good will.

The process of controlled deidealization is not, however, confined to the revelation of hitherto unsuspected components of the hero's personality. It also manifests itself in a related but more radical dynamics, aiming at more than a qualifying effect, namely, a gradual redefinition of previously communicated traits, which are now given either a new twist or different weight and emphasis or both. The combination of the two devices is particularly noticeable in the processing of Odysseus's heroic stature or status—in the "control of respect."

This section does not content itself with bringing Odysseus's heroic qualities down to earth, as it did with his attitude to home. That process is not especially risky, for no reader will lose his admiration for the hero at the sight of the momentary ebbing of his courage in face of the unleashed fury of the elements (pp. 81, 83). On the contrary, the realistic touch only adds luster to the usual indomitability of his spirit. These books go much further than that. They suggest that the complexity of Odysseus's character largely consists in its basic duality, in the coexistence of strictly heroic qualities with others that are generally regarded—by the standards of his own comrades and other codes of honor—as too "low" to be compatible with the truly heroic nature. It now first begins to emerge that though indeed eminently endowed with all the qualifications required of a typical Greek hero (an Achilles or an Agamemnon), Odysseus's character is far more complicated in that he radically deviates from the norm. He is not warmly frank or rashly blunt but prudently circumspect and at times even unpleasantly devious; not the slave of passion but coldly calculating and self-controlled; not rigidly and ostentatiously heroic but adaptable and versatile. In Phaeacia, Odysseus actually displays his heroic mettle only when driven to it by Euryalus's taunts (pp. 106-8); and even when roused to anger he does not lose control of his emotions. But as a rule, though justly confident of the military prowess celebrated in books 1-4, he is now shown to refrain from rushing into battle, preferring to bide his time and make the most of his genius for craftiness.

Books 5-8 offer varied illustrations of the Autolycan behavior that justifies one set of the formulaic epithets intermittently attached to his name here: "the nimble-witted Odysseus" (p. 79), "the wise and subtle Odysseus" (p. 98), or "the resourceful Odysseus" (p. 101). The Ithacan king also shows himself to be a versatile adventurer, who can build a boat in a craftsmanlike manner or trick his way home as well as fight the stormy seas or stand up to a haughty nobleman in a foreign country. The problem confronting Homer, however, was how to bring these "unheroic" aspects to the fore without forfeiting the reader's belief in the unity of Odysseus's character or his respect for the unconventional hero.

It is in terms of the counteraction of these dangers that the order of presentation and the patterns of distribution of the material relating to Odysseus's character are to be explained. The impact of the preliminary and prolonged hymn to the hero could be uprooted, as in the *Light in August* model, only if the subsequently imparted information were of such a drastic nature as not only to counterbalance but overweigh, discredit, or invalidate it. In the present case, however, a number of effective measures have been taken to prevent this from happening and to ensure that it will be the protagonist's heroic facet, not the Autolycan, that will operate as the primary frame of reference.

First, Odysseus is (scenically again) presented throughout this intermediate stage as worthy of the admiration of goddesses, princesses, and kings. He is variously shown to live up to his heroic reputation so as to confirm the nostalgic characterizations of his friends and justify the application of the complementary set of formulaic epithets to his name: "Odysseus, the royal sacker of cities" (p. 103), "the stalwart Odysseus" (p. 78), or "the heroic Odysseus" (p. 103). The sea adventure impressively establishes his courage and powers of endurance, and the scene of the games, his athletic prowess as well; even after being knocked about by the seas for twenty days he beats all the Phaeacian champions at disk-throwing and offers to match himself against all comers at boxing and wrestling too. As the "peerless Laodamas" points out, "the man is mighty strong" (p. 106). But it is Demodocus's song about the Wooden Horse—the acme of Odysseus's military achievements—that does most to reinforce the reader's consciousness of Odysseus's stature, both directly and indirectly; apart from evoking him in heroic action, it recalls the other Odyssean exploits narrated at Sparta, and implies that his fame has spread even so far as Phaeacia, "the outposts of mankind" (p. 90).

The reinsistence on this facet of the hero's personality confirms the primacy effect, gives the reader the sense of continuity of characterization, and precludes any possibility that the Autolycan complex of traits, concurrently worked in, may get such a strong hold of his mind as to jeopardize the desired response to Odysseus's figure as a whole. Moreover, in order to establish the heroic aspect even more firmly as the dominant frame of reference, Odysseus is not allowed, throughout books 5-8, to commit even a single deed that may be denounced as dishonest, mean, or undignified. On the contrary, though as crafty as ever, he is shown at his most considerate and urbane, his conduct being favorably contrasted with the boorishness of the "heroic" Euryalus. The deeper exploration of the more unsavory sides of his character has wisely been delayed to books 9-12.

Even if Homer left it at that, the reader would thus be able to integrate satisfactorily the two poles of Odysseus's nature in terms of the centrality of the heroic traits and the comparative marginality of the Autolycan. But· in fact—unlike the psychological experiment described—the order and modes of presentation are not simply devised to relegate the latter set of traits to a position of subordination to the primary frame of reference, as discordant elements in an otherwise homogeneously heroic portrait. The work aims at a much subtler and tighter mode of dynamic integration. It leads the reader to the realization that the points at which Odysseus's figure diverges from the heroic norm do not constitute newly revealed qualities but only natural extensions or new manifestations of the very characteristics that have made him the formidable warrior that he indisputably is. They were already latent in the foregoing presentation of his character, only they were elaborately camouflaged. Have not Nestor, Menelaus, and Helen sung the praises of Odysseus's military resourcefulness and versatility as well as his other soldierly assets? While following their expositional accounts, the reader could not have predicted that Odysseus is wont to make use of these same qualities in less than heroic circumstances and in more prosaic struggles for existence; but now he retrospectively perceives that the present expositional extension is highly probable.

For example: during his infiltration into the Trojan citadel, Helen alone—we were told in book 4—penetrated through his beggar's disguise, but he was careful to evade her questions about his true identity till she "had solemnly sworn that [she] would not disclose his name to the Trojans" (p. 60). This expositional incident now functions as a dramatized preparation for Odysseus's displaying the same crafty attitude throughout books 5–8 in a series of strikingly analogical but low-key cases: his refusal to take advantage of Calypso's promise to release him till she has sworn to plot no mischief against him; his abstention from making use of Ino's veil, in spite of his desperate situation at sea, except as a last resort; and his evasive answers to Alcinous's implied questions about his identity. These are now grasped as different manifestations of the previously depicted craftiness, not as exemplifications of a new facet of personality. They redefine the same basic trait by showing it to be capable of flexibly assuming different forms or dimensions in different conditions. The reinforced heroic frame of reference, though, prevents the reader at this stage from giving equal weight to the different manifestations of this quality. On the contrary, it drives him to provide a circumstantial extenuation for the "lower" instances of wiliness: as long as Odysseus is surrounded by strangers and potential enemies, he cannot be blamed for being on his guard against the sudden generosity of a Calypso or even an Ino, or the inquisitiveness of an Alcinous.

The story of the Wooden Horse is the control center at which most of these devices meet. Its delayed communication (compare Menelaus's account on p. 60 with Demodocus's on pp. 114–15) is far from accidental. It was sorely needed precisely at this point. This exploit, by which Odysseus gained universal renown as the author of the Greek victory, dramatically foregrounds on the one hand the more conventional, and hence immediately prestigious, aspects of his military prowess—the Phaeacian bard goes so far as to claim that during the decisive hand-to-hand battle he looked like the God of War himself (p. 115). On the other hand, as the Wooden Horse forms the greatest deception in military history, it drives home the heights to which Odysseus's guile can rise and the spectacular results it can yield where the conventional heroism of a whole army has been of no avail for years. So, when juxtaposed with the pettier ruses of books 5–8, this episode both dwarfs them (thus safeguarding the primacy effect) and at the same time brings out the "family resemblance" that marks them as deriving from the same fundamental trait. Last, this retrospect also mitigates the effects of Odysseus's inveterate suspiciousness by concretely suggesting the fatal results of the opposite line of conduct. The Trojans (the reader now learns) argued about what was to be done with the Wooden Horse the Greeks had left behind: "Some were for piercing the wooden frame with a bold stroke of the spear; others would have . . .

hurled it down the rocks; while others again wished to let it stand as a signal offering to appease the gods—and that was just what happened in the end." Unlike Odysseus, who whenever in doubt always acts on his worst suspicions, the trustful Trojans finally decided against looking the gift horse in the mouth and were consequently destroyed.

Books 5–8 thus mark a considerable progress in the delineation of the hero's character and the manipulation of the reader's response. The tricky process of twofold deidealization has been warily launched, mainly through a strategy of patterned expositional distribution. The unfolding of character has involved not only a reliance on the tenacity of first impressions but also a delicate dynamics of stretching, balancing, counterbalancing, and interrelating expositional motifs of "negative" and "positive" normative import. Accordingly, the reader can no longer consider Odysseus a paragon of virtue or a strictly conventional hero; but due to the efficacy of the control devices, the first stage in the complication of character and response has been accomplished at a low price both from the viewpoint of unity and that of retention of sympathy and respect.

This part of the epic, however, forms only a transitional stage, in the control strategy as well as in the action. The main, and infinitely bolder, step is still to be taken in books 9–12, where various facets that have only been hinted at so far are brought into the open to be further molded and defined. To cite one suggestive instance, the grounds for Odysseus's distrust of Calypso, Ino, and Alcinous are progressively weaker than those on which his suspicion of Helen are based. He was of course fully justified in distrusting Helen; subsequently, he is somewhat less justified in suspecting Calypso of treachery—though her jealousy may make her dangerous, she is after all in love with him; his suspicion of the help offered by the gentle Ino, a total stranger, is a bit more groundless; and his distrust of the hospitable Phaeacians, almost wholly gratuitous. Significantly, moreover, in the cases of Calypso and Ino Homer throws some ironic light on Odysseus's instinctive suspiciousness by informing the reader beforehand that the goddesses mean well. Through this nicely gradated succession of analogical incidents Homer subtly alludes to a basic antipathetic tendency of the hero's. But at the present phase he confines himself to touching lightly on this trait so as to pave the way for the full exploration of its depths in the sequel, where its insidious effect on Odysseus's moral fiber is openly dramatized.

IV

Since the vital but lengthy flashback (pp. 117–71) by which the manipulation of character and attitude is further complicated and rounded off impedes the natural flow of the action and the final resolution of the reader's anxieties, Homer reinforces the effect of his having lowered the pitch of suspense at the start of book 5 by rekindling our curiosity, throughout books 5-8, about the long-standing expositional gaps. This is mainly accomplished through numerous passing allusions—generalized (p. 79) and specific (p. 77), dramatic (p. 97) and authorial (p. 113)—to Odysseus's wanderings. So by the time Alcinous, himself intrigued by his guest's personality and allusions to an eventful past, calls on the stranger for a true account of his wanderings (p. 116), the reader is as prepared as Odysseus's internal audience to attend to the long-deferred story of the fabulous adventures.

We soon discover, however, that the tale's intrinsic charm is its strongest recommendation. Not only are the adventures fascinating but Odysseus's gifts as raconteur make the most of them. The power of this double appeal is reflected in the spellbound response of his audience, Alcinous going so far as to claim that his guest is endowed "with all the artistry that a ballad-singer might display" (p. 153). The Phaeacians are so captivated that, when the wanderer breaks off his tale in the middle, they bribe him to proceed with it. Nor is this bardic skill to be simply attributed to Homer himself. It should be viewed as another of the talents with which this versatile hero has been invested, as is indicated not only by the otherwise superfluous dramatized response of the audience but also by the significant points at which Odysseus's mode of narration is made to diverge from that typical of the omniscient narrator himself.[13]

In fact, Odysseus's bardic artistry has made such an impression on critics that he has even been accused of usurping the poetic licence of free invention as well. Troubled by the sudden predominance of the fabulous elements in an otherwise comparatively realistic work, as soon as Odysseus takes over as narrator, they try to account for it by the hypothesis that he simply concocted a pack of cock-and-bull stories in order to impress his hosts and ingratiate himself with them.[14] I should certainly not put this past Odysseus, who shows himself at Ithaca to be a master improviser. And if he were here too not simply a humanly and unconsciously unreliable narrator, like his friends with their partial versions of him, but deliberately mendacious, this perspectival ambiguation of the inset tale and the expositional past of its frame would have serious implications for the whole control strategy. But though there are indeed grounds for this suspicion, the evidence demonstrating that the arch-deceiver happens for once to be telling the truth is overwhelming. Without venturing into the alluring byways of Homeric scholarship, I wish to point out that the whole problem is resolved by the indisputable fact that we have already heard about four of the central episodes (Cyclops, Circe, Oxen of the Sun, and Calypso) and part of another (the Agamemnon tragedy) from an independent, reliable source—the omniscient narrator himself. And the two versions agree at all points.

Moreover, if we follow the direction in which Odysseus's expositional presentation has been moving, we realize that perhaps the strongest argument in favor of the veracity of his tale is based not on factual but on purely artistic grounds. In the light of this nicely gradated progression so far, the sequel of book 8 is the logical place for a disclosure of his conduct in fabulous surroundings. We first saw him—through the eyes of his friends—among his fellow-kings at Troy, where life was regulated by a strict, stylized code of honor. Next we observed him—directly—against the background of secluded Phaeacia, which partakes both of the fabulous and the civilized world: its inhabitants "are the outposts of mankind and come in contact with no other people" except chance travelers, and what is more, they are as near to the gods as "the Cyclopes and the wild tribes of the Giants" (pp. 90, 98).[15] After this transitional phase, what is more natural than to proceed to the other extreme, to the fabulous sphere proper as refracted through the hero's own eyes? This twofold advance is almost predictable. And in retrospect, its artistic rightness should be evident.

Furthermore: the gradated geographical and perspectival movement dovetails beautifully into the gradated expositional presentation of Odysseus—likewise composed of three stages. The increasingly "internalized" refraction of Odysseus's movement through increasingly barbaric or fabulous surroundings realistically motivates the principles of distribution of his antecedents: it accounts for the emergence of different facets of his personality at different phases of the work. At Troy, it is psychologically convincing that he should display only his heroic, socially acceptable side. Later, in Phaeacia, where his success considerably depends on his appearing as a distinguished personage, the heroic elements are naturally brought into play to some extent; but as he is surrounded by strangers, as he is neither in strictly heroic surroundings nor watched by the suspicious eyes of his fellow-warriors, and as his ends cannot be encompassed here by military prowess—he instinctively puts his trust in his nimble wits and urbanity. And at the third stage it is as natural that the traits that come to the fore should mainly be those opposed to the conventionally heroic. In the world of witches, monsters, and ogres, Homer persuasively implies, to adhere to heroic etiquette is to commit suicide. Even the most superior soldiership is of no avail against a Cyclops, a Circe, or a Scylla. So here the protagonist, bound by no special laws because there are none and fighting for survival, not only can but must give free rein to the wily side of his nature.

This circumstantial motivation of the distributed disclosure of the expositional material does not, of course, account for the *order* in which the three stage are presented. It does not explain Homer's decision to place Telemachus's interviews with Nestor and Menelaus before his father's chronologically simultaneous adventures in Phaeacia, or the adventures in Phaeacia before the chronologically anterior wanderings, or most other deviations from the fabula order. All this is to be accounted for not so much in the realistic terms of the "natural" dynamics of the action as in the aesthetic terms of presentational dynamics, particularly control of distance and thematic development. On the other hand, the geographical movement devised also functions as one of the overall control measures in that it has an extenuating effect on our view of Odysseus's increasing deviation from the heroic norm; this sequential patterning of fictive space suggests that his conduct is determined by the increasingly wild surroundings and desperate circumstances in which he finds himself. So by sending Odysseus into the dangers of wonderland Homer can—as he could not in Phaeacia—show him at the height of his Autolycanism, even present him as something of the Wily Lad of folklore, without forfeiting the reader's respect for his hero; at the same time he can also positively increase our admiration for this versatile figure by demonstrating that due to his keen wits Odysseus emerges triumphant from trials which could not but prove fatal to the conventional hero.

Thus, the concurrent progression ("dynamics") of the four parallel lines of spatial movement, perspectival shifting, expositional distribution, and control strategy may be roughly represented as follows:

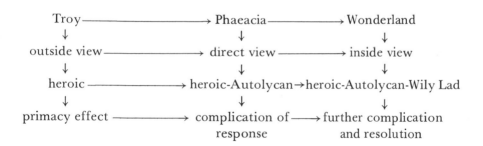

V

In the series of expositional episodes composing books 9–12, Homer proceeds to push to the extreme both poles of Odysseus's heroic nature, searchingly explores them, and firmly fixes our attitude to hero and heroic norm through a complex of persuasive devices that are as effective as they are subtle. On the one hand, he presents Odysseus at his craftiest. The instances of guile worked into the foregoing phase are child's play compared with the trickery Odysseus resorts to throughout his adventures in the fabulous world, where, moreover, he does not even once extricate himself from trouble by conventionally heroic action. Homer even presses the nonheroic facet of character so far as to lay bare the archetypal Wily Lad elements latent in it, incorporating in his epic a number of folk-tales in which Odysseus is made to figure instead of the traditional Wily Lad. This notably happens in the Cyclops episode, where the protagonist is driven to devise spectacular ruse after ruse. He first meets the monster with deceit when asked where he has moored his ship. Later, despite the horror inspired by the sight of the Cyclops devouring his men, Odysseus at once begins to look for the best way of escape. An "heroic" solution first occurs to him: "Now my manhood prompted me to action: I thought I would draw my sharp sword from the scabbard at my side, creep up to him . . . and stab him in the breast" (p. 124). But he wisely restrains this impulse, realizing that this is no time for heroics; to kill the giant is to be buried alive in the blocked cave. So, though still determined to have his revenge, he falls back upon his genius for trickery. He secretly prepares the weapon that is to be plunged into Polyphemus's eye; he inebriates the giant, far-sightedly taking care to mislead his befuddled host as to his true name; blinds him with the aid of his surviving comrades; and finally extricates all of them from the cave under the bellies of the outgoing sheep. Odysseus himself chuckles in retrospect over the ingenuity of his stratagems.

At this stage, however, Homer can afford to bring into the open the full extent of Odysseus's Autolycanism without forfeiting or even noticeably decreasing our respect for him as an heroic figure. The prolonged primacy effect, the gradated presentation of this facet of character as well as the situational context are a set of powerfully counteracting factors. And to this one should add the brilliance and monumental dimensions of the victories narrated here: to defeat the Cyclops—by a stratagem that has aptly been described as the Wooden Horse in reverse—is an achievement of quite another order than to play it safe with Calypso. But at this point the author is no longer content with control devices that are merely preventive or precautionary, effective as they prove even in themselves. Attack being the best form of rhetorical defence, he not only establishes Odysseus's heroic stature more impressively than ever before but also takes a decisive step forward by exposing the code of honor itself to searching criticism.

Most of these new measures are located in the Underworld episode, though to be fully appreciated they must be viewed against the background of this expositional section as a whole. (It is surely no accident that this adventure comes after a series of instances in which Odysseus has cleverly tricked his way through a variety of tight spots.)

First, if books 9–12 present Odysseus at his most wily, the Underworld episode evokes his martial greatness as a counterweight, thus redressing the balance. And since the fabulous context hardly offers any opportunity for conventional soldiership, the more distant past—the Trojan War again—is harked back to. The Wooden Horse exploit, which has by now become a rhetorically charged objective correlative of Odysseus's heroic mettle in general, is brought up for the third time (p. 157); here, however, Homer sees fit to stress that Odysseus was in command of the Greek champions during the fateful battle. But it is the repeated showing of the extent to which he is accepted as a perfect equal by the greatest of the great—Agamemnon, Achilles, even Heracles—that mainly impresses on the reader that Odysseus is, above all, a king among kings and a hero among heroes. From this viewpoint, his address to the spirit of Telamonian Aias (pp. 157–58) fulfills a particularly important function. It operates as a timely reminder that when Thetis decided to award the arms of her dead son Achilles to the bravest Greek left alive before Troy, only Aias and Odysseus dared come forward to claim the prize; and the arms fell to Odysseus.

The re-setting of the protagonist among his peers thus counterbalances any diminution of his heroic image in the contiguous, framing episodes. This is further counteracted by the author's driving home to us that in certain circumstances a rigid adherence to heroic etiquette is fatal as well as stupid. Thus, in the fabulous world heroism should unhesitatingly be relegated to the position of a last resort. Odysseus usually serves as the vehicle of this warning; but even he, qua hero, occasionally becomes the object of irony. First, Odysseus checks his vindictive impulse to stab the Cyclops just in time to save himself and his comrades from death. Later, when bravely setting out to rescue his men from Circe, he sees no other course of action open to him except the heroic. So he slings his bow over his shoulder and his big bronze sword in its scabbard, only to learn from Hermes that such weapons would have been of no avail against the goddess, who can be overcome by cunning alone. Later still—note the gradated, increasingly ironic manner in which the limitations of conventional heroism are exposed through the temporal ordering—Odysseus makes elaborate warlike preparations before reaching the cave of Scylla, whom he was determined to fight in spite of Circe's warnings that it would do no good, in order to save his comrades: "I put my brave harness on, seized a couple of long spears, and took my stand on the forecastle deck" (p. 166). But he was able to do no more than helplessly watch Scylla snatch the six ablest hands he had on board and listen to their screams as they were being devoured.

The Underworld episode, moreover, goes on to question the very foundations of the heroic code. This criticism is forcefully and persuasively projected through Odysseus's encounter with Achilles, who when alive was the staunchest upholder of the heroic values, indeed their epitome. The memorable exchange forms one of the thematic cores of the epic:

> "Achilles, the most fortunate man that ever was or will be! For in the old days when you were on earth, we Argives honoured you as if you were a god; and now, down here, you are a mighty prince among the dead. For you, Achilles, Death should have lost his sting!"
>
> "My lord Odysseus," he replied, "spare me your praise of Death. Put me on earth again, and I would rather be a serf in the house of some landless man, with little enough for himself to live on, than king of all these dead men that have done with life." (P. 156)

This is surely an unforgettable occasion, the effect of which—from the viewpoint of control of distance and development of theme—can hardly be overestimated. One should have expected this to be a confrontation not simply of two persons but also of two conflicting codes. What one discovers, however, is that the very foundations of the heroic code are undermined by Achilles's belated realization that the supreme value, to which all others are to be subordinated, is neither honor nor reputation—and certainly not a glorious death—but simply life itself, even in its lowest form. It is accordingly by this criterion, essentially inimical to the heroic view of life, that conduct is to be regulated; for death, however glorious, can offer no compensation even to the mightiest of its phantoms.

But the reader's amazement at the shift in Achilles's attitude must be negligible compared with that of Odysseus, who, having assumed for the moment the values of the code epitomized by his friend in his lifetime, finds himself rebuffed and then repudiated out of hand in an eloquent hymn to life that directly vindicates the values to which he alone of all his comrades has subscribed all along. This comedy of errors contributes of course to the tremendous rhetorical effectiveness of Homer's stroke. The persuasiveness of the hierarchy of values thus established primarily derives, however, from Homer's usual practice of impelling the reader to the desired normative judgments by backing them with the testimony of unimpeachable authorities. Nobody can withstand the affirmation of life as the supreme norm when invested with the imprimatur of the prototype of classical heroes.

This crucial encounter, moreover, is framed by two others, each exposing specifically the fatal results of a blind adherence to the heroic code. It was Aias's rage at what he regarded as a slight to his honor (the award of Achilles's arms to Odysseus) that finally led to his suicide. This excessive regard for heroic values, however awe-inspiring, is of course denounced by the normative context of the episode. And the reader is also offered a direct contrast to this line of conduct in Odysseus's readiness to undergo, or even impose on himself, worse indignities in order to survive—whether the inglorious escape from the Cyclops's den under a ram's belly or the adoption of a beggar's disguise at Troy and Ithaca.

The confrontation with the late commander-in-chief is even more pregnant. Agamemnon and Odysseus, who have so far been collocated only by way of analogy, are finally brought together in terms of the action; and Agamemnon enlightens his friend about the circumstances of his death. Odysseus learns to his surprise that the "illustrious son of Atreus, king of men" did not fall, as befits so great a hero, in battle or by a god's hand. He was ingloriously struck down like "an ox at its manger" and saw his men slaughtered "like white-tusked swine" (note the pejorative implications of the similes). Agamemnon is honest enough to admit that his murder is due to his stupid overconfidence and unthinking overtrust-fulness, which rendered him an easy prey to the treachery of his wife and her lover. He "had looked forward to a rare welcome" (p. 155), and he got it with a vengeance. Like Achilles, who has belatedly come to appreciate the value of sheer living, Agamemnon has been taught by death the need for craftiness. What is most ironic about his speech is his pathetic attempt to share with his living friend the dearly bought moral:

> "Let this be a lesson to you also. . . . Never be gentle even with your wife, nor show her all that is in your mind. Reveal a little of your counsel to her, but keep the rest of it to yourself. Not that *your* wife, Odysseus, will murder you. Icarius's daughter is far too sound in heart and brain for that. The wise Penelope! . . . Do not sail openly into port when you reach your home-country. Make a secret approach. Women, I tell you, are no longer to be trusted." (P. 155)

Agamemnon has evidently gone from one extreme to the other. The need for deviousness and general mistrust—even with regard to Penelope, despite his polite disclaimer—has become an obsession with him. Dignity be damned, he now claims; stealing by the back door into one's own kingdom is preferable to an open approach and a sumptuous welcome, suspiciousness is preferable to credulity, if one wishes to stay alive. In this case, however, he is forcing an open door. Odysseus must have been brought up short and perhaps wryly amused (though also warned to be on his guard more than ever) at the sight of the former champion of heroic conduct hotly vindicating Autolycanism and preaching it to the grandson of Autolycus.

The importance of tracing the play of literary analogy all along the continuum of the text, from first structural impressions to final unfolding, should now be evident. The rhetorical effectiveness of the confrontation of Agamemnon and Odysseus at this point derives to a decisive extent from the analogy between them having now come full circle. In its temporal development along the sujet, this spatial pattern has gradually undergone an instructive metamorphosis—starting as a straight analogy and ending now as a full-fledged contrasted one—having fulfilled different functions at different phases. While books 1–4 misleadingly highlighted the unity in variety, in the interests of suspense, the present encounter foregrounds the variety in unity, exploring the difference in the outcome of the two analogical stories in the interests of normative control. It leaves the reader no choice but to account for this disparity in terms of character or conception of life in relation to heroic norms; and the conclusions one is impelled to draw from this confrontation cannot but redound to Odysseus's credit. The differences between the two heroes are now conspicuous in direct proportion to the initially elaborated correspondence between the circumstances of the respective returns.

From the rhetorical viewpoint, therefore, Agamemnon's fate affords another powerful justification, anticipatory as well as retrospective, of Odysseus's conduct. The specificity and dynamics of the linkages between the two kings render it a much more persuasive control device than the generalized tales, smuggled into the preceding stage, about the fall of Troy owing to the trustfulness of its people or about the public shame inflicted by (the similarly cuckolded) Hephaestus on the God of War himself—though all these expositional precedents operate in the same direction. When our hero hoodwinks all comers and goes so far as to trust nobody at all (he does not reveal to his wife even "a little of [his] counsel")—we might have been repelled by his trickery and morbid suspiciousness had we not had the Agamemnon memento mori in general, and the lesson embodied in his speech in particular, so vividly placed before our eyes.

Odysseus thus gains rather than loses in stature in the successive confrontations with his illustrious friends amidst the terrors and deprivations of death. Life among one's own people and family being firmly established as the supreme good (note the eager inquiries after sons), all strictures based upon deviations from the artificial code of honor lose their force whenever life is at stake, as it continually is with Odysseus.

The dearly bought hindsight of Odysseus's comrades is, moreover, unfavorably contrasted with his own foresight. He did not have to die first in order to come to appreciate the sweetness of mortal life—we have even seen him spurn immortality in its favour. And he did not have to be treacherously slain first in order to comprehend the shortcomings of the heroic code and the need for circumspection, in the so-called civilized world as well as the lawless jungle. He is therefore their equal by their old, heroic standards, and their superior by their newly adopted ones.

At the final stage of the control strategy Homer has thus effected a radical change in our conception of the heroic figure. He has gradually led up to the demonstration that the versatility of the protagonist's talents is not an embarrassing peculiarity but a valuable asset. Odysseus may be less conventionally heroic than his comrades but he is invariably victorious and hence more truly heroic; less uncompromising but more far-seeing; less dignified but alive. As the almost-oxymoronic formulaic epithet applied to him in this final section indicates in miniature,[16] he is "Royal son of Laertes, Odysseus of the nimble wits"—the man perfectly equipped for coping with all kinds of danger, adapting himself to all circumstances, turning effortlessly from one set of accomplishments to another or bringing all of them to bear upon the problem in hand, determined to triumph by heroic hook or Autolycan crook.

VI

The vindication of Odysseus's versatility naturally shifts our attention from the martial frame of reference to the moral, turning them into two facets of the same (normative and artistic) problem. For while the text leaves no doubt about the expediency and necessity of Autolycanism, it has not settled the question of its limits. Should trickery, circumspection, and deviousness be condoned, or even admired, in all circumstances? Is mere existence so important as to justify all measures taken to ensure its continuance? Has Odysseus no object beyond survival?

Indeed, Homer concurrently plays a dangerous game with the complication of our response to the protagonist as a moral and social being. The hints interspersed throughout the previous phase are now fully articulated; Odysseus's character-traits are boldly brought into the open to be defined or redefined; and sympathy is manipulated by a deft expositional distribution, producing quite a few new variations on the balanced and complex effects typical of the *Odyssey* as a whole.

Odysseus's moral nature is largely explored thorugh his relations with his Ithacan followers. He is now repeatedly shown to be endowed with most of the qualifications required of a leader; and his loyalty to friends in need—already singled out for praise by Menelaus—is now scenically dwelt on when he endangers his life to rescue his men from Circe's trap, having contemptuously dismissed the entreaties of the only survivor to leave the victims to their fate and look after the safety of his own skin. Such conduct, fully confirming and as usual even intensifying the primacy effect, establishes his moral as well as his heroic stature.

What his narrative, however, now reveals is that though conscious of his social obligations, Odysseus is essentially a lone wolf who not only keeps his own counsel but carries it out regardless of cost. Our attitude to his rather unpleasant egotism—a trait fully disclosed for the first time—is controlled with special care; Homer does not rely only on the confirmed primacy effect to counteract the consequent increase in distance but introduces some new counterbalancing factors as well.

As we constantly discover, the hero's secretiveness and mistrust are so deep-rooted that he takes his men into his confidence only when he has no other choice, especially where his own safety is concerned. In one fateful case, moreover, the urge to keep things to himself brings disaster on the heads of them all. I refer to his inexplicable failure to disclose to his followers the nature of the mysterious leather pouch with which Aeolus presented him. Odysseus, who came near jumping overboard in despair when he saw Ithaca vanishing astern, ascribes this misfortune to "a rascally crew and a fatal sleep," or at most to "our criminal folly" (pp. 132, 131). In fact, he has mainly himself to thank for this catastrophe, which ultimately results in the death of the whole crew and the prolonged postponement of his own homecoming. And what makes his conduct particularly reprehensible is that he was not dealing with enemies or potential enemies (such as Helen or even Calypso) or strangers (such as Ino) but with his own compatriots and fellow-warriors.

It is easy to imagine the rhetorical consequences that would attend the presentation of this incident near the beginning, where it chronologically belongs. By eschewing the "natural" order, Homer ensures that the reader's response to Odysseus's error of judgement, and to the trait it springs from in general, is more lenient and balanced. The one-sided primacy effect functions not to exculpate him from guilt but to place this episode in the proper perspective. Having by now been persuaded by the expositional dynamics that Autolycan conduct is indispensable for survival and that some of Odysseus's greatest exploits could be achieved in no other way, the reader cannot at this point denounce suspiciousness outright. And this stage of the *Odyssey* continues to deter him from doing so by reimpressing on him that most often—as in the Cyclops episode—it is Odysseus's very distrustfulness that carries the day and saves the lives of others. Moreover, the nicely gradated unfolding of the inveteracy of the hero's deviousness makes the Ithacan crew appear an almost natural or predictable addition to the list of progressively innocent objects of suspicion, ranging from Helen (or together with the recent arrivals, from the Cyclops and Circe through Helen) to the Phaeacians, and ultimately extending to his own family, including even his loyal son.

Due to these control-devices, the reader is manipulated into seeing this incident in its true light—not as a categorical condemnation of Autolycanism, in the moral as well as heroic context, but as a qualifying criticism of it projected through one of the rare occasions on which Odysseus overreaches himself. If so far the work has exposed the basic limitations of the heroic code, it now proceeds to round out and persuasively balance its theme by suggesting the dangers of the other extreme. Previously we saw

the hero averting a series of actual or potential threats by prudent, sometimes overprudent, behavior; now we are made aware that his morbid mistrust, prevailing even when prudence should have dictated confidence in
his men, is a weapon that cuts both ways.

Our response is further complicated by the concurrent (and even more
startling) revelation that this egotism also takes an opposed form—that of
selfish foolhardy risks as well as selfish overprudence. Wherever Odysseus
lands, nothing—not even the lessons of previous disasters to his crew—can
deter him from finding out "what kind of men are over there, and whether
they are brutal and lawless savages or hospitable and god-fearing" (p. 121).
He thus penetrates into the Cyclops' den despite—or owing to—the foreboding that he is going to confront "some being of colossal strength and
ferocity, to whom the laws of man and god meant nothing" (p. 122). And
he turns a deaf ear to his followers' entreaties to take possession of the
absent monster's supplies and set sail at once. Determined to await the
cave dweller's arrival, Odysseus adduces the transparent pretext that he
has "hopes of some friendly gifts from him."

But Homer does not let the matter rest here. Indeed, he counteracts
our condemnatory response to Odysseus's selfishness by implicitly opposing to it a number of cases in which Odysseus walks open-eyed into fatal
traps in order to rescue his men. (Order of presentation—within a single
continuous segment as well as with regard to distributed pieces—is as
revealing in the sequence of adventures as in Proteus's list of casualties or
the series of Underworld confrontations: textual contiguity heightens the
effect of spatial patterning in terms of similarity. For instance, immediately after hearing about the trap laid for them by Circe, Odysseus overrides
his men's entreaties not to risk his own life just as a short time before he
disregarded their entreaties to spare theirs.) But of even greater importance
is the repeated suggestion, also by way of contrast, that this very form of
egotism constitutes one measure of the protagonist's superiority to his
followers. They are concerned with filling their bellies, whereas his hunger
is spiritual. They are interested in the Cyclops's cheeses; he, in the
monster itself. They cannot restrain their physical appetite even in the
face of their leader's warnings (e.g., in the Sun-oxen episode), while he
takes similar risks to satisfy the craving of the soul. The irresistibility of
this intellectual curiosity is, moreover, highlighted by Odysseus's need to
overcome his deep-rooted circumspection in order to gratify it. Compared
with the transitional-phase procedure of counteracting negative revelations
by means of positive counterparts, this is a measure of the rhetorical and
psychological daring often displayed by the final phase: it is the two
opposed forms of Odysseus's egotism that are, in a typically balanced
structure, made to extenuate one another.

Odysseus's lust for knowledge, however, not only affects an equally newly revealed facet of personality but also propels a long-launched and specially charged deidealizing trend—the question of his attitude to home. If the primary impression of his homesickness has been somewhat qualified in book 5, it is now drastically complicated by the cumulatively evoked tension in him between the love of home and the desire to make the most of his journey. Sensual pleasure and high living have at times the power to detain him (his affair with Circe being analogized with his stay on Calypso's island); but his curiosity never fails to do so. For him the journey home is also an end in itself. And it is his *wanderlust* that causes the death of part of the crew and also the prolonged delay of his own homecoming (and this in turn results in his mother's death of grief, as we now learn in the Underworld episode, and makes possible the present complications at Ithaca); had Odysseus listened to the pleading of his men to stay away from the Cyclops, he would not have incurred Poseidon's wrath. This reshuffling of chronology and causal links is a new variation on presentational dynamics: opening of a crucial gap → temporary play of hypotheses → authoritative-looking closure → retrospective invalidation, reopening and reclosure. For the ten-year delay, which previously communicated exposition misled us into attributing to an unjustified external intervention, is now retrospectively disambiguated by the discovery that it is, in fact, a product of the protagonist's own nature, or to be more precise, of his not holding home as the only value in life.

This surprising disclosure would, again, deeply prejudice our view of Odysseus were it made much earlier—say at the beginning of the epic, where Poseidon's wrath is first mentioned. Its protracted delay to the third stage, however, enables the author to add a complex touch to Odysseus's character at a minimal price from the viewpoint of unity and control. And much of its interest consists in its structural similarity to the dynamics of hypothesizing that Faulkner effects for markedly different ends, with regard to the gap about Christmas's malignity, when he abruptly substitutes external causality (the pressure of society, etc.) for internal (the stereotyped racial lures) so as to heighten rather than decrease sympathy; or in even more general terms, so as to disintegrate a fallacious rather than complicate a one-sided first impression. It is only now that the reader fully grasps the reason for Homer's having lavished such unusual care, throughout books 1–8, on drawing our notice to the strength of Odysseus's homesickness, through explicit commentary and direct dramatization, through the testimony of reliable eye witnesses and the painting of withstood temptations in the brightest colours: the tendentious distribution of antecedents functions to subordinate the recency effect to the primary frame of reference. The present section, moreover, reaffirms rather than negates the conclusion that the protagonist's *wanderlust* takes only second place to the dominant desire to get home.

The dangers he is prepared to undergo in order to regain rocky Ithaca—notably the awe-inspiring descent into the Underworld—eloquently testify to the potency of his resolution, dramatically bearing out the implications of his incredulous comment about the men he has to drag back by force from the land of the Lotus-eaters: "All they now wished for was . . . to browse on the lotus and to forget that they had a home to return to" (p. 119). Furthermore, Odysseus's craving for knowledge has concurrently been presented as far from contemptible. So the tension between the two pulls involves a minimal loss of sympathy also because Odysseus is revealed to be torn between two positive values.

In conclusion, having traced the "negative-negative" and "positive-positive" patterning of the unfolding antecedents, let us observe how the text also specifically counteracts the unfavorable effect of this retrospective light by opposing to it another retrospection of a highly favorable kind. When we watch Odysseus take in the impressions of the awful privations of death—crystallized first in his mother's and later in Achilles's words—we cannot but admire him the more for rejecting Calypso's offers of immortality. Significantly, the Calypso episode is chronologically posterior to the descent into the Underworld; it is only due to the "artificial" ordering that it has been placed in an anterior position. When Odysseus rejects the goddess's proposal, then, he has already witnessed the abjectness of death. But the reader did not know this at the time (book 5). So when he now makes this discovery he experiences a retrospective shock of sympathy for the man who could consciously spurn immortality in favor of home and mortal life. This affords us another good example of Homer's juggling with temporal sequence and expositional distribution in the interests of control. He wisely judged it superfluous to introduce this piece of Underworld information into book 5, where our liking for Odysseus as a cherisher of home was at its height anyway, preferring to reserve its disclosure for the account of his temporally anterior adventures, where the need for sympathetic twists is more pressing, partly in view of the equally postponed disclosure of the details of the encounter with the Cyclops.

However, the temporal potentialities of fiction are exploited for manipulating attitude not only through the manifold patterning and repatterning of the expositional past per se but also through the subtle linkage of narrative past (Odysseus's expositional adventures) to present and future (the turbulent state of affairs at Ithaca). Homer gives our sympathy for the hero a final heightening touch by variously forcing on our notice the temporarily suspended dynamics of the action—the dangers that threaten him at home and the depravity of the Suitors. And by reminding us of an aspect of the overall situation whose normative implications are, for a change, absolutely unambiguous, he both plays afresh on our pity for the wronged man and makes his character shine by contrast.

Thus, our suspense about Penelope is enhanced during the Underworld episode, since what has so far been kept implicit is now insistently articulated. The first note is struck, quietly enough, when Odysseus is for the first time warned of the dangers awaiting him. Like Zeus, Tiresias confines himself to prophesying Odysseus's rout of the Suitors, without even alluding to the problem that troubles the reader most at the moment (pp. 147–48). And it soon emerges that the prophet's ominous silence disturbs the husband even more than the reader. For in the immediately following colloquy with his mother, Odysseus himself anxiously inquires about Penelope's fidelity: "'And what of my good wife? How does she feel and what does she intend to do? Is she still living with her son and keeping our estate intact? Or has the likeliest of her countrymen already married her?'" (p. 149). And lest we should think that Odysseus's doubts spring merely from his incorrigible mistrust, the whole confrontation with Agamemnon is made to revive, develop, and intensify the sinister implications of the previously established analogies. The selection and distribution of the expositional premises is again seen to be highly controlled: in Agamemnon's own account of his murder—the fifth round!—the role of "that foul traitress Clytaemnestra" is magnified beyond all previous reports (pp. 154–55). On hearing the shocking story, moreover, it is Odysseus himself who makes the first explicit linkage in the epic between the perfidy of the two sisters married by the Atreidae ("'From the beginning [Zeus] has worked his will through women's crooked ways. It was for Helen's sake that so many of us met our deaths, and it was Clytaemnestra who hatched the plot against her absent lord'"); and Agamemnon presses the tripartite analogy another step forward. He not only enunciates a warning against female treachery in general ("'Women, I tell you, are no longer to be trusted'") but also specifically couples Penelope with the two fatal sisters ("'Let this be a lesson to you also,'" etc.) and relates women's past criminality with regard to overtrustful husbands to the dangers of the present and the line of action to be taken in the future ("'Make a secret approach'"). His polite demurrer ("'Not that *your* wife, Odysseus, will ever murder you'") is even particularly disturbing, since it forms the first explicit indication that Penelope may indeed attempt to dispatch her husband to Hades to join his comrades.

In this case, again, suspense is not created just as an end in itself, but is exploited for the control of sympathy since it reinforces our sense of the dangers threatening the hero. What is most remarkable about this scene, however, is that it combines these effects by evoking a situation that is in point of absolute chronology nonexistent as yet—for the Underworld adventure antedates the beginning of the suit by four years at least. It is only through his deliberate deformation of the fabula order that Homer can now not only canalize the reader's reactions into the

desired grooves by such devices as Agamemnon's warnings but can constantly make the reader understand the implications of a fictive scene
much better than the characters who figure in it. Thus, the answer given
by Odysseus's mother to his inquiries about his wife (" 'There is no question of her not staying in your house. . . . She has schooled her heart to
patience'"; p. 149) is viewed by the reader as considerably less reassuring
than by the agents themselves. For Odysseus has only just been forewarned by Tiresias of the danger that is to arise, while we are at this point
already aware, in a way that he cannot possibly be, of the developments
that are chronologically to take place years later as well as disturbed by
the series of analogies that are soon to be foregrounded and recollocated.

The same potentialities of the literary work are exploited in another,
and even more interesting, sympathy-heightening device with perspectival
implications, namely, the oblique evocation of the Suitors in the course
of Odysseus's story. They cannot be directly introduced into it, or even
referred to, since, qua Suitors, they have not come into existence yet. So
they are brought in by way of analogy—fiction's favourite device for
bridging temporal discontinuities and evoking the physically absent. As in
the encounter with Agamemnon, the analogies in which the Suitors figure
can be appreciated by nobody in the fictive world, including the narrating
Odysseus himself, but by the reader alone.

The subtlest, most curious, and most denunciatory of the analogies
we are affected by due to the discrepancy between order of occurrence
and order of presentation is the collocation of the Suitors with the one-
eyed Cyclopes. Let us take the three related touchstones of piety, order,
and hospitality by which the Suitors have been judged before (by reference to norms concretely established in the behavior of Telemachus's
hosts) and found culpable: they neglect to offer sacrifices to the gods; they
have upset all social and political order in Ithaca by paralyzing all civic
institutions and infringing all laws; and they fail to observe the sacred rites
of hospitality. The Cyclopes commit exactly the same crimes and sins; the
fact that with them these offences assume monstrous proportions should
not blind us to the essential similarity. They are merely displayed as more
consistent than the Suitors in that they draw the reprehensible conduct of
their analogues—or its implications—to its "logical" conclusion. What is
implied by the behavior of the Suitors is openly declared by the Cyclopes;
and what is metaphorically suggested by the actions of the Suitors is
literally practiced by their fellow-criminals. To take the three touchstones
one by one: the metaphorical godlessness of the Suitors corresponds to
the literal godlessness of which the Cyclopes are proud ("We Cyclopes
care not a jot for Zeus with his aegis, nor for the rest of the blessed gods";
p. 123); the hackneyed or dead metaphor suggested by the Suitors' scorn
for laws and legal institutions is revitalized by way of realization in the

literal lawlessness of the Cyclopes, who "have no assemblies for the making of laws, nor any settled customs" (p. 119); the Suitors fail to welcome guests, the Cyclopes literally eat them.

The Suitors have often been shown up before, both by way of contrasted analogies (with Menelaus or Nestor) and straight ones (with Aegisthus). But never has their depravity been impressed so forcibly as through this suprasequential collocation, which retrospectively presents them in an inhuman light. It is now implied that what the Cyclopes are in the wilderness, the Suitors are in civilized Greece; and compared with the monsters who are intent on destroying his house, Odysscus is a paragon of virtue. Against them he may direct his Autolycan talents with our full approval; and we gladly note that in its relation of narrative past to present and future, the analogy foreshadows that he will do so with resounding success.

Odysseus is a static character, but his characterization is remarkably dynamic. He does not develop in the course of the action, but the reader's acquaintance with him incessantly does. In our movement through the three phases of his expositional presentation we gradually progress from a stock-response to an idealized portrait of a conventional hero to a highly complex, subtly balanced valuation of a unique character. And due to the brilliance of Homer's control strategy—turning mainly on the modes of distribution and ordering of antecedents—it is indeed a nice question at which of these stages our respect and sympathy for the protagonist are at their most profound. There is not much doubt, however, that our final attitude toward him would have considerably varied had the text organized the fabula materials in any different way.

As it is, the reader has now been fully prepared for the long-awaited representation of the greatest of Odysseus's ordeals. He is intimately acquainted with his many-sided character, his qualifications and his ways, about which the sequel indeed adds but little information that is radically new;[17] he has been manoeuvred into the desired attitude toward the hero, one that is so complex, balanced, and firmly established on thematic and psychological grounds that it is very difficult to shake; and the internal canons of probability have been strongly impressed on his mind. So in spite of the lawlessness now rampant at Ithaca and in spite of the quantitative advantage of the Suitors, the reader has full confidence in Odysseus's ability to cut his way to victory. For the integrated heterogeneity of the hero's talents renders him the most formidable opponent imaginable, just as from another viewpoint it stamps him as a true product of the creative imagination, which reveals itself, in Coleridge's phrase, in the balance or reconciliation of opposite or discordant qualities.

CHAPTER FIVE

THE RHETORIC OF ANTICIPATORY CAUTION: FIRST IMPRESSIONS IN "FIRST IMPRESSIONS" AND THE POETICS OF JANE AUSTEN

> "I quite doated on you the first moment I saw you. But so it always is with me; the first moment settles everything. The very first day that Morland came to us last Christmas—the very first moment I beheld him—my heart was irrecoverably gone."
>
> Jane Austen, *Northanger Abbey*

> Jane Austen was instinctive and charming. . . . For signal examples of what composition, distribution, arrangement can do, of how they intensify the life of a work of art, we have to go elsewhere.
>
> Henry James, "Gustave Flaubert"

In *Light in August,* the primacy effect is demolished by subsequently disclosed expositional material; in the *Odyssey* it is developed and modified. But in both models the impact of the recency effect(s) and the operation of the control strategy in general decisively hinge, though for different reasons, on the reader being initially encouraged, even lured, into a deep emotional and normative commitment or into forming a solid opinion about a certain object in the fictive world. In each case, accordingly, the primacy effect is homogeneous, fundamentally unqualified, and powerfully driven home, so that only in retrospect does the reader come to spot the discordant anticipatory hints that have been smuggled into the preliminary account right from the start though temporarily submerged by its overall import or dissimulated by specific means.

Most of Jane Austen's novels, however, illustrate a third model of dynamic control through expositional manipulation and temporal ordering in general: the rhetoric of anticipatory caution. Here the primary effect itself—and hence our attitude to the protagonist, whose information or view largely gives rise to it—is perceptibly qualified from the beginning.

Emma, Northanger Abbey, even *Sense and Sensibility,* afford interesting variations on this strategy; but the novel originally entitled *First Impressions* has of course an irresistible claim to analysis.

The rhetoric of anticipatory caution, like the other control strategies I have presented, is of course defined in terms of the relations (i.e., degrees of tension or clash) devised between the reader's primacy and recency effect. But what makes *Pride and Prejudice* even more representative outside Jane Austen's own work is that it devises in addition a correspondence between the reader's and the protagonist's impression formation. The dynamics of response, hypothesis-construction, and chronological reconstruction, within the rhetorical framework consisting in the relationship between author and reader, has a concurrently sustained dramatic equivalent, within the fictive world itself, in the dynamics of the heroine's own perceptual adventure. This major complication introduced by Jane Austen has a variety of implications for narrative technique and structural dynamics in general. Historically, the manipulation of parallel lines of development, and particularly of expositional quest, has since become a recurrent feature of the modern novel—whether in the form of Henry James's "crooked corridors," Ford Maddox Ford's and Joseph Conrad's "impressionistic" method, or even the external process of inquiry instituted by the detective story. Theoretically, it raises and sharpens a set of such crucial questions as (1) the relations between the uses of first impressions as theme, as psychological habit or occasional lapse on the part of the characters, as causal factor in the action, and as rhetorical pattern; (2) the relations between hypothesis-construction in "life," in fictive "life," and in the literary play of expectations; and (3) the relations between temporal structure or informational distribution and narrative perspective.

The main object of informational manipulation in *Pride and Prejudice* is Darcy's expositional character, that is, his character before the point in time at which the action proper starts (his arrival at Netherfield), particularly as manifested in his past relations with Wickham. The bulk of this complex of factual, moral, and psychological antecedents is communicated to the reader as late as the scene of anagnorisis and peripety located towards the middle (chaps. 35–36), the first half of the sujet (our "first impressions") consisting in a piecemeal distribution of reported bits and dramatized glimpses of Darcy's character and a false, damaging version of his conduct to Wickham. Naturally, this mode of unfolding considerably influences our attitude to him. Interestingly enough, however, though Darcy's figure (like Christmas's in *Light in August*) forms the main object of expositional manipulation, it is Elizabeth's figure that forms the main object of the control strategy based on this manipulation. For here the operation of first impressions is exploited not only as a rhetorical device directed towards or even against the reader, but also as a major dramatic and thematic pattern in an action which traces the tenacious hold that first impressions have over the heroine's beclouded mind and their painful uprooting in the sequel.

During her first visit in Derbyshire, from the meeting at Pemberley on, Elizabeth is repeatedly "surprised," "astonished," and "amazed" to discover the "change" or "improvement" exhibited in Darcy's behavior.[1] But, though Darcy's character (unlike Odysseus's) is indeed far from static, it has changed rather less than she now fancies. She herself has somewhat earlier given a more accurate account of the matter when, after the fateful developments at Hunsford, she tells Wickham that "Mr. Darcy improves on acquaintance," promptly going on to quash Wickham's attempt to weaken the force of her comment ("Is it in address that he improves? . . . I dare not hope . . . that he is improved in essentials") by the cutting reply: "Oh, no! In essentials, I believe, he is very much what he ever was" (pp. 216–17). It is not so much (and certainly not only) Darcy that has developed as her knowledge of him.

And significantly, perhaps nowhere outside the anagnorisis episode itself does the text so insistently suggest as in the first Pemberley scene that Elizabeth's increasing "astonishment" derives largely from her initial ignorance of Darcy's character and the tortuousness of her way to knowledge. The circumstance that, as the visitors are looking at the house, "the owner of it himself" (whose conduct is soon to confirm much of the suspiciously glowing account of him just elicited from the housekeeper) should "suddenly [come] forward from the road, which led behind it to the stable" (p. 229), is, structurally, psychologically, and thematically, as appropriate a symbol as (in *The Ambassadors*) the dawning of the expositional truth on Strether through the agency of a boat rounding a "bend" in the river. The manifold suggestiveness of this occurrence, relating to the "owner" himself, is heightened by the implications of a quick succession of equally appropriate metonymic analogues relating to his property. The metonymic frame is first established as early as the beginning of the visit, when Elizabeth's eye is "caught by Pemberley House, situated on the opposite side of a valley, into which the road with some abruptness wound" (p. 223)—the link between the spatial sinuosity of the scene and the temporal sinuosity of the action being soon tightened and pinpointed beyond doubt by Darcy's similarly "abrupt . . . appearance" (p. 229). Then, in even closer reference to the heroine's ongoing process of discovery, we learn that "every step [down the "beautiful walk by the side of the river"] was bringing forward a nobler fall of ground, or a finer reach of woods . . . but it was some time before Elizabeth was sensible of any of it" (p. 230); or that, on seeing "a narrow walk amidst the rough coppicewood," she "longed to explore its windings" (p. 231). Finally, owner and scenery are brought together when, noticing Darcy's second

approach to them, the "astonished" Elizabeth wonders about his intentions as long as "a turning in the walk concealed him from their view;
[but] the turning past, he was immediately before them" (p. 232).[2]

In the tortuousness and chronological disrepair of the route gradually
leading each from first impressions to full expositional enlightenment,
there is thus a marked correspondence between reader and protagonist.
But this correspondence is by no means perfect, especially in all that concerns the specific order and dynamics of impression formation. It is not
that we have from the beginning a complete rounded portrait of Darcy but
that, though largely kept in the dark, we are from the beginning prevented
from blindly subscribing to Elizabeth's unfavorable first impressions of
him, and particularly to Wickham's slanderous reports, which give rise to
her major misjudgments and misdeeds in the first half of the novel. What
seems to Elizabeth an established fact is to the reader a glaring informational gap; what seems to Elizabeth the obvious truth is impressed on the
reader as no more than one (and not even the most probable one) of
several expositional hypotheses. To establish such a disparity in awareness,
even by way of negative anticipation, is to establish two distinct perceptual
sets or frames of reference, leading to a variety of differences not only in
the ongoing interpretation of the data but even in the consciousness and
primary selection of the very data to be interpreted. And with these seemingly modern problems of perception Jane Austen shows herself instructively familiar—in her general compositional artistry, in the recurrent figure of "blindness," and even in such explicit formulations as that following Harriet Smith's disclosure to Emma of her matrimonial hopes with
regard to Mr. Knightley: "Much that lived in Harriet's memory, many little
particulars of the notice she had received from him, a look, a speech, a
removal from one chair to another, a compliment implied, a preference
inferred, had been unnoticed, because unsuspected, by Emma" (*Emma*,
chap. 47).

Since Jane Austen sees to it that such jarring clues should be "noticed,
because suspected" by the reader from the start, her primacy effect
markedly differs from that of the two previous models in its plausibility,
and hence force, and in its relations with the future recency effect.
Consequently, when the delayed exposition giving rise to the recency
effect is finally divulged, Elizabeth's surprise is much more violent than
the reader's, in direct proportion to the disparity in the homogeneity of
their respective first impressions of Darcy; it is mainly she who views the
two successive sets of data as conflicting, while the forewarned reader has
little difficulty in reconciling and integrating them.

I should like to start by tracing the remarkably ramified network of
cautionary measures by which this preventive effect is produced, the
reader's perceptual set established and the initial discrepancy in awareness

manipulated, throughout the first half of the novel. For apart from its specific functions with regard to the heroine, this network also has a wider theoretical significance. It richly illustrates both the operation of the distinctive feature of our third model of control and some features and problems that attend the complication of parallel progress; it also variously brings out a major but hitherto little-treated aspect of temporal structure—the operation of verbal dynamics in relation to the dynamics of such large compositional units and patterns as character, event, or analogy; and, as with other works belonging to this model (e.g., *The Ambassadors*), it directly relates to the heart of the matter—forming part of the novel's structural principles (linear, spatial, perspectival, and stylistic) and combinations of principles, developing the overall thematic pattern, and concretely establishing much of the normative groundwork and the structure of probabilities.

II

Mark Schorer has noted that *Persuasion* has a metaphorical base "derived from commerce and property, the counting house and the inherited estate"; David Lodge has acutely commented on the "vocabulary of discrimination and evaluation" in *Mansfield Park*.[3] What I believe of equal importance, however, is that Jane Austen's novels, again like the late James's, reverberate with various clusters of words or phraseology (mostly nonfigurative) drawn from the general semantic field of the characteristically human quest for knowledge and ordeal of knowledge, with all their concomitant difficulties, limitations, setbacks, and painfully slow progression. As subfields of this language of quest, we have the language of clue and inquiry (e.g., *sign, symptom, hint, motive, information, report, inquire, detect, testify, witness*); the language of conjecture and hypothesis (*opinion, view, supposition, surmise, inference, conjecture, ingenuity, deduce, impute, conclude, follow, imply, sure, reasonable, (im)possible, (im)probable, incredible*), the language of expectation and frustration (*hope, wish, fear, prognostics, expect, foresee, calculate, anticipate, disappoint, surprise, wonder, startle, amaze, shock, incredulous*); the language of appearance and reality, deception and self-deception (*seem, appearance, looks, portrait, character, description, true, evident, false, imaginary, secret, mean, design, scheme, premeditate, sincere, artful, guarded, reserve, affectation, duplicity, deceive, self-deception, pass oneself off as, disguise, conceal, dissemble, (un)conscious, blind, (im)partial, prepossession, prejudice*); the language of mistake, doubt and bafflement (*error, wrong, misunderstand, fancy, undervalue, do injustice to, escape one's notice, doubt, suspect, hesitate, disputable, disagree, contradict, confuse, puzzle, ignorance, curiosity, suspense*); and the language of discovery, validation, and enlightenment (*disclose, expose, discover, perceive, comprehend, see through, quickness of observation, clear-sighted, establish, confirm, prove, explain, justify, clear from guilt,* etc.). It is sufficient to open at random a novel by Jane Austen, and for that matter a volume of her letters, to see how pervasive these word clusters are and how inseparable from the idiom of her mind; and a comparison with other novelists, including those I have dealt with above, will readily reveal that this is not always the case. In what follows I shall often have occasion to trace the interaction between the linguistic substratum and the other levels of the text. Now I only wish to note that, just as the dark colors applied throughout the depiction of Balzac's pension in *Père Goriot* give the reader an overwhelming sense of a dehumanized world, so does the cumulative effect of these word clusters give him a sense of a world that is limited, groping, and fallible. Even in themselves, therefore, they establish a perceptual set that keeps the reader on his guard and constantly invites independent inferential activity on his part. And given the kind of reader envisaged by Jane Austen ("I do not write for such dull elves / As have not a great deal of ingenuity themselves"), such an invitation will not be issued in vain.

These "vocabularies" are not, however, left to operate by themselves but enter into different combinations with a complex of mutually reinforcing cautionary measures. In retrospect this complex is perhaps best described as a series of ever-narrowing but concurrently drawn and analogically interlinked concentric circles—with Elizabeth's initial view of Darcy, crystallized after Wickham's arrival, as center—progressing from the widest circumference, namely the nature and tendencies of the fictive world as a whole, through the group of characters who generally or more occasionally resemble the heroine in their powers and limitations of vision, to her own habitual attributes, as displayed in her relations with characters other than Darcy. It is by such indirections, so typical of her exacting method, that Jane Austen conveys to the reader, among many other things, the various expositional premises, terms, or antecedents that he needs in order to form his view of Elizabeth, and particularly of the probability of her view of Darcy. The analogical links of similarity and contrast (the unifying "radii") between the different circles establish their common relevance to the resolution of the central expositional crux. But the further each frame of reference is from the center, the more oblique, though not necessarily the less significant, its expositional relevance—the more inclusive and sometimes more inescapable the canons of probability operating in it. Or, to use a complementary metaphor, if at one extreme of the rhetorical scale leading from the most implicit to the most explicit devices we locate the omnipresent word clusters with their essentially insidious effect, then at the other extreme we have a nucleus of relatively generalized, or rather semigeneralized, pronouncements on the obstacles to human insight. And in between we have a series of concretely dramatized and variously patterned warning-signals that elaborately point the same moral with regard to the fictive world as a whole, to different groups or types belonging to it, and to the heroine herself, their position on the scale varying of course with the directness and specificity of their implications for Elizabeth's "primary" view of Darcy.

It is surely no accident that one striking cluster of more explicit or generalized warnings should be placed in the preliminary stages of the novel. The very first chapter is characterized by a cautionary frame. As has often been observed, the famous opening pronouncement ("It is a truth universally acknowledged that a single man in possession of a good fortune, must be in want of a wife") first seems to be backed by the authority of the narrator herself. But by a sudden ironical twist, this universal is immediately relegated to the status of a "well fixed" selfish prejudgment on the part of the neighborhood, typically exhibiting a complete lack of knowledge of as well as regard for the prospective catch: "However little known the feelings or views of such a man may be on his first entering a neighbourhood, this truth is so well fixed in the minds of the surrounding families, that he is considered as the rightful property of some one or other of their daughters." (This primarily stylistic twist given to the very first of our "first impressions," remarkably parallel to the "turnings" and "windings" of the larger dramatic patterns, is only one manifestation of the structural and functional correspondence in Jane Austen between stylistic or syntactic microcosm and compositional macrocosm.) The bulk of the chapter then illustrates the adherence to this "truth" in and through the representative conduct of Mrs. Bennet (whose periphrastic references to Bingley as "a young [or "single"] man of large fortune" ironically echo the opening sentence), while her husband's deflationary retorts embody the subsequent twist. And finally, the closing paragraph goes on to play another variation on the theme. It turns the recent conversation between the Bennets to new account by using it to suggest that failures of insight may happen not only in reference to strangers (such as Bingley) but to intimates as well: "Mr. Bennet was so odd a mixture of quick parts, sarcastic humour, reserve and caprice, that the experience of three and twenty years had been insufficient to make his wife understand his character."

This expositional observation is further borne out by the immediately ensuing events: "Mr. Bennet was among the very earliest of those who waited on Mr. Bingley. He had always intended to visit him, though to the last always assuring his wife that he should not go" (p. 17). And having made the new point, the second chapter reverts to the earlier one so as to link the two. Mrs. Bennet, unaware of the surprise in store for her, complains to her husband that it is "impossible" that she should cultivate the newcomer, let alone introduce him to her friends at the ball due in a fortnight, as long as she is not "acquainted with him" herself. Thereupon Mr. Bennet, dexterously playing on the double meaning (social versus psychological) of "acquainted," deliberately misunderstands and mock-seriously compliments her in a speech that, apart from its explicit cautionary force, ironically harks back to the beginning and end of the opening chapter at once: "I honour your circumspection. A fortnight's acquaintance is certainly very little. One cannot know what a man really is by the end of a fortnight" (p. 18). And this generalization (including the ambiguity of "acquaintance" and "know") is in turn harked back to, in a more serious spirit, during the exchange between Elizabeth and Charlotte Lucas concerning Jane and Bingley (chap. 6). The whole colloquy (typically charged with what I called "the language of quest," etc.) is highly suggestive in this context, since it is constructed as a series of variations on the theme of the possibility of a person's "real" character and feelings being penetrated—by the "world" in general, by certain better-equipped observers, or by the couple in question itself. Particularly notable, however, is the fact that Elizabeth finally echoes (and perhaps applies) her father's generalization from Bingley's case, saying that their four evenings together "have enabled [Jane and Bingley] to ascertain that they both liked Vingt-un better than Commerce; but with respect to any other leading characteristic, [she does] not imagine that much has been unfolded": after all, Jane "has known him only a fortnight. . . . This is not quite enough to make her understand his character" (p. 31).[4]

The very opening section thus establishes a small system of cautionary cross-references, which is further ramified in the sequel. Far from obtrusive and rarely pronounced *ex cathedra* by the narrator herself, these variously generalized warnings are woven into concrete scenes, coming from the dramatis personae and often partly discredited by the speaker's cynicism (as in Mr. Bennet's case), his excessive innocence or sweetness of temper (as with Jane's "It is often nothing but our own vanity that deceives us" [p. 132]), his occasional pomposity (as with Darcy's "Nothing is more deceitful than the appearance of humility" [p. 54]), or his habitual fatuity (as with Collins's "We are all liable to error" [p. 144]). And it is again no accident that such camouflage should be particularly typical of the first half of the work (in the second, the narrator can already afford to ridicule openly that "interesting" response "arising on a first interview with its object, and even before two words have been exchanged" [p. 253]). Here, throughout the "first impression" phase, such pregnant comments derive most of their force and validity not from their intrinsic authority but—like the implications of the linguistic substratum, which they activate, articulate, and fill out—from their cumulative effect, their compositional interconnections, and above all, their dramatic ("inductive") corroboration and development. Once we consider the novel in these terms, we are struck by the unusual multiplicity and variety of represented events, including seemingly trivial episodes and comic digressions, that concretely project the difficulty of attaining knowledge and the continual liability to error within the particular framework or "probability-register" postulated by the work. Furthermore, like the early prefigurations of the Return theme that similarly establish the expositional norms and premises specific to the work, this is not a more or less repetitive projection of the same general point, but a complex, thematically and normatively polyphonic exploration of human fallibility from a number of complementary viewpoints—in terms of its constant and variable causes, manifestations, and effects on the characters.

As this study in perception and perceptual ambiguity slowly unfolds, it emerges that the limitations and fallibility typical of the fictive world as a whole stem from four closely related causes or sources: either inherent in the human condition as such and/or specifically adhering to the observer and/or to the object of observation and/or to the relations between the two. Of these the first is effectively reimpressed on our minds as the most basic and inescapable—reimpressed because one may (and in some works one is allowed to) lose sight of it in practice, as the characters themselves tend to do. The omniscient and omnipresent narrator alone is exempt from the limitations of vision inherent in the human condition. But she is of course exempt by artificial convention, and her exemption only throws into relief the condition of mortals. None of her characters, however perceptive as human beings go, has that easy access to privileged information, and their way to knowledge (often even of the most elementary kind) is an arduous and gradual business, largely characterized by guesswork and trial-and-error methods.

One of Jane Austen's favorite devices for bringing this home is to play different points of view off against each other (a device with a considerable unsettling effect, which modern novelists doctrinally committed to consistency of point of view were driven to replace by such perspectively oblique cautionary measures as the Jamesian "supposititious observer" or, in Ford's *The Good Soldier,* the dramatized narrator's lamenting refrain "I don't know; I don't know. . . . Who knows?") Another is to spring a piece of news on a mixed group of characters so as to show the intelligent and the impercipient equally startled. Still another is to depict the general hunting for news launched by the arrival of strangers on the scene. To illustrate again from the opening chapters: in order to draw from Mr. Bennet a description of Bingley, his wife and five daughters "attacked him in various ways; with barefaced questions, ingenious suppositions, and distant surmises" (p. 20); and it is only by degrees that they get to "know" the new officers: "Every day added something to their knowledge of the officers' names and connections. Their lodgings were not long a secret, and at length they began to know the officers themselves" (p. 37). First-hand "intelligence" often being unavailable, the characters naturally make do with hearsay, which repeatedly proves superficial, exaggerated, or simply false; two early, typically comic examples are Lady Lucas's "highly favourable" account of Bingley (p. 20) and the successive "reports" (first "twelve ladies and seven gentlemen," and then "five sisters and a cousin") as to the size of the party he is to bring with him to the ball (pp. 20–21).

The effect of this perceptual constant is, however, sometimes counteracted and more usually aggravated by a number of variables. One variable, relating to the object of observation, is explicitly indicated in Elizabeth's distinction (roughly corresponding to E. M. Forster's binary classification of characters into "flat" and "round") between simple and "deep, intricate" characters (p. 49). It is not quite true that "Elizabeth's vision of the world as divided between the simple and the intricate is, in *Pride and Prejudice* at least, Jane Austen's vision also."[5] For the work precisely demonstrates that such dichotomies, whether psychological or moral, should be turned into continuums or else they will fail to accommodate the variety and complexity of life, even of comically stylized life. But the distinction has vital implications for the problem of expositional reconstruction of character. The simpler the agent, the greater the homogeneity of his traits and the more of a piece his past (or expositional) with his present actions; therefore, his character is proportionally more easily seen through and his conduct less puzzling and more predictable than is the case with his "intricate" counterpart. (What starts the whole discussion is Elizabeth's remark to Bingley: "That is exactly what I should have supposed of you.") Since to wholly divest a character of his unpredictability is to divest him of a basic verisimilar feature, the relatively simple characters are occasionally shown to be capable of surprising or baffling us and their human environment. In her fear that the scheme of catching Collins will come to nothing for lack of further opportunity, for instance, the usually perceptive Charlotte "did injustice to the fire and independence of his character, for it led him to escape out of Longbourn House the next morning with admirable slyness, and hasten to Lucas Lodge to throw himself at her feet" (p. 120). But the "amusement" that we, with Elizabeth, derive from these characters is primarily one of recurrent recognition, of watching them run true to (early and easily discovered) expositional form in the face of various checks and pressures. The intricate characters, on the other hand, prove far more incalculable as well as unfathomable, especially since their "mixture" of traits includes "reserve"— whether Mr. Bennet's ironic reserve, Jane's natural reserve (her main claim to complexity), or Wickham's (and other Austenian rakes') artful reserve, disguised by his apparent "openness."

It is thus especially with the latter type of character that another complex of variables, relating to the observer himself and to the specific conditions in which he forms his opinion, comes to the fore. In its dramatized spectrum of observers, the novel clearly subscribes to the Jamesian view that, though the human predicament is indeed inescapable, there are nevertheless "degrees of feeling—the muffled, the faint, the just sufficient, the barely intelligent, as we may say; and the acute, the intense, the complete, in a word—the power to be finely aware and richly responsible. It is those moved in this latter fashion who 'get most' out of all that happens to them."[6] But even the handful of "finely aware" agents are only potentially so, and the reliability of each may greatly vary in practice according to his situation vis-à-vis the object—for example, the degree of "acquaintance" between the two. As with the perceptual constant of the human condition, Austen does not let us lose sight of this variable but rather activates it by a variety of compositional and stylistic means. Starting from her juvenilia, one can trace a steady line of ridicule at the speed in which "acquaintance" ripens into "intimacy" with some people: in *Northanger Abbey,* we encounter Miss Thorpe "loitering . . . between two of the sweetest girls in the world, who had been her dear intimate friends all the morning" (chap. 14); and in *Mansfield Park,* Mr. Yates is introduced as "a new intimate friend of Mr. Bertram's"—his "'particular friend', another of the hundred particular friends" (chaps. 11, 19). But these passing digs at minor and usually comic characters also function, by way of analogical linkage, as parodistically highlighted-and-dissimulated warnings directed against more serious excesses on the part of such generally perceptive observers as the main figures—whether Elizabeth's diametrically opposed reactions to Wickham and Darcy (to be dealt with soon) or, in *Sense and Sensibility,* Marianne's overconfidence in her first impressions of Willoughby. When her sister Elinor ventures to point out that Willoughby is "so little, or at least so lately known to her," Marianne's rejection of the equation of "little" with "lately" is so vehement—and its consequences so disastrous—that it negatively testifies to the weight Jane Austen ascribes to the variable of "acquaintance" in her structure of probabilities: "You are mistaken, Elinor . . . in supposing I know very little of Willoughby. I have not known him long indeed, but am much better acquainted with him than I am with any other creature in the world, except yourself and mama. It is not time or opportunity that is to determine intimacy; it is disposition alone. Seven years would be insufficient to make some people acquainted with each other, and seven days are more than enough for others" (chap. 12). In this Marianne is startlingly implied to resemble Mrs. Palmer, surely the silliest character in the novel, who when similarly questioned by Elinor whether she is "intimately acquainted" with Willoughby, unhesitatingly replies: "'Oh! dear, yes; I know him extremely well. . . . Not that I ever spoke to him indeed" (chap. 20).

The danger of confusing the two senses of this key-word, with their different implications for perception and conduct, is clearly projected in *Pride and Prejudice,* even outside the Darcy affair itself. That this complicating factor does not apply only to the likes of Mrs. Bennet is (as I argued) suggested as early as the opening chapters. The point is then developed in chapter 6, where Elizabeth contrasts what is "generally evident" about the relations between Bingley and Jane (namely, "that he *did* admire her") with what she, with her superior knowledge of her sister and her better opportunities for observation, finds "equally evident" (namely, that Jane "was in a way to be very much in love"); and where her subsequent self-contradictions pave the way for Charlotte's shrewd warning that Bingley's knowledge of the reserved Jane, just like the world's in general, cannot be compared to her own, etc. Later, our awareness of this factor is maintained by verbal signals as well (e.g., the reference to various newcomers, notably Wickham, as "strangers").

No doubt is left in the reader's mind, however, that the most potent source of prejudgment and misjudgment in the world of the novel is the observers' "prejudice" or "partiality" in its various forms and combinations—personal, familial and social, negative and positive, emotional and intellectual, conditioned by "interest" and originating in "pride." Sometimes the narrator herself helps to lay bare the influence of the observer's wishful thinking on the valuations of character and event—for instance, that of Charlotte's "wishes" with regard to Elizabeth and Darcy (pp. 170, 171). More often, the characters themselves are made to point out the dangers of partiality, explicitly relating them to their own views, usually by way of polite demurrer (e.g., Mrs. Bennet, praising Jane's beauty: "It is what everybody says. I do not trust my own partiality" [p. 51]; or Miss Bingley, disclosing to Jane her hopes of a marriage between her brother and Miss Darcy: "A sister's partiality is not misleading me, I think, when I call Charles most capable of engaging a woman's heart" [p. 177]), or, naturally more trenchantly, to the views of others (e.g., when Elizabeth contemptuously dismisses Caroline's "interested wishes" with regard to her brother [p. 199]). And again, the semigeneralized or explicit warnings are "inductively" warranted, elaborated, and reinforced in instance after instance. Mrs. Bennet is obviously the most ridiculous victim of narrowly partial "views," part of the comic effect deriving from the abrupt shift of valuation with the shift of interest. But, as with other comic characters in literature, her excesses are only a parodistic, and hence rhetorically perspicuous, version of a basic tendency that no character wholly escapes—whether relatively innocent or malicious, socially high or low, intricate or simple, conscient (in Jamesian parlance) or semiconscient or nearly inconscient.[7] In this fictive world, a "disinterestedness" such as Jane's is indeed "really angelic" (p. 131), but it does not save her from errors of judgment since it only drives her to the opposite extreme of general prepossession.

The cautionary import signaled by the exploration of the causes of human error and bewilderment is, moreover, rounded out and intensified by the concurrent foregrounding of their different manifestations, which are again sometimes pure and simple, sometimes mixed and complex. It is thus in terms of the aim to throw into doubt the validity of interpretations of conduct and character that the numerous scenes of misunderstanding are largely to be accounted for. The same is true of the recurrent differences of opinion within the fictive world—whether obliquely and negatively suggested (as when Bingley says that the prettiest woman in the room is "the eldest Miss Bennet beyond a doubt, there cannot be two opinions on that point" [p. 28]) or, more often, directly represented (ranging from the comic dispute between the Bennets as to whether their children are "silly" or "clever" [pp. 37-38], through the "characteristic" disagreement between Darcy and Bingley about the Meryton assembly [pp. 26-27], to the full-scale, inconclusive argument between Elizabeth and Jane after Bingley's departure [pp. 117-20]).

The same is even more conspicuously true of the prevalence of partial and downright error, the errors consequent upon the tendency to rely on or give way to first impressions occupying an uncommonly prominent position here. It is not the hero and the heroine alone who are characterized by the tendency to form one-sided expositional portraits or conceptions of character. In the first half of the novel we find first impressions taking a large variety of analogical forms: collective (even "universal") and individual; favorable and disapproving; personal and social; purely comic and more serious; produced by a direct observation of the object and consisting in a prejudgment based on hearsay evidence (e.g., the "universally acknowledged truth" of the opening or the inevitable accomplishments of every "young lady spoken of for the first time" [p. 46]). But, whatever their form and origin, most of them are sooner or later invalidated, directly challenged, partly qualified, or at least rendered questionable. The frequent use of the qualifier "first" is one cautionary device—part of its force, like that of "acquainted," deriving from the tension between two meanings (chronological versus hierarchical priority). Another is the relation of the first impression to the cause producing it, such as "pride," "resentment," or "interest"; this device manifests itself first in the title, then (in a less generalized though still relatively "universal" form) in the two opening paragraphs, then (more concretely) in the presentation of Mrs. Bennet's typical views, and so on. Another power-ful warning-signal appears throughout chapters 3–5 (where the introduc-tion of the dramatis personae to one another affords us a polyphonic col-lection of first impressions), namely, the clash between different first impressions of the same object, whether Darcy, Bingley's sisters, or the Meryton assembly as a whole. Even more direct is the effect of Elizabeth's overt attacks on the absurdity or injustice of first impressions (those formed by others, of course), whether favorable ("the first effusions . . . of the generality of travellers" [p. 148]) or the reverse (notably what she is pleased to call Darcy's "implacable resentment" [pp. 63, 83, 95]). Perhaps the most unsettling and persuasive measure of all is the light retrospectively thrown by further information (on rereading Jane's letters after Colonel Fizwilliam's disclosures, "Elizabeth noticed every sentence conveying the idea of uneasiness, with an attention which it had hardly received on the first perusal" [p. 177]); or, more drastic still, the dramati-zation of various first impressions formed by variously endowed ob-servers (e.g., the "world's" view of Darcy, Darcy's of Elizabeth, Elizabeth's of Bingley, or Jane's of Miss Bingley) being later immediately retracted or gradually revised by the observers themselves.

Finally, whatever their causes and manifestations, these failures of perception have some ever-recurrent effects on the characters. In few novels is the "disappointment" of expectation given so conspicuous a position as in the Austenian world; the event sometimes surpasses and generally falls short of the character's expectations, but only rarely does it realize them. Surprise, a related symptom of lack of information or mistaken conception, is similarly one of the key-phenomena in the novel, just as the word "surprise" (with its synonyms) is one of its key-words. Characters are surprised on almost every page, sometimes owing to their peculiar deficiencies and sometimes in the company of others (not exclud-ing the reader), sometimes more and sometimes less justifiably, some-times by trivial and sometimes by momentous discoveries, the latter simultaneously evoking deeper feelings as well, such as joy, alarm, or regret. But nobody is exempt from this emotion—nor from doubt, curiosity, and suspense—including those whose judgment is thought by some to be infallible, as Darcy's is by his sister, and those who, like Elizabeth, pride themselves on never being taken by surprise.

III

It is against this dramatically and thematically disturbing background (or "probability-register") that the novel concurrently explores the heroine's own general powers and blind spots, carefully interrelating the outer and inner "circles" by means of analogical links. The procedure is thus not dissimilar to Homer's manner of enveloping his hero in the *Odyssey*'s world of Suitors and Returners, in the interests of control of distance and probability. But this only brings out the marked difference in expositional and rhetorical implications between the handling of the primacy effect in the two models: there the depiction of the surrounding world is designed to allay our suspicions for the moment (about Odysseus's problematic side) or to counteract disbelief (about his powers), while here it is designed to arouse and sustain suspicion and to promote disbelief. And the difference between the rhetoric of initial diversion or dissimulation and the rhetoric of anticipatory caution continues to show itself in the portrayal of the heroine.

What complicates matters in Elizabeth's case is that, unlike the "fools," she is far from invariably wrong in her estimates of character, including her prejudgments and first impressions. This is suggested by her early (distributed and expositionally illustrative) tests of judgment. On several occasions she is emphatically shown to be right—emphatically because favorably contrasted with others. Collins's first epistolary masterpiece, for example, elicits a variety of typical reactions from the Bennet family (pp. 67–69). Catherine and Lydia are simply not interested, it being "next to impossible that their cousin should come in a scarlet coat"; Mrs. Bennet is mollified by the writer's readiness "to make [the girls] every possible amends"; Jane is charitable as usual; while Mary opines that the letter (olive branch and all) is not stylistically "defective." Elizabeth alone (before Mr. Bennet supports her) finds the style pompous, the gratuitous apologies absurd, and the man "an oddity." Significantly, the narrator does not content herself with letting the ensuing events vindicate her heroine's perspicacity, but goes out of her way to stress the point by giving us a formal expositional sketch of the clergyman. This (otherwise superfluous) authoritative characterization bears out Elizabeth's first impression not only by its general purport but even by the very evaluative epithets used; Elizabeth's rhetorical question whether Collins can be "a sensible man" (p. 68) is made to rhyme with the narrator's opening formulation that "Mr. Collins was not a sensible man" (p. 74), just as Mr. Bennet's finding him "a mixture of servility and self-importance" (p. 68) is echoed by the narrator's "a mixture of pride and obsequiousness, self-importance and humility" (p. 74).

Since Elizabeth, however, takes most pleasure and pride in the study of intricate characters—and since Darcy (unlike Collins) soon evinces clear signs of intricacy—it becomes both generally and specifically revealing that Jane Austen should take pains to prevent her having much to show for it. On the one hand, the full authorial disclosure of Elizabeth's long-accomplished and not inconsiderable achievement in penetrating her father's psychological make-up is (otherwise inexplicably) delayed to the second half of the work (pp. 218–19). During the first half, on the other hand, her most glaring misjudgment is committed with regard to an intricate figure, namely Charlotte Lucas. Austen's handling of this episode is even more brilliant than is usually thought. The first hint of a possible lack of comprehension on Elizabeth's part is given as early as chapter 6, in her summary dismissal of Charlotte's prudential generalizations about marriage: "You make me laugh, Charlotte; but it is not sound. You know it is not sound, and that you would never act in this way yourself" (p. 92). And Charlotte's encouragement and acceptance of Collins, testifying to her determination to practice at the first opportunity what she has preached here, establishes before long the groundlessness of this confident valuation. What is more, it also suggests, first, the disparity between Elizabeth's professed interest in psychological intricacy and her bafflement in the face of its ostensible contradictions; second, the "romantic" nature of her outlook on life; and third, her tendency to shape others in her own image. (The two latter points are somewhat differently conveyed in and through her exchange with Jane about the possibility of Bingley's return, which actually frame the Collins-Charlotte episode. The contiguous location of the two rhetorically complementary and mutually illuminating fiascos, one with a simple and the other with an intricate character, is another striking example—as striking as the sequential framing of the *Odyssey*'s Underworld episode—of the interaction of the temporal and spatial dimensions in Jane Austen.)

As with many erroneous characterizations, then, this initial mistake is designed to reveal the observer's expositional self rather than the object of observation; and Austen again takes the greatest care to drive the point home. To start with, she creates an ironical discrepancy in awareness between reader and protagonist by obtrusively deviating from the latter's perspective so as to give us an inside view of Charlotte's mind. Elizabeth is thrice grateful to Charlotte for the "good nature" (p. 103), "civility" (p. 115), and "kindness" (p. 120) she shows in "[engaging] Mr. Collins's conversation to herself"; and on the first two occasions this reading seems plausible enough. But on the third, when Elizabeth goes so far as to thank Charlotte for keeping the rejected suitor "in good humour" and receives the assurance that "her satisfaction in being useful . . . amply repaid her for the little sacrifice of her time," the narrator lets us into the secret: "Charlotte's kindness extended further than Elizabeth had any conception of;—its object was nothing less than to secure her from any return of Mr. Collins's addresses, by engaging them towards herself" (p. 120). This informational discrepancy, moreover, besides retrospectively illuminating character and action, also enables us to appreciate to the full the ironies of the scene in which Charlotte breaks to her friend the news of the engagement. And the effect of the scene is further intensified by being presented as a re-enactment after the fact, so to speak, of the earlier and more academic exchange. The "astonished" Elizabeth now disbelieves the deed just as she previously disbelieved the thought, her incredulity being "so great as to overcome at first the bounds of decorum": "'My dear Charlotte,—impossible!'"[8] while Charlotte calmly restates her opinions and implicitly points the moral of the heroine's failure of insight: "'You must be surprised, very much surprised. . . . But when you have had time to think it all over, I hope you will be satisfied with what I have done. I am not romantic you know. I never was. I ask only a comfortable home" (pp. 123-24).

But the author does not let the matter rest here. Elizabeth's first pained "impossible," with regard to the past, is immediately followed by another, with regard to the future—by "the distressing conviction that it was impossible for that friend to be tolerably happy in the lot she had chosen" (p. 124). And the rashness of both "impossibles" is shown up by Jane Austen's favorite device of startling analogical collocation, especially (in James's terms) of the "free spirit" with the "fools." One effect of the informational discrepancy is that it retrospectively reveals another link between the two opening chapters and the sixth—between the perception-proud heroine who misjudges her "intimate friend" (p. 27) and none other than that woman of "mean understanding" who is ridiculed for failing to understand her own husband's character after twenty-three years of marriage. The fortnight's acquaintance explicitly disparaged in both contexts is indeed very little, but is long experience always so much more? Moreover, as soon as the engagement is announced, the analogy is specifically carried further, temporarily bridging the gap between the one's sense of betrayal and the other's narrow egotism. For just as Elizabeth's initial incredulity is soon parodistically echoed by her mother (who "persisted in disbelieving the whole matter" [p. 125]), so does the subsequent prediction place her again in the same uncongenial company (Mrs. Bennet "trusted that they would never be happy together" [p. 125]).[9] Finally, the similarity is not confined to the conditions or symptoms of misjudgment but is made to extend to its very causes. For when confronted with a piece of conduct that is contrary to their expectations, it does not occur to either mother or daughter to explain it in terms of the intricacy of the character involved, but both tend to see it as inexplicable and usually reprehensible. Mrs. Bennet thus attributes Elizabeth's rejection of Collins to her "perverseness" (p. 135); Elizabeth herself, going one better, takes Charlotte's acceptance of him ("'It is unaccountable! in every view it is unaccountable!'") as evidence for "the inconsistency of all human characters" (p. 139).[10] It takes her a long time to come to admit that her friend "seems perfectly happy . . . and in a prudential light, it is certainly a very good match for her" (p. 169).

In her liability to prejudice, the heroine similarly proves no exception to the fictive rule. She is indeed quick, sometimes too quick, to spot partiality or animus in others and to ridicule their biased views—Miss Bingley's hopes, Collins's account of his benefactress ("I suspect his gratitude misleads him" [p. 86]), or Bingley's "blind partiality" (p. 91) to his friend. But she is much less aware of the analogy between them and herself in this very regard. When Jane disclaims the "extraordinary merit" with which Elizabeth invests her and attributes this ardent praise to sisterly "warm affection" (p. 131), she does little more than articulate a source of error that has been amply manifested before, even outside and prior to the Darcy-Wickham affair. What is more, even when the heroine's valuations turn out to be essentially correct and her superiority to others seemingly established by way of contrast, it is sometimes implied that she may be right for the wrong reasons.

Thus, on the very occasion when she apparently goes out of her way to endorse Elizabeth's first impressions of Bingley's sisters, the narrator states that "with more quickness of observation and less pliancy of temper than her sister, and with a judgment too unassailed by any attention to herself, she was very little disposed to approve them" (p. 25). The expositional cogency of Elizabeth's view is first straightforwardly ascribed to her superior "quickness of observation." But, by a typical twist of the primacy effect, the narrator then goes on to offer another and less favorable reason. What the text ostensibly says (and critics have taken at face value) is that Elizabeth was in a position to judge the newcomers more objectively than her sister. But what the peculiar phrasing (note the multiple negatives and qualifiers in "*too un*assailed by *any* attention") ironically implies is that she was at least equally influenced by personal prejudice. And the significance of order of presentation within the syntactic microcosm again reveals itself in the second reason being placed immediately before the main clause, which reinforces the ironical effect through its correspondingly emphatic (and formally unexplicit) negative phrasing and its subjectively coloured verb: "She was very little disposed to approve them." In her susceptibility to the distorting influence of social "attention" or its absence, Elizabeth is thus indicated to resemble the other inhabitants of her world: Collins, who pronounces the vulgar Mrs. Philips to be a most "elegant" lady on the grounds that he has "never met with so much attention" (p. 78); the ladies of the neighborhood, happy to get "their share of Mr. Wickham's attentions" (p. 87); Bingley, who enthusiastically says of the Meryton assembly that he has "never met with pleasanter people or prettier girls in his life; every body [has] been most kind and attentive to him"; or even Darcy, who disparages the same people, having "from none received either attention or pleasure" (pp. 26–27). As is often the case with Jane Austen's compositional *and* syntactic patterns, including that of the title itself, formal parataxis or juxtaposition has in the last two instances strong hypotactic (e.g., causal) implications: (no) attention and hence (no) pleasure.

Finally, the whole weight of the outer circles, with their cumulative and increasingly specific projection of expositional probabilities, is from the beginning brought to bear on the innermost one of Elizabeth's attitude to Darcy. Even in their light alone, Darcy's case immediately stands out as quintessentially tricky, and the wariest hypothesis-construction is accordingly indicated—he being a reserved and intricate stranger and she (once her first impression is formed after the gratuitous insult at the ball: "She is tolerable; but not handsome enough to tempt *me*" [p. 22]) being strongly predisposed against him. But Jane Austen leaves nothing to chance. She closely interlinks the various circles, thus establishing beyond doubt their relevance to the central expositional problem; progressively calls attention to the causes and symptoms of possible misjudgment; and lays the ground for future developments.

The structural measures—such as spatial linkage, whether in the form of straight or contrasted analogy—again prove Jane Austen's rhetorical forte. That the heroine's initial conception of Darcy and his pride is at best oversimplified is suggested, for example, by the identity of the other people sharing it. Elizabeth is thus coupled with the "world" in general, whose highly favorable first impression of Darcy, ironically deflated from the start, as quickly and amusingly veers to the opposite as soon as he is "discovered to be proud, to be above his company, and above being pleased." Then, of course, "his character was decided. He was the proudest, most disagreeable man in the world" (p. 21). What is more, Jane Austen typically exposes the unreliability of the "world"—the equivalent of Faulkner's "townview"—by concurrently showing that even their impressions of the objective facts of Darcy's physical appearance are drastically modified during the evening. On his arrival, Darcy impresses everybody "by his fine, tall person, handsome features, noble mien. . . . The gentlemen pronounced him to be a fine figure of a man, the ladies declared he was much handsomer than Mr. Bingley"; but once he is "discovered to be proud," nothing can "save him from having a most forbidding, disagreeable countenance, and being unworthy to be compared with his friend" (p. 21). This is essentially Elizabeth's attitude too, her collocation with the narrow and superficial collective viewpoint being facilitated (and the effect produced on the reader by Darcy's insult softened) due to the gradual unfolding of her attractive figure. At that early stage she is to the reader little more than "one of [Mrs. Bennet's] daughters," just as Darcy is simply "another young man" (p. 21).

Even less complimentary is Elizabeth's more specific collocation with her mother (as in the cautionary, analogical instance of Charlotte Lucas). The narrator is not content with establishing Mrs. Bennet as infallibly fallible in general but reminds us of this with particular reference to Darcy. After the ball, the lady characterizes Bingley's sisters as "charming women" and Darcy (whose rudeness she describes "with much bitterness of spirit and some exaggeration") as "disagreeable" and "conceited" (p. 24). However, since no later than on the next page we have the narrator's word for it that her "charming women" are in fact "proud and conceited," it stands to reason that her, and Elizabeth's, "conceited" man may turn out not wholly uncharming. (And to one familiar with Jane Austen's fondness for expositional—and other—validation, development, and ironic reversal by way of verbal and situational rhyming sequences, it is almost predictable that Mrs. Bennet should finally come to enthuse over Darcy in the following terms: "'Such a charming man!—so handsome! so tall!'" [p. 343]). This very soon becomes even more probable when the narrator herself, insistently using Bingley's "easiness, openness and ductility" as foil, describes Darcy as "clever . . . haughty [not 'conceited'], reserved, and fastidious" (p. 26)—a valuation that, despite or perhaps because of its cautious phrasing, is subtly more favorable, and certainly more promising, than any hitherto given by the characters. And the ensuing developments (not least the dialogue scenes sensitively analyzed by Reuben Brower[11] and others) proceed to suggest that he is too intricate to be "simply" reduced to the Bennet formula. Nor can his character accommodate both this formula and the reader's initial view of him (however incomplete), for then he would be too intricate to be true. To heighten the reader's awareness of conflict and gaps, to prevent him from integrating the sequence of clues and versions into a unified, homogeneous conception of personality, is to save him from the primacy effect blinding the characters.

More revealing and complex though hardly more flattering than the mother-daughter relationship is Elizabeth's being implicitly placed in the company of Collins, whose "resentment" of her rejection of *him* and whose inability to comprehend her character and motives are repeatedly indicated to spring from "angry pride" as well as stupidity. Besides serving as another warning-signal, this ironic collocation of the rejected also throws light on Elizabeth's psychology and particularly suggests an important motive for Elizabeth's listening to Wickham's allegations "with all her heart" (p. 81). As Collins pompously puts it when he gives up his suit, "Resignation is never so perfect as when the blessing denied begins to lose somewhat of its value in our estimation" (p. 114). Moreover, Collins, however stupid and vain, in a sense learns more from experience than she; in his courtship of Charlotte he shows that he has become "comparatively diffident since the adventure of Wednesday" (p. 120), while she does not even begin to see the implications of the Charlotte fiasco for her confident judgment of the unknown Darcy "from the very beginning, from the first moment" of their "acquaintance," even before she has "known [him] a month" (p. 181).

Furthermore, the progressive juxtaposition of Elizabeth's first impressions of Darcy with Darcy's first impressions of her affords us a much more illuminating manifestation of the same pattern of unity in variety and especially of variety in unity. In the three previous collocations, the spatial patterns of analogy implicitly serve as "deep" inside views or privileged comment since they highlight, and in Collins's case even lay bare, motives and probabilities of which the heroine herself is unconscious. Here the analogy fulfills the same function, but what makes it possible in the first place is a privileged inside view of the reserved stranger, juxtaposed with one of the heroine's mind. Darcy, who "at first scarcely allowed her to be pretty" and "looked at her only to criticise," gradually becomes aware of her attractiveness—first of the beautiful expression of her dark eyes, then of the pleasing lightness of her figure, and finally of the easy playfulness of her manners. It is stressed that these changes in what is to us expositional valuation do not come easily to him ("he was forced to acknowledge," "he was caught by"). But this only renders it all the more creditable that once he makes each "discovery," however "mortifying," he should modify his original view, and that the more he learns the more he "wish[es] to know" (p. 32). In contrast, Elizabeth (as the same early passage begins to indicate) simply shuts her eyes to whatever is inconsistent with her first impressions, including Darcy's growing interest in her: "To her he was only the man . . . who had not thought her handsome enough to dance with." Due to her "mortified" pride, she is not only unable but unwilling to see his peace overtures and pointed, admiring observation otherwise than as attempts to intimidate or find fault with her" (pp. 33, 57, 165). As she tells Charlotte: "Heaven forbid! . . . To find a man agreeable that one is determined to hate (p. 92); and in Jane Austen's novels many a true word is spoken in jest. Her "arch" statement to Darcy on the same occasion about the "great similarity in the turn of [their] minds" (p. 93) is, in all that concerns their liability to prejudice, another true word, though the analogy thus suggested is rather different in its nature and implications from what she imagines it to be; it is indeed straight as well as contrasted, and insofar as it is contrasted, it reflects as much credit on him as on herself. For Darcy frankly tells her that his temper is "too little yielding" and "resentful," so that his "good opinion once lost is lost forever," while she is unconscious of her own "tendency to [this] particular evil" (p. 63). Accordingly, the reader cannot but view in an ironic and cautionary light Elizabeth's pejorative rephrasing and repeated criticism of his self-avowed failings ("Implacable resentment *is* a shade in a character" [p. 63]), her rather impertinent questions ("[You] never allow yourself to be blinded by prejudice?" [p. 95]), and her solemn admonitions ("It is particularly incumbent on those who never change their opinion, to be secure of judging properly at first" [p. 95])—all of which might with more justice be addressed by Darcy to herself.

Nowhere is this more evident than in her relations with Wickham. From the moment of his arrival, the initial discrepancy in perspective increasingly widens. For while Elizabeth eagerly swallows his story though explicitly warned against him, the reader is given every reason to distrust this channel of information. When viewed in terms of the perceptual set established by the work, most of the dramatic warning-signals are too perceptible to require more than passing mention: Wickham's version of the expositional events being mere "report"; his bias; his anxiety to find out beforehand whether his fair auditress is "much acquainted" with Darcy (p. 80); the inconsistency of so many of his professions with his actual behavior; the differing views of Jane and the Bingleys; etc. Compositionally, moreover, Elizabeth's first impressions of Wickham are nicely contrasted not only in nature but also in cause (*here* we have "attentions" galore) with those she has formed of Darcy as well as of Bingley's sisters. The text also provides us with subtle sytlistic clues, in particular thematically charged but unobtrusively patterned key-words. For instance: in view of the inglorious twist given to our first impressions of the "truth universally acknowledged" as early as the opening, Wickham's very description as "universally liked" (p. 92) is contextually invested with disturbing implications. And while the narrator has no hesitation in straightforwardly describing the male figures as "gentlemanlike" (Bingley [p. 21] or Mr. Gardiner [p. 135]), she reserves for Wickham the ambiguous phrase "of most gentlemanlike appearance," goes on to say that "his appearance was greatly in his favour" (p. 75), contrasts him with others in this very respect ("The officers . . . were in general a very creditable, gentlemanlike set . . . but Mr. Wickham was . . . beyond them all in person, countenance, air and walk" [p. 79]), and repeatedly indicates that for Elizabeth "there was truth in his looks" (p. 83). That appearances may be deceptive, in Wickham's case as in Darcy's, the reader is already well aware. But this is precisely the lesson Elizabeth herself has to learn the hard way in the second half of the novel, where both anagnorisis and peripety are appropriately brought about by the painful expositional discoveries at Hunsford and where her development may best be described in terms of her progressive expositional revaluations.

IV

Since each of the three models of control (which, as suggested, may be ranged upon a scale according to their distance from the fabulaic norm of straightforward chronological communication) accommodates a large number of variations and gradations, the borderlines between them tend to be blurred; and with such differences of degree, it is not always easy to determine to which category a certain work belongs. The question on which the whole matter turns is whether the warning-signals worked into the primacy effect are discordant enough to mar its homogeneity and be immediately detectable, or whether they have been so camouflaged or neutralized at the time as to be perceived only in retrospect. Take, for instance, the initial *outside* view of an object of expositional presentation —an almost inescapable perspectival device (common, as we have seen, to all three models of control) for producing a more or less one-sided primacy effect with any show of probability, avoidable only when the narrator or author is ready to face a charge of plain cheating (as in *The Murder of Roger Ackroyd*). To lay it down categorically that such a view, whether scenically or more subjectively conveyed, is suspect by definition, is to carry distrust much too far. But it is as clearly true that not a few works, both ancient (e.g., Shakespeare's *Julius Caesar,* with its opening alternation of indirect and direct views of Caesar) and modern (notably the ambiguities of James's fiction), have in effect provoked controversy as to the degree or even kind of credence we are supposed to give to certain outside views relayed through certain channels of information. And the resolution of such problems is not merely an exercise in pigeonholing. When the reader's being thus left in doubt (temporarily or permanently) is established as a deliberate choice on the author's part, it may provide an important clue to the intentions of the work; when less than deliberate, it may indicate a discrepancy between intention and execution.

Pride and Prejudice, however, is no borderline case. Here the problem does not arise at all, since the discordant elements introduced into the primacy effect are so varied, pervasive, and interconnected, the duration of the preparatory strategy so long (compared, say, with the four chapters that Faulkner devotes to *his* primacy effect), and its cumulative expositional implications so firmly grounded on stylistic, compositional, psychological and thematic norms—that the heroine's primary view of Darcy has little chance of being accepted at face value. Jane Austen's strategy of anticipatory caution is as persuasive as the system of diversions, baits, and misleading hypotheses designed to prevent the reader from anticipating the revelations about Christmas or Odysseus.

Moreover, it is not just that the reader is directed to note and properly integrate a great deal of information—including negatively enlightening and gap-producing clues—that is overlooked, rejected, or misinterpreted by the prejudiced heroine. Austen's strategy of propelling the two processes of discovery is also representative in that the discrepancy in perspective devised throughout the first-impression phase largely derives from the greater resources, variety and authoritativeness of "literary" as opposed to "everyday" hypothesizing. First, some of the factual clues offered to the reader consist in privileged information to which no human observer can have access (such as reliable inside views of other characters, notably Charlotte and Darcy)—a procedure that would for this very reason be categorically spurned by the late James, though indeed not by the author of *The Portrait of a Lady*. Second, and more important, the play of hypotheses informing the reading-process is maintained through the distribution of indicators and warning-signals to which one naturally ascribes more significance in the determination of probabilities in literature than in life (and to Elizabeth, the Wickham-Darcy affair is of course "life"): temporal ordering, analogical collocation, metonymic transfers, patterned verbal echoes, or stylistic manipulation, in their various forms and mutually reinforcing combinations.

In fact, the resultant disparity between the order and dynamics of Elizabeth's impression formation and those of the reader corresponds exactly to the pronounced disparity between our first and third models; it is Elizabeth alone on whom the disclosures composing the recency effect come as violent, humiliating shock, while the reader finds in them a series of confirmations of what he has long been led to suspect. And in view of this ever-increasing initial disparity, the surprising thing is not that Elizabeth should be seen from the start as overconfident and sometimes curiously blind, but rather that in spite of this she should retain so much of our sympathy throughout.[12]

Part of this effect is no doubt explainable in terms of expositional selection—of the intrinsic attractiveness of many of the character traits with which Elizabeth has been invested from the beginning (such as her wit, vivacity, independence, and the courage and honesty she displays throughout, not least in her recognition of the truth and her expiatory suffering). It is mainly this, I think, that Jane Austen had in mind when she called her "as delightful a creature as ever appeared in print," adding that she did not know how she should "be able to tolerate those who do not like *her*." Most of the rhetorical job of control is done, however, not by the principles of selection but of combination and distribution, not by the mere introduction of intrinsically charged materials into the fabula but by the contextual manipulation of problematic materials within the sujet.[13] These recurrent compositional devices naturally assume even greater importance in a novel like *Emma*, where the rhetorical game Austen plays is far more dangerous precisely because it centers in a heroine who—like Odysseus—is intrinsically far less sympathetic than Elizabeth ("a heroine whom no-one but myself will much like"). But the difference, however significant, is ultimately one of degree.

What I believe of particular theoretical interest about the counter-balancing retention of sympathy in Jane Austen (as well as about the rhetorically opposed, and in the first half concurrent, distancing strategy outlined so far) is the manifold interaction of spatial, sequential, and perspectival principles. Each of the forms of spatial structure is again made to contribute its share. Many of the contrasted analogies (or the contrasted aspects of the more complex analogies) that Elizabeth figures in serve to throw her attractive facets into higher relief; and there are few agents who are wholly exempted from this service, though some foils (like Darcy, Mr. Bennet, or Jane) are indeed worked more thoroughly and some (e.g., such lightning-rods as Miss Bingley) more shamelessly than others. But many straight analogies (or points of similarity) are rhetorically even more vital and potent. For they serve not to reinforce what would be sympathetic enough even in itself but to mitigate what would otherwise, out of compositional context, be ridiculous, deplorable, and even reprehensible about Elizabeth.

The very spatial collocations that I have so far described as cautionary and ironic are in fact made—individually and collectively, successively and simultaneously—to work both ways. On the one hand, they do indeed tend to increase our distance from the heroine by keeping us on the alert and by throwing an ironic light on her faults and errors; but on the other hand, they also produce the opposite effect by concretely demonstrating that these faults and errors are part of the human predicament. And the more numerous, varied, "universal" (within the projected fictive world), and firmly established these couplings are, the more persuasive the rhetorical set-off and the stronger its extenuating force.

Moreover, since most of these analogical relationships are neither wholly straight nor wholly contrasted but complex, the resultant variety in unity not merely extenuates the heroine's initial mistakes but positively redeems them in varying degrees. Elizabeth's collocations with her mother (for instance), however startling and revealing, ultimately only heighten our awareness that theirs—like Strether's and Pocock's raptures about Paris—are two different orders of response. Exactly the same function is served by the remarkably unflattering analogy between Elizabeth, who prides herself on being "a studier of character" (p. 43) and her silly sister Mary, always "deep in the study of thorough-bass and human nature" (p. 65). And such differences become increasingly conspicuous once the turning point is passed and we move into the second half of the work. Here Jane Austen takes full advantage of the fact (as little appreciated by her critics as by Homer's) that, owing to the sequential nature of the verbal medium, even such suprasequential ("spatial") patterns as analogy not only necessarily unfold in time but are as amenable as plot to dynamic manipulation and development.

Analogy is an essentially spatial pattern, composed of two fictive components at least (two characters, events, strands of action, etc.) between which there is at least one point of similarity and one of dissimilarity; the point (or points) of similarity affords the basis for the spatial linkage and confrontation of the analogical components, while that of dissimilarity makes for their mutual definition, illumination, qualification, or simply concretization. But though a spatial pattern, the relations between analogues may change in line with the information we possess at each stage. And in narrative, this sequential transformation of analogical couplings may be a function, not only of the dynamics of presentation (the suppression and distribution of antecedents, as in the *Odyssey* with its static hero) but of the dynamics of the action—notably the development of a character beyond his expositional self.

Accordingly, the implications of the analogies constructed in the novel's opening half are no longer expositional and ironic here. On the contrary, one of the author's major devices for bringing home to us the unusual extent (unusual within this particular fictive framework) to which Elizabeth has recognized, repented and benefited by her mistakes and has outgrown (or is outgrowing) her expositional self is to show how her relations with her previous analogues have become (or are becoming) increasingly contrasted. The development of the analogies both reflects and derives from the development of character; and the static terms of the various analogies constantly give us a concrete measure of the progress made by their dynamic counterpart. A typical manifestation of this spatiotemporal technique is the implied contrast—in depth, seriousness, and consequent self-knowledge—between Elizabeth's revision of her first impressions of Darcy after his first proposal and the nature of the corresponding "expositional revaluations" made by different members of her family, notably Mr. and Mrs. Bennet, after his second.

This brings us to the general problem of the interaction between different compositional principles or dimensions, in the interests of control. Several modes of interaction (complementing those brought out through the *Odyssey*) have already been amply illustrated in the foregoing analysis. We have seen more than one structural and functional parallel between style or syntax and overall composition. We have seen how the spatial patterns of similarity and equivalence (whether in the form of word-clusters, verbal and situational rhyme, interlinked referential "circles," or specific analogical collocations) help to create and maintain the ironic discrepancy in awareness between reader and heroine, thus fulfilling in effect the perspective functions of multiple inside views and authorial commentary; just as, on the other hand, such perspectival adjustments as the occasional inside views and comments help to link, establish, or round out not a few spatial patterns (e.g., Elizabeth-Darcy). We have also seen how the various spatial structures constantly have temporal implications in that they either retrospectively illuminate the past (whether expositional or more recent) or foreshadow the future or interrelate these two temporal directions (e.g., by way of implied causal linkage, rendered probable by the multiplicity of analogical precedents). And we have also seen how the spatial dimension is in turn determined by the temporal progression or unfolding of both the continuum of the text and that of events—for instance, how order of presentation affects, and even effects, the dynamic shifts and rhetorical twists of analogy.

For a novelist accused by the Master of "wool-gathering," this is no mean achievement, even by the standards of his own work.[14] But the most impressive (and historically, the most original) mode of interaction between the temporal, the spatial, and the perspectival principles of the text is perhaps that by which Austen maximizes the distance-decreasing force of what I have just called the rhetorical set-off. What happens is that the reader himself is compositionally dragged, as it were, into the network of universalizing analogy; and this is accomplished through the dovetailing of the narrator's largely self-restricted perspective with her strategy of expositional distribution, or, more precisely, through the overall (though not strictly consistent) quasi-mimetic motivation of the principles of distribution and temporal ordering in terms of the protagonist's own process of vision. The author, while leaving the heroine herself in the dark and slowly propelling her forward to the anagnorisis scene, could of course easily manage to make the narrator fully enlighten *us* at an early stage as to the expositional truth—as is often done in Trollope and as she herself does in Charlotte's case. Jane Austen's habitual abstention from this logically-chronologically "natural" system of presentation—her tendency to enlighten the reader more negatively than positively and to apply the staircaselike construction of progressive discovery to reader as well as protagonist through the motivating device of the self-limited point of view—is another central feature of her art in general and her expositional rhetoric in particular.

When the parallel lines of discovery, disambiguation and reconstitution are manipulated within the framework of the first and second models of control, with their misleadingly homogeneous or homogeneously misleading first impressions (which is rarely the case previous to the modern novel), the reader's potentially adverse judgment of his fellow inquirer is fairly easily counteracted. Since the disparity between primacy and recency effect can then be made at least as pronounced and sometimes as humiliating for us as for our dramatic counterpart, the informational (and hence also normative) superiority we enjoy in straightforward chronological communication is drastically minimized, if not reversed. But even when, as in such a specimen of the dynamics of anticipatory caution as *Pride and Prejudice,* the reader can often make better use of the information relayed through the vessel (not to speak of the inside views and other privileged material accessible to the narrator alone) than the vessel himself does, irony and distance are still kept under tight control. For even then the general and more specific expositional antecedents are not fully and authoritatively conveyed by the narrator at the very start but are on the contrary delayed, distributed and submerged, fragmentary and often temporarily or even permanently ambiguous, at best less than wholly reliable, and never conclusive. Consequently the reader can fill in the gaps only by dint of a laborious process of selection, rearrangement, and reinterpretation of data (e.g., by incessantly comparing and differentiating, temporarily combining and then readjusting the implications of the different circles concurrently drawn round Elizabeth)—a process characterized by setbacks, surprises, consciousness of lacunae and weak spots, and continual doubt. In short, he has a firsthand understanding of the agent's perceptual predicament, since his superior insight into the developing situation is ultimately based on more or less tentative hypotheses and he is seldom as sure of his ground as when enjoying the privilege of Trollope's confidence.

It is precisely this point that Wayne Booth fails to appreciate in his fine essay on *Emma,* when he claims that Jane Austen withholds from us the information about the secret engagement between Frank Churchill and Jane Fairfax because "she chooses to build a mystery," that for her unwillingness to sacrifice the mystery she pays the heavy price of lessening "our pleasure in observing Emma's innumerable misreadings" of the situation, and that her choice is therefore "perhaps the weakest aspect of this novel."[15] In fact, the author's main problem here was not to choose between the unrelated or even clashing interests of "mere mystification" and heightened irony, but to maintain the delicate balance between sympathy and irony, involvement and detachment; to disclose the antecedents at an early stage would be to destroy one of the most powerful means of control. As W. J. Harvey succinctly puts it: "*Emma* is a novel which constantly tempts us into surmise, speculation, judgment; the process of reading runs parallel to the life read about. Hence the need for mystification and hence the delayed revelation which shows us how we, too, are liable to mistake appearances for realities and to arrive at premature conclusions."[16]

Like many other novelists, Jane Austen is indeed intent on creating narrative interest—curiosity, suspense, surprise—through expositional distribution and other temporal deformations. But like some great storytellers, including the notoriously masculine Homer and Fielding, she also skill-fully interweaves these with her other interests and makes them reinforce one another in different means-end combinations. One measure of her art is that, though most of her novels are characterized by the temporary suppression of at least one crucial piece of information, the particular order and modes of presentation (and the consequent play of hypotheses) flexibly vary with the overall ends of each work. Compare, for instance, the different manipulations of the Darcy-Wickham affair here and the secret engagement in *Emma*. In *Pride and Prejudice*, where the author can afford to heighten the irony without forfeiting our sympathy for the charming heroine, the anticipatory expositional hints are numerous and insistent, the informational gaps are perceptibly opened and handled, and the predominant narrative interest is accordingly that of curiosity as to "what really happened." In *Emma*, on the other hand, where the heroine has more faults and fewer intrinsic merits, such an increase of distance would greatly endanger the balance aimed at. Therefore, as far as Emma's most prolonged and perhaps most reprehensible misjudgment is con-cerned, the reader is largely reduced to sharing the heroine's state of ignorance. The anticipatory warning-signals relating to the engagement are fewer in number and much better camouflaged; the revelation of the "mystery" startles us almost as much as Emma; and the predominant nar-rative interest is accordingly not curiosity or suspense, hinging on the reader's early awareness of informational gaps, but surprise, hinging on a more or less imperceptible suppression of temporally anterior material and then a sudden retrospective illumination of what has gone before.

Jane Austen's novels thus afford various specimens of the third model of control, differing in the degree of correspondence between the two concurrently propelled processes of discovery: between rhetorical struc-ture and dramatic pattern, between the dynamics of the reading-process and the dynamics of the action centered in the heroine. That the four novels employing the strategy may be theoretically gradated in these terms—with *Northanger Abbey* and *Emma* serving as limiting cases and *Sense and Sensibility* and *Pride and Prejudice* in between—is only one of their further claims to notice. An even stronger claim is the coincidence of rhetorical gradation and historical progression—the later the novel, the closer the correspondence—so that the development of Jane Austen's art may be as profitably traced in these very terms. But in each case, the narrative strategy of creating and maintaining no more than a quantitative and (especially towards the end) variable discrepancy between reader and protagonist is designed to make the best of both worlds. On the one hand, the foreshadowing devices place the reader in a position where he is able to enjoy the human comedy of errors, to comprehend the heroine's fallibility against the background of her world as a whole, to

penetrate her rationalizations and relate them to her subjective predicament, and to trace her development in terms of her progression in expositional awareness, including self-awareness. On the other hand, the modes
of temporal ordering—keeping the reader, too, in a crooked corridor of
curiosity, suspense, bafflement, or surprise—help to ensure our participa-
tion and counteract the temptation we may feel to smile down condescendingly on the heroine, even when we are fairly convinced that she is
misguided in her reading of character or event.

CHAPTER SIX

RETARDATORY STRUCTURE,
EXPOSITIONAL SUSPENSION, AND
THE DETECTIVE STORY

> This postponement of the point put Florence
> in a flutter; and she looked from Cousin
> Feenix to Walter in increasing agitation.
>
> Charles Dickens, *Dombey and Son*
>
> Is all good structure in a winding stair?
>
> George Herbert, "Jordan I"
>
> What we call the beginning is often the end
> And to make an end is to make a beginning.
> The end is where we start from.
>
> T. S. Eliot, "Little Gidding"

One of the prime means of creating, intensifying, or prolonging suspense consists in the author's temporarily impeding ("suspending") the
natural progression of the action, especially its onward rush toward some
expected climax, by the interposition of more or less extraneous matter.
In all good murderous melodramas, Dickens observes,

> We behold, with throbbing bosoms, the heroine in the grasp of a
> proud and ruthless baron, her virtue and her life alike in danger, draw-
> ing forth her dagger to preserve the one at the cost of the other; and
> just as our expectations are wrought up to the highest pitch, a whistle
> is heard, and we are straightway transported to the great hall of the
> castle, where a grey-headed seneschal sings a funny chorus with a fun-
> nier body of vassals . . . carolling perpetually. (*Oliver Twist,* chap. 17)

Fielding's treatment of Fanny's abduction in *Joseph Andrews* perfectly
illustrates this procedure, though largely by way of parody. When the
myrmidons of the lecherous squire have carried the girl off, after a mock-
heroic battle with Joseph and Adams, the narrator is in no hurry to allay
the reader's anxiety about her fate. On the contrary, he states, in words
strongly reminiscent of Dickens's, that "before we proceed any further in

this tragedy we shall imitate . . . the wise conductors of the stage, who in the midst of a grave action entertain you with some excellent piece of satire or humour called a dance."[1] The reader, whose "expectations are wrought up to the highest pitch," is accordingly kept on tenterhooks till two chapter-length retardations (pp. 203-9) have run their course. The first introduces "A discourse between the poet and the player; of no other use in this history but to divert the reader"; and is immediately followed by "The exhortations of Parson Adams to his friend in affliction; calculated for the instruction and improvement of the reader." It is only at this point that the narrator reverts to Fanny, but not before he has first poked fun at our growing tension: "Neither the facetious dialogue . . . nor the grave and truly solemn discourse . . . will, we conceive, make the reader sufficient amends for the anxiety which he must have felt on the account of poor Fanny, whom we left in so deplorable a condition. We shall therefore now proceed to the relation of what happened to that beautiful and innocent virgin" (p. 210).

The retardatory material, however, may comprise intrusive commentary as well as occurrences in the fictive world. Earlier in the same novel (bk. 3, chap. 6), as soon as the squire has set his pack of hounds on Adams, the narrator intercalates no less than three retardations of this kind in order to prolong our comic fears for the fleeing parson. He first indulges in an elaborate mock-heroic invocation to the omnipotent Muse—who has, among her other feats, "without the assistance of the least spice of litera-ture, and even against his inclination, in some pages of his book, forced Colley Cibber to write English"—calling upon her to aid him in doing justice to Joseph's gallantry on this memorable occasion. The first inter-ruption over, the narrator hardly manages to state that, on perceiving the danger his friend was in Joseph grasped his cudgel, when he flies off at a tangent again, throwing Adams to the dogs. This second mock-heroic suspension, evidently a parody of the celebrated portrayal of Achilles' shield in the *Iliad,* is concerned with the mighty cudgel in Joseph's hands—specifying its history (his grandfather got it "when he broke three heads on the stage"), its appearance ("On its head was engraved a nose and a chin, which might have been mistaken for a pair of nut-crackers"), and so on. Finally, no sooner has the narrator resumed his account of Joseph's rush to the parson's rescue just as one of the dogs is laying hold of his cassock than he suddenly leaves the excited participants frozen in mid-stride, announcing that he would "make a simile on this occasion" were there not weighty reasons against it.[2] And he naturally feels obliged to set these reasons forth in full. The funniest thing about this is that among the considerations adduced we find that a mock-epic simile "would interrupt the description which should be rapid in this part." But, the narrator adds, "that doth not weigh much, many precedents occurring for such an interruption." Under the pretence of doing justice to both sides of the question, he first retards the action by a proretardatory and then by an antiretardatory argument.

Retardatory structure relates directly to the temporal nature and potentialities of literary art. Since the continuum of the text is necessarily apprehended by the reader in a continuum of time—elements on all levels being communicated and patterns unfolded not simultaneously but successively—a certain delay in the disclosure of relevant or desired information is inevitable by definition. But this property of the medium is also deliberately exploited by literary artists, first, in order to create and manipulate the reader's expectations as to the final form that different patterns will assume—be the expectation aroused by the beginning of a rhyme pattern, by the sustained development of a complicated metaphor or figurative cluster, by an ongoing sequence of events, by a constantly shifting analogical pattern, or by a gradually resolved thematic pattern. Second (by a similar though more complex manipulation of information), this property is exploited to create a clash between different expectations, or in other words, to play off different retardatory structures against one another so as to give rise to a more colorful play of hypothesis and effect. Such temporary blocking or suspension of the development of one pattern in favor of another also manifests itself on all the levels—but also between all the levels—of the literary text. It manifests itself, for example, in the clash produced at the end of a run-on line by the preferential treatment accorded to the meter and/or rhyme at the expense of the suspended syntax; or the clash between our interest in the outcome of the dramatic developments and our interest in the comic-parodistic gambols offered by Fielding during such episodes as the battle of the dogs; or the clash between different, alternately pursued generic structures or qualities, such as the tragic and the comic in mixed dramas of the Elizabethan age.

The means which may, among their other functions, serve retardatory ends are thus remarkably numerous and various[3]—since the literary text as a whole must to a considerable extent be viewed as a dynamic system of competing structures and lines of interest. Even on a single textual level, the representation of the fictive world, they assume such different forms as the suspension of the expected ending (or of certain actional landmarks) in terms of the "natural" logic of the given action with its given constituents; temporal shifts (whether in the form of doubling back into the past or plunging into the future); spatial shifts to analogical scenes, to a different actional strand or another ramification of the same strand; authorial commentary (descriptive, moral, aesthetic); and syntactic or stylistic tortuousness. In general, retardatory devices may be described and compared from the following complementary viewpoints:

1. The nature of the retarding material (action, description, commen-

tary relating not to the fictive world but to the modes of narration, language, typographical space, or different combinations of these elements).

2. The magnitude of the retardation (from a sentence or even less to whatever lies between the beginning and the end of the work) and the correlations between its different manifestations within a single work.

3. The location of the device in the text (e.g., to what extent its presence is "annoying" precisely there).

4. The structural and rhetorical relations or tensions between the retarding material and the retarded pattern (e.g., as regards their relative force or attraction, or their manipulated interdependence).

5. The mode in which the retardation is intercalated into the text and its presence motivated.

6. The functionality of the device within the framework of the whole text.

7. The relations between the nature, form, and dynamics of the specific retardatory device on the one hand and generic structure, conventions, expectations and effects on the other.

8. The relations between the specific retardatory device and the basic properties or conditions of the medium, as compared with other arts.

These general statements about the constants and variables of retardatory structure will be elaborated and exemplified here through the intercalation of delayed exposition, whether arising from the action in the fictive world or conveyed directly by the narrator.

First, like all other retardatory measures in the literary text, the operation of this particular device is highly contingent; and unless properly handled, it may prove a double-edged weapon. In such time-arts as the theater or the cinema, when the action is abruptly broken off at an exciting point and the scene shifts, nothing in the spectator's power can do away with the impeding material—say, a flashback—or even accelerate its tempo. Whether he likes it or not, he is compelled to sit it out, waiting for the piece to revert to the suspended strand and resolve his suspense. The same is essentially true of all the arts of performance, whether music or even—what saved Scheherazade's life—oral narration. With a written text before him, however, the reader can, if he finds the interposition intolerable, skim through it or even skip it altogether, and return to it later or not at all. In fact, the literary artist can implicitly count on the success of his retardations only when relying on such extrinsic factors as the conditions of serial publication, which involve a long lapse of time between every two installments and are indeed often exploited for holding the reader in suspense from one monthly or weekly part to another. [4] But within the framework of the literary medium proper, the operation of such devices hinges on the artist's own skill in counteracting the reader's natural inclination to dash forward—for example, by keeping him amused as Fielding does.

Expositional retardation, however, suffers in addition from two peculiar drawbacks I have already touched on in different contexts. First, the material in its "natural" form and function is intrinsically dull; second, the delay of exposition arouses and ultimately gratifies an interest that in itself is by its very nature opposed to suspense—namely, curiosity—or, in terms of chronological order, delayed exposition is related to a temporal direction diametrically opposed to that of suspense, namely, narrative past. It is this direct chronological rivalry that on the one hand distinguishes the expectations dynamized by narrative (or rather the narrative dimension of temporal art) and on the other hand, makes narrative retrospection an illuminating case of retardatory structure in general.

Curiosity and suspense cannot be defined merely in terms of a "lack of information" contrived at a certain point upon the continuum of the text about some developing pattern and the consequent pitching forward of the reader's attention in the hope of closing the breach, completing or stabilizing the pattern, or at least validating the initial tentative hypotheses. For this definition applies to any expectation on any level of the literary text (and other temporal arts), whether generated by the beginning of a rhyme pattern, a syntactic structure, a psychological conflict, an analogical collocation, or a thematic development. The fact that the text is communicated and apprehended along a continuum makes possible (and to some extent entails) a gradual and controlled unfolding of information, and hence a lively play of expectations throughout. An expectation, whatever the pattern it adheres to, is then nothing but a temporary and continuum-conditioned hypothesis—a function of the relevant (phonic, verbal, actional, ideological, compositional, generic, etc.) information possessed by the reader at a given point. As such it can be specified and traced in terms of the nature and textual level of its object, the kinds of information that determine its rise, metamorphoses and possible fulfilment within the context of the work in question, and of course the modes in which this information unfolds during the reading-process.

What distinguishes curiosity and suspense from all other expectations is their common reference to the continuum of events, located on the level of the work's fictive world. Any text and reading-process, any expectation aroused, and any progressively disclosed pattern that is the object and the cause of expectation, may be described in terms of "past," "present," and "future": whatever has already appeared is "past" and whatever awaits us in the sequel is "future" in relation to that point upon the continuum of the text at which we find ourselves at any given moment—the "present" point. This use of temporal terminology is, however, clearly figurative, since the components of a rhyme, a sentence, or a theme do not lend themselves as such to chronological organization and reconstitution. In themselves, outside their sequential ordering in the reading-process, with its own retrospections, foreshadowings, and bi-directional cross references, none of them necessarily belongs to the past or future to a greater extent than the other. But this no longer obtains in a work with a narrative strand, where the level of fictive world is by definition informed by a quasi-mimetic logic of development; apart from the dynamics of presentation, deriving from the temporality of the medium, we have here the dynamics of the action, deriving from the temporality of the represented events. Here, then, we can speak at each stage about past and future in literal, chronological terms too, denoting not a heterogeneous rhetorical complex of experienced and expected "developments" but also strictly referential processes and directions. And though, as we have seen, curiosity and suspense are affected by the presentational sequence no less than any other kind of expectation, it is to the latter sequence, with its inherent chronological dimension, dynamics, and deformability, that they distinctively adhere in an hypothesis-object or effect-cause relationship. And it is also in terms of the relations devised between time as chronological sequence (or order of occurrence) and time as communicative sequence (or order of presentation) that these two primary narrative effects can themselves be differentiated.

In the fabula there is a perfect correspondence between textual-figurative and mimetic-narrative past, present, and future. At each point, not only the general temporal directions but also the narrative materials belonging to each are fixed and definite, since whatever precedes or follows this point chronologically also precedes or follows it presentationally. A work that resorts to the fabulaic order, therefore, always creates suspense but not curiosity. It creates suspense, because as long as the end has not been reached, the reader necessarily lacks information about the future resolution of events. But it does not create curiosity, because the reader possesses at each stage all the relevant information about the past.[5] While the ambiguation of the narrative future naturally arises from the dynamics of the action, the ambiguation of the past can arise only from the dynamics of presentation, perceptibly manipulating and distributing some antecedents so as to turn what is chronologically "past" into a hoped-for textual "future." The opposed displacement in the form of "anticipation" or "foreshadowing" (turning chronological future into presentational present and past) may indeed heighten, modify, or canalize suspense. But it is an optional device rather than a necessary compositional condition; moreover, the more explicit and authoritative it is, the more does it mingle suspense with curiosity, for to present some future development as a foregone conclusion is to produce a gap subsuming all that intervenes.

Among its other claims to notice, therefore, expositional retardation involves not only the tension inevitably generated whenever a text concurrently pursues more than one kind of expectation and suddenly blocks one in favor of the other (say, syntax and meter in the case of *enjambement*), but a head-on clash between ongoing expectations or interests that relate to the same overall pattern on the same level of the work—the sequence of events—while pulling the reader's attention in opposite chronological directions: narrative past versus future. What is more: it involves a clash between expectations which are far from equipollent, one being "natural" and the other "artificial," compositionally stimulated, and hence more contingent. Consequently, if the operation of any prolonged retardatory device turns on the reader's blocked interest being counterbalanced by some other interest, that of expositional retardation depends particularly on curiosity being brought into equilibrium with suspense. Before this device is embarked upon, either the reader's curiosity with regard to the impeding expositional material must be heightened or (less often) actional suspense played down to some extent. Otherwise, one will bring off no more than short stabs of retardatory suspense. At the climax of "Barn Burning," Faulkner thus daringly segments the scene of the boy's desperate escape from his confinement at home, intent on frustrating his father's plan of burning down Major de Spain's property, by the interpolation of almost irrelevant expositional material about the two bovine sisters:

> Then he was free. His aunt grasped at him but it was too late. He whirled, running, his mother stumbled forward on her knees behind him, crying to the nearer sister: 'Catch him, Net! Catch him!' But that was too late too, the sister (the sisters were twins, born at the same time, yet either of them now gave the impression of being, encompassing as much living meat and volume and weight as any other two of the family) not yet having begun to rise from the chair. . . . Then he was out of the room, out of the house. . . .

But as the briefness of the parenthetical suspension shows, Faulkner is well aware that in the circumstances he must not try the reader's patience overmuch.

On the other hand, Thackeray's abortive bid for a protracted retardation in the eighth chapter of *Pendennis*—as the heading declares, "Pen is kept waiting at the door, while the reader is informed who little Laura was"—may illustrate the possible consequences of unskilled preparation for the interposition of delayed antecedents. Thackeray does not fail for want of trying. On the contrary, in the preceding chapter he insistently points to a number of gaps concerning Laura. We are first informed in passing that Major Pendennis "had his private reason for disapproving of her; which we may mention on some future occasion";[6] during Mrs.

Pendennis's conversation with the Major, she attacks first long engagements (p. 68) and then unequal marriages (p. 71), instancing in both
cases the misfortunes of "poor Laura's father"; and when she sighingly
repeats her objection to premature engagements, the narrator makes a
direct attempt to pave the way for the retrospect on Laura's history, commenting that "as she has made this allusion no less than thrice in the
course of the above conversation, and seems to be so oppressed with the
notion . . . and as the circumstance we have to relate will explain what
some persons are anxious to know, namely, who little Laura is, who has
appeared more than once before us, it will be as well to clear up these
points" (p. 72). But the ensuing bulky account leaves the reader cold
because Thackeray has not managed, despite his belated efforts to force
the expositional gaps open, to strike the proper balance between curiosity
and suspense. As the reader's mind has so far been focused on Pen and the
family crisis to which his infatuation has given rise, he takes a definite
interest in the suspended narrative future ("Pen waiting at the door") but
none whatever in the immediate textual future offered in exchange—the
delayed antecedents of the shadowy Laura, who has as yet established no
claim on his attention.

And even Homer sometimes nods. Book 2 of the *Iliad* is constructed
so as to gather momentum throughout its gradual progression towards the
first full-scale battle scene of the epic. Suspense mounts from moment to
moment as Homer evokes the councils of the Greeks, their cheers and war
cries, and their deployment in battle formations. When the armies seem to
be on the point of engagement, however, he drastically frustrates our expectations by intercalating an enormous retardation, heralded by the invocation "Tell me, ye Muses . . . who were the leaders and rulers of the
Danaans? . . . Now I shall name the captains of the ships." What follows is
the famous Catalogue of Ships—a long census list, each item usually consisting of the name of a Greek leader, some biographical details, a short
description of his native country and the strength of the contigent ac-
companying him to Troy; and no sooner has this roll-call come to an end
than Homer embarks on that of the Trojans.

I for one cannot but regard this retrospective interpolation as a
blemish. The contemporary audience may possibly have greeted a catalogue with enthusiasm since what are to us meaningless geographical labels
were for them vital realities; to follow the names of places on this list was
to make a circuit of the Greek world.[7] But this does not materially affect
my objection, which relates not so much to Homer's principles of expositional selection as to his order of presentation.[8] This essentially informational catalogue may have had some interest if placed at the start of the
poem—where it chronologically belongs—as preliminary exposition, or at
most at a point where our interest in the narrative future is still but mild.

It is hard to imagine, however, that even for the contemporary audience its interest at the point to which it has actually been delayed could be intense enough to counterbalance, for the duration of no less than half a Book, the cumulative force of the suspense previously generated. The intrinsic attractiveness of the expositional material may be greater than in Thackeray's case, but so is the suspense impelling us forward to the battle scene, and so is the length of the suspension.

The imbalance may thus take different forms, but with much the same result: the reader is strongly, and justifiably, inclined to skip the annoying impediment. Whenever this happens, the retardation has a boomeranglike effect, for neither has the reader been put in possession of the necessary information nor has the development of the action been impeded. And the sense of artistic failure is obviously not diminished even when the reader conscientiously withstands the temptation to skip.

On the other hand, to catch the reader between the Scylla of curiosity and the Charybdis of suspense is to achieve two desired effects at the same time. An excellent example is the opening books of the *Odyssey,* where, as I argued, our interest in the narrative past has been so deftly stimulated and so closely interrelated with the absorbing interest in the outcome of the future struggle, that we positively welcome the prolonged retardation produced by Telemachus's journey in quest of exposition. And Homer's subsequent success in balancing and interweaving the two conflicting interests constantly reduces the reader anew to the unenviable—but artistically ideal—position of being able to appease his pressing need for exposition only at the expense of heightening his retardatory suspense, and vice versa. Consequently, far from skipping or skimming through the distributed expositional material, he carefully scrutinizes the past in order to discover its implications for the different hypotheses revolving in his mind about the future turns that Odysseus's adventure may take.

The interposition of Mrs. Bennet's narrative in *Amelia* shows, moreover, how the reader may be similarly cornered into a state of mutually retarding interests through the dynamics of the action as well as that of the reading-process. To ensure the effectiveness of this expositional block, Fielding reinforces the reader's interest in it not only by the preliminary opening of gaps but also by investing the tale with actional or propulsive value, that is, turning its very communication into a crucial developmental motif. Being thus integrated with the action, this harking back (like Darcy's peripeteic letter in *Pride and Prejudice*) forms a much more effective retardatory device than the commentarylike interpolation of which the unsuccessful instances I have cited are composed. As soon as Amelia identifies the handwriting of an anonymous note warning her of "a dreadful snare . . . laid for virtuous innocence, under a friend's false pretence,"[9] she rushes in distress to Mrs. Bennet's house, begging her to allay her anxiety, "for I am more and more convinced that something of the utmost importance was the purport of your message" (p. 298). Mrs. Bennet hopes she will be able to save Amelia from the impending catastrophe, but adds that "to disclose all my fears in their just colours, I must unfold my whole history to you. Can you have patience, madam, to listen to the story of the most unfortunate of women?" (p. 299). Amelia, needless to say, assures her of the highest attention. However, before letting Mrs. Bennet embark upon her history, Fielding further stimulates our interest in it through an intriguing temporary gap: Mrs. Bennet suddenly bursts into tears and shocks Amelia with the avowal that she has been guilty of adultery and murder. So when Mrs. Bennet finally recovers her spirits, the reader—filled with anxiety for the sympathetic heroine and therefore eager to have the expositional narration despite its dilatory nature, and in addition tantalized by the promising beginning—needs must curb his impatience and say, with Amelia: "Indeed, madam, you have raised my curiosity to the highest pitch, and I beg you will proceed with your story" (vol. 2, p. 3).

II

The second way of achieving the necessary equilibrium is not—or not only—through the heightening of curiosity but through the temporary playing down of suspense. This sort of balance is usually resorted to when the intercalated exposition is mainly designed to serve other ends than the intensification of the reader's sense of retardation. I have already shown, for example, how book 5 of the *Odyssey* reduces our anxiety about Odysseus's ultimate fate in order to pave the way for the prolonged, subtle unfolding of his character in books 5-12—notably the expositional block of books 9-12—thus transforming what was previously dramatic tension into psychological interest; and how, once this task is accomplished, Homer soon finds an opportunity to galvanize suspense into life again.

Fielding's handling of his interpolated expositions offers an even more varied example. Since the eighteenth century, these digressions have been an object of acrimonious criticism even more often than Homer's. In "An Essay on the New Species of Writing" (1759), for instance, Francis Coventry concludes that "the most glaring Instance of [dullness] in all this Author's Works is the long unenliven'd Story of *the man of the hill;* which makes up so great a Part of a Volume. A Narration which neither interests nor entertains the Reader, and is of no more Service than in filling up so many pages."[10] The grounds for these strictures are as readily apparent, the digressions consisting of fairly extensive histories narrated by minor or even marginal characters, often but newly introduced, to one of the main agents; and with few exceptions, such as Mrs. Bennet's tale, they have little influence on the subsequent course of events.

However, had these critics paid attention either to Fielding's acute awareness of what I called the quantitative indicator or even to his explicit warning to the "little reptile" of a critic "not too hastily to condemn any of the incidents in this history as impertinent and foreign to our main design, because thou dost not immediately conceive in what manner such incident may conduce to that design,"[11] they would have been less rash in dismissing these episodes as mere padding. What they actually did was to judge the functionality of the intercalated tales by the Aristotelian criterion of causal concatenation: "The plot . . . must imitate one action and that a whole, the structural union of the parts being such that, if any of them is displaced or removed, the whole will be disjointed and disturbed"; and finding (to continue the quotation) that their "presence or absence makes no visible difference" to the progression of Fielding's plot, jumped to the conclusion that they can by no means form "an organic part of the whole."[12] As Fielding's admonition implies, however, a literary text is amenable to different modes of organization or, from the reader's viewpoint, to different modes of integration; and the less we can integrate it or parts of it in terms of one organizing principle, the more is our attention drawn to the alternative modes. The creator of one of the most perfect plots in history can hardly be imagined ignorant of the digressive nature of his interpolated tales. On the contrary, it is the eloquent testimony of the tight causal structure characterizing the bulk of these novels that reinforces the conclusion that Fielding deliberately wishes to heighten the reader's consciousness of these expositional narratives as digressions on one level of the work, the level of the action, so as to send him in quest of their functionality on other levels. He deprives most of these episodes of actional or propulsive value precisely in order to direct the reader to integrate them with the rest of the work not in terms of plot but of theme;[13] he temporarily retards or suspends the linear progression of his story in order to indicate that for the time being he is going to resort to spatial development.

Despite the difference in expositional form, the thematic and normative functionality of these bulky digressions resembles in some ways the operation of the *reassembled* Agamemnon story in the *Odyssey* when considered in isolation from the variety of purely narrative ends this contextual "precedent" is made to promote. In each case Fielding establishes an analogical relationship between the narrator of the intercalated tale and his audience or, more seldom, some other major agent.[14] At times some aspects of the analogy are even explicitly commented on by the participants themselves, either prior to the beginning of the narration or at some later stage. The Man of the Hill prefaces the story he is about to narrate at Tom Jones's request with the remark that "in what little hath dropped from you there appears some parity in our fortunes," just as Fanny Matthews compares herself with Amelia Booth. And in the course of the narrative many additional correspondences are suggested. As it turns out, however, the points of similarity so insistently driven home do not serve as bases for an overall straight analogy, but are on the contrary designed to throw into relief the fundamental contrast between the ostensible analogues. Most of these expositional histories—Mr. Wilson's tale in *Joseph Andrews* being the major exception—dramatize an alternative way of reacting to such circumstances as the major agent finds or has found himself in; and as the alternative may sometimes appear attractively feasible but is always negated by the normative framework of the novel, it favorably illuminates by way of contrast the character and choice of the protagonist who has (explicitly or implicitly) rejected it, and enriches the thematic import of the work. When Tom is confronted with the misanthropic recluse, Sacks rightly claims, "We already know too much about him to think him capable of anything but complete commitment to the fortunes and misfortunes of his fellow men. [However,] Fielding's deft manipulation of the relationship between Tom and the old man permits him to embody dramatically important ethical comments; it allows him to incorporate the presentation and rejection of what he considers an important attitude toward evil in the external world into the world of the novel at a rhetorically effective moment."[15] And in *Amelia,* Mrs. Bennet's narrative reveals and defines the contrast between Amelia and her hostess, whose flirtatious conduct in the face of the identical temptation awaiting the heroine—and withstood by her—has resulted in her husband's undoing as well as her own. The transformation of the initially straight analogies into contrasted ones is thus as important here as in the *Odyssey,* since, in James's apt phrase, "We get the interest and the tension of disparity when a certain parity may have been in question."[16]

A thoroughgoing account of the analogical import of Fielding's digressions would lead me far afield and would involve in addition much theoretical overlapping with my analysis of the *Odyssey.* Therefore, having suggested that their main function significantly diverges from that of the previously mentioned instances of retardation in that they promote thematic rather than narrative interest, I wish to concentrate on that aspect of the problem which I have not yet had occasion to treat, namely, the way Fielding overcomes the peculiar difficulties that stem from the spatial operation of these retardatory episodes. The Agamemnon story in Homer, for instance—or for that matter, the nonexpositional analogical strand centering in Gloucester in *King Lear*—is sure to receive proper attention because, among other reasons, it is closely related to the linear progression of the action or at least to our expectations about the narrative future. On the other hand, the danger of the reader's impatiently thumbing through Fielding's interpolated expositions is in direct proportion to their being extremely unamenable to integration in such terms. To counteract this lack of dramatic value, reduce the reader's sense of retardation, and ensure his attentive, leisurely, and pleasurable perusal of what Coventry denounces as "long, unenliven'd" narratives, Fielding accordingly takes a surprising variety of mutually reinforcing precautions.

First, in direct contrast with his retardatory practice in such episodes as Fanny's abduction, he takes care to introduce these digressions at points where suspense is at a particularly low ebb. In Booth's and Miss Matthew's narratives, no suspense has as yet been generated since the action proper has hardly been launched, so that in this respect their effect is curiously comparable to that of preliminary exposition. In a sense, as I shall soon indicate, the dynamics of both action and expectation is set going here through the process of expositional narration. In most other cases, however—such as the history of Mr. Wilson or the Man of the Hill—the retrospective digression is interposed at a stage where the main line of action more or less stands still for the time being and no fateful issue is immediately imminent. The only exception is Mrs. Bennet's tale, but then its communication is indeed endowed with actional value as a counterbalancing inducement.

However, since in view of the tangential position of these tales a mere balance of curiosity and suspense with a ratio of nil to nil (as often happens with preliminary exposition) will evidently not do, the former interest must be made to outweigh the latter. So in conjunction with this essentially preventive device, Fielding resorts to the positive measure of heightening our curiosity about the past history of the prospective narrator, an interest that is appropriately dramatized in each case in and through the reactions of the prospective auditor. Booth catches a glimpse of the handsome, well-dressed Miss Matthews being ushered into the prison. When he confidently expresses his disbelief in the rumour that she is guilty of murder, he is amazed to witness the joy of the genteel girl at what she calls her revenge: "'Murder! oh! it is music in my ears! ... Yes, my old friend, this is the arm that drove the penknife to his heart.'" As she, moreover, constantly alludes to the "many extraordinary things" that have happened to her since their last meeting and culminated in her imprisonment, it is no wonder that Booth (like Alcinous) is so intrigued that he admits that "curiosity was too mean a word to express his ardent desire of knowing her story" (vol. 1, pp. 19–20 [bk. 1, pp. 5–6]).[17] Mrs. Bennet's narrative is prefaced with a similar manipulation of expositional gaps; and so is, though with less success, that of Mr. Wilson, who is finally told by Parson Adams that "his literary goodness as well as that fund of literature he was master of, which he did not expect to find under such a roof, had raised in him more curiosity than he had ever known. 'Therefore,' he said, 'if it be not too troublesome, sir, your history if you please'" (p. 154 [3.2]); and so is the Man of the Hill's.

The two devices discussed so far are preparatory in that they are designed to produce in the reader the necessary incentive to embark on the inset digressions. Throughout the narratives themselves, however, Fielding employs a special mode of distribution as a complementary measure for facilitating the absorption of the retardatory material, counteracting its tediousness and driving its significance home.

Apart from the variety of functions that the distribution of exposition may fulfill—creation of curiosity, suspense, and surprise; control of distance and credibility; semantic processing and thematic development; perspectival tension and adjustment; emphasis of problematic points; shifts in patterning and significance; or structural linkage (sequential or spatial) —it always achieves an additional effect. Discontinuous communication makes—simply by virtue of its discontinuity, if not for other reasons—for better and pleasanter assimilation of information. But in all the cases dealt with in the previous chapters this effect was a side-issue or by-product, the main function of the distribution depending not so much on the mere discontinuity of exposition as on the ambiguation, temporary withholding and delayed disclosure of parts of it. There are, however, cases of distribution for distribution's sake—in which the concentrated, continuous blocks of the fabula are broken up into numerous small units in order to sugar the expositional pill. The difference in the principal goal of distribution, moreover, involves a marked disparity in the form of exposition, i.e., in the degree of informational discontinuity. In the previous cases both the chronological and the presentational discontinuity between related units that are immediately contiguous in the fabula is conspicuous; not a few years and some hundreds of pages intervene, for instance, between the first and last bit of exposition concerning Odysseus. But when the main effect turns not on delay but on segmentation, the distributed exposition is discontinuous only in the sense that it does not constitute a solid block but a succession of smaller units thinly separated by a variety of interpositions.

Fielding is one of the novelists who have pounced upon the opportunity thus offered to make the best of both worlds—to retain the advantages of expositional concentration (e.g., concision) and yet reap the rhetorical benefit of formal distribution. Particularly notable are three devices of informational segmentation, each creating its own miniature retardation within the wider retardatory framework. The first kind of segmental measure derives from the circumstances of the inset, dramatized epic situation.[18] The flow of Booth's narrative, for example, is broken up scores of times by the inquiries or interjections of Miss Matthews. In some works (especially plays, which, owing to the exigencies of theatrical performance, do not lend themselves too well to continuous informational monologues) the block of summary is cut up into bits and passed off as a genuine dialogue scene. A notorious case in point is the nineteenth-century drawing-room comedy that more often than not opens with a butler and maid having a gossipy chat about their master, or in earlier drama, the colloquy of First and Second gentleman. Booth's retrospect, however, is so bulky that its presentation in dialogic form would take up most of the novel. Fielding, therefore, must needs content himself with segmenting it through the frequent interruptions of the addressee; in a similar situation, Shakespeare ingeniously breaks the awkwardly long expositional tale narrated by Prospero to Miranda in the first act of *The Tempest* by making the narrator interrupt himself.

Fielding, moreover, reinforces the relevance—and hence also the interest—of Miss Mathews's interpositions by investing them with actional, structural, and thematic value. First, he adds a subsidiary line of interest to the communication of exposition by showing these interruptions to reflect not only her character but also the steady progression in the relations between the secondary narrator and his fair auditress. Throughout her own narration, the lady has already alluded to her admiration for Booth; but his recital offers her even better opportunities "to soften, to allure, to win and to inflame" (p. 161 [4.1]); and her compliments, sighs, and amorous glances grow increasingly unambiguous. And as Booth is far from insusceptible to her innuendos, it is little wonder that when they are finally left alone the omniscient narrator does not think it proper to expose the ensuing scene to the eyes of the public. In short, while the bulk of Booth's account throws light on the narrative past, its own retardatory segmentation propels the action forward to the future.

The rest of Miss Matthews's comments serve significant functions of other kinds. Thus, her many observations on the behavior of women and Amelia in particular firmly establish the contrast between her and the heroine; and her argument with Booth about the validity of Mandeville's philosophical theses (3.5) not only reveals the moral nature of the two disputants but directly relates to the thematic core of the novel.[19] During Mrs. Bennet's tale, Fielding variously endows Amelia's interpositions with structural value, one of them notably serving to hammer home the closeness of the analogical relationship between her present imbroglio and Mrs. Bennet's expositional temptation. On hearing how her hostess first met the deceitful lord at the oratorio, Amelia excitedly exclaims "that she herself had first seen the same person in the same place and in the same disguise. 'O, Mrs. Bennet!' cried she, 'how am I indebted to you! . . . I look upon you, and always shall look upon you, as my preserver from the brink of a precipice, from which I was falling into the same ruin'" (7.7).

Partridge's frequent interruptions of the Man of the Hill's tale, on the other hand, fulfill a more purely segmental function in that they provide comic relief. His retardations within retardation take the form of parading his scraps of classical erudition, and even interpolating a funnily pointless tale of his own. In this they radically differ from Tom's thematically and structurally pregnant interpositions. In Parson Adams's comments on Mr. Wilson's history, the comic and the serious are often combined. Adams constantly breaks the continuity of the inset recital by reinforcing the narrator's adverse judgment of his own past conduct, but the moral efficacy of his remarks stems precisely from the blissful childlike innocence they manifest. But all these instances of local segmentation, however diverse, have in common a salient compositional and functional feature that distinguishes them from those cited in the opening part of this chapter. In all of them, it is not (or not only) that the unfolding of the past suspends the present and retards the progression toward the future, but that the materials relating to the present and future retard the unfolding of the past. Therefore, in terms of the dynamics of expectation, it is not suspense that is intensified, but curiosity.

A second, and much more drastic and prolonged, mode of segmentation consists in the irruption of the fictive frame into the inset epic situation; the flow of exposition is impeded owing to the temporary breaking up of the epic situation as a whole. Such an interposition separates, for example, Miss Matthews's tale from Booth's: no sooner has she wound up her retrospect and he is about to begin his, than "the keeper arrived and acquainted the lady that dinner was ready" (vol. 1, pp. 45–46 [1.9]). The dinner scene over, the two return to the lady's apartment, where she keeps Booth to "his promise of relating to her what had befallen to him" since their last meeting (pp. 51 ff.). Later, Booth is again "interrupted in his narrative" by the sudden entrance of the keeper, who brings the happy tidings that Miss Matthews can now be bailed, since the man she has stabbed is not even mortally wounded (p. 88). So the harking back to the past temporarily gives place to the affairs of the present (to "a scene of a different kind from any of the preceding"; p. 89), and the action proper progresses for a while. Finally, however, Miss Matthews, "who had very impatiently borne this long interruption prevailed on the keeper to withdraw," claiming: "'The first account I heard [of her approaching release from jail] . . . did not make me amends for the interruption of my curiosity. Now I hope we shall be disturbed no more till you have finished your whole story'" (p. 93). And the author in his mercy realizes her hope.

A comic equivalent of this pattern of retardation in reverse manifests itself when Mrs. Bennet falls into a fit of grief in the middle of her tale and, in answer to Amelia's shouts for help, Sergeant Atkinson burst into the room. Mrs. Bennet pretends to be astounded at his presence in the house, but the maidservant gives the show away by innocently exclaiming, "'Why, 'tis only master, madam.'" This interruption also marks a progression in the action, for Amelia and the reader learn to their surprise that the bluestocking and the honest soldier have been clandestinely married (vol. 2, pp. 49 ff.).[20]

Both distributive measures mentioned so far consist in quasi-mimetic breaks in the quasi-mimetic pattern of epic situation. The interruptions are, in other words, dramatized in that they are dissimulated as occurrences inside the fictive world itself, forming part of the ongoing action and affecting the characters no less than the reader. The breaks in what is to the reader the flow of exposition derive from corresponding breaks in what is to the characters the continuity of narration. There is, however, a third segmentary device that radically diverges from the others in its purely artistic, distinctively nonmimetic nature. It is not related at all to the continuum of represented events but only to the continuum of the text—the flow of words and other typographical symbols—that project them.

The division of the continuum of the text into paragraphs, chapters, or books, neither affects nor reflects the course of events in the fictive world.[21] Its effect, if any, is purely rhetorical in the sense that it is produced only upon the reader, to whom alone the fictive action is presented in the form of a written text. The pursuit of a thief does not stop every time the author breaks up its description in order to start a new paragraph or chapter, for the progression of the two continuums is not necessarily interdependent. The action may be continuous and its typographical representation discontinuous, and vice versa.

Fielding himself made manifold use of this mode of segmantation.[22] He exploits it, for instance, to reinforce the relations between sequential contiguity and suprasequential similarity, drawing the reader's notice to the contrapuntal parallelism between two scenes by devoting a special chapter to each and placing them in succession (the amorous overtures Mrs. Slipslop makes to Joseph Andrews are presented immediately after Lady Booby's attempt to seduce her virtuous servant, etc.). For the problem that concerns us at present, however, Fielding's views "On Divisions in Authors" (*Joseph Andrews*, 2.1) are of particular relevance:

> There are certain mysteries or secrets in all trades, from the highest to the lowest, from that of prime-ministering to that of authoring. . . . Among those used by us gentlemen of the latter occupation, I take this of dividing our works into books and chapters to be none of the least considerable. Now, for want of being truly acquainted with this secret, common readers imagine, that by this art of dividing we mean only to swell our works to a much larger bulk than they would otherwise be extended to. . . .

But in reality the case is otherwise, and in this as well as all other instances we consult the advantage of our reader, not our own; and indeed, many notable uses arise to him from this method; for, first, those little spaces between our chapters may be looked upon as an inn or resting-place, where he may stop or take a glass or any other refreshment as it pleases him. . . . As for those vacant pages which are placed between our books, they are to be regarded as those stages where in long journeys the traveller stays some time to repose himself. . . . A volume without any such places of rest resembles the opening of wilds or seas, which tires the eye and fatigues the spirit when entered upon.

Exactly—plus retardatory gains. So during the long journey of Booth's tale Fielding provides the reader with a great many breathing spells by breaking it up into two books and no less than twenty chapters—on average, a ratio of five pages to a chapter. In terms of Fielding's development, the expositional segmentation in *Amelia* thus differentiates it from the early *Joseph Andrews,* where Mr. Wilson's whole autobiography is crammed into a single chapter, running without a break for twenty pages (3.3); and is carried even further than in the midway *Tom Jones,* where the chapter divisions of the Man of the Hill's tale are much more widely spaced.

Finally, Fielding often draws the reader's attention to this technique of textual segmentation—laying bare rhetorical difficulty and device so as to anticipate possible objections—before passing on to the next chapter. Sometimes he even goes so far as to declare outright the purpose for which he has chosen to suspend for a moment the flow of the text, drawing a parallel between external and internal audience or narrator: Amelia "recovered her spirits, and begged her [hostess] to continue her story, which Mrs. Bennet did. However, as our readers may likewise be glad to recover their spirits also we shall here put an end to this chapter" (vol. 2, p. 36); or, in *Tom Jones,* the Man of the Hill "proceeded to relate what we shall proceed to write after we have given a short breathing-time to both ourselves and the reader" (8.13). On other occasions he adduces such transparent pretexts as, "We will make a gap in our history, to give [the critical reader] an opportunity of accurately considering whether this conduct of Mr. Booth was natural or no" (vol. 1, p. 63). Thus his disarming awareness of the tediousness of concentrated exposition and his evident efforts to counteract or at least to minimize its retardatory effects add another coating to the pill. One can only wish that more novelists showed the same solicitude for the reader's nerves.

III

So far I have focused on the manifold employment of expositional retardation as a local device, whether the unfolding of the past blocks or is blocked by the developments of the present and the future. A similar principle may, however, be contracted into the miniature form of a sentence (as in the passage cited from Faulkner's "Barn Burning") or expanded into a major structural pattern, overarching the whole action or large parts of it. I have already indicated that, owing to the sequential nature of the literary medium, retardatory structure is much more common than may appear at first sight, so much so that the literary text may be viewed as a dynamic system of competing and mutually blocking retardatory patterns. And this is particularly conspicuous in the narrative work, with its sequentiality of fictive developments as well as of communicative medium. Large-scale retardatory structure on the level of action characterizes, in fact, that comprehensive, almost all-inclusive category of stories—usually tracing a conflict—in which an end is postulated, and suspense is generated and sustained owing to the reader's "prescience of something definite to come; and it is this alone that articulates and vivifies future time for us, so that it no longer seems a mere impersonal process, or a vacant succession, but becomes a presence, hostile or auspicious, capable of destroying our peace, or of bringing us happiness."[23] When —or as long as—our apprehension of the end to which everything is borne forward remains vague, as in *Wuthering Heights,* or the outcome of the conflict doubtful, as in the first parts of the *Odyssey* or in *Sons and Lovers,* our suspense during the development of the action primarily consists in the clash between hope and fear combined with the sense of impeded catastrophe or equilibrium. The more definite our foreknowledge and the predominance of the "how" over the "what" hypotheses, however, the more purely retardatory the suspense; all the reader does is eagerly or resignedly await the inevitable end as it draws nearer and nearer with each twist of the action that retards it.

The purest case of this kind of tension occurs when the narrator is not content with the expectations arising from the work's structure of probabilities but simply anticipates, early in the sujet, a climax that is to be fully dealt with only much later—say, old Karamazov's "tragic and mysterious death . . . which I shall relate in its proper place," referred to on the first page of *The Brothers Karamazov.* But the reader's prescience and suspense may derive from generic as well as concrete foreshadowing, whether overt or dramatized. In many a comedy, for instance, we have little doubt that the love story will end in the merry ringing of marriage bells; but the happy ending must be postponed to the last scene, or else, as Trollope mischievously asks, "Where would have been my novel?"[24] The author, therefore, strews the path of the lovers with such obstacles as the disapproval of parents, misunderstandings, or even shilly-shallying on their own part, so that much of the interest of the story is made to turn on the lovers' cutting their way to the altar through the tangle of difficulties; and the more numerous or formidable the obstacles, the greater the retardatory suspense. And the same applies to the popular adventure story, from the primitive folktale to *The Guns of Navarone*, where the postulated ending—the hero's accomplishment of an arduous task—is constantly impeded through a similar "staircase-like construction."

I shall again illustrate the problem by showing how the delay of exposition operates as an overall retardatory principle in the detective story, a genre in which this kind of structure reaches perhaps its most conventionalized form. A good way of bringing out its distinctive functional organization is to compare it with Elizabethan revenge tragedy.[25] In both, the beginning of the sujet and particularly its end are predetermined by generic convention. The revenge play opens with the disclosure or discovery of a crime—usually murder—and is brought to a close with the criminal's death at the hands of the revenger, at times amidst a general holocaust; the detective story starts with the commission or discovery of a crime—also murder as a rule—and ends in the unmasking of the culprit. In a sense, therefore, the answer to such questions as, "Why does Hamlet delay?" is simply that the generic premises preclude prompt reprisal; the revenger must be prevented from polishing the criminal off in act 1, and the detective from spotting him after his first survey of the scene of the murder, or else there would be little action and no work. The artist is consequently compelled in either case to impede the climax by interposing a middle between the predetermined beginning and end; and, moreover, to relate it dramatically and dynamically to these points of reference so that it will result from the one and issue in the other, that is, to account for the necessary retardation in quasi-mimetic terms by placing the causes for delay within the fictive world itself and turning the middle into the bulk of the represented action. This retardation is of such magnitude that any interpolation coming from the narrator himself will obviously be unacceptable, as in most fictive works organized on similar principles, except as a distinctly minor device.[26]

One way of motivating the staircase-like construction is common to both genres, namely, the explanation of the delay in the execution of revenge or the unmasking of the criminal in terms of the revenger's or the detective's ignorance of the identity of the evildoer or the doubtful nature of the evidence he does possess. The climax is postponed, then, owing to the lack of what is to the reader expositional information. At this point, however, the two genres diverge in two related respects.

First, while in the detective story this dramatized ignorance invariably forms the primary if not exclusive "justification" for the delay, in the revenge tragedy it is combined with—and sometimes altogether replaced by—a host of other retardatory devices, such as the revenger's inability to secure legal justice due to the lack of tangible proof or the high rank and power of the criminal, who often desperately tries to escape detection by putting obstacles in the avenger's way (Hieronimo and Lorenzo in Kyd's *The Spanish Tragedy,* or Hamlet and Claudius); the fits of grief or madness from which he suffers as a result of brooding over his wrong and which temporarily sap his will to act (Hamlet, or Antonio in Marston's *Antonio's Revenge*), and so on.

Second, though both genres are marked by strong narrative interest, the dominant interest in each differs due to a radical disparity in the temporal disposition of materials and the manipulation of expectations. The revenger himself may for some time grope in the dark—as Hieronimo or Titus Andronicus do—frantically seeking to identify the criminal or establish his guilt. The reader or spectator, however, is usually—Hamlet being one of the rare exceptions—placed at an informational vantage point; he is authoritatively informed about the antecedents of the crime soon after the beginning, at any rate long before the revenger has managed to resolve his doubts. The preclusion of curiosity accordingly reinforces the generic premises and the concrete progression of the work in pitching our attention forward to the future, where the outcome of the conflict is shrouded. But the future is at some points almost as opaque to the reader as to the hero. The generic conventions only foreshadow that the murderer will eventually fall and that the revenger himself cannot wholly escape punishment; but the circumstances of the revenge and most of its consequences are variable and amenable to dynamic ambiguation. Therefore, the prolonged postponement of the catastrophe produces a complex of different forms of suspense—retardatory, actional, and psychological—which becomes especially intense when the revenger is a rounded and sympathetic character—a Hamlet, for example.

The detective story, on the other hand, exploits what is in essence the same type of overall structure not for the stimulation of suspense but primarily of curiosity. While in the revenge tragedy the narrative future is opaque compared with the translucence of the past, here the opposite is true: if any discrepancy in awareness is created between us and the detective, it relates not to the past but to the future. We know in advance that the criminal is to be apprehended in the last chapter and that the detective is sure to come to no harm; but we are kept in ignorance all along of the circumstances leading up to the crime, particularly the identity of its perpetrator. Indeed, it is precisely the necessity to unravel the expositional mysteries that propels forward both the action (within the fictive framework) and our attention (within the rhetorical) from beginning to end and justifies the constant postponement of the climax; whereas even in such exceptional revenge plays as *Hamlet* the detective theme, such as it is, peters out about the middle, the conclusive resolution of our uncertainties coinciding with that of the hero. In the detective story, therefore, the reader's attention is impelled backward to the narrative past. And if he looks forward in suspense to "future" developments—both chronologically or literally future, as is the case with all actional retardatory structures, and textually or figuratively future, as with all retardatory structures in art—it is mainly with a view to comprehending the past, the very climax constituting a final retrospective illumination. The dominant interest is, in short, curiosity; the very *raison d'être* of the retardatory structure, consisting in the delay of exposition, is its increasing intensification, and to reach the top of the staircase is to be rewarded by its final satisfaction.

It is in terms of this fundamental disparity between desired effects that the difference between the overall orders of presentation employed by the two genres is to be explained. The revenge play, interested above all in tracing the development of a conflict toward a catastrophe, follows an essentially chronological sequence, with possible minor deviations. The detective story, on the other hand, is the only genre that cannot but resort to radical chronological deformation, since its whole effect depends on the creation and manipulation of temporary gaps.

The reader's mind is drawn to the suppression of antecedents and to the centrality of the expositional gaps already at the outset, as soon as the murder is discovered. For in order to fathom the mystery the reader must reconstruct a whole complex of expositional relationships, notably those between the criminal and his victim, so as to fill in two or three vital expositional gaps: the murderer's identity, his motive, and the means by which he managed to commit the crime undetected.[27] But these are precisely the author's most jealously guarded secrets. So the foreknowledge that by generic convention these invariably temporary ambiguities are to be authoritatively dispelled toward the end turns the detective story from the start into a battle of wits between the curious reader, who endeavors to beat the author (or rather his delegate, the amateur or professional sleuth) to the solution, and the author who does his utmost to mystify, misdirect, and baffle him. The challenge to the reader's ratiocinative and reconstructive powers is already implicit in the generic premises and order of presentation; but the gage is at times publicly thrown down—as in the authorial footnotes scattered throughout John Dickson Carr's provocative *The*

Reader Is Warned, or the short notice with which Ellery Queen occasionally prefaces the end of the race:

> At this point in the story you are in possession of all the facts needed
> to build up a complete and logical solution of the crime. Your job is to
> spot the vital clues, assemble them in rational order, and from them
> deduce the one and only possible criminal. It can be done; it has been
> done, as you will see.[28]

Having opened the central expositional gaps, the author is faced by the
intriguing problem of how to accomplish his ends within the limitations
of the fair-play convention, that is, how to communicate to the reader all
the information that ought to enable him to anticipate the solution and
yet prevent the mystery from leaking out.[29] The difficulty is overcome by
the representation of the hunt for the murderer carried out by the police,
the detective, and occasionally some of the suspects who are intent on
clearing themselves or establishing the guilt of others. It is thus the exigencies of the investigation, with its twists, turns, and momentary setbacks, that form the stable means of accounting in realistic terms for the
generically determined retardation of the solution and at the same time
enable the author to *distribute* the exposition throughout the work in the
form of a host of fragmentary of even conflicting bits and pieces, so that
we are placed throughout before the same problems confronting the detective and in the same form and order. Delay, distribution, order: the
overall generic end determines and the overall generic structure motivates
all of these presentational necessities.[30]

In and through the process of detection, the reader is thus provided
with a steady flow of expositional material, which he tries, at each stage,
to piece together into a coherent exposition. To be valid, his reconstruction of the past must convincingly disambiguate the major gaps and a wide
variety of minor ones—all related to the expositional state of affairs—that
incessantly emerge in the course of the investigation. Whenever a clue
comes to light, the reader must reexamine his current expositional
hypothesis to see whether it is compatible with the new discovery. And
since unexpected, complicating clues keep cropping up, he is continually
kept busy checking and modifying the tentative hypotheses he has put
together. Indeed, most of the fun of the story consists in the successive
construction of such theories, some of which are immediately discarded,
while others, which for some time seem to hold water, are suddenly upset
by new revelations: the cast-iron alibi is disproved, a hitherto unsuspected
motive is ferreted out, an eye-witness account establishes the innocence
of our favorite suspect. And so to work again, on a new trail.

As a rule the (actual as opposed to implicit) reader eventually comes up against a deadlock that completely baffles him. (The stupid policemen of the genre's golden age have by now evolved *their* expositional theory and arrested the character to whom it points.) Lost in the labyrinth of apparently unconnected and incompatible details, he either gives up in despair the attempt to fathom the mystery or has his eye upon one of the dramatis personae (the least unlikely person, of course, or, taking into account the possibility of a sophisticated double bluff, the most likely one), without being able to validate his suspicion logically by means of a coherent reconstruction. So he looks forward to the surprise that is to be sprung on him in the last chapter, in which the detective brings his investigation to a successful conclusion by triumphantly unmasking the criminal and explaining to the astonished audience every link in the chain of reasoning that led to the dramatic denouement.[31] In the course of this delayed and *concentrated* exposition the clues distributed throughout are reexamined and sifted. Some of them turn out to be red herrings, while others, having been reinterpreted and fitted into their true place, cast new light on the whole sequence of events. Seeming contradictions are reconciled; implications are fully articulated; overlooked clues are shown to be invested with significance; the host of fragmentary bits of information are woven into a net of proof. And no gap is left open. As Jane Eyre exclaims upon the discovery that St. John is her cousin, "Circumstances knit themselves, fitted themselves, shot into order: the chain that had been lying hitherto a formless lump of links, was drawn out straight—every ring was perfect, the connection complete" *(Jane Eyre,* chap. 33).

The detective story may thus be defined as a retardatory structure that achieves its effects—sustained curiosity and suspense—by distributing the expositional material piecemeal throughout while postponing the concentrated, true exposition—the opening part of the fabula—to the end of the sujet. The variations that can be introduced into this genre are, of course, innumerable. But it would be difficult to conceive of an innovation—whether the permanent ambiguation of the gaps (the Jamesian twist), the restriction of the "detective's" powers or the questioning of his motives (as also in Kafka), the charging of clues and quest with psychological and thematic meaning (as already with Sophocles' inquirer), or the transposal of informational discrepancies *(Crime and Punishment)*—that could dislodge expositional manipulation from its key position without radically infringing the basic generic premises. It would be no exaggeration to claim that in this genre the expositional game is the be-all and the end-all—so much so that its detractors have often complained, as I shall indicate in the next chapter, that it leaves little scope for other, and superior, interests.

CHAPTER SEVEN

A PLEA FOR PRELIMINARY AND CONCENTRATED EXPOSITION: THE CASES OF TROLLOPE AND BALZAC

"Just a moment," said Wimsey, "I do like a story to begin at the beginning."

Dorothy Sayers, *The Unpleasantness at the Bellona Club*

In view of the numerous advantages I have so far analyzed of the "artificial" over the "natural" order, of delayed over preliminary and of distributed over concentrated exposition, one is liable to jump to the conclusion that differences in modes of expositional presentation have far-reaching normative implications. One might even be tempted to divide novelists into two categories—the masters of expositional rhetoric, temporal manipulation, and narrative strategy in general being honored with a place in one, and the crude, slipshod, plodding authors who, unconscious of the subtleties and potentialities of their craft, begin by shoving down the reader's throat whole lumps of expositional matter, being ignominiously relegated to the other. This temptation must, however, be strenuously withstood. I shall argue in this chapter that not a few novelists advisedly incur the drawbacks of chronological ordering because either their general conception of their art or the aims and needs of a particular work or both dictate the preliminary location, concentrated form, and orderly disclosure of exposition; and that the price thus paid is at times not too high, considering the artistic gains. Furthermore, preliminary expositions may vary widely in their temporal structure and in their materials and functions; in their relations with the rest of the work or the rest of the expositional information contained in it; and in their degree of rhetorical success. And disparities in presentational choices must not be automatically invested with normative significance, not only because preliminary and concentrated expositions, just like the delayed and distributed varieties, cannot be lumped together but also because they may serve ends that cannot otherwise be encompassed.

I propose to start by examining several statements made by Anthony Trollope, one of the inveterate users of preliminary exposition:

As Dr. Thorne is our hero . . . and as Miss Mary Thorne is to be our heroine . . . it is necessary that they shall be introduced and explained and described in a proper, formal manner. I quite feel that an apology is due for beginning a novel with two long dull chapters full of description. I am perfectly aware of the danger of such a course. In doing so I sin against the golden rule which requires us all to put our best foot foremost, the wisdom of which is fully recognised by novelists, myself among the number. It can hardly be expected that any one will consent to go through with a fiction that offers so little of allurement in its first pages; but twist it as I will I cannot do otherwise. I find that I cannot make Mr. Gresham hem and haw and turn himself uneasily in his arm-chair in a natural manner till I have said why he is uneasy. I cannot bring in my doctor speaking his mind freely among the bigwigs till I have explained that it is in accordance with his usual character to do so. This is unartistic on my part, and shows want of imagination as well as want of skill. Whether or not I can atone for these faults by straightforward, simple, plain story-telling—that, indeed, is very doubtful. (*Dr. Thorne*, chap. 2)

I would that it were possible so to tell a story that a reader should beforehand know every detail of it up to a certain point. . . . In telling the little novelettes of our life, we commence our narration with the presumption that these details are borne in mind, and though they be all forgotten, the stories come out intelligible at last. . . . But such stories as those I have to tell cannot be written after that fashion. . . . The story must be made intelligible from the beginning, or the real novel readers will not like it. The plan of jumping at once into the middle has been often tried, and sometimes seductively enough for a chapter or two; but the writer still has to hark back, and to begin again from the beginning—not always very comfortably after the abnormal brightness of his few opening pages; and the reader who is then involved in some ancient family history, or long local explanation, feels himself to have been defrauded. It is as though one were asked to eat boiled mutton after woodcocks, caviare, or maccaroni cheese. I hold that it is better to have the boiled mutton first, if boiled mutton there must be. . . .

Before I can interest readers in the perplexed details of the life of a not unworthy lady, I must do more than remind them that they do know or might have known, or should have known, the antecedents of my personages. I must let them understand how it came to pass that so pretty, so pert, so gay, so good a girl as Mary Lovelace, without any great fault on her part, married a man so grim, so gaunt, so sombre, and so old as Lord George Germain. It will not suffice to say that she had done so. A hundred and twenty incidents must be dribbled into the reader's intelligence, many of them, let me hope, in such a manner that he shall himself be insensible to the process. But unless I make each one of them understood and appreciated by my ingenious, open-hearted, rapid reader—by my reader who will always have his fingers impatiently ready to turn the page—he will, I know, begin to masticate the real kernel of my story with infinite prejudices against Mary Lovelace. (*Is He Popenjoy?*, chap. 1)

Perhaps the method of rushing at once "in medias res" is, of all the ways of beginning a story, or a separate branch of a story, the least objectionable. The reader is made to think that the gold lies so near the surface that he will be required to take very little trouble in digging for it. And the writer is enabled,—at any rate for a time, and till his neck has become, as it were, warm to the collar,—to throw off from him the difficulties and dangers, the tedium and prolixity, of description. This rushing "in medias res" has doubtless the charm of ease. "Certainly, when I threw her from the garret window to the stony pavement below, I did not anticipate that she would fall so far without injury to life or limb." When a story has been begun after this fashion, without any prelude, without description of the garret or of the pavement, or of the lady thrown, or of the speaker, a great amount of trouble seems to have been saved. The mind of the reader fills up the blanks,—if erroneously, still satisfactorily. He knows, at least, that the heroine has encountered a terrible danger, and has escaped from it with almost incredible good fortune; that the demon of the piece is a bold demon, not ashamed to speak of his own iniquity, and that the heroine and the demon are so far united that they have been in a garret together. But there is the drawback on the system,—that it is almost impossible to avoid the necessity of doing, sooner or later, that which would naturally be done at first. It answers, perhaps, for half-a-dozen chapters;—and to carry the reader pleasantly for half-a-dozen chapters is a great matter!—but after that a certain nebulous darkness gradually seems to envelope the characters and the incidents. "Is all this going on in the country, or is it in town,—or perhaps in the Colonies? How old was she? Was she tall? Is she fair? Is she heroine-like in her form and gait? And, after all, how high was the garret window?" I have always found that the details would insist on being told at last, and that by rushing "in medias res" I was simply presenting the cart before the horse. But as readers like the cart the best, I will do it once again,—trying it only for a branch of my story,—and will endeavour to let as little as possible of the horse be seen afterwards. (*The Duke's Children*, chap. 9)

Whatever one's opinion of Trollope's expositional practice—which I briefly discussed in Chapter 2—or of the cogency of his present arguments, which I propose to consider now, it would be difficult to dismiss him as naively unconscious of the problems involved. I shall start with his attempt to defend preliminary exposition by fighting the plunge *in medias res* on its own ground—the creation of narrative interest.

In his endeavor to disparage the prevalent claim that any comparison of delayed and preliminary exposition will show, to apply James's phrase in another context, the poor concussion of positives on one side with negatives on the other, Trollope doubtless raises an interesting rhetorical point. But the conclusion he reaches after having weighed the pros and cons of each order of presentation, that the game of putting the chronological cart before the horse is ultimately not worth the candle, has only a limited validity. As shown in the previous chapter, it is only when the work has failed to stimulate the reader's interest in the narrative past that delayed exposition shares all the disadvantages of the preliminary, and forms (one might add) an annoying retardation into the bargain. In such cases, the brightness of the opening pages definitely renders the perusal of "some ancient family history, or long local explanation" even more irritating than usual. Trollope, however, erroneously equates the abuse of the *in medias res* system with the system as a whole, failing to take into account several important variables. He seems to be totally unaware of the effect that a skillful handling of gaps may have on the reader's interest in the antecedents—an effect that can be produced only through temporal deformations. To exploit Trollope's own metaphor—argument by false analogy is a double-edged weapon—the opening scenes may serve as appetizers that give relish to the expositional boiled mutton following them; indeed, exposition itself (e.g., the last chapter of a detective story) may in this way be transformed into a choice morsel. Nor does Trollope consider the possibility that an author may plunge *in medias res* precisely in order to have "a certain nebulous darkness gradually [seem] to envelope the characters and the incidents"; and that the realization of various artistic goals (e.g., the creation of suspense, spatial manipulation, or the dynamics of judgment) may decisively turn on "the reader's mind [filling] up the blanks,—if erroneously, still satisfactorily." Finally, his main objection to this plunge—that it ultimately results in the reader's frustration— is glaringly incompatible with his admission in *The Duke's Children* that he is going to resort to this device for once, against his better judgment, because "readers like the cart the best." Having once postulated the reader's response as touchstone, he obviously cannot have it both ways.

The deficiencies of Trollope's argument as to the form of exposition are as significant as those vitiating his views on the effects of its location. He does not seem to conceive of exposition, whether delay or preliminary, as other than concentrated into "two long dull chapters full of description," thus both failing to explain why it should be so lengthy and simply overlooking the possibilities of distribution open to the novelist. Distribution in the form of segmentation is particularly relevant in this context, since it would enable Trollope to counteract the tediousness of concentrated exposition without incurring what he would consider the penalty of *delay* that distribution usually involves.

One is forced to conclude that Trollope's attempt to vindicate preliminary exposition on the grounds of narrative interest is not particularly successful. In itself, however, this line of defense hardly accounts for such strong language as "twist it as I will I cannot do otherwise." In fact, the statements cited above raise not one but several points. And theoretical discrimination hardly being Trollope's forte, he himself seems to be unconscious of the ramification of his argument. Thus, in the second quotation he opens his comparison of preliminary and delayed exposition by declaring that "the story must be made intelligible from the beginning, or the real novel readers will not like it"; but in support of this claim he proceeds to point out that delayed exposition leads to failure in the maintenance of narrative interest—without realizing that "intelligibility" and "interest" are theoretically two distinct issues. Moreover, as soon as the shortcomings of the plunge *in medias res* have been demonstrated, as it were, Trollope's argument curiously shifts its ground again. For in the immediately ensuing commendation of chronological progression he reverts to the question of intelligibility: "But before I can hope to interest readers in the perplexed details of the [heroine's] life . . . I must let them understand how it came to pass," etc. In the excerpt from *Dr. Thorne,* on the other hand, the whole argument is based on the need for "naturalness"— an issue that is close to "intelligibility" but definitely not identical with it.

Trollope's practice is, however, more defensible than he seems to realize; and in its light, even his present vindication of preliminary exposition is considerably more cogent than may appear from his own muddled conduct of it. But to be properly appreciated, his expositional strategy must be viewed against the wider background of his conception of narrative art as a whole. Trollope's distaste for temporal deformation will then be seen to relate not only to the heart of his craft but also to some of the dominant goals and compositional principles that characterize a type of structure of which his own novels are fairly representative specimens.

II

One striking feature of Trollope's *Autobiography* is the consistency with which it views the art of fiction in terms of the creation of characters and the delineation of character. Trollope confesses that after a number of false starts he finally came to perceive, with the publication of *The Warden* (1855), "wherein lay whatever strength I did possess. The characters of the bishop, of the archdeacon, of the archdeacon's wife, and especially of the warden, are all well and clearly drawn. I had realised to myself a series of portraits, and had been able so to put them on the canvas that my readers should see that which I meant them to see."[1] As time went on he became increasingly convinced that "the highest merit which a novel can have consists in perfect delineation of character, rather than in plot, or humour, or pathos" (p. 143), an attitude crystallized in the definition: "A novel should give a picture of common life enlivened by humour and sweetened by pathos. To make that picture worthy of attention, the canvas should be crowded with real portraits, not of individuals known to the world or to the author, but of created personages impregnated with traits of character which are known" (p. 109).

Nowhere in the book does Trollope offer a definition of the tricky key-term "real";[2] and his whole treatment of the formidable issue of realism is at times amusingly cavalier. But despite frequent shifts of emphasis, his prescriptions ultimately boil down to three. First, the characters must be lifelike in their universality, possessing traits common to all human beings as human beings, regardless of time, place, or social position. They must walk upon the fictive stage "as they do walk here among us,—not with more of excellence, nor with exaggerated baseness, —so that my readers might recognise human beings like to themselves, and not feel themselves to be carried away among gods or demons" (p. 125). He proudly cites, for instance, Hawthorne's praise that his novels, though intensely English, are "just as real as if some giant had hewn a great lump out of the earth and put it under a glass case, with all its inhabitants going about their daily business, and not suspecting that they were being made a show of" (p. 125). Second, the characters must at the same time conform to generally accepted conceptions of local types. Trollope was thus gratified when competent judges pronounced his Dr. Grantly "to be a real archdeacon down to the very ground" (p. 80). Last, the agents must also be real in the sense of concretely rendered, from the visual as well as psychological viewpoint. It is this criterion that is implied in Trollope's constant reference to characters as "portraits" or "real portraits," which must be "made to stand before the reader's eye by the aid of such portraiture as the author is able to produce."[3]

What makes the problem of characterization so crucial for Trollope is the dilemma no novelist can evade: "The writer of stories must please, or he will be nothing. And he must teach whether he wish to teach or no. How shall he teach lessons of virtue and at the same time make himself a delight to his readers?" (*Autobiography,* p. 190). This view of the double function of literary art is, of course, hardly original. Its interest rather consists in the claim that the realization of either function hinges on the novelist's modes of characterization. The reader cannot be touched by gods and demons, nor amused by wooden blocks. To be affected, he must be convinced that "men and women with flesh and blood, creatures with whom we can sympathise, are struggling amidst their woes. It all lies in that" (p. 196). Realistic characterization is accordingly the supreme criterion by which Trollope evaluates particular works and ranks their authors. Thackeray is the greatest English novelist, and his *Esmond* the greatest novel, since "his characters stand out as human beings, with a force and a truth which has not, I think, been within the reach of any other English novelist" (pp. 209, 160). George Eliot comes second; and consciously running counter to the collective opinion of the world of readers—a very unusual thing with him—Trollope relegates Dickens, the most popular English novelist of any time, to third place, owing to the artificiality of his puppets (pp. 212-14).

Trollope's insistence on the primacy of character correlates with an extreme depreciation of "plot," since Aristotle the element generally regarded—not least, by many of Trollope's contemporaries[4]—as the life and soul of fiction. Trollope never wearies of repeating that plot (in the sense of action, the set of represented events, or *story,* a term he uses interchangeably with *plot*[5]) is "the most insignificant part of a tale" in that it is no more than a vehicle for dramatizing, illustrating, and bringing out character (p. 109); he even goes so far as to claim that the worth of a narrative hardly depends on the coherence or probability of its plot, since there are few structural faults that are so bad as to be irredeemable by lifelike characterization. Speaking of his own novels, he admits that "nothing could be less efficient or artistic" than the plot of *Framley Parsonage,* but he nevertheless maintains that this "hodge-podge" is more than compensated for by the handling of the characters" (p. 123). He is, on the other hand, perplexed at the success of *Dr. Thorne* ("the most popular novel I have ever written"), which contains no single memorable figure but only an efficient plot (pp. 108-9). And finally, though aware that "the plot of *Orley Farm* is probably the best I have ever made," he disagrees with his friends in judging this work to be inferior to *The Last Chronicle of Barset* with its admittedly improbably plot but more penetrating characterization (pp. 143-44, 236-37).

Trollope, moreover, often gives the impression that he does not even regard character and plot as interdependent components of one whole. In such novels as *Crime and Punishment* or *Emma,* the protagonists can hardly be conceived of apart from the concrete complex of events in which they are entangled; the development of the characters depends to such an extent on the concrete terms of the plot and the progression of the action on the traits of the agents as to make the two dynamic elements practically indissoluble. Trollope, in contrast, speaks of his characters as if they existed apart from any particular plot or could equally be projected through a number of alternative plots; and they are indeed carried over from novel to novel, changed by nothing but time. At any rate, however causally interwoven in the finished product,[6] the two elements were sharply distinct in his mind during the first stages of the process of composition. He frequently declares, not without pride, that at the time he began a novel he was thoroughly impregnated with his dramatis personae but had only a faint notion of what was to happen to them. This, however, did not discourage him in the least. Plot being of so little importance, he did not trouble to work it out beforehand, but simply improvised it as he went along: "As to the incidents of the story, the circumstances by which these personages were to be affected, I knew nothing. They were created for the most part as they were described. I never could arrange a set of events before me," while "the evil and the good of my puppets, and how the evil would always lead to evil, and the good produce good—that was clear to me as are the stars on a summer night" (p. 274). In the rare cases he made an effort to plan everything ahead, he always had to give up the unequal struggle after "some hours of agonising doubt, almost of despair"; and then, "with nothing settled in my brain as to the final development of events, with no capability of settling anything, but with a most distinct conception of some character or characters, I have rushed at the work as a rider rushes at a fence which he does not see. . . . At such times I have been able to imbue myself [so] thoroughly with the characters I have had in hand . . . till it has been my only excitement to sit with the pen in my hand and drive my team before me at as quick a pace as I could make them travel" (pp. 151–52).[7]

Trollope's expositional practice may thus, first of all, be accounted for genetically, in terms of compositional exigencies. He cannot plunge straight into the middle of the fabula for the simple reason that he starts with no clear idea of it; and he can hardly afford to jump into space. So he is in effect forced to open his sujet with a preliminary and concentrated exposition, in which he will try to convey to the reader his clear conception of a set of characters placed in a particular setting. For him, moreover, this is as much of a virtue as a necessity, since it is from the introduction of the characters that he can derive the necessary inspiration or impetus for the coming improvisation of his plot.

To dismiss Trollope's expositional procedure in these terms, however, and accuse him of merely wishing to erect his personal shortcomings into universally binding laws, is to do him less than justice. Whenever an author has a private axe to grind—and when does he not have one?—the borderline between personal inclination and artistic theory tends to become blurred or tortuous. Yet there are some strong indications that Trollope's disparagement of plot is grounded on a fundamental conviction that the narrative interests stimulated by plot per se, in isolation from character, and especially by plot in the sense of a causally concatenated series of events turning on a mystery and culminating in a sensational denouement, are essentially inferior. He depreciates, in other words, the very effects that depend to no small extent on chronological deformations in general and the manipulation of expositional gaps in particular.

A convenient starting-point for discussing his low opinion of this cluster or class of interests is his evaluation of Wilkie Collins, perhaps the greatest mystery-plot contriver of the nineteenth century:

> Of Wilkie Collins it is impossible for a true critic not to speak with admiration, because he has excelled all his contemporaries in a certain most difficult branch of his art; but as it is a branch which I have not myself at all cultivated, it is not unnatural that his work should be very much lost upon me individually. When I sit down to write a novel I do not at all know, and I do not very much care, how it is to end. Wilkie Collins seems so to construct his that he not only, before writing, plans everything on, down to the minutest detail, from the beginning to the end; but then he plots it all back again, to see that there is no piece of necessary dove-tailing which does not dove-tail with absolute accuracy. The construction is most minute and most wonderful. But I can never lose the taste of the construction. The author seems always to be warning me to remember that something happened at exactly half-past two o'clock on Tuesday morning; or that a woman disappeared from the road just fifteen yards beyond the fourth milestone. One is constrained by mysteries and hemmed in by difficulties, knowing, however, that the mysteries will be made clear, and the difficulties overcome at the end of third volume. Such work gives me no pleasure. I am, however, quite prepared to acknowledge that the want of pleasure comes from fault of my intellect. (Pp. 220–21)

Evidently, Trollope damns Collins with faint praise. But what is here modestly advanced as a possibly subjective distaste is elsewhere laid down as an objectively valid judgment, grounded on the primacy of character in fiction. In such forthright statements as "the novelist has other aims than the elucidation of his plot. He desires to make his readers so intimately acquainted with his characters that the creations of his brain should be to them speaking, moving, living, human creatures" (p. 199), he postulates or tries to establish a hierarchy of literary interests in which suspense, curiosity, and surprise are relegated to the lowest position. The normative conclusion he constantly drives at is that whenever the achievement of any of these allegedly inferior, short-lived effects may clash or interfere with what cannot but be the main line of interest, the novelist should not have a moment's hesitation as to which kind of interest must be sacrificed.

In his adherence to this view Trollope displays unexpected firmness and courage. He has too often laid himself open to accusations of best-sellerism to be suspected of ignoring the taste of the reading-public. In his principles of selection, for example, he repeatedly exposes his readiness to cater to his contemporary readers. As he candidly admits with regard to *Phineas Finn:* "I was conscious that I could not make a tale pleasing . . . by politics. If I wrote politics for my own sake, I must put in love and intrigue, social incidents, with perhaps a dash of sport, for the sake of my readers" (p. 272). And yet he has enough self-respect (and, one must bear in mind, enough awareness of his weak and strong points as a novelist) to draw the line at what he considers the only right compositional strategy. He knows only too well that, at a time when the sensational mystery novel was at the height of its vogue, plot "will most raise [a tale] or most con-demn it in the public judgment" (p. 109); but he is determined not to jug-gle with his fabula simply in order to generate pleasures that are so shal-low and weak that they cannot survive a peep into the last chapter and are destroyed by their very enjoyment (*Barchester Towers*, chap. 14).

Trollope's quarrel with Wilkie Collins and other masters of the elab-orately plotted novel is, then, that they deliberately construct their works on such principles as not only give rise to a clash of interests but even turn the "proper" hierarchy of values upside down by sacrificing—or at least strictly subordinating—the superior to the inferior and the enduring to the ephemeral. He especially objects, in effect, to their incessant manipulation of expositional gaps, which diverts the reader's mind from the unfolding of character to that of the intricate plot. The reader has no attention—or patience—to spare for the portrayal of character since, "constrained by mysteries and hemmed in by difficulties," it is wholly occupied by the ambition to memorize and pattern a multitude of details (such as the dis-appearance of a woman "just fifteen yards beyond the fourth milestone") or is simply riveted on the end, where "the mysteries will be made clear and the difficulties overcome." More important still, even if the reader did have some attention to spare, he would find nothing to bestow it on. Trollope's claim that Collins's novels are "all plot" (p. 216) may be exaggerated. After all, the creator of Count Fosco and Sergeant Cuff not infrequently practices what he preaches about the indispensability of convincing characterization to any kind of narrative,[8] though most of his characters too are, in T. S. Eliot's phrase, constructed rather than created.[9] But there is no doubt that this description perfectly fits the modern detec-tive story, the purest form of the novel of plot, in which the exigencies of the expositional game certainly leave very little scope for "realistic" characterization and natural development of character. This limitation has indeed gradually evolved into one of its generic features.

Of all literary genres, the detective story is most conspicuous for the "purity" of its effects. Unlike the revenge play, say, its retardatory structure is not devised as a convenient framework for the elaboration of a wide variety of interests, but is exclusively designed to generate curiosity appealing to our ratiocinative faculties. As any emotional coloring of the represented facts may divert the reader's mind from the intellectual challenge of piecing together the jigsaw puzzle of clues, this genre not only handles gaps in the tantalizing way I outlined but also resorts to a number of drastic preventive measures to preclude any possible distraction or distribution of interest. In order to leave our minds detached, it cheerfully pays the price of psychological and thematic shallowness by divesting the tale of any potentially profound human interest, in a way even Collins would be chary of doing, let alone openly admitting to. Crime is presented not as a moral or social problem but as a necessary logical premise, which, like the Point in Euclid (as a modern mystery writer wittily puts it), has position but no magnitude. Love interest is introduced as another datum or as an interlude. The dramatis personae have such characters, and so much character, as the intricate plot requires. Many of them are ciphers or conventional types; and even the potentialities of those endowed with some degree of rotundity are rarely pursued in excess of the exigencies of the plot. Significantly, if any care is lavished on characterization, it manifests itself in the portrayal of the detective, the only figure that is as a rule emotionally detached, his concern in the case being professional or scientific. As a vehicle of the intellectual interest, it is he (not the victim, not the criminal, not any of the suspects—the natural objects of psychological interest) that is the hero of the work. But even here, what the author mainly places in the limelight is the detective's analytical powers as displayed in his special methods of detection.

When Trollope, therefore, debunks the genre for sacrificing the verisimilitude of its characters to what I called the expositional contest ("You have the vehicle without the passengers, a story of mystery in which the agents never spring to live," p. 109), he is forcing an open door. As Edmund Crispin bluntly declares, "orthodox detective fiction is in its essence artificial, contrived and fantastic. In trying to make it less artificial, contrived and fantastic you do not improve it: you simply cease to write it," since "only by making a game of it, by shifting it to a level perceptibly artificial, patently *removed* from reality—only in this way can we decently allow the squalid divagations of the mad or the anti-social to provide regular matter for our entertainment."[10] Trollope and the detective story writer simply postulate, as I shall argue in the next chapter, different kinds of readers (or different faculties of the same reader's mind) with different kinds of interest as well as different talents on the part of the author. The detective novel envisages and implies an alert reader, with a sportsmanlike spirit, a keen interest in mystery, ambiguity, and analytical reasoning (what Trollope derogatorily dismisses as "a patient reader, and one who can content himself with a long protracted and most unemotional excitement"[11]), and a frank enjoyment of craftsmanship in the form of virtuoso literary engineering;[12] whereas Trollope envisages an "open-hearted, rapid reader . . . who will always have his fingers impatiently ready to turn the page" or "the hasty normal reader" (p. 126), one who reads fiction from an interest in the characters, conflicts, and fortunes of human beings like himself and, having little taste for either mystery or craftsmanship and even less inclination to exert himself, demands a straightforward, *lucid*[13] handling of the plot.

What I think most illuminating about this opposition of the poetics of lucidity and the poetics of ambiguity is the way that the disparity in the postulated scales of interest dictates radically different orders of presentation in general and expositional communication in particular. While the detective story necessarily turns on sustained deformations of chronology, with Trollope the possibility of plunging into the middle is ruled out almost automatically, as is any other form of withholding information, since he is determined that no gaps should deflect the reader's attention from the all-important psychological center of interest. A continuous, overmastering manipulation of curiosity and suspense would, of course, be unthinkable; but there must not even be a temporary clash of interests. Therefore, just as the detective story resorts to certain extreme preventive measures to preclude any undesirable distractions, so does Trollope; only the measures taken and the effects they are designed to promote are diametrically opposed. Trollope is more flexible in practice (especially in the handling of suspense, which by its nature depends less than curiosity on the play of temporary gaps) than in theory. Still, he gives some signal instances of the lengths he is prepared to go in order to ensure that the reader's mind should be neither pitched forward to the narrative future nor pulled back to the past but left free to dwell on the succession of narrative presents. In *Barchester Towers,* he takes what many novelists would consider an unthinkable step when he authoritatively dispels a major line of suspense—concerning the matrimonial snares yawning at the heroine— soon after it arises, and repeatedly thereafter, by the reassuring anticipatory comment that "the gentle-hearted reader should be under no apprehension whatsoever. It is not destined that Eleanor shall marry Mr. Slope or Bertie Stanhope" (chap. 15). Conversely, in a defiant statement towards the end of the exposition in *Dr. Wortle's School,* Trollope admirably clarifies his stand with regard to the equally prevalent retardatory practice of heightening curiosity by "artificially" suppressing information:

And now, O kind-hearted reader, I feel myself constrained, in the telling of this little story, to depart altogether from those principles of story-telling to which you probably have become accustomed, and to put the horse of my romance before the cart. There is a mystery concerning Mr. and Mrs. Peacocke which, according to all laws recognized in such matters, ought not to be elucidated till, let us say, the last chapter but two, so that your interest should be maintained almost to the end,—so near the end that there should be left only space for those little arrangements which are necessary for the well-being . . . of our personages. It is my purpose to disclose the mystery at once, and to ask you to look for your interest,—should you choose to go on with my chronicle,—simply in the conduct of my persons, during this disclosure, to others. You are to know it all before the Doctor or the Bishop,—before Mrs. Wortle or the Hon. Mrs. Stantiloup, or Lady de Lawle. You are to know it all before the Peacockes become aware that it must necessarily be disclosed to any one. It may be that when I shall have once told the mystery there will no longer be any room for interest in the tale to you. That there are many such readers of novels I know. I doubt whether the greater number be not such. I am far from saying that the kind of interest of which I am speaking,—and of which I intend to deprive myself,—is not the most natural and the most efficacious. What would the "Black Dwarf" be if every one knew from the beginning that he was a rich man and a baronet? . . . Therefore, put the book down if the revelation of some future secret be necessary for your enjoyment. Our mystery is going to be revealed in the next paragraph,—in the next half-dozen words. Mr. and Mrs. Peacocke were not man and wife. (Chap. 4)

The ordering procedure so boisterously heralded here is in most cases unobtrusively resorted to, as a matter of course. One can imagine, for example, what a mystery a Wilkie Collins would spin round Mary Thorne's birth. Trollope, however, lays all the circumstances before the reader in *Dr. Thorne,* even before the Thornes "become aware that [the mystery] must necessarily be disclosed to any one."

When Trollope chooses for some reason to refrain from neutralizing such potential diversions in advance, he generally sees to it that little doubt should be left as to the filling in of the expositional gaps temporarily kept open. In *Orley Farm,* the reader is not definitely told, until he is more than halfway through the novel, whether Lady Mason has indeed forged the codicil to her husband's will. But since, far from finding the mystery thickened from moment to moment by the distribution of ambiguous clues, the reader is increasingly made morally certain of her guilt, this expositional suppression maintains curiosity at a very moderate pitch. As it later turns out, this device is mainly exploited for dramatic effect; the formal disclosure has been reserved for the climax of the key-scene in which Lady Mason confesses her crime to the incredulous Sir Peregrine. That this mode of handling gaps—strikingly similar in technique, effect, and underlying view of fiction to Hawthorne's concealment of the identity of Hester Prynne's lover in *The Scarlet Letter*—was consciously employed, is established by the comment the narrator makes as soon as Lady Mason has thrown herself at the feet of her fiancé:

> I venture to think, I may almost say to hope, that Lady Mason's confession . . . will not have taken anybody by surprise. If such surprise be felt I must have told my tale badly. I do not like such revulsions of feelings with regard to my characters as surprises of this sort must generate. That Lady Mason had committed the terrible deed for which she was about to be tried, that Mr. Furnival's suspicion of her guilt was only too well founded, that Mr. Dockwrath with his wicked ingenuity has discovered no more than the truth, will, in its open revelation, have caused no surprise to the reader—but it did cause terrible surprise to Sir Peregrine Orme. (Chap. 40)

The categorically rejected "revulsions of feeling" on the reader's part are of course none other than the dynamics of retrospective illumination and progressive revision in which our three control strategies consist.

Trollope does not, of course, always set forth his aims so explicitly. Usually, the full preliminary presentation of exposition is in itself judged sufficient to indicate to the reader at once the kinds of interests the author intends to pursue as well as those to be forgone. To anticipate my argument in the chapter on point of view, by sharing with the reader from the very start the authorial privilege of omniscience, Trollope effectively precludes the state of bafflement from which the reader (as well as the agents) usually suffers and which is deliberately exploited throughout the mystery story for the purpose of maintaining narrative interest. And by thus freeing the reader from the limitations inherent in the human condition, Trollope elevates him to a godlike vantage point that not only prevents what he considers undesirable distractions but is also flattering and enjoyable in itself and, what is more, affords us a rare opportunity of comprehending every shift and twist of the drama played out by the unenlightened characters below.

Trollope, then, may lightheartedly or resignedly advise the reader to "put the book down if the revelation of some future secret be necessary for [his] enjoyment," but in fact he does his best to prevent the threatened rejection by immediately offering an alternative source of potential interest. To avoid falling between two stools, however, he must at all costs ensure that our interest will indeed be captured *at once* by the characters and their interrelations, for we will put up with the absence of one sort of "allurement" in the opening only provided that it is amply compensated for by another. Hence Trollope's constant recourse to preliminary exposition as the only means of straightway immersing the reader in the fictive world and at the same time pulling him up to the desired informational vantage-ground. By starting his sujet with the portrayal of a group of strikingly "real" (and hence, in his opinion, necessarily interesting) characters, with promising points of friction between them, he endeavors to break through or at least reduce our habitual reluctance—discussed in chapter 2—to make the effort required to absorb a mass of preliminaries as long as the essentially generalized and deconcretized situation it depicts and the agents it statically introduces still have to make good their claim to our attention. And for this nucleus to be effectively established, by Trollope's exacting canons of verisimilitude, the exposition clearly must be concentrated and fairly detailed as well as preliminary.

So the setting is usually disposed of with a few broad strokes, and most of the exposition is devoted to planting the dramatis personae upright on their feet. Predictably, these novels differ from the detective story not only in the location and form of exposition but also in the nature of the expositional material selected for presentation, i.e., in the ratio of incident to character. There, most of the exposition consists of a chain of antecedent events; here Trollope moves at a leisurely pace from one character to another, trying to realize each one for us in the strongest, most verisimilar terms. The pattern is more or less uniform: he analyzes at some length the unique combination of universal traits and concrete peculiarities that constitutes the kernel of personality, and fixes the reader's response to it through overt rhetoric; he integrates the character with his environment, gives a short account of his past history, and adds a paragraph or two describing his appearance. These character-sketches are seldom as brilliant as those of George Eliot, the early James, or Dostoyevsky; as James aptly puts it, Trollope gratifies the taste for recognition rather than surprise[14]—and this is as true of his characterization as of the structure of his plots and sentences. But they are for the most part vivid and shrewd, sometimes surprisingly penetrating. Each full-length portrait, at any rate, is designed to impart to the reader all the data necessary for a thorough comprehension of a certain character; it forms an authoritatively stated generalization of which the action or "plot" itself is only a particular dramatized manifestation. And it is his possession of the sum-total of portraits that elevates the reader to his quasi-divine observation post, from which he can catch more than a glimpse of the future as well as see the present in the round.

There is usually no need for Trollope to go out of his way (as he does in *Barchester Towers*) to anticipate the future actions of his characters with a view to endowing the reader with that degree of foreknowledge he judges necessary for his preventive or constructive purposes. The exhaustive preliminary exposition in itself largely invests the reader with prescience, closely interweaving narrative past and future in a straightforward, "natural" structure of probabilities. The extent to which our foreknowledge is certain, however, varies in proportion to the given agent's complexity or heterogeneity of traits. In an important digression in *The Eustace Diamonds,* Trollope formulates the conception of two types of personality (strikingly like Elizabeth Bennet's binary classification of characters into the "simple" and the "deep, intricate" and also E. M. Forster's into the "flat" and the "round") that is, in fact, implicit throughout his work:

> Within the bones and flesh of many of us, there is but one person, a man or woman, with a preponderance either of good or evil, whose conduct in any emergency may be predicted with some assurance of accuracy by any one knowing the man or woman. Such persons are simple, single, and perhaps generally safe. They walk along lines in accordance with certain fixed instincts or principles, and are to-day as they were yesterday, and will be to-morrow as they are to-day. Lady Eustace was such a person, and so was Lucy Morris. Opposite in their characters as the two poles, they were each of them a simple entity; and any doubt or error in judging of the future conduct of either of them would come from insufficient knowledge of the woman. But there are human beings who, though of necessity single in body, are dual in character; in whose breasts not only is evil always fighting against good, but to whom evil is sometimes horribly, hideously evil, but is sometimes also not hideous at all. . . . Such men or women may hardly perhaps debase themselves with the more vulgar vices. They will not be rogues, or thieves, or drunkards, or perhaps liars; but ambition, luxury, self-indulgence, pride and covetousness will get a hold of them, and in various moods will be to them virtues in lieu of vices. Such a man was Frank Greystock. (Chap. 18)

With reference to the first kind of character, our prescience is virtually unlimited (and our suspense, accordingly, purely retardatory). The essentially fixed homogeneity of his traits precludes surprises; and the full introductory analysis of his personality gives us such an intimate knowledge of it that his conduct in any future emergency may indeed be "predicted with some assurance of accuracy." We have little doubt that when faced by a concrete painful choice, Lucy Morris will act nobly, while Lady Eustace will take the easy, mean, or underhand way out. The pleasure we derive from these characters is primarily—as with their Austenian equivalents—one of recurrent recognition, of watching them run true to expositional form in the face of various trials. But this type of character is, in its pure manifestation, seldom enough encountered in Trollope's gallery of portraits too, for to divest a character of his complexity and consequent unpredictability is to divest him of a basic verisimilar feature. Most of Trollope's figures, therefore, not infrequently even the secondary ones, are to a certain extent "dual," and proportionally unpredictable. Whenever the duality takes the form of realistic touches that merely round out the dominant impression of character, we are in effect on as safe a ground as with the "simple entities." In *The Warden,* for instance, the reader is morally certain that, however vehement Archdeacon Grantly's opposition to Mr. Harding's "pusillanimous" resignation of the wardenship, he will not abandon his father-in-law; that however sincere Eleanor Harding's determination to give John Bold up, she will not be able to withstand his entreaties; or, in *Barchester Towers,* that even though Eleanor may like Bertie Stanhope and doggedly stand up for Slope, she is not in much danger of marrying either of them. The only cases of genuine suspense occur when the duality is a fundamental feature, as it is with Frank Greystock, or when the pressure of circumstance on character makes the issue doubtful, as with Mr. Harding, forced into a painful choice between his wish to do the right thing and his horror at having his name bandied about in the press, on the one hand, and his loyalty to the church and fear of the Archdeacon, on the other. Here the preliminary character-sketch foreshadows the outcome of events in a somewhat different way. Its function is to lay the ground for the future conflict by analyzing in generalized terms the latent tensions which are subsequently dramatized in a concrete chain of events, and to narrow down the spectrum of possibilities by indicating the circumstances in which one side or the other, one pull or the other, may dominate; in short, to suggest roughly lines of future conduct. In the exposition of *The Warden,* the narrator, apart from highlighting the general sweetness, generosity, and uprightness of the warden's character, lays such stress on the old man's having so far enjoyed the modest fruits of what his attackers will call his snug clerical sinecure only because it has never occurred to him that "he had received a pound from Hiram's will to which he was not entitled"—that the reader is justifiably led to suspect that in case of a public scandal Mr. Harding is not likely to cling to his wardenship, and that if the Archdeacon tries to oppose that decision he is not going to find the warden as pliant as usual.

The straight sequential interweaving of narrative past, present, and future into a general-particular, premise-proposition, or cause-effect relationship is also calculated, in line with the other aspects of Trollope's compositional strategy, to place the unfolding of character in the limelight. Even the suspense generated by the partial incalculability of the outcome is mainly psychological; among other contributing factors, in Trollope it is mostly plot, including the resolution of events, that bends in response to the pressure of character, not vice versa. The interrelation of temporal directions thus radically differs from that in the *Odyssey,* for instance. There it is brought about so as to dynamize suspense and judgment, the canons of probability being accordingly established not explicitly and authoritatively but implicitly and dubiously, not in a concentrated but in a distributed and discontinuous form, not prior to the action proper but in and through it.

To return to the opening excerpts: as Trollope stakes everything upon his characters appearing on their first introduction to be "living, moving, human creatures," it is no wonder he resolutely maintains that, though fully conscious of the dangers of adhering to the "natural" order, "twist it as I will I cannot do otherwise" than start with a portrait of Dr. Thorne or Mary Lovelace. He considers this the only way of securing the closely related effects of "naturalness," "intelligibility," and "interest" all at once while at the same time canalizing the reader's attention and expectations into the desired grooves.

III

Trollope's expositional modes have thus their artistic grounds. His procedure is doubtless far from exciting, and at times one cannot help feeling that it carries caution and exclusiveness to the point of pusillanimity and narrowness. It is this very extremity, however, that makes Trollope's theory and practice so illuminating an example of both the poetics of disambiguation (profabulaic or even ultrafabulaic "lucidity") and the limitations inherent in any artistic choice. It appears that there may be some important interests or particular forms of interests in the pursuit of which the novelist may be inclined or even compelled to forgo to a smaller or larger extent those effects that decisively depend on a prolonged, deliberate, and perceptible suppression of antecedents. Trollope's lesson is, therefore, particularly applicable to those works that postulate a center of interest that does not go well with the constant pull of attention away from the narrative present, or from the specific way the text unfolds from moment to moment, to the expositional past. This, strangely enough, is true even of works that refrain from opening with a preliminary exposition or from adhering throughout to the chronological sequence.

To mention one instance, in spite of Thackeray's frequent plunges *in medias res* and the numerous temporal doublings and redoublings in which he indulges,[15] his deviations from chronology in general and his delay and distribution of exposition in particular differ significantly in manner and effect from Homer's or Dickens's. The sustained manipulation of gaps in the interests of curiosity and suspense presupposes, as I have explained, a tight causal concatenation of the plot, for it is insofar as the reader is made aware of having been plunged in the midst of a causal chain that he feels the lack of the antecedent premises or links. However, Thackeray's ambition of painting a panoramic picture of society is of course hardly compatible with the limitations imposed by a rigid causal sequence. On the contrary, he was right to conclude that his goal could best be realized within a structural framework that is loose and comprehensive enough to lend itself to the incessant introduction, grouping, and regrouping of a host of characters from various social strata, some of whom are rarely, if ever, brought into contact in terms of the action.[16] Moreover, since a novel like *Vanity Fair,* qua "picture," turns more on spatial than temporal development, Thackeray is justifiably chary of resorting overmuch to effects that exclusively depend for their resolution on the linear progression of the sujet. To keep the reader in a perpetual state of curiosity and suspense would be to distract his attention from the postulated focus of interest—the slow unfolding of the panorama with its multitude of components, the combination and interaction of characters, the shift and twist of analogical relationships, and the constant flow of commentary poured out by the philosophizing, reminiscential, gossipy showman of the human comedy.

These exigencies largely account for Thackeray's habitual order of presentation and expositional modes. Unlike Trollope, he is by no means contemptuous of such effects as curiosity and suspense, but he rarely keeps them at a high pitch or pursues them over long stretches of the tale.[17] He may choose for example to open his novels (*Vanity Fair* or *Pendennis*) by rushing into the midst of a dramatic scene; but while Homer proceeds to manipulate the gaps opened early in the *Odyssey* for about half of the epic, Thackeray hastens to double back as soon as he has tied a knot in time and captured the reader's interest. The same applies to the delay of nonexpositional passages of summary to a point where the occasion they are designed to illuminate retrospectively is already well under way. Similarly, while in retardatory structures most overt anticipations are calculated to arouse suspense, Thackeray's narrator exploits his foreknowledge primarily to enable the reader to see all round an incident by juxtaposing or stringing together its present and future repercussions. It is appropriate, finally, that Thackeray's favorite narrative interest should be surprise, an effect that hinges on a previously imperceptible suppression or ambiguation of information. Its mode of operation being retrospective, this effect (e.g., the springing of Becky's marriage on Sir Pitt Crawley *and* the reader) does not distract the reader's attention from the panoramic tour through society in the way curiosity or suspense might do.[18]

Thackeray's temporal strategy is thus more flexible than Trollope's, but the difference in their attitude towards the complex of purely narrative interests is ultimately one of degree.[19] With authors who actually stick to the chronological order when society is their protagonist (e.g., Graves's *I, Claudius*), the correspondence is even closer.

In a sense, however, not only Thackeray but even Trollope and Graves seldom fail to delay and distribute a great deal of exposition. By its very nature, the portrayal of a social panorama presupposes a large cast of characters from different locations and classes, or in other words, several loosely interwoven strands. The author, therefore, cannot possibly begin by introducing all of his dramatis personae. He must start with a single set, spatial arena, or social nucleus from which the action later branches out into other groups, whose delayed entrance is prefaced with such chapter headings as "New Faces," or some equivalent. *Vanity Fair,* for example, begins with Amelia and Becky, and then passes on to the Sedleys, George Osborne, Dobbin, the Crawleys, the O'Dowds, Lady Southdown and her daughters, etc., each of whom is separately presented in a more or less proper, formal manner. However, the various expositional blocks thus intercalated are delayed in name—since they obviously belong to that part of the fabula preceding our temporal point of reference in the sujet—but not necessarily in effect. They are formally delayed but not suppressed, the delay deriving from the compositional exigencies of what may well be a chronologically propelled action (e.g., in a picaresque, spatially variegated novel with a single line of progression) and/or the limitations of the verbal medium (which, being linear, cannot simultaneously represent two or more actional strands). The definition of delayed exposition must then be further qualified, in terms of the functionality of informational unfolding —not least (see Section 7 on Balzac below) the unfolding of fictive space. A datum or sequence of motifs is really delayed only if the reader expects or misses it before it is actually imparted to him; or—when its disclosure comes as a surprise—if it retrospectively illuminates what has gone before, reshaping the reader's response to the action, the characters, or the fictive framework. The suppression of Odysseus's heroic powers may serve to illustrate the first possibility; that of his Autolycan traits, the second.

In conclusion, when such novelists as Trollope and Thackeray try to transcend their limitations by delaying exposition and manipulating referential gaps, they usually come a cropper. I have already commented on Thackeray's handling of gaps and retardatory structure in *Pendennis.* His attempt in the same novel to construct a small-scale mystery plot also results in a pathetic failure. As Thackeray is not too adept in the distribution of ambiguous clues, the reader all too soon penetrates the secret of Colonel Altamont's identity and the nature of his hold on Sir Francis; and the last-moment discovery that Amory, alias Altamont, is a bigamist into the bargain (cf. Trollope's *Dr. Wortle's School*) is so artificially contrived that one can only shut one's eyes in despair.

The mystery plot in *The Last Chronicle of Barset* is equally botched but even more detrimental. It forms a superlative demonstration of its author's fictional theory, including the admission that he has "never been capable of constructing with complete success the intricacies of a plot that required to be unravelled" (pp. 236–37). He himself notes its implausibility (p. 236), but does not appear to see that its gravest deficiency goes much deeper. The exploration of Crawley's tortured mind is conducted with so sure a hand and so delicate a touch that it cannot fail to monopolize the reader's attention and would therefore make the introduction of a line of detective interest infuriatingly distracting even in the best of cases. But the very insight Trollope gives us into the clergyman's psychology nullifies the interest of this sideline in advance. We cannot for a single moment believe Crawley capable of stealing a check, just as, in a diametrically opposed case, the revelation of Lady Mason's guilt indeed causes us no surprise. So given Crawley's ordeal as the dominating center of interest, the whole detective theme—the persistent suppression of the circumstances in which the check came into Crawley's hands, and particularly the plodding investigation, held by Mr. Toogood soon after the establishment of his relative's innocence, in order to unmask the real culprit, a person totally unrelated to the main theme—loses its raison d'être. And the worse than amateurish handling of the plot only heightens our sense of waste. It is a pity indeed that the predictable failure attending Trollope's endeavor to out-Collins Wilkie Collins (aided and abetted by the inept subplots) should have fatally marred what I think was potentially one of the finest psychological studies of the nineteenth century.

IV

Revealing as Trollope's case is, however, it illustrates only some of the possible functions of preliminary and concentrated exposition. And since in Trollope these modes of presentation are more preventive than constructive, it is perhaps no wonder that I have not found even a single introduction of his interesting enough to merit thorough analysis. What I believe of prime importance are the theoretical implications of his lesson as a whole. In order to demonstrate how similar modes of presentation may be constructively exploited for purposes that are more various, flexible, and daring, I wish to cross the Channel and turn to Balzac.

Of the writers addicted to preliminary and concentrated exposition, Balzac is generally considered the worst offender. Henry James, one of his earliest and most penetrating critics, used to shudder at "the custom of the seated mass of explanation after the fact, the inserted block of merely referential narrative, which flourishes so, to the shame of the modern impatience, on the serried page of Balzac, but which seems simply to appal our actual, our general weaker, digestion."[20] And there are few readers, I think, that will entirely fail to sympathize with this complaint. He must be stout-hearted indeed who does not quail, momentarily at least, at the prospect of sweating through two or three dozen closed-packed expositional pages, almost unrivaled for their density of evocation, before he can catch a glimpse of the relatively short "real kernel" of the tale. At the beginning of *Père Goriot,* for example, the reader is informed that the novel will be concerned with the "hidden sorrows of Père Goriot";[21] but before being introduced to Goriot even by way of exposition, he needs must traverse a formidable introductory tract. As anybody acquainted with his work knows but too well, Balzac is rarely content with a condensed account of his dramatis personae's careers combined with brief character-sketches, but feels it incumbent upon him thoroughly to evoke their environment as well. The quarter and the street in which Madame Vauquer's boardinghouse is situated are first represented in all their gloom, dreariness, and squalor (pp. 4–5). Balzac goes on to describe in more detail the house itself and its precincts—the walk running parallel to it, the door with its noisy bell, the garden and its meager produce, the ugly yellow façade with its small windows, and even the drain at the back (pp. 5–6). The reader is then led into the house itself and treated to a depiction of its interior. The somber salon is rendered with gusto—the faded upholstery, the marble-topped table, the ugly blue clock, and the close, rancid smell. Next, the even more horrible dining room is systematically tackled, with the layers of dirt on the walls, the clipped carafes, the stained napkins, the engravings so nauseating "as to spoil one's appetite," the greasy oilcloth, the rickety chairs, and the indented red tiles of the floor (pp. 6–8). An outline of the boarding-house routine follows, accompanied by a masterly evocation of the frowsy, obese landlady and her sharply individualized lodgers—the angular and disfigured Mademoiselle Michonneau with the dirty shade of green taffeta over her eyes; the machinelike, spindle-shanked Poiret; the sweet, suffering Victorine Taillefer; the pious Madame Couture; the handsome, ambitious Rastignac; and the robust, gregarious, cynical Vautrin (pp. 8–18). It is only at this late point that the reader reaches the account of Goriot's career in the pension and his relations with its inmates (pp. 18–31); and the first discriminated occasion soon ensues.

Owing to its length, density, and preliminary location, this typical Balzacian exposition doubtless proves hard going even for the patient reader, while to the impatient it offers a liberal chance to be bored. On the other hand, there is no doubt either that Balzac knows what he is about in his bulky expositions and that, like Trollope, he consciously takes the risk of incurring the reader's displeasure by ostensibly robbing his opening pages of their potential allurement. Having completed his exhaustive evocation of the Vauquer dining room, for example, Balzac wryly comments, in one of his rare humorous asides, that "to explain how old this furniture is, how cracked and rotten and shaky and worn, how deformed, how lopsided, and sick and dying, we should have to embark upon a description which would too long delay our start on the story and which hurried readers would not pardon" (p. 8). And at the start of *La Recherche de l'absolu* he earnestly insists on the need for "these didactic preparations against which some ignorant and voracious persons see fit to protest." The rhetorical disadvantages this procedure involves are evident. What remains to be discovered is, again, its goals and gains.

Henry James was among the first critics to take Balzac's historical pretensions at face value, accounting for the wealth of detail in the Frenchman's works in terms of his heroic ambition to leave a full record of contemporary society and manners, with each story an integral piece in the vast mosaic of the Human Comedy. According to him, the key to the understanding of Balzac lies in the tragic duality of his nature:

> Of imagination on one side all compact, he was on the other an insatiable reporter of the immediate, the material, the current combination, and perpetually moved by the historian's impulse to fix, preserve, and explain them. One asks one's self as one reads him what concern the poet has with so much arithmetic and so much criticism, so many statistics and documents, what concern the critic and the economist have with so many passions, characters and adventures. The contradiction is always before us; it springs from the inordinate scale of the author's two faces; it explains more than anything else his eccentricities and difficulties. It accounts for his want of grace . . . his bristling surface, his closeness of texture, so rough with richness, yet so productive of the effect we have in mind when we speak of not being able to see the wood for the trees.[22]

James readily admits that Balzac's unequaled power of setting his figures on their feet and immersing the reader in his world is to be attributed to this very solidity of specification. But the trouble is, he claims, that Balzac does not know where to stop. Incapable of subordinating his ogre's voracity for facts and encyclopedic knowledge of society to his artistic aims, he constantly succumbs to the historian's urge to record and preserve whatever happens to meet his eye. He fails to realize (James argues) that the historian and the creative artist operate according to two different laws of selection, which "can with no sort of congruity or harmony make, for the finer sense, a common household." While art thrives, as James never wearies of reiterating, upon rigorous, economical, strictly functional selection, in the interests of thematic significance and compositional beauty, the historian in Balzac incessantly impels him to indulge in the accumulation and inclusion of facts as facts, in the interests of historical completeness: "To be colossally and exhaustively complete—complete not only in the generals but in the particulars—to touch upon every salient point, to illuminate every typical feature, to reproduce every sentiment, every idea, every person, every place, every object, that has played a part, however minute, however obscure, in the life of the French people—nothing less than this was his programme."[23] In his ambition to outdo professional historians and supply their omissions as concerns the preservation of the manners of the day, he pounces on every opportunity for the evocation of background and social phenomena, human and inanimate, as an end in itself. Everything is grist to his mill; with his inimitable descriptive talent he squeezes every orange dry "till it cries out, we hardly know whether for pleasure or pain." His inordinate hunger for facts even drives him to invent pretexts for giving rein to his passion for detail. A minor character is as fully presented, with his whole bunch of concomitants, as the major agents; a place that fleetingly appears upon the fictive stage is dwelt on out of all proportion to its contextual significance. "He moves always in the mass; wherever we find him, we find him in force; whatever touch he applies, he applies it with his whole apparatus. He is like an army gathered to besiege a cottage equally with a city, and living voraciously in either case on all the country about."[24]

So compositional tightness is frequently cast to the winds; aesthetic effects are subordinated to—or at best mingled with—scientific or social ends; the creative imagination spends its strength in warming arrays of factual data into life; the dragging in of superfluous background descriptions often throws the work out of focus and diverts the reader's attention from the inner life of the characters to their environment; the habit of striking too many matches paradoxically produces obscurity; and waste reigns supreme. It is this irreconcilable duality, usually resulting in the triumph of the insatiate historian, social philosopher, and man of business over the novelist (James sadly concludes) that accounts for the anomaly that "the first and foremost member of his craft" and "the father of us all" is,[25] in spite of the magnificence of his achievement, a failure as an artist.

I have chosen to dwell on James's strictures because, apart from their embodying a number of oft-repeated claims that it would be worthwhile to examine, they at the same time afford us another opportunity of witnessing how the clash between general conceptions of the art of fiction entails differences in the handling of such compositional problems as exposition and temporal structure. The excerpt with which I started this section might give the impression that what James finds objectionable about Balzac's preliminary and concentrated expositions is the "digestive" complications to which they are liable to give rise: that he mainly finds fault with them—as Trollope seems to do with regard to the opposite procedure of the plunge *in medias res*—on the grounds of narrative interest. In fact, James's objections too are much more fundamental, deriving from preconceived hierarchies of significance. It turns out that he denounces the minuteness of Balzac's expositions largely because he is opposed to some of Balzac's most cherished aims, the legitimacy of which as potential artistic interests he is simply not prepared to admit—neither in Balzac's case nor in that of the younger English novelists of his own day.[26] With his own artistic ideals constantly before his eyes and his customary monistic approach, he deprecates a priori any attempt to shift even part of the reader's interest, let alone its center, from the arena of the mind, the subtle interplay of motive and the ordeal of consciousness, to the social panorama with its material background, the "packed and constituted, the palpable, provable world."[27] In his own politely scathing idiom, Balzac's universe smells so much of *things* that "the larger ether, the diviner air, is in peril of finding among them scarce room to circulate."[28]

James cannot, in short, bring himself to concede that the disparity between his own and Balzac's principles of expositional selection and combination may derive from their different, but equally legitimate, interests and aims, or from their preference for different compositional strategies by which similar ends are to be encompassed. Whatever fits in with his own view of the novel is artistic; whatever fails to conform to this exquisite Procrustean bed is damned with faint or ardent praise and dismissed in terms of a vicious, wasteful, irresistible historical urge.

It is true that in Balzac's weaker works, some of which are cited by James, the procession of expositional lumps forms a rambling, ill-placed agglomeration of details that contributes not a little to the general sense of failure. It is also true that in most of his works the massive exposition is designed to immerse the reader in a world that is lifelike in its dense specificity and to promote his belief in the reality of the minutely evoked figures. After all, Balzac is said to have called for his own Dr. Bianchon when on his deathbed, just as Trollope claimed to have spent much of his time in the company of Mrs. Proudie. I intend to argue, however, that to explain Balzac's procedure in terms of historical or realistic fullness of presentation is not only to oversimplify his aims but also to fail to do justice to the manifold artistic functionality of the combination of preliminary location and concentrated form that characterizes most of his expositions.

V

It may at first appear that, in order to encompass as much as possible of the material and human background, the exposition in *Père Goriot* digressively proceeds by purely metonymic transitions—that is, quasi-mimetic transitions based on contiguity in time or space or both—from street to house, from house to rooms, from rooms to landlady, and so on, each represented object being dwelt on sufficiently to meet the author's standards of realistic evocation.[29] What may further reinforce this suspicion is that the metonymic logic of progression indeed characterizes many concentrated expositions, whether preliminary or delayed. Trollope's *Dr. Wortle's School,* for example, starts with an account of the headmaster, proceeds to introduce his wife and daughter, and then passes on to the setting. The next two chapters concentrate on one of the schoolmasters, Mr. Peacocke, and his wife, shifting back and forth from their appearance and character to their history at Dr. Wortle's school, and ending with the disclosure of their guilty secret. By the beginning of chapter 4, Trollope has thus managed, through a succession of essentially metonymic transitions, both spatial and temporal, to embrace the whole of the bulky expositional nucleus from which his action is to branch out. At times, moreover, the metonymic principle of progression and elaboration indeed forms a convenient, transparent device or pretext for the author's giving rein to what James calls the historian's impulse to record and preserve. The unreasonably long introduction to the Thornes of Ullathorne in *Barchester Towers* (chap. 22) is a good case in point. The reason why these indisputably minor figures should be accorded a more detailed portrayal than any of the principal agents is suggested from the start: "Wilfred Thorne, Esq., of Ullathorne . . . was a fair specimen of what that race of squires has come to in our days which, a century ago, was . . . fairly represented by Squire Western." His chief interest, then, is that of a social type. Trollope accordingly gives an exhaustive account, liberally interspersed with anecdotes, of his foibles, his old-fashioned literary taste, his exaggerated regard for blood and pedigree, his extreme political conservatism, etc. The following portrayal of his sister, the "living caricature of all his foibles," proceeds along similar lines but is considerably shorter, taking up no more than three close-packed pages. From this point on, the purpose underlying the frequent metonymic transitions becomes increasingly conspicuous. As soon as he has finished with Miss Thorne, Trollope observes: "While we are on the subject of the Thornes, one word must be said of the house they lived in. . . . By those who love the peculiar colour and peculiar ornaments of genuine Tudor architecture it was considered a perfect gem. We beg to own ourselves among the number." And so he embarks on a description of Ullathorne Court with a view to rousing

Englishmen to an appreciation of their national art treasures. Then he comments: "Such was the interior of Ullathorne Court. But having thus described it, perhaps somewhat too tediously, we beg to say that it is not the interior to which we wish to call the English tourist's attention. . . . It is the outside of Ullathorne that is so lovely," etc. But the guided tour is not over yet, as we learn a page later: "Such is Ullathorne Court. But we must say one word of the approach to it, which shall include all the description which we mean to give of the church also." And the chapter ends on the same note as it has begun: "Such, we believe, are the inhabitants of many an English country-home. May it be long before their number diminishcs."

In *Père Goriot,* however, as often in Balzac, the concentrated exposition is organized on tighter and more significant principles. Its movement is not centrifugal but centripetal; and its line of progress is not accidental but carefully calculated, so that the stages it passes through are not largely interchangeable as in Trollope. The novel does not start with the presentation of a single figure and then push outward in the direction of other characters or the setting by indiscriminate widening strokes. Here the principle of expositional development may be described in terms we have used for *Pride and Prejudice* to describe the *reconstitutive* structure of probabilities rather than the *actual* progression or unfolding of the text: namely, as the successive drawing of ever-narrowing concentric circles, starting from what is under the circumstances the widest possible circumference—the quarter in *Père Goriot,* or in novels of provincial life, such as *Eugénie Grandet,* the town as a whole—and proceeding to the street, the façade of the house and its garden, the interior of the house (rooms and furniture), the dress of the dramatis personae, their physical appearance, and their character.

Moreover, although the transitions from one expositional circle to another are ostensibly either metonymic or, in most cases, synecdochic, the links between them are at the same time metaphorical or analogical, too. For the relations between the different objects presented are based not on contiguity alone but also on similarity. The text closely interconnects the various circles by suggesting numerous correspondences between them—some common to all and others only to a few, some serving purely compositional, unifying functions and others thematically significant as well. The striking recurrence of certain colors, for example, mainly operates as a linking device. Thus, the two monuments located in the quarter, the Val de Grâce and the Panthéon, impart a *yellow* tone to the atmosphere (p. 4); the façade of the boarding-house is daubed with yellow (pp. 6, 18); the teacups in the drawing room have faded gold bands around them (p. 7); the dining room engravings are framed in varnished wood with gold stripes (p. 9); Madame Couture's curtains are of yellow calico (p. 19);

Poiret's cane has a knob of yellow ivory (p. 13); and Victorine resembles a shrub with yellow leaves (p. 14).

In themselves, linking radii of this kind are of little actional or thematic import; but their abundance encourages the reader to look for additional, and more significant, correspondences between the different concentric rings, such as the actual or metaphorical filth and disfigurement that are common to all of them. In some of Balzac's tales these implicit linkages are all the reader has to go upon, and he is compelled to do most of the integrative work by himself. But here the narrator considers it so essential to put the reader on the scent that he once goes out of his way to comment on the close similarity between the shabby clothes of the lodgers and the recently evoked look of the rooms: "The disheartening spectacle of the appearance of the rooms of the boarding-house was repeated in the costumes of the residents, all of them seedy and worn. The men wore frock-coats so faded that their color was doubtful [cf. pp. 8–9: "The dining room . . . was long ago painted in some color which cannot be discerned today"], shoes such as are seen lying in the gutters of the more fashionable districts [cf. "those indestructible pieces of furniture proscribed from every other place"], linen which had frayed [cf. "carafes which are dirty and chipped," "rickety chairs," "broken footwarmers"]— in a word, costumes in which only the idea survived," etc. (pp. 11–12).

The network of analogical links spread all over the opening already indicates that the various objects presented in it have not been selected at random, nor merely by virtue of their realistic vividness. Their function, moreover, is not confined to the establishment of compositional and tonal unity but also relates to Balzac's modes of characterization.

Balzac may give the impression of being an artist who operates in a loud, explicit manner, leaving little to be conveyed by implication. But a comparison of his character-sketches with those of other novelists—Trollope or Dostoyevsky for example—brings out a striking difference. Direct characterizing epithets are relatively scarce in Balzac's dossiers; and when they do appear, the reader is not asked to accept them on the narrator's more or less gentlemanly word of honor, but finds them warranted and reinforced by situational chapter and verse. Balzac tends to characterize his agents largely in an indirect way, so as to suggest their inner traits through the outer circumstances enveloping them; if the exposition forms a series of concentric circles, its ever-narrowing centripetal movement indicates that the kernel of character is their center and focal point. The principle of progression, then, is significant in the same way as the cinematic close-up. And the firm analogical relations between the circles, including those of dress and appearance, strongly imply that the environmental contexts form a complex of objective correlatives for the elusive, hardly formulable traits of personality. Itself part of the represented reality, the spatial arena is used to signify and round out another part of that reality.

In the case of Madame Vauquer, the first character to be introduced, this metaphorical relationship is elaborately established:

> Her plump little hands, her body fat as a church rat's, her prominent pendulous breasts, are all in harmony with [the dining] room which is dripping with unhappiness, vacant of all speculation, and full of warm stale air which Madame Vauquer breathes without any sense of disgust.
>
> That face of hers, as nipping as the first autumn frost, those wrinkled eyes . . . indeed her whole person gives the clue to the boarding-house, just as the boarding-house implies such a mistress as Madame Vauquer. You cannot imagine a jail without a jailer. The unhealthy obesity of this little woman is a product of this life of hers, just as typhus fever is the product of the exhalations in a hospital. Her skirt is made of an old dress, and through its rents the wadding projects; beneath it falls her woollen petticoat; and these clothes sum up the drawing room, the dining room, the little garden, explain the kitchen and give an idea of the boarders. The moment she is here, the spectacle is complete. (P. 9)

The idea of the close relationship between environment and character has by now become an integral part of modern man's world view; but it largely goes back to Balzac, who constantly insists on it in his pseudo-scientific treatises, in comments scattered through his stories,[30] and especially in his techniques of characterization. In this quotation we have the theory in a nutshell. The reciprocal interaction of character and milieu forms a complicated two-way causal relationship, where each factor is simultaneously cause and effect. On the one hand, Madame Vauquer has, qua landlady, made the pension what it is—she has chosen, furnished, and managed it according to her own ideas and nature. On the other hand, the pension has left its mark upon the landlady in that it has sustained, brought out, and developed some features that were latent in her—most conspicuously, her unhealthy obesity and disgusting dowdiness. The creation has as it were assumed a life of its own, which has imposed itself on its creator. So the two have merged into each other to the extent that neither can be described or understood in isolation; in Balzac's favorite metaphor, they are oyster and shell. Both the causal relationship and the close analogical correspondences between the two imply, moreover, that the establishment is a projection of the personality of its mistress in a more than merely physical sense; they persuasively suggest that the filth, mustiness, dilapidation, and stench pervading the pension are external, dramatized analogues of corresponding moral and psychological traits that characterize the landlady.[31]

Balzac's indirect mode of characterization in *Père Goriot* takes subtler forms as well. I have emphasized that Balzac is not content with evoking a character's outermost shell but makes a point of drawing a set of concentric circles round him. This structured specificity is designed to suggest some fine differentiations between the various inmates. Of all these it is ultimately Madame Vauquer alone who has freely chosen to live in the boarding-house, who is responsible for its appearance and management, and who is fairly satisfied with her life and even proud of her position as queen of this "private almhouse" (p. 18). Whereas the fact that this or that lodger is reduced to living there reveals in itself his finances rather than his character; it merely implies that he has been "condemned to carry a load of misfortunes more or less obvious" (p. 11). The outer rings, therefore, can be regarded as metonymic equivalents of character-traits only when corresponding to the inner, those closer to the kernel of personality—those for which the lodgers themselves can be held responsible (such as dress) and particularly that immanent in them, namely, physical appearance.

With one group of lodgers—composed of Mlle. Michonneau and Poiret —there is basically a one to one correspondence between quarter, house, furniture, dress, and appearance, e.g., in point of ugliness, dirtiness, and decrepitude. So the mutually reinforcing set of analogical indicators establish their nature beyond doubt, as effectively as any series of epithets could do. It is suggested that they partake of the nature of everything enveloping them: their lives are as rotten as the furniture and as stained as their dress; their passions as dried out or unnaturally bloated as their bodies, etc. This conclusion is further validated by the multiplicity of analogical links connecting them with Madame Vauquer, the embodiment of the boarding-house spirit. The dress of all three is dirty or crumpled; their past is shrouded in mystery; Poiret's fleshless legs correspond to Michonneau's skeletal figure and his swollen face to Vauquer's obese body; and, as I shall later show, they are all projected in terms of pejorative animal imagery.

With the rest of the characters, on the other hand, the disparity between narrower and wider circles implies that they have not yet been submerged by the spirit of the boarding-house and are to some extent out of place there. This is especially noticeable with the two youngest lodgers, Rastignac and Victorine. Their clothes, cheap and worn but not filthy, and their handsome looks set them apart from the previous trio—indicating that they have not yet fallen prey to the general atmosphere of stagnation and decay. For them there is still some hope. At the same time, it is implied that due to the conditioning effect of environment on those long exposed to it, they had better extricate themselves from the place before it is too late. Victorine's temper and what may be called her existential fiber or vitality are already being undermined. She has already acquired the unhealthy complexion "which had a likeness to the pervading suffering which formed the background of the picture"; and she is subtly compared to "a shrub whose yellowed leaves show that it has just been planted in a soil that does not suit it" (p. 14). Yellow being one of the dominant colors in the evocation of setting as well as the conventional color of decay, the yellowing leaves of this delicate shrub suggest that her growing resemblance to the "yellow" pension is identical with her gradual withering.

To the functions of other instances of a clash between personality and environment I shall refer later. What I now wish to stress is that, though the concentration of exposition involves the introduction of a multiplicity of details and characters and endows Balzac's spatial arena with a remarkable solidity of specification, there is little danger of the reader's failing to see the wood for the trees. On the contrary, the analogical links that interweave the fictive objects presented, living and inanimate, produce a strong sense of unity in variety, highlighting similarities and contrasts of character and situation, or contrasts of character in face of the unifying similarities in situation. Balzac's devices of indirect characterization, moreover, are not only economical but also particularly suited to his purpose, since in the exposition at least he is interested in evoking modes of existence rather than modes of consciousness, or more precisely still, in evoking a dominant mode of existence to which several characters fail to conform precisely because its nature is incompatible with theirs. The whole weight of the exposition is thus implicitly brought to bear on the presentation of each character, though in different ways— with some suggesting collapse, stagnation, or resignation, and with others, notably Rastignac, bringing into relief present malaise and laying the ground for future rebellion. The former, of course, serve as foils to the latter, as static elements almost invariably do in relation to their dynamic counterparts.

The artfulness and flexibility of Balzac's selective procedure are revealed in the information withheld as well as in that communicated. Although the introductory summary seems to be at least as exhaustive as any of Trollope's, the narrator, far from telling us all he could—or should, according to James's presentation of his aims and habitual practice—actually opens a considerable number of expositional gaps of varying importance, giving rise to multiple hypotheses (or systems of gap-filling) about character and event. While with Trollope the three aspects of temporal structuring (location, form, and order) are concomitant and mutually implicative, with Balzac preliminary and concentrated exposition is perfectly compatible with chronological displacement and referential ambiguity, temporary and permanent. He has chosen, for instance, to refrain from imparting to the reader the histories of Vauquer, Michonneau and Poiret, thereby creating a notable discrepancy in specification between the temporal and spatial dimensions of his fictive arena. Thus, while reporting Michonneau's own account of her past life ("she had looked after an old man suffering from catarrh of the bladder," etc.) and strongly intimating that he doubts its veracity ("Her story was . . ."), the narrator pretends to be as ignorant as her fellow-lodgers as to the true circumstances of the degeneration of the once beautiful woman into the present harridan: "What acid had taken away from this creature a woman's contours? . . . Was it vice or grief or cupidity? Had she loved too well, had she been a dealer in second-hand clothes, had she been a courtesan? Was she expiating the victories of an insolent youth packed with pleasure by an old age so horrible that passers-by avoided her?" (p. 12). Similarly, after depicting Poiret's repulsive appearance, the narrator deliberately draws the reader's attention to his suppression of the truth concerning the boarder's past career: "What sort of work had worn him down to this? What passion had ruined his swollen face, which, had it been a caricature, would have been judged incredible? What had he been?" And he again puts forward a number of hypotheses—Poiret may have worked "in the office where executioners send in their expense accounts. . . . Perhaps he had stood at the gate of an abattoir or been a subinspector of sanitation" (p. 13)—without, however, deciding between them.

Unlike some modern novelists, Balzac does not confine himself to this conjectural presentation of antecedents in order to circumvent such self-imposed limitations as a rigorously restricted point of view or an abstention from "telling" and overt commentary. On the contrary, the fact that his narrator usually flaunts his omniscience and freely indulges in intrusive address throws these sudden lapses of knowledge into relief.

In fact, where the ideal of historical completeness or realistic fullness should have dictated as thoroughgoing a report of the past careers of his dramatis personae as of their present surroundings, Balzac prefers to leave a tantalizing gap in order to produce a purely aesthetic effect. He shows himself as aware as James himself that leaving a gap open and throwing out suggestions or conjectures about how it should be filled in often makes for much more effective characterization and manipulation of response than explicitly and authoritatively disambiguating it with a "weak specification." As James admirably puts it when explaining his decision to refrain from specifying the villainy of the dead servants in *The Turn of the Screw*:

> Portentous evil—how was I to save that, as an intention on the part of my demon-spirits, from the drop, the comparative vulgarity, inevitably attending, throughout the whole range of possible brief illustration, the offered example, the imputed vice, the cited act, the limited deplorable presentable instance? . . . There is for such a case no eligible *absolute* of the wrong; it remains relative to fifty other elements,

a matter of a appreciation, speculation, imagination—these things, more-over, quite exactly in the light of the spectator's, the critic's, the reader's experience. Only make the reader's general vision of evil intense enough, I said to myself . . . and his own experience, his own imagina-tion, his own sympathy (with the children) and horror (of their false friends) will supply him quite sufficiently with all the particulars. Make him *think* the evil, make him think it for himself, and you are released from weak specifications.[32]

Different as the gaps in James's *nouvelle* and those mentioned here are in point of referential and thematic centrality, their function and manner of operation are not dissimilar. It is owing to Balzac's indirect mode of characterization that he can not only free himself from total dependence on colorless epithets but also leave some of the gaps sugestively open. Instead of committing himself to a single "limited deplorable presentable instance," he impels the reader's imagination, already kindled by the intense evocation of background, to brood on the spectrum of possibilities offered by the narrator, discover the compatibility of *all* of them with the implications of the concentric circles that envelop these characters, and consequently accept and be affected by the *sum-total* of hypotheses, however factually heterogeneous, and perhaps even add some of his own. Through this deft interrelation of (conspicuously realized) space and (conspicuously gapped) time, the sense of the two characters' shameful, shady, possibly vicious careers is richly and economically conveyed.[33] Moreover, by leaving these ambiguities open Balzac achieves a density of suggestion of another kind as well. He partly divests Poiret and his female analogue of their "concreteness" and turns them into illustrative types that stand for a wide variety of failures and frustrations, all of them finding their natural refuge at Madame Vauquer's.

So far I have dealt only with permanent gaps. The temporary gaps, however, that the narrator opens in his preliminary exposition only to resolve the consequent play of hypotheses definitely and authoritatively later on, are equally functional. When communicating Goriot's anteced-ents, for instance, Balzac again restricts himself, as it were, to the collec-tive point of view of the pension—imparting to the reader only what the inmates have ferreted out or conjectured. So the reader learns about Goriot's initial prosperous appearance; the failure of Madame Vauquer's matrimonial designs; her hostility to him, increasingly coming into the open from the first manifestations of his financial decline; and the success of her petty plan of revenge owing to the ready cooperation of the lodgers, who have reduced Goriot to the position of local butt of raillery and horseplay. But since the boarding-house world has not been able to get the taciturn Goriot to talk about his early career, the reasons for his growing impoverishment, or his occasional lady visitors, the reader is only treated to the numerous conjectures in which the inquisitive boarders indulge: Goriot has ruined himself with speculations; Goriot is a gambler; a police spy; a usurer; an old libertine with perverted tastes, sucked dry by the mistresses he tries to pass off as daughters in order to keep up appearences (pp. 26 ff).

The narrator repeatedly notes that these speculations are no more than "fairy tales" (p. 26); but he nevertheless chooses to leave the reader temporarily in the dark as to the true explanation of Goriot's career and conduct. And he reaps a number of benefits from this combination of a false preliminary outside view and a delayed true exposition. First, by strongly stimulating the reader's curiosity about this central gap, he paves the way for the disclosure "of the hidden sorrows of Père Goriot" promised right at the outset of the novel (p. 4). Second, the delay of the reliable retrospect enables Balzac to insinuate the abnormality of Goriot's passions, while its communication (pp. 77–80, 90–93) powerfully throws Goriot's selflessness into relief against the malicious gossip of the pension and reinforces the theme of the cynicism and heartlessness of society (epitomized by the pension). The effect of the distribution and the delay of the expositional material relating to Goriot might have been stronger still had Balzac, like Faulkner in *Light in August,* first induced the reader to give credence to the lodgers' libelous hypotheses and then drastically demolished the primary impression by springing the sad truth upon him. However, in spite of the narrator's anticipatory hints, the contrast between the two expositional versions effectively manipulates our response to Goriot vis-à-vis his milieu and drives home the thematic point.

Third, and perhaps most noteworthy, the narrator's choice of Rastignac to disambiguate Goriot's antecedents in a dramatized process of gap-filling settles the controversial question of the identity of the protagonist in this novel.[34] The distribution of expositional material suggests that the center of interest is neither Parisian society nor even Père Goriot himself but the initiation and development of the young student who, determined "to fathom the mysteries of a terrible situation" (p. 11), learns the first lesson about the corruption of the fashionable world through the moral pointed by Goriot's tale (pp. 76 ff). The fact that the reader is in effect limited to Rastignac's perspective, sharing his ignorance when, like the rest of the boarders, he is baffled by the mystery that shrouds the retired merchant and then gradually discovering the truth as the youth gropes his way towards it, indicates that, in Rastignac's case as well as that of James's own (and much more consistently employed) centers of consciousness, it is all "*his* vision, *his* conception, *his* interpretation. . . . He therefore supremely matters; all the rest matters only as he feels it, treats it, meets it."[35]

VI

The expositional strategy exemplified by Balzac does not share, more-over, the Trollopian dislike for sequential "revulsions of feelings." On the contrary, it is precisely by placing the exposition at the beginning of the sujet that Balzac produces a set of important primacy effects—some operating as preventive or preparatory measures and others as deliberately misleading implications, some molding the reader's response to various characters and others manipulating his hypotheses about broader aspects, such as the whole fictive world projected in the work, its thematic and causal pattern, or its overall tone. To comprehend the other functions served by this exposition, one must then take into account—apart from its principles of selection—the significance of its preliminary (though not nec-essarily chronological) ordering and the force of its concentrated form, and analyze their mutually reinforcing effects on the dynamics of the reading-process.

Balzac opens the novel with a dense exposition because, among other reasons, he is as eager as Trollope to ensure the reader's belief in the reality of the fictive scene and the figures populating it before he raises the curtain upon his tumultuous drama. The ambition to plant every character firmly on its feet partly accounts for the difference between Balzac, who, in James's phrase, is always "charging with his heavy, his heroic lance in rest, at every object that springs up in his path,"[36] and writers like Jane Austen, whose minor agents are sparingly characterized by an epithet or two. In Balzac's case, however, this expositional practice is especially imperative since, unlike Trollope at his most typical, Balzac is not a realist pure and simple. His apprentice work consists in the spinning of thrillers and sensational yarns after the manner of Walter Scott; and even his mature work manifests the tension between "realistic" and "romantic" pulls—between the urge to represent contemporary man-ners as they actually are and the yearning for the bizarre and the improb-able, for violent action and melodramatic intrigue. He represses neither of the conflicting tendencies, however, but often seeks, and sometimes manages, to reconcile them by artfully dissimulating the gaudiness of the sensational element. As Lubbock shrewdly observes, Balzac endeavors to mitigate the violence of his drama by absorbing "the extravagant tale into a study of actual life. If he can get the tale firmly embedded in a back-ground of truth, its falsity may be disguised, the whole work may even pass for a scene of the human comedy; it may be accepted as a piece of real-ity."[37]

For this illusion to be produced, the exposition must be not only con-centrated but preliminary as well. The prolonged, cumulative effect of the continuous blocks of circumstantial evocation with which *Père Goriot* opens produces a primacy impression of realism that is intense enough to compel belief in the whole of the ensuing action, the more so since it is later variously reinforced. The preliminary solidity of specification tones down and dissimulates, above all, the sensational effect of the unmasking of Jacques Collin, nicknamed Cheat-death, alias Vautrin—the lodger who turns out to be an escaped convict and arch-criminal in disguise—thus going a long way towards lending credibility to what would otherwise have appeared a loudly melodramatic strand of the action.

Lubbock, however, goes on to claim that this ambition to bridge the chasm between the realistic and the romantic poles ultimately breaks down: "The trouble is that Balzac's idea of a satisfying crime is as wild as his hold upon facts is sober, so that an impossible strain is thrown upon his method of reconciling the two. Do what he will, his romance remains staringly false in its contrast with his reality." According to Lubbock, then, Balzac's thoroughgoing realism, far from disguising the improbability of his romance, finally throws it into high relief.

This raises a problem of more than merely local interest. For whenever primacy and recency effect are opposed—as is of course the case, in varying degrees, with each of the three basic models of control—the introduction of the hitherto withheld elements, premises, and patterns does indeed require wary handling on the author's part in several related respects. First, both their previous suppression during the primacy-effect phase and their subsequent disclosure or disambiguation have to be quasi-mimetically accounted for—this motivation of the temporal ordering usually taking the form of perspectival shifts, notably from indirect or external to direct or internal presentation (as in the cases of Christmas, Odysseus, Darcy, or Goriot). Second, the resultant tension between conflicting, sequentially unfolded indicators, views, and hypotheses (whether between antipathetic and sympathetic response, straight and contrasted patterning of analogical relationships, or "realism" and the reverse) must somehow be resolved, or else the unity of the work might be seriously endangered. This reconciliation of factual, structural, affective, and normative opposites may be variously effected—either in quasi-mimetic or purely rhetorical terms, by way of anticipatory preparation, transitional shift, or retrospective readjustment. But resolved they must be, the need for integration growing of course with the (logical, habitual, or contextual) incompatibility of the initial and the subsequent hypotheses. This directly relates to the present case in point, since the reader usually finds it easier to reconcile conflicting views of the hero (in such terms as the fallibility or relativity or restrictedness or ambivalence of human vision or, moving from the fictive channel to the object of perception, the complexity, many-sidedness, or changeability of human character) than conflicting accounts of the canons of probability (e.g., realism versus the fantastic) operating in the fictive world as a whole.

In fact, Balzac shows himself instructively aware of the problem of integration. In making the cited strictures, Lubbock fails to do justice to the variety of Balzac's preparatory and transitional techniques in *Père Goriot,* and (as his question-begging terms *truth* and *falsity* indicate) this failure derives from a basic confusion between different kinds of "realism" and reality-models, different ways of producing a realistic effect, and different modes of probability.

There is no doubt that where the fictive world established early in the work is indeed verisimilar in the sense that its laws of probability are recognized by the reader as essentially correspondent with those operating in the world as he knows it, the subsequent introduction of fantastic or sensational elements gives rise to a jarring effect that is most inimical to credibility. Cases of perfect correspondence are of course rare; but it is sufficient that the internal and the external canons of probability should overlap at all important points to make the reader as reluctant to give credence to miracles or apparitions in fiction as in life. As the clash between the typically verisimilar and the improbable can at best be no more than partly reconciled (e.g., through conventions, as in Elizabethan drama), it is understandable that such novelists as Jane Austen, who wish the reader to believe implicitly in the verisimilitude of their fictive world, should avoid this clash of probability-registers like the plague. Other writers, however, have the improbable burst upon a verisimilar frame of reference for a variety of rhetorical and generic purposes. Henry James, for instance, infused new life into the genre of the ghost story by embedding the supernatural in "prosaic prosperous conditions" and recording its impact on flesh-and-blood characters. For in this way he invested the fantastic elements with a degree of credibility sufficient to produce a thrill or horror undreamt of in the Gothic philosophy of Mrs. Radcliffe.[38] Gogol largely springs his inimitable grotesque effects by first evoking a humdrum setting, out of which the fantastic later erupts like a cannon-ball. "The Nose" opens with an account, liberally interspersed with expositional details, of the preparations for breakfast made by two ordinary people upon an ordinary day. The narrator proceeds at a leisurely pace, going even into such marginal, "realistic" expositional details as the appearance of the sign on the barber's shop and the delicacies favored by his spouse. All of a sudden, however, reader and characters alike find themselves in the midst of a fantastic situation which cannot but leave them gaping:

> Suddenly he [Ivan Yakovlevich] stopped, surprised. There was something whitish in the middle of the roll. He poked at it with his knife, then felt it with his finger.

"It's quite compact . . ." he muttered under his breath. "Whatever can it be?"

He thrust in two fingers this time and pulled it out. It was a nose.

He almost fell off his chair. Then he rubbed his eyes and felt the thing again. It was a nose all right, no doubt about it. And what's more, a nose that had something familiar about it.[39]

In *Dead Souls* the role played by expositional disclosure and temporal ordering in the metamorphoses of the overall generic response is even more notable. The narrator first takes advantage of Chichikov's arrival at the provincial capital to overwhelm the reader with torrents of expositional detail, relevant and irrelevant, concerning the carriage in which the hero rolls into the town, the appearance of its occupant, the inn, and the servants. There is nothing remarkable about any of these nor about any of the immediately ensuing scenes. On the contrary, everything is all too common: Chichikov goes sightseeing, calls upon the town officials, and speedily makes friends with these worthies. Soon, however, the reader is jolted out of his tranquillity. Bedlam breaks loose from the moment Chichikov sets out on his round of visits to the neighboring landowners, asking each in turn to sell him his "dead souls"—the serfs who have died since the last census. The peaceful town is in no time infested with wild rumours, the officials are filled with vague fears and consternation—one even dies of a heart attack. And the reader is as baffled as any of them, since the "primary" canons of probability established in and through the opening can by no means accommodate the fantastic, and yet the leisurely, circumstantial build-up lends it some eerie reality. But Gogol has still another expositional card up his sleeve: unlike "The Nose" and the Jamesian ghost story, the ambiguation of the probability-register here turns out to be temporary rather than permanent. Having produced the desired generic effect through the clash between reality and fantasy, he winds up his novel by mischievously deflating the balloon of fantasy— accounting for Chichikov's conduct by a highly naturalistic explanation, which, had it been presented at the beginning of the sujet, where it chronologically belongs, would have precluded altogether the overall grotesque effect.

In all of these cases, at any rate, the reader's judgment as to the improbability of the fantastic elements is fully confirmed by the internal premises of the work itself. The point Lubbock misses in regard to *Père Goriot*, however, is that the probability ("truth") of the Vautrin strand is to be judged not by external but mainly by internal norms. And the reason for such oversights is fairly clear: the unobtrusiveness of the internal logic. In the *Odyssey*, for instance, the modern reader, who is not particularly inclined to believe in the divine paraphernalia of classical literature, is automatically put on his guard against imposing his own canons of probability on the work from his first encounter with the assembly of deities squabbling and pulling strings on Olympus. Balzac's reputation as historian of contemporary manners may, on the other hand, blind us—as it does Lubbock—to the variety of means by which his preliminary exposition, however ostensibly one-sided, paves the way for the subsequent introduction and integration of sensational motifs.

First, the lifelike appearance of the pension and its inmates is to be attributed not so much to their commonness as universal phenomena as to the specificity and concreteness of their evocation. Character, like all other components of the literary work, is, in W. K. Wimsatt's phrase, a concrete universal.[40] Particular fictional characters, however, may differ in their position on the scale that ranges form the concrete to the universal. Flat characters tend to find their place at one of the poles (say, Dickens's Mrs. Micawber as opposed to Bunyan's Ignorance), while the round stand somewhere in the middle, acting "by the influence of those general passions and principles by which all minds are agitated" and yet "ever kept . . . distinct from each other."[41] Some of the lodgers (Poiret or Michonneau) are portrayed as so warped and dehumanized that— though endowed in the sequel with some degree of rotundity—they hardly appear to be "the genuine progeny of common humanity, such as the world will always supply, and observation will always find."[42] On the contrary, the narrator himself describes them as "curious monstrosities" that escape the notice of most observers (p. 14). To the question of their relatedness with general human nature as projected in this novel I shall return later; what I wish to stress is that if Balzac's "truth" indeed appears to be so "true" here, as Lubbock maintains, it is not because we know it to be true from our own experience of life but primarily because Balzac sets his people on their feet with such solidity and intensity of specification that he compels the reader's belief in them in the face of their comparative lack of inherent verisimilitude. While James and Gogol lure the reader into applying his habitual canons of probability to their works by initially showing their fictive worlds to correspond to his own reality-model, Balzac's expositional section thus impresses on the reader's mind that though the fictive world established in it is "true," it is nevertheless so peculiar that one must beware of automatically judging it by any external register. So the distinctive realism of the preliminary evocation of setting and characters, far from widening the chasm between Balzac's "truth" and his "romance," provides an almost natural transition between them.

Apart from the general impression produced by the fictive world, a number of more specific devices are employed throughout the introductory part in order to lay the ground for the delayed recency effect: the sensational denouement of the unmasking of Vautrin.

The terrible dilapidation of the boarding-house makes it a suitable haven for "the refuse of humanity" (p. 8)—just as the similar state of Dickens's Jacob's Island indicates that "they must have powerful motives for a secret residence, or be reduced to a destitute condition indeed, who seek a refuge" in it (*Oliver Twist,* chap. 50). And indeed, the pension and its boarders are constantly associated, literally and metaphorically, not only with destitution but with crime as well. One of the functions served by the narrator's pointed abstention from filling in the gaps relating to the antecedents of some of the lodgers is to shroud them with an air of mystery; each of them has some secret to hide, and (as the description of Michonneau, for instance, implies) this secret often concerns something shameful, vicious, or downright criminal.

This impression is powerfully reinforced by the expositional imagery, which is largely drawn from the figurative fields of crime, jail, and justice. The pension as a whole is recurrently (and concentrically) projected as a kind of prison. The walls of the houses in its street "make one think of a prison" (p. 4); the windows on its ground floor "have the decoration of bars" (pp. 6, 7); Madame Vauquer is head keeper—"you cannot imagine a jail without a jailer" (p. 9); and, as one can by now safely predict, the lodgers are "criminals condemned to life imprisonment" (p. 18).

With regard to some of the inmates, moreover, the prison imagery is not designed to evoke the reader's pity but to imply that they have the makings of a criminal or have actually been involved in crime. Michonneau may have been a courtesan (p. 12), while Madame Vauquer has "the innocent air of a procuress who will put on a show of indignation in order to get a better price, but in every other way is . . . ready to inform on anyone in hiding" (p. 9). With Poiret, a whole cluster of images associated with crime and retribution is dragged in, though only indirectly related to him: "Perhaps he had been a clerk in the Ministry of Justice, in the office where executioners send in their expense accounts, carrying such items as black veils for parricides, grain for the headsman's basket, strings for the blades of the guillotine" (p. 13).

The abundance of crime imagery, the portrayal of all the lodgers as prisoners and some of them as real or figurative offenders subtly prepares the reader for the discovery that the pension contains within its precincts another, and very substantial, convict and criminal. The addition of Vautrin to the existing list of "criminals" in his new capacity as arch-criminal involves only a shift from the petty to the monumental, from the metaphorical to the literal, or from moral to legal wrongdoing. In escaping from penitentiary to pension, we retrospectively perceive, the prison celebrity has merely exchanged one jail for another, with little to choose between them. Even the betrayal of a criminal in hiding is prefigured or foreshadowed already in the expositional imagery,[43] only as it later turns out it is not the procuress that squeals on Vautrin, but the courtesan. Among these thieves there is even no honor.

Balzac's control strategy thus illustrates still another device—as prevalent as those typical of Homer and Austen—for moderating the clash between primacy and recency effect while forcefully bringing out the true, modified conception of character or event against the background of the initial hypothesis—namely, the transition from a figurative to a literal reading of a fictive feature, or vice versa. The counterpart of the present manifestation of this dynamic principle can be found in the unfolding of Goriot, who is (somewhat less surprisingly) "transformed" during the reading-process from what the world of the pension views as the elderly, unnaturally lustful lover of his beautiful visitors into the figurative but indeed morbid and unnatural lover of his daughers.

The preparations for the ultimate disclosure of Vautrin's identity culminate in his own expositional presentation (pp. 15–17). Balzac has, in fact, distributed throughout this character-sketch all the necessary clues, only most of them are so cunningly registered as part of the general set and atmosphere of the boarding-house that their full or true significance can be appreciated only in retrospect.[44]

Vautrin differs from other lodgers in that he does not quite merge into the broader concentric circles enveloping him; but then Rastignac and Victorine do not either. The strong, genial man, with enough money to pay for extra delicacies and make loans to his fellow-boarders, does not seem to be a failure in any sense; but neither did Goriot during his first years at Vauquer's. Against any normal background, amenable to the reader's habitual canons of probability, moreover, Vautrin's cynicism, scorn of law and high society, and unaccountable nightly disappearances would doubtless make him stand out as the criminal he is; but within the peculiar framework of the pension he is just another lodger with a carefully concealed mystery at the bottom of his life. One of Vautrin's most conspicuous features, his dyed whiskers (pp. 10, 16), is in the same way passed off as no more than a realistic touch revealing the small weaknesses of the man, of no more significance than Vauquer's ill-arranged false hair (p. 9) or Goriot's powdered hair (p. 29).[45]

Balzac's communication of dissimulated clues, verbal and situational, goes even further. He dwells for a moment on Vautrin's expertness at fixing locks, but immediately covers up his tracks by presenting it as a mere item in a miscellaneous list of accomplishments: "He knew about many other sorts of things, ships, the sea, France, foreign countries, business, men, current events, laws, hotels and prisons" (p. 16).[46] And then we come across the crowning diversionary touch: "Even in the way he spit he disclosed an imperturbable coolness which would not prevent him from engaging in crime if it would help him out of an equivocal position." Here Balzac is in effect laughing in the reader's face. This broad hint should have given the whole show away, only the reader cannot take it at face value owing to the operation of three counteracting factors. First, the other lodgers have recently been portrayed in terms of criminal imagery. Second, the very relation of spitting to crime weakens the force of the suggestion, making the whole sentence appear an exaggerated ("metaphorical") comment on the coolness of the man, not an indication of his actual criminality. Third, and most audacious, in the sentence that immediately follows Vautrin's eyes are said to be "like those of a severe judge in penetrating to the heart of every matter" (p. 16): the implications of the concluding simile—derived from the same figurative field but connoting the opposite side of the legal fence—temporarily neutralize those conveyed by the initial statement.[47]

No less typical is the set of precautions taken to establish the internal probability of Goriot's own tragedy. The heartless conduct of the daughters to their loving father is so extreme in its unnaturalness that it is liable to be dismissed as incredible or at least grossly exaggerated. So, the reader retrospectively discovers, Balzac exploits the preliminary location of the exposition to prepare another (tonal and thematic) perceptual set that will compel belief in the coming events.

The depressing depiction of milieu operates like a prelude to a piece of music by setting the tone for the whole piece. As the narrator himself notes, "the Rue Neuve-Sainte-Geneviève, above all, is like a frame of bronze, the only frame appropriate to this story for which the mind cannot too thoroughly be prepared by dark colors and serious ideas" (p. 5). The appropriateness of this environmental frame consists both in the atmosphere or mood it evokes and in the eerie fictive world it establishes. The dark colors liberally (too liberally, perhaps) applied throughout the depiction of the pension and its inmates give the reader, from the very outset, an overwhelming sense of a world characterized by egotistic existence, warped, almost dehumanized inclinations, and pervasive suffering. And Goriot's tragedy later fits naturally into this initially prepared framework, with its immanent laws.

To focus this general manipulation of mood and expectation, Balzac intersperses the preliminaries with brief specific prefigurations of the theme that is to be fully unfolded in the tale of Goriot and his daughters. The degeneration and disintegration of family ties is ironically suggested by the imagery supposed to elucidate the relations between the inmates of the pension—vitiated by callous indifference ("like old married couples, they had nothing more to say to one another," p. 17) and self-interest.

Breakfast at the boarding-house, the narrator comments, "had the air of a family gathering," with Madame Vauquer—honored by Vautrin with the title "Mama" (p. 16)—acting as mother. But he immediately gives his metaphor an unexpected twist—reminiscent of Jane Austen's "microcosmic" reversals of verbal meaning and impression—when he goes on to explain that the seven lodgers were "Vauquer's spoiled children, and her care and regard for them was in wonderfully exact proportion to the size of their bills" (p. 11).

Moreover, the early set of portraits contains various familial details which first seem to possess only limited referential value but later turn out to have fulfilled important prefigurative functions. Victorine has been repudiated by her father, whose cruelty she repays with love (pp. 14-15); the same theme is cunningly suggested in passing apropos of Poiret, the conjectural employee in the office where "executioners send in their expense accounts, carrying such items as black veils for parricides"; and at more length, of Michonneau, whose "story was that she had looked after an old man suffering from catarrh of the bladder and deserted by his children who believed he was penniless" (pp. 12-13).

The multiplicity of expositional prefigurations, paving the way for the problematic future discoveries and developments by way of shifts from the figurative to the literal or the cursory to the intensive, insidiously impresses on the reader that, within the particular framework postulated by the text, Goriot's tragedy is far from unique. This is a fictive world where fathers are in the habit of repudiating their children, and children their fathers; relations between the various members of a family can be regulated only on a pecuniary basis and are thus reduced to mercenary dealings; and normal family feelings—such as those implied by Madame Couture's taking care of Victorine "as if she were her own child" (p. 15)—are not the rule but the exception. As often in narrative and drama, it is the internal universalization of the theme that gives the main action its credibility.

VII

This brings me to a related primacy effect, one that is first elaborately contrived and then surprisingly shattered, with enormous thematic profit. While the handling of Goriot's antecedents shows how preliminary and concentrated exposition may, through suitable chronological dislocation and actional development, accommodate and exploit the dynamics distinctive of our third ordering strategy ("The Rhetoric of Anticipatory Caution") and the handling of the "realism-sensationalism" clashes shows its adaptability to the second ("Primacy Effect Complicated and Qualified"), the drastic manipulation of the initially suggested relationship between character and milieu will now demonstrate the flexibility and functionality of these presentational modes with regard to the first model of control ("The Rise and Fall of First Impressions").

The cumulative effect of the preliminary exposition induces the reader to ascribe the threatened darkness of the action proper that is to ensue to the influence of environment—of the setting whose material and moral decrepitude is so luridly evoked at the start. And the minuteness of the preliminaries seems at this stage to be explained in terms of the establishment of the internal canons of probability peculiar to this queer locality. The narrator is not, moreover, content to let the queerness of the fictive world and the characters populating it speak for itself. He further reinforces the impression that the exposition is related to the story proper as premises to a proposition by a variety of means. He claims that the Rue Neuve-Sainte-Geneviève is the only frame appropriate to this tale (p. 5); he promises that the scene will abound in peculiarities and local color (p. 3); and, most persuasive of all, he explicitly presents the Pension Vauquer as a collector's piece: "The handsome side of Paris knows nothing of such faces, pale with moral and physical suffering. But Paris is a veritable ocean. . . . No matter how many or how eager its explorers be, there will always be some unknown cavern, some flowers and pearls and monsters, something unheard of, something forgotten by the literary divers. The Maison Vauquer is one of these curious monstrosities" (pp. 13–14).

Throughout the exposition, moreover, the rest of Paris (especially the fashionable world) looms in the background as something far-off and alien, by implication always contrasted with the world of the pension, into which it secretes its refuse—of dress, furniture, and people. The lodgers are described as wearing "shoes such as are seen lying in the gutters of the more fashionable districts" (p. 12); the dining room is furnished with "these indestructible pieces of furniture, proscribed from every other place, and resting there just as the refuse of humanity comes to rest in homes for the incurable" (p. 8). And the recurrence of prison, almshouse, and hospital imagery seems to confirm this impression.

Furthermore, one of the central figurative fields in the opening—the animal imagery[48]—suggests that the world of the boarding-house is so anomalous or monstrous that the laws by which normal human life is regulated may not apply to it at all. The multifunctional device of the concentric circles manifests itself again. The boarding-house contains some real animals—the rabbits, pigs, and fowls in the court (p. 6) and the landlady's cat prowling about the house (pp. 8–9). Part of the drawing room furniture is covered with horsehair (p. 7); the dining room has a tortoise-shell clock case (p. 8); Goriot owns a porringer with two billing doves on the cover (p. 20) and he wears a goatskin vest (p. 29). But the inmates themselves are also presented in animal terms. Two rooms are always kept for "birds of passage" (p. 10). Madame Vauquer has a "parrot's nose," a body as "fat as a church rat's" (p. 9), and "magpie eyes" (p. 20); she is "more suspicious than a cat" (p. 22; her pet is a cat); and when she arrayed herself for the conquest of Goirot's heart, her bovine appearance suggested "the sign at the Boeuf-à-la-Mode restaurant" (p. 22). Michonneau has "the sharp voice of a grasshopper" (p. 12). Poiret has a "thin turkey neck" and seems "to have been one of the donkeys in our great social treadmill" (p. 13). The old lodgers, who themselves "lived in the house as oysters live on a rock," hold that Goriot's "sinful excesses had made a poor limpet of him, an anthropomorphic mollusk" (pp. 30, 31); while Madame Vauquer yearningly thinks that Goriot, "a beast of solid substance," can still give a woman a great deal of pleasure (p. 22). Of all these it is Victorine alone— the "wounded dove" (p. 15)—that is projected in terms of an image that does not carry pejorative implications.

In this metaphorical jungle or zoo, moreover, most of the human beasts behave even worse than the animals cooped up in the yard; for while the "rabbits live amicably with pigs and fowls" (p. 6), the boarders are remarkable for their callousness and downright cruelty. So this network of images gives the crowning touch to the impression of uniqueness produced by the opening presentation of the pension. And the fact that this figurative field is drawn on not by the narrator alone but by the fictive agents as well further heightens the unity of effect: in this peculiar world people even think in terms of animal imagery.

This primacy effect is so forcefully impressed that the subsequent demolition of the link between character or conduct and environment cannot but bring us up short. It is not that the pension is suddenly revealed to be human, but that the rest of society is revealed to be at least equally inhuman. The animal imagery, which the reader has so far been misled into viewing as the epitome of the distinctive dehumanization of the boarding-house, is discovered to embrace the whole of Paris; it links high and low, the rich and the poor, the law-abiding and the criminal, the Faubourg Saint-Germain and the Rue Neuve-Sainte-Geneviève, thus projecting a somber view of the whole of human society as an assemblage of animals—insensible, greedy, selfish, or simply disgusting.

On the one hand, the pension continues to be a "frightful den" (p. 196) and the lodgers "animals at a trough" (p. 84) or "filthy beasts" (p. 165), who appropriately amuse themselves by imitating animal sounds (p. 183). Michonneau is an "old bat" (p. 52); she reminds Bianchon of a "long worm" (p. 52) and has a "viper's glance" (p. 207). Poiret is a louse (p. 165); Vautrin has "a chest as hairy as a bear's back" (p. 106); and Madame Vauquer sleeps like a dormouse (p. 40). At the same time, however, Balzac often denotes the different worlds and their inhabitants not only by the same figurative field but by similar specific metaphors as well, thus impelling the reader to construct a wide variety of interrelated analogical patterns, to compare and contrast their components, and to draw the desired normative and semantic conclusions. If, for example, Vauquer is bovine and Vautrin stronger than an ox (p. 210), Baron de Nucingen is "a calf's head set on a pig's body" (p. 179). Goriot and Poiret are constantly described in terms of dog imagery, usually connoting such favorable attributes as canine intuition or devotion; but de Marsay is "a dirty dog" (p. 136). And if Michonneau is a "regimental horse" (p. 48) and Goriot's room "as filthy as a stable" (p. 263), Madame de Beauséant is, like all women in love, more sensitive than a courser (p. 170), and Goriot finally repents not having kept his daughters (one already characterized as a "thoroughbred" and "high stepper") under "bridle and spur like wily horses" (pp. 35, 269).[49]

We have already seen (and will soon continue to see) that the represented fictive space as well as the "spatial" patterns of analogy are no less amenable to dynamic manipulation than fictive time and the temporally developmental patterns of action and character. The referential dimension of space is indeed not to be reconstituted and explained in the light of normative indicators comparable in precision to the correspondence between either representational and represented time or the chronological and the actual sequence. Still, it forms not only an object of selection (compare the generalized reference to Job's setting with the specificity of Calypso's, not to speak of Vauquer's) but also, like any other element in the literary work, of combination, distribution, and ordering—including sequential displacement, discontinuity, and progressive unfolding. Thus, the gradated, tripartite geographical progression in the *Odyssey* or the delayed portrayal of the sinuous Pemberley scenery in *Pride and Prejudice* are discovered to be part and parcel of the work's presentational (temporal, perspectival, verbal) logic. But the present instance—the sudden widening out of the initially circumscribed arena—is of special interest since it demonstrates that even in a "social" novel, where numerous classes and settings and simultaneous, multilinear action seem to be dictated by the very terms of the case, space may be so distributed and ordered as to have a drastic effect on the dynamics of response.

The systematic uprooting of the elaborate pseudo-sociological primacy effect, though somewhat less startling than in *Light in August,* proves here too the most efficacious means of driving the thematic point home. Contrary to our initial impressions (aided and abetted, again, by social prejudice), we become increasingly aware that penury and dilapidation are not to be automatically equated with egotism and malice, nor rank and elegance with a sense of honor and goodness of heart. A Madame de

Beauseànt is as rare a phenomenon in high society as a Goriot in the world of the boarding-house. What appeared to be, throughout the expositional phase, a bitter travesty of family relations, intended to show up still another aspect of the general degeneracy of the boarding-house world, is later revealed as typical of family life at all strata of society, finding its most complete expression in Goriot's treatment at the hands of his rich, titled daughters. In several instances, moreover, the poor and the criminal are represented as more loyal and honorable than their aristocratic analogues. The broken-down Poiret adheres to Michonneau when everybody else has turned against her, while d'Adjuda-Pinto, de Marsay, or de Trailles jilt their mistresses or even cause their downfall and then leave them to face the music. Vautrin is, according to his enemy the chief of police himself, a man of honor who is quite incapable of walking off with the treasury entrusted to him by the underworld; the respectable banker de Nucingen is a swindler and an embezzler.

Retrospectively, therefore, the reader again comes to realize that (*pace* James and many others) the preliminary evocation of background is designed to serve artistic rather than scientific ends. It forms an indirect mode of characterization and control, not a philosophical or sociological treatise on the ineluctable causal relationship between environment and personality. It may indicate that some of the lodgers are at the end of their tether; but, in spite of its deliberately deceptive implications, it does not, and cannot, explain in terms of a particular milieu the core of character and the sources of passions, which are universal. Only in retrospect does the reader fully decode such early clues as "such an assemblage was bound to offer and did offer a microcosm of a whole social world" (p. 18), which —like the two-pronged simile early applied to Joe Christmas: "He carried with him his own inescapable warning, like a flower its scent or a rattle-snake its rattle"—could at the time be contextually interpreted in different ways and were subordinated to the overall pattern. Contrary to what is suggested by the opening as a whole, the threatened "darkness" of the action proper derives not so much from the peculiarities of the pension environment as from the surprising discovery of the equal dehumanization of the rest of society. The reader is forced to perceive that, despite what he now views as superficial differences, there is really little to choose between the world of fashion with Madame de Beauseànt as queen, the world of the pension with Madame Vauquer as mock-queen, and the world of crime ruled by Vautrin; the appearance may vary but the human reality behind it is essentially the same. So every deviation from the law of the jungle common to all three worlds, as well as the prevalent conformity to it, is to be accounted for in terms of what Johnson calls the uniform simplicity of primitive qualities rather than distinctions superinduced and adventitious.

VIII

Balzac thus infuses new life into the old theme of appearance and reality by first tricking the reader into the belief that appearance *is* reality and subsequently smashing the false impression to pieces. It should be noted, however, that not only does the preliminary and concentrated exposition concurrently launch the three strategies of control with regard to different fictive objects, but, what is theoretically no less illuminating, it even manipulates them into mutually reinforcing one another in various means-end combinations. For instance: the reader's surprise at the twist given to the "environmental" primacy effect has a dramatic equivalent inside the fictive world itself—Rastignac's growing amazement at the discovery that the loathsome boarding-house is no more than a microcosmic reflection of the whole social order. And it is this correspondence between reader and protagonist—initially much closer than in *Pride and Prejudice* or *Emma*—that structurally relates the broad thematic functions of the fallacious primacy effect (of model 1) to the crucial role it plays in the balancing control (model 2) of our distance from Rastignac and his initiation.

Both the preliminary location and the concentrated form of the exposition are also explainable in terms of Balzac's aim to create an anticipatory extenuation of our adverse judgment of Rastignac's efforts to conquer a place in high society by impressing on us right at the start the strength of his motives, the grounds for his fatal mistake, and the depth of his inexperience. Had our first encounters with Rastignac been scenically staged in the gilded salons of the Parisian nobility, the primacy effect would in all probability have been extremely—and to some extent unjustifiably—unfavorable. He would probably have been dismissed as an unscrupulous social pusher and contemptible gigolo, a valuation which, though doubtless true as far as it goes, hardly does justice either to the young man's personality or dilemma or conflict. To delay the evocation of circumstances would accordingly be, in Trollope's phrase, to let the reader "masticate the real kernel of [the] story with infinite prejudices" against the hero. And the point is that in this case the author cannot risk an unfavorable primacy effect because, unlike Faulkner in *Light in August* or Heller in *Catch-22*, he simply does not have up his sleeve a card strong enough to ensure its timely reversal.

As it is, the cumulative force of the preliminary portrayal of the disgusting material and moral atmosphere in which Rastignac is enveloped, coupled with a favorable account of his character and plans, calls forth the reader's sympathy for the resolution of the young, sensitive, ambitious nobleman from the provinces to break out of the stifling prison to which he is condemned by his poverty, before it is too late. It is strongly suggested that such a change of environment is imperative, for if he does not extricate himself in a hurry the tainted atmosphere of the pension is sure to engulf him by degrees. The danger signals are all there: Victorine, his "yellowing" analogue, has already been affected; and the device of the concentric circles turns the striking similarity between the ugly and the worn dress of the lodgers, particularly Poiret's (pp. 12, 13), and Rastignac's own—"an old frock coat, an ugly vest, a miserably worn, badly knotted student's black tie, trousers in keeping with such a costume, and resoled boots" (p. 15)—into a warning that the infection may creep beyond externals.

Subsequently, therefore, the reader cannot but sympathize with Rastignac when, during the first stages of his ordeal, he is dazzled by the brilliance of the houses of Parisian nobility, the exquisiteness of their dress and equipage, and the polished elegance of their manners. It is no wonder that as he stands gaping at the beauty of Madame de Beausèant's salon, "the madness of luxury seized him; the thirst for gold parched his throat. He must live on a hundred and thirty francs for the space of three months" (p. 71). As the narrator himself persuasively observes, in view of "the evidences of his poverty . . . could he have done otherwise?" (p. 37). When launching his campaign, Rastignac in his innocence still labors under the illusion that wealth and distinction constitute happiness— he associates, for instance, de Traille's cabriolet with "all the happinesses of Paris" (p. 56). And as during the first phases of the action proper the reader still shares Rastignac's misconception, due to the misleading presentation of the pension as the exclusive source of misery and evil, our distance from him diminishes even further.

The controlled dramatization of the reversal of the reader's thematic expectations through Rastignac's ordeal thus requires that the preliminary exposition should contain on the one hand a partial, biased ("deformed") picture of social realities and on the other a full account of Rastignac's position amidst and vis-à-vis them. It retrospectively emerges that the view of society initially projected has been tailored to coincide with the hero's own in order to extenuate our response to his error of judgment by establishing its plausibility. The reader, far from being elevated to a quasi-divine (Trollopian) or even superior (Austenian) coign of vantage, is deliberately made to share the hero's all-too-human defects of vision as a drastic means of demonstrating to him that, if placed at the same starting-point as the inexperienced youth, he too would be liable to fall into the same trap. The apparently objective ("historical") evocation of static ("spatial") human and social phenomena also carries, then, significantly subjective and dynamic implications. Instead of directly rendering the inner process that led to Rastignac's decision to push his way into high society—a line at which he rarely excels and which might preclude the production of other desired effects—Balzac typically chooses to achieve much the same result by evoking the hopelessness and menace of the milieu in a way that will indirectly throw some favorable light on the propulsive forces in the agent's soul.[50] This procedure may not be to the taste of either James or Trollope, but its effectiveness and economy are undeniable.

The extenuating perceptual set of the exposition is, moreover, exploited not only for conditioning in advance the reader's response to Rastignac's initial break out of the boarding-house world but throughout the work as well. As Rastignac's ordeal progresses, he encounters a succession of obstacles or temptations that threaten to set at nought his resolution to keep straight. In spite of his qualms and good intentions and in spite of his momentary decisions to forgo the shortcuts to wealth and fame and make his way to distinction by dint of honest labor, he usually succumbs to temptation. It is obvious that the reader neither can nor is meant to adhere to his original sympathetic attitude toward a hero whose highest ambition is to become a kept man, who is despicable enough to fleece his mother and sisters in order to cut a dash in drawing rooms, and whose final challenge to society—about which he is completely disillusioned by the end of the novel—ironically takes the form of going to dine with the Baroness de Nucingen.[51] On the contrary, as the expositional primacy effect gives way to the recency effects of the action proper, our norms and his increasingly tend to diverge rather than (as in Jane Austen) to converge. And in view of the inroads made on it by his conduct, the surprising thing is that so much of our sympathy should remain to the end. This saving effect, too, should largely be accounted for in expositional terms.

The reader's judgment of Rastignac's aberrations is influenced all along by the tremendous impact of the preliminary exposition; as the action goes forward the pension looms large in the reader's mind—even larger than the Agamemnon precedent in the *Odyssey* or Charlotte's capitulation in *Pride and Prejudice*—constantly acting as a reminder of the probable alternative to Rastignac's goal. Even the reversal of the appearance-and-reality theme cannot do away with our horror at the pension milieu—particularly because this development is effected not only gradually but also through the protagonist's own point of view. Balzac, moreover, does not content himself with the initial impression but frequently reinforces or extends it by contrasting the squalor of the pension with the luxury of the rich and dramatizing the contrast in and through Rastignac's inner conflict. It is indicated time and again, for instance, that one of the decisive causes of Rastignac's backsliding is the sight or memory of the pension, the epitome of everything he wishes to escape from, at moments of crisis. On two occasions this is especially noticeable. Returning from his first visits to Madame de Restaud and Madame de

Beausèant, with the latter's merciless exposure of high society ringing in his ears, he is still undecided about his future course: "His imagination, carried into the high places of Parisian society, planted a thousand evil thoughts in his heart and at the same time enlarged both his mind and his conscience. He saw the world for what it is: law and morality impotent among the rich" (p. 84). Thus poised between the temptations of wealth and the urge of conscience, between ambition and disillusion, it is the immediately following drop into the dilapidation of the pension, now seen for the first time with the film of familiarity removed ("the nauseating dining-room where the eighteen boarders engaged in feeding met his eyes and struck him as so many animals at a trough"), that tips the scales ("The transition had been too abrupt, the contrast was too complete to pass without giving an exorbitant stimulus to his ambitious feelings," p. 84). Consequently, he commits himself to launch his campaign by writing to his family for money, "draining the last drops of their blood" (p. 94).

On another fateful occasion, when Rastignac has been so taken aback at the realization of the enormities attending the social climb that he is inclined to give it up altogether, his dinner with Madame de Beausèant determines him to revoke his decision. This time it is the sumptuousness of her dining room that overrides his scruples: "His thoughts carried him back for a moment to the boarding-house, and he felt such disgust that he swore to himself he would leave it in January" (p. 124). So when he meets Delphine de Nucingen at the theater the same night, he at once makes up to her with a view to installing himself as her gigolo. This illustrates again the Balzacian *principle of convertible dimensions*, variously projecting the statics of space into the dynamics of time so as to propel, suggest, and justify inner process by outer shell.

The first impression is thus reactivated in different ways throughout— as a means of controlling the dynamics of the reader's judgment, as a device for indirectly rendering the dynamics of the hero's own spiritual ordeal, or as a thematic counterpointing measure. In each role, moreover, it conduces to a remarkable economy of representation. Due to its protracted effect, the reader is so permeated, once for all, with the sense of squalor characterizing the boarding-house that later there is no need to evoke this milieu again in order to ensure its continually affecting our response to Rastignac or its illuminating his motives for action. Whenever he leaves the pension, returns to it, or recalls it, the briefest reference to it or to one of the inmates that epitomizes its spirit is more than enough to bring it to our minds, bristling with its multiplicity of atmospheric, thematic, psychological, and dramatic implications.[52] This procedure even saves Balzac the trouble of going into an exhaustive account of the elegance and opulence of the houses of the nobility, for the vividness of the introductory portrayal of the boarding-house implicitly rounds out the picture by way of contrast. The concentrated force of the preliminary exposition makes its weight felt at every point of the action proper.

To conclude: there is no justification whatever for categorically dismissing chronological progression and/or preliminary exposition as sloppy, inartistic, static, and necessarily inferior modes of presentation. Nor may all their manifestations be indiscriminately lumped together. Even the instances I have discussed reveal a remarkable range of variability in function, ordering, texture, ratio of preliminary to delayed exposition and reasons for the different location of elements, and interrelationship with the action proper. To mention some closely related variations: preliminary exposition may form a complex of preventive or constructive measures or both; it may contain only a fraction of the sum-total of expositional material spread over the work, as in the *Odyssey* and many a detective story, or outweigh the delayed exposition, as in Trollope; its starting-point may coincide with the chronological beginning or involve a marked plunge *in medias res,* as in the *Odyssey,* or an initially less pronounced one, as in *Père Goriot;* it may be exploited for opening gaps with a view to the stimulation of various narrative interests, or for anticipatorily closing them, or for both, as in Balzac, the disparities in procedure drawing the reader's attention to the different focuses of interest; it may be partial or incomplete so as to accommodate a deliberately biased presentation of a character or situation, or exhaustive so as to preclude a one-sided response, or both with regard to different expositional objects, as in Balzac—each choice giving rise to different relations between the preliminary exposition on the one hand and the rest of the sujet (including the delayed or corrective exposition) on the other; and its principles of selection may also vary, according to the work's hierarchy of meaning and the different aspects of the expositional state of affairs on which the author wishes to lay stress.

Preliminary expositions are also far from homogeneous in point of tedium or assimilability. Here one must take into account another complex of variables—length, style, vividness of the presented objects or the manner of presentation, and the artist's consciousness of what he is doing. As regards stylistic felicity, expositions may range from Balzac's plodding, graceless language and occasionally vulgar tone, which often sets one's teeth on edge, through Trollope's businesslike approach, to James's graceful glide into the action proper of *Washington Square* or Jane Austen's pungently witty introduction of the Elliots in *Persuasion.* From another viewpoint, some of Balzac's queer creations or Walter Scott's historical scenes capture the reader's attention far more successfully than more humdrum objects. The crazy gambols of Gogol's exordiums—the boisterousness of "The Tale of How Ivan Ivanovich Quarrelled with Ivan

Nikiforovich," or the waywardness of "The Overcoat"—make most preliminary expositions unbearably dull by comparison; but then few writers can afford to postulate such narrators as Gogol's. They may, though, resort to other vivifying devices, some of them strikingly unconventional; in J. D. Salinger's *Zooey,* some of the necessary antecedents are relegated to a long footnote, and in George Orwell's *1984,* to an appendix. Last, the author's awareness of the dangers of preliminary exposition may also counteract the usual tediousness of this procedure in that it has a disarming effect on the reader. This consciousness may take an explicit form, as in Trollope's defiant apologetics or Salinger's brief humorous comments in *Zooey* ("All this data, I think, is to some degree relevant"); but it may also be suggested through the artist's handling of his material. The more functional a preliminary exposition is and the more the reader is convinced of its indispensability in the given circumstances, the more is he inclined to condone its lack of narrative allurement and accept its other gains as fair compensation.

Each case must, then, be judged on its own merits. There may conceivably be readers who share James's distaste for "the seated mass of explanation" as such to the extent that they regard its drawbacks—even where related to the heart of the matter—as categorically irredeemable. But it is precisely to them that one of the best pieces of advice ever given to a reader is directed, curiously enough by the same mentor: "We must grant the artist his subject, his idea, his *donnée:* our criticism is applied only to what he makes of it. Naturally I do not mean that we are bound to like it or find it interesting: in case we do not our course is perfectly simple—to let it alone."[53]

CHAPTER EIGHT

EXPOSITIONAL MOTIVATION, TEMPORAL STRUCTURE, AND POINT OF VIEW (1): VARIETIES OF OMNISCIENT NARRATION

> *Decius.* Most mighty Caesar, let me know some cause. . . .
> *Caesar.* The cause is in my will.
>
> Shakespeare, *Julius Caesar*

I have so far classified expositions, in descriptive and functional terms, according to three presentational criteria. I have distinguished between preliminary and delayed expositions (i.e., differentiation by position in the sujet) and between concentrated and distributed expositions (i.e., differentiation by degree of formal continuity). Exposition may thus be preliminary and concentrated (as in *Père Goriot*), delayed and concentrated (as the flashback tracing Christmas's history in *Light in August*), delayed and distributed or segmented (as in the body of the detective story or in Fielding's digressive tales), or in effect even preliminary and distributed (in such egregiously contrived opening scenes as the colloquies of gossipy servants, or such mixtures of antecedent and anticipatory elements as the opening of Ford's *The Good Soldier*). I have also indicated the complementary relations between the pair of terms denoting the textual location of exposition on the one hand and the chronologically oriented pointers *in medias res* and *ab ovo* on the other; for instance, a work may open with preliminary exposition and yet, owing to the noncoincidence of the actual with the fabulaic starting-point, produce various effects that turn on the delayed communication of information. These types of exposition are clearly amenable to many combinations (though their basic functions are limited); and even in a single work one may locate a variety of expositional techniques. The *Odyssey*, for instance, despite its plunge *in medias res*, starts with a concise preliminary exposition. The bulk of the expositional material is, however, delayed: some of it is distributed in and through the dialogue and action of the initial discriminated occasions; the main expositional section is subsequently presented in the form of a condensed history narrated by the protagonist; while in book

19, as soon as Eurycleia recognizes Odysseus, the scene is retrospectively illuminated by the story of the scar communicated by the omniscient narrator himself. The reconstituted sequence of all these local expositions composes the exposition of the epic. Most important, as I have demonstrated throughout, whatever the nature and variety of the expositional modes characterizing a work, a structural type or a genre, the question of the resultant temporal ordering of the information presented is of crucial importance in determining semantic formation and rhetorical effect:

1. The ordering of the text as a dynamic whole, as a sequentially unfolding synthesis of temporally heterogeneous materials (expositional and nonexpositional, foreshadowing and retrospective, successive and simultaneous, atemporal, static and developmental, generalized or habitual and scenic), substantively heterogeneous materials (e.g., verbal, actional, thematic, and generic), and formally and functionally heterogeneous or even rival patterns in terms of which they are interrelated.

2. The ordering of the expositional blocks and elements vis-à-vis one another (as with distributed antecedents whose progressive integration and reconstitution determines the play of curiosity or normative response).

3. The ordering of elements within a single continuous block or any other distinct segment (as in Odysseus's series of fabulous adventures with its sequential frames, balances and counterpoints, or in Balzac's variously propelled opening).

4. The ordering within what I called the verbal microcosm as well as along the whole verbal continuum (whether in the form of the tripartite shift in Odysseus's epithets, Balzac's figurative distributions, ramifications, and ambiguities, or Jane Austen's syntactic and stylistic turns).

The different combinational, distributive and ordering strategies, each with its own clearly definable dynamics of the reading-process, may serve to distinguish in compositional terms not only a variety of genres, authors, and individual works that pursue—or are discovered to pursue—radically different goals (e.g., Trollope versus the detective story). They can also be sharply subdivided to bring out and explain a variety of subtler similarities between the professedly dissimilar (e.g., the "crooked corridors" in Jane Austen and Henry James, the exploitation of social stock-responses in Balzac and Faulkner, or the interaction of narrative and normative dynamics in Homer, Austen, and Balzac) and dissimilarities between the similar (e.g., in terms of the predominant narrative interest, between the retardatory structure in the revenge tragedy and the detective story, or between Trollope and Thackeray, *Emma* and *Pride and Prejudice,* or even books 1–4 and 5–12 of the *Odyssey;* in terms of basic presentational choices, between preliminary exposition versus chronological progression in Trollope and Balzac; in terms of ostensibly equally dynamic control of response,

between *Light in August,* the *Odyssey,* and Jane Austen's structural variations, themselves theoretically gradable). The principles and variables of
temporal structure have thus, apart from their other theoretical and interpretative uses, not a few typological implications for poetics, which often
cut across conventional boundaries.

Finally, I believe the argument has sufficiently established the role of
exposition as the basis of the narrative structure of probabilities and the
extent (in narrative and drama, truly decisive) to which the literary text
in all its aspects as a dynamic system—whether formal integration,
semantic processing, or rhetorical control—turns on gaps in general and
expositional gaps in particular. It turns, first of all, on the author's basic
attitude to gaps and the consequent play of hypotheses (Trollope's doctrinal objections being indeed one of his major claims to notice); and,
more usual, on his specific handling of them. The main variables of the
latter process of referential ambiguation and disambiguation—whose
distinctive multifold past-present-future development and bi-directionality
of expectation, retrospection and cross reference are by no means confined to a handful of esoteric writers—can now be concentrated and
reformulated under the following heads.[1]

Temporary and Permanent "Systems of Gap-filling"   Multiple hypotheses about the fictive world and its components are produced, not by
permanent gaps alone but whenever the reader is made aware of a gap of
either kind. For as long as the withheld information is not authoritatively
communicated—and owing to the text's sequential nature, the reader can
rarely be sure that it will be—any gap must for the time being be regarded
as virtually permanent. The more so since, if the reader is to make sense of
what is happening—organize the heterogeneous materials into some
semblance of order, link word to deed and character to action, or relate
narrative past to present and future in a structure of probabilities—he cannot forgo gap-filling even when fairly convinced that the text will sooner
or later double back to dispel its referential ambiguities. Accordingly, the
reader cannot but construct different hypotheses and revise, rearrange, or
replace them even where confronted by such questions as Odysseus's
soldierly powers, Wickham's allegations, or old Karamazov's murderer—
all of them gaps that turn out to be temporary. But the reverse is also
true: the reader can no more (actually, even less) determine in advance
which gaps will ultimately prove to be permanent. And this uncertainty
is equally amenable to dynamic exploitation, whether as a factor in the
play of narrative interest (as with Penelope's attitude to the Suitors); as a
spur to propel the reader forward in the hope of obtaining the information
that will do away with the awkward need for multiple or even incompatible hypotheses (as with the ambiguity concerning the ghosts in *The Turn*

of the Screw); as a bait to inveigle the reader into believing that he has finally discovered the definitive filling, a belief that is later disintegrated so as to drive home some crucial point (as repeatedly with Raskolnikov's motives and Christmas's race); or for any other end whose accomplishment depends on the reader's erroneously entertaining the possibility that the gap or system of gaps is only temporary.

As long as the terminal point in the reading-process (subsuming of course the process of chronological reconstitution) has not been reached, therefore, the distinction between temporary and permanent gaps is far from crucial to the reader. It sometimes even happens that gaps that have apparently been filled in once for all (e.g., the reason for the delay in Odysseus's homecoming, or the identity of Tom Jones's mother) are suddenly reopened at a later stage; while others that seem destined to remain permanently ambiguous are suddenly closed at the last moment (e.g., through the prevalent device of resolving doubts, complications, and improbabilities by the disclosure that the whole story is nothing but a dream). One must of course take into account such variables as authoritative statements about the temporariness or permanence of the ambiguity (say, the narrator's initial promise in *Père Goriot* to unfold Goriot's secret sorrow as opposed to the declaration in *The Ambassadors* that the mysterious article manufactured by the Newsomes is never to be specified) or established generic and authorial conventions (say, the expectation of having a clearing-up chapter in the detective story as opposed to the expectation that a Shakespearean tragedy will seldom definitely formulate the motives of leading characters, whether Brutus, Macbeth, Hamlet, or for that matter Iago). But as far as the constant of the sequentiality of the reading-process is concerned, the question whether the clash of referential hypotheses is temporary or permanent can never be decided a priori, with the opening of the gap, but only a posteriori, with its final closure or nonclosure by the text.

The conditions of "temporary permanence" and "permanent temporariness" have, then, far-reaching implications for the extent and flexibility of the distributive and persuasive options at the disposal of the literary artist. But this by no means neutralizes the effects of the disparity between the two types of ambiguation, which come to the fore when the reader looks back on some reconstituted temporal segment and above all on the text as a whole.

First, the significance of these effects manifests itself in the basic difference between the devices by which the suppressed or delayed information is foregrounded. For what turns out to be a permanent ambiguity is retrospectively highlighted against the background of the text's principles of selection, the gap being a chronological blank in the fully reconstituted *fabula* as well as in the unfolding *sujet*; whereas what turns out to be a temporary gap is highlighted against the background of the text's principles of combination, the sujet creating the gap by dislocating and relocating some coherent fabula segment. Consequently, the opening of each type of gap and its further ambiguation or disambiguation in the sequel are revealing in a different way. With the first type the reader asks, Why has the author chosen to leave out this information altogether while going counter to the quantitative indicator in actively drawing attention to its absence and importance? And he is recurrently directed to work out such various (though often complementary) answers as:

1. In order to avoid weak specifications and instead give scope to the reader's imagination (as with the evil to which the children are exposed in James's *The Turn of the Screw* and Aziz and Miss Quested in Forster's Marabar caves).

2. To deconcretize a fictive element in the interests of structural linkage, normative density, and thematic universalization (as with Balzac's Michonneau and Poiret).

3. To dramatize the theme that what really matters is not the objective truth (e.g., whether Christmas is white or black) but the subjective view of the environment or, even more general, that factual truth (e.g., the relations between and motives of the characters in *The Good Soldier*) is unattainable and that only subjective impressions of reality are given to man.

4. To counteract the dangers of sentimentality (as with Milly Theale's mysterious illness in *The Wings of the Dove* or Iona's repeatedly delayed and finally suppressed tale in Chekhov's "The Lament").

5. To produce the delights and tensions of ambiguity for their own sake (this indulgence in the game of art is carried to an extreme in Robbe-Grillet's *La Maison de rendez-vous,* perhaps the closest referential equivalent in fiction to the wildest gambols of verbal ambiguity in poetry).

6. Possibly even to elide materials to which the author feels unequal, as with Jane Austen's notorious shirking of serious love scenes ("What did she [Emma Woodhouse] say? What she ought, of course. A lady always does").

With the second type of gap, on the other hand, the reader asks, Why has the author chosen to complicate the process of communication, through the delay, distribution, and at least partly misleading patterning of antecedents, when he could easily have avoided all this and was determined to fill in the gaps anyway? And the reader is thereby directed to the various functions I have dealt with throughout—including (as long as the ambiguity is unresolved) temporary, less drastic, or fallacious versions of those that have just been cited as typical of permanent gaps.

Second, the temporary gap involves by definition not a single but at least a double chronological displacement—both when opened and when filled in—not to speak of such gradual, partial, or dubious closures as characterize innumerable instances of the plunge *in medias res,* distributed and false exposition, or subjective refraction and outside view. Therefore, apart from the two questions that arise with the discovery of each type of gap (Why has the gap been opened? And why at this point?) and apart from the selectional question that retrospectively arises in each case (Why has the text ultimately chosen to close or to perpetuate the informational breach?), there arises in retrospect another, combinational question that is peculiar to the temporary gap: Why has the author chosen to divulge the withheld information, and thus put an end to the play of hypotheses, at precisely this point or series of points? The previous chapters have amply demonstrated not only the variety of ways in which this choice too can be explained but also the extent to which the answers, whether in terms of generic predetermination (as in the detective story) or more particular exigencies and functions (as repeatedly in the *Odyssey*), throw light on the compositional, semantic, and affective potency of temporal ordering.

The Object of the Multiple Systems   The dynamics of referential ambiguity, whether temporary or permanent, are launched and controlled by the suppression of antecedent materials of the most diverse kinds. The informationally gapped object may consist in:

1. *Actional segments or causal links* (whether in the temporary form of Darcy's treatment of Wickham or the permanent one of Karamazov's treatment of his first wife), including of course the *internal action* of motive and feeling (compare for instance the detective story's progressive disambiguation of the tensions leading to such a drastic act as suicide with its recurrent permanent ambiguation in canonical literature, ancient and modern: Achitophel's self-strangulation in the Book of Samuel, Skarp-Hedin's resigning himself to being burnt together with his father in *Njal's Saga,* Smerdyakov's hanging himself in *The Brothers Karamazov,* or the suicides of Faulkner's Quentin and Woolf's Septimus).

2. *Character-traits* (Odysseus's or, permanently, Julius Caesar's or the dramatized narrator's in *The Sacred Fount*), whose unfolding and integration often turn on basic views of character (e.g., the flat-round opposition).

3. *Personal relations* (between Odysseus and Calypso, Christmas and Miss Burden, or the Dowells and the Ashburnhams in *The Good Soldier*).

4. *Descriptive details,* which, though in themselves static, may be manipulated into serving propulsive roles in the action as well as in the reading-process (e.g., the temporarily delayed Pemberley scenery, with its suggestive beauties and sinuosities, or the permanently suppressed physical

features of the face that launched a thousand ships); and the equally manipulable limits and contents of the spatial arena, including the very existence of individual agents, actional strands, and parts of the fictive world (as with the shifting geography of the *Odyssey,* the initially invisible and by implication idealized high society in *Père Goriot,* or the never-reached top of Kilimanjaro in Hemingway's tale).

5. The premises, canons, and tendencies composing the *probability-register of the fictive world* as a whole (Is this logic "realistic" or "melodramatic"—as in Balzac; "realistic" or "grotesque"—as in Gogol; "realistic" or "supernatural"—as in the ghost story; "realistic" or "comic" —as in Fielding? In what sense, case or degree is it "realistic" or the reverse? What is the relative weight of external—universal, contemporary, or artistically conventional—and internal probabilities; and what of essentially mimetic and essentially compositional hypothesizing? And even when this general, sometimes generic, reality-model is not especially problematic or has been roughly reconstructed by the reader, there still remains the formidable problem—as in the *Odyssey,* in Jane Austen, even in Trollope—of applying the text's unique structure of probabilities to each crux and expectation, with its variable interplay of character, event, and circumstance.)

At this stage it is only necessary to add five further comments on this aspect. First, the manifold dynamization to which even inherently static fictive objects are amenable (in forms as complex and multifunctional as Balzac's principle of "convertible dimensions") not only explains my insistence on incorporating and placing them in such a developmental pattern as the fabula rather than in a separate, atemporal or spatial, fictive framework, but also forcefully brings out the fundamental difference between material and function.

Second, no more justified would be the equation of the fictive object of temporal manipulation with the object of the rhetorical strategy grounded on the resultant play of expectations. With Odysseus or Faulkner's Sutpen in *Absalom, Absalom!* the two are indeed more or less identical; but Darcy's past is temporarily ambiguated and recontextualized mainly in order to control our response to Elizabeth, the question of Becky Sharp's innocence in the affair with Lord Steyne is permanently gapped to drive home a general thematic point, and Chichikov's motives are withheld for generic purposes.

Third, multiple systems of gap-filling may also relate to different components of the narrative act of communication (and of smaller acts framed by it, such as interpolated tales, interior monologues, or dialogue scenes), whether located within or without the projected world. A case in point is the question of Odysseus's reliability as autobiographical teller, or the discovery that, contrary to the first impression, the source of *Pride and Prejudice*'s opening sentence is the collective viewpoint of the country families rather than the narrator herself. But as this is essentially a problem of narrative perspective, it will be separately dealt with below.

Fourth, texts, authors, and genres may be collocated and distinguished according to the nature of the suppressed referential, especially expositional, material. In the detective story, for instance, the object of reconstitution is a series of events and a network of superficial personal relations (and the genre itself may be subclassified according to the relative position of the three major gaps); in Shakespearean tragedy, the reconstructive emphasis falls on motive; in the stream of consciousness novel, the reader is constantly directed to puzzle out the pressure of past experience on present association; while in Gogol, Kleist, or the post-Jamesian ghost story, it is often a question of deciding between (or integrating) opposed probability-registers, reality-models, or perceptual sets that relate to the whole universe of discourse.

Fifth, the gaps and shifts in the reader's reconstitution of the various fictive objects both affect and are affected by the no less eventful unfolding of patterns on all other textual levels—whether verbal ambiguity, literal and figurative sequence, analogical development, thematic twists, or generic metamorphoses. Still, just as the causally propelled dynamics of the action within the represented world is the backbone of the narrative work, so is its actual ordering the backbone of the dynamics of presentation. It is in terms of the relations devised between these two sequences and their contextual centrality vis-à-vis the others that many diachronic changes (including modern novelistic aspirations to the condition of drama, poetry, or music) as well as synchronic differences are best described.

The Relative Probability of the Multiple Hypotheses   Different cases of gap-filling also vary widely in the relative weight of the different hypotheses, their degree of probability ranging from something like zero (no contextual support or even explicit invalidation) to a factual or quasi-factual status (as when the gap is finally disambiguated and the clash resolved by a reliable omniscient narrator). This variability has a double significance. From the comparative and typological viewpoint, it affords an important basis for the opposition of various poetics. A possible scale: Trollope, who goes out of his way to maneuver the reader—through a full disclosure of the narrative past and occasional anticipations of the future—into holding a single, authorially validated "hypothesis" throughout about each potential crux; Homer, James, Nabokov, or the detective story, each striving after his own fashion to generate prolonged and hard-contested clashes between hypotheses, temporary and permanent, through different strategies of temporal distribution, informational coloring, structural misdirection, and verbal equivocation; and in between the poles, Jane Austen, whose recourse to the rhetoric of anticipatory caution consists on the one hand in alerting the reader to at least two conflicting hypotheses where the heroine only sees a single sequence of established facts and on the other hand in consistently rendering this "factual" sequence less plausible than the alternative reading. From the complementary, interpretative viewpoint, to trace the shift of probabilities along the continuum of the single work is to lay bare a crucial dimension of its semantic and rhetorical art (as with the dynamics of narrative interest in the "Telemachia," the rise and fall of first impressions in Faulkner and Balzac, or any other case of retrospective revision).

Simultaneity and Successiveness in Hypothesis-Construction The complex of narrative interests in literature—and the more "respectable" functions and manifestations of each—has been progressively disentangled in close reference to various principles of distribution and ambiguation. Our distinction between the two clashing components of suspense, hope and fear, relates to two possible expectations about the future resolution of a conflict; that between curiosity and suspense relates to the chronological direction of the missing and desired information (narrative past versus future); while that between curiosity and surprise relates to the perceptibility of the process of gapping and gap-filling. With "curiosity gaps," the reader is at once alerted to the deformation of antecedents; with "surprise gaps," in contrast, his awareness of the gap's very existence and/or relevance and/or true significance is retrospective, being delayed to the point of closure rather than heightened at the point of opening. To distinguish in these terms between perceptible and camouflaged suppression or anticipatory and retrospective ambiguity is not of course to preclude the possibility of interaction between the two types of displacement (as in Jane Austen) any more than between curiosity and suspense; nor the possibility of mixed gaps (whose opening is highlighted, while the timing, manner, or substance of their filling is unexpected, as—often—in the detective story); nor even the possibility of dynamic variations in the status of a single gap as the result of such textual developments as the turning of hitherto unsuspected blanks into intriguing informational cruxes (a central feature of Faulkner's unfolding of the Sutpen saga, for instance) or the invalidation of apparently settled linkages (e.g., the abrupt reopening of the question of the delay in Odysseus's homecoming). It is only to refer another basic difference in function and effect to a difference in the distribution of material and the consequent relations between the hypotheses—this time to the order in which they are made to emerge.

The distinctive feature of the "curiosity gap" is that its opening simultaneously gives rise to no less than two legitimate possibilities of closing the glaring informational breach. The number of hypotheses, their object, compositional grounds, logical or existential relations, relative probability, and correspondence with those entertained by the dramatis personae—all these vary widely even within and along a single text, as we have repeatedly seen. What remains constant is the consciousness of referential ambiguity and the active play of expectations, lasting till the gap is definitively closed at any point or (if permanent) definitively left open at the end.

What characterizes the pure "surprise gap," however, is that the different hypotheses emerge not simultaneously but successively, often in a widely spaced sequence. More precisely, one of them is made to arise immediately upon the hidden opening of the gap—as the automatic, self-explanatory, or at least overwhelmingly probable explanation; so that it may be effectively demolished and replaced by a subsequently sprung explanation, with a superior intrinsic authority or contextual power of accounting for the facts. This is, then, the most extreme case of shifts in probability during the reading-process. For the position of the successive hypotheses within the text's structure and hierarchy of probabilities is not simply changed, but turned upside down: what at first seemed the only possibility, to the extent that the reader may have unconsciously filled in the gap in passing, is later eliminated or at least drastically demoted, and what at first may not have occurred to him at all is later decisively established. But, as suggested, there are also various cases of mixed ambiguation and less drastic dynamics; the scale on which the three basic control strategies have been ranged largely corresponds in fact to that leading from "surprise gaps" to "curiosity gaps."

The Logical Relations between the Hypotheses The logical relations between the multiple hypotheses are no less variable, both comparatively and sequentially speaking. These relations range from the pole of mutual exclusiveness to that of complementariness or even partial overlapping. In some instances, briefly, to accept one of the hypotheses is to reject the other(s), since they are mutually incompatible in purely logical terms, or in terms of generally accepted views of reality, or in terms of the work's internal logic, or in any combination of these normative models, including deliberately manipulated tensions between external and contextual incompatibility. Is the world of *The Turn of the Screw* realistic or supernatural? Is Joseph K. or the suspect in the detective story guilty or innocent? Is Wickham a gentleman or a cad of gentlemanly appearance? And which of the five men in her life did Gudrun of the *Laxdaela Saga* love best? It is precisely such either/or choices that literature often suspends and forces the reader to hold in combination, for a variety of purposes, not only successively but also simultaneously, not only temporarily but also permanently.

In other instances it is equally evident that the rival hypotheses are heterogeneous, independent of each other and often practically unlimited in number (e.g., those concerning Milly's mysterious illness in *The Wings of the Dove* or, in a more comic key, the unnamed article produced by the Newsomes in *The Ambassadors,* which critics have made futile attempts to disambiguate), and are primarily to be integrated in rhetorical terms, such as density of insinuation. And in still other instances, they are variously reconcilable even in logical or mimetic terms as well—whether fully or partly, literally or figuratively, factually or psychologically, a priori or a posteriori, into chronological sequence or simultaneity—though it may ultimately turn out that only one of them is valid.

This is the case, for example, with expositional gaps as different as the antecedents of Balzac's pension trio (Michonneau may have lost her looks through both prostitution and avarice, or first through one and then through the other), the complex probability-register shaping the fate of Returners in the *Odyssey,* or the motives activating Iago (possibly a combination of envy, vindictiveness, and sheer love of evil). With regard to the latter gaps of psychological ambiguation, it is particularly noteworthy that even hypotheses that appear contradictory or incompatible in the abstract may be contextually rendered inextricably complementary—in terms of the agent's complex or paradoxical make-up. The tense love-hate relations between Dostoyevsky's figures, with the resultant actional surprises and complications, are a conspicuous case in point. And so is the Jamesian principle of propelling protagonist as well as reader towards an insight into the mixtures and paradoxes of the expositional situation and the human predicament in general—into what Strether in his last confrontation with Madame de Vionnet belatedly recognizes as the "fine, free range of bliss and bale." Common to all such cases is the synthesis of previous existential opposites in terms of a single inclusive hypothesis.

II

But in order to see the problem of the temporal disposition of narrative materials, notably exposition, in the round, one must view it in still another perspective by distinguishing between two modes of motivation. When making this additional discrimination, one is not concerned with the position or form or ordering of exposition per se but with the different ways in which the work may choose to account either for its general principles or for isolated instances of expositional dynamics.

The term *motivation* as used here diverges from its customary designation in criticism, that is, "the combination of circumstances (or the art of their combining) that makes plausible the actions of a character by supplying them with a reasonable basis in past events."[2] The motivation I shall deal with is not psychological but compositional: it does not explain the actions of the characters but primarily the strategy of the artist.[3] For my present purposes I shall define *motivation* as the explicit or implicit justification, explanation, or dissimulation of an artistic convention, device, or necessity either in terms of artistic exigencies, goals, and functionality (aesthetic or rhetorical motivation) or in terms of the referential patterns of the fictive world (realistic or quasi-mimetic motivation). It is the network of motivations crisscrossing a work that gives it its unity and coherence, for an unmotivated motif or group of elements is obviously a redundancy.

As the provision of antecedents is an artistic necessity *par excellence,* the author must always find a way of motivating his temporal structure so as to integrate this material, sequentially and/or retrospectively, with the other elements of the work. He must, then, justify three aspects of his expositional presentation, namely, the existence of the expositional material or rather of each of the parts composing it (What is this piece of information doing in the work? Why has it been selected or specified or disambiguated while others have been kept out or left open?); the particular location of each part in relation to the others (Why has this piece of information been presented at this point when it seems properly to belong to that? Why is its location preliminary—or why is it not? Why has it not been delayed like some of the other expositional motifs? etc.); and what I have called its form (Why has this complex of motifs been concentrated, distributed, or segmented in the way it is?). The basic modes of expositional motivation may, however, vary not only from work to work, and not only from instance to instance within the same work, but even from one aspect of a single instance to another.

What characterizes expositions that are motivated in purely aesthetic terms is that their communication has no existence on the level of the fictive reality and the represented action but takes place exclusively within the framework of the rhetorical relationship between narrator and reader. The narrator has no recourse to the mediation of his dramatis personae but addresses the exposition straight to the reader, as part of his narrative duties and artistic aims. Frequently, no effort is made to disguise its informational or other functions. On the contrary, they are at times brought into the open to be excused, explained, or simply stated. Trollope's defiant vindications of his temporal principles are perhaps the best example. But they have rarely been rivaled in length and detail. Overt aesthetic motivations of one or more of the three aspects of presentation mentioned above are usually formulated much more concisely. In the first chapter of William Godwin's *Caleb Williams,* for instance, the narrator prefaces the introduction of preliminaries with the comment that there are "some circumstances deserving to be mentioned as having influenced the history of my future life"; in Salinger's "Zooey," the narrator observes that the title character is so complex that "at least two dossier-like paragraphs ought to be got in" right upon his first appearance, and he later apologizes for "the aesthetic evil of a footnote" in which the rest of the family is lumped together; whereas chapter 33 of Dickens's *Old Curiosity Shop* states that "as the course of this tale requires that we should become acquainted, somewhere hereabouts, with a few particulars connected with the domestic economy of Mr. Sampson Brass, and as a more convenient place than the present is not likely to occur for that purpose, the historian takes the friendly reader by the hand, and springing with him into the air . . . alights with him upon the pavement of Bevis Marks."

Most expositions that have a purely aesthetic motivation, however, dispense with formal preambles, suchlike explanatory phrases being, as I argued in my first chapter, implicit in the very nature of the information conveyed and the manner of its insertion and integration: "There was a man in the land of Uz, whose name *was* Job; and that man was perfect and upright, one that feared God, and eschewed evil"; or "The Brangwens had lived for generations on the Marsh Farm, in the meadows where the Erewash twisted sluggishly through alder trees" (*The Rainbow,* chap. 1).

While in all these cases, however, the purely artistic justification of the communication, form, or order of the antecedents and the consequent structural dynamics is at least partly borne out by the represented facts, in other cases the aesthetic motivation explicitly adduced by the narrator is only designed to dissimulate the real aims (or real aesthetic motivation) guiding his narrative strategy. The real aesthetic motivation is then not simply implicit but deliberately camouflaged by the false. This often happens, as one might well expect, when the narrator wishes to account in artistic terms for his flagrant suppression or delay of some material that should, logically and chronologically, have been communicated at the point where the motivation is introduced or much earlier in the sujet. In *The Brothers Karamazov,* the presentation of Smerdyakov is thus abruptly cut short with the remark that "I should really say something more about him, but I am ashamed to keep my reader's attention occupied with common servants too long, and I am therefore going back to my story in the hope that all the relevant facts about Smerdyakov will somehow or other emerge in the course of it" (pt. 3, chap. 2). As we retrospectively discover, however, Smerdyakov, far from being just another of the "common servants," is (both dramatically and thematically) one of the novel's main figures; and the narrator's assumed impatience with him, his professed reluctance to waste space on so insignificant a character whom he can afford to realize "somehow or other" in the sequel, and his desire to get on with the central line of the action, are not manifestations of artistic selectivity but cunning mystification devices that further (e.g.) the detective theme. The false aesthetic motivation, in fact, throws dust in the reader's eyes by distracting his attention from the future parricide and centering it on Dmitri; as such it should be sharply distinguished from such genuine motivations of expositional location as "I'm afraid I shall have to give some preliminary description of [Alyosha], too, to explain at least one very strange fact, namely, the fact that I am forced to introduce my future hero to the reader in the very first scene of my novel wearing the cassock of a novice" (pt. 1, chap. 3), on the one hand, and from such inadequate (or even partly erroneous) but truly meant overt aesthetic motivations as some of Trollope's, on the other.

When portraying Sir Francis Clavering, Thackeray resorts to the pretext of artistic economy to justify his marked suppression of relevant information, though for a wholly different reason—to achieve the density to which I referred in the previous chapter. Having effectively discredited the Baronet by putting forward a number of hypotheses to explain his avoidance of the officers of his regiment, the narrator motivates his real purpose in leaving this gap permanently open by the claim that "it is not our business to inquire too closely into the bygones of our characters, except in so far as their previous history appertains to the development of this present story" (*Pendennis,* chap. 25). In *Dead Souls,* on the other hand, the motivation of the prolonged ambiguity of Chichikov's antecedents has the rich comic flavor typical of Gogol's art. The perfectly naturalistic explanation of the hero's seemingly mad business deals is postponed to the last chapter—though it chronologically antedates almost everything else—since there was no other way of maintaining the overall grotesque effect. But before springing the truth on us—at a time when we have already despaired of understanding Chichikov's motives and at an appropriately inappropriate place, namely, during the flight from town with which the novel ends—Gogol innocently accounts for this unconscionable delay in terms of the overwhelming amount of work he has had on his hands since the beginning of the novel: "The author confesses that he is actually very glad [that Chichikov has fallen asleep in his troika], since it will afford him an opportunity of saying something about his hero, inasmuch as up to now, as the reader has seen, the author has been incessantly hindered now by Nozdrev, now by balls, then by ladies, then by the tittle-tattle of the town, then finally, by thousands of these trifles which seem trifles only when they are put into a book but which, while they are in circulation in the world, are held to be quite important matters. But now let us put absolutely everything to one side and get right down to business."[4]

Mostly, however, the true artistic functionality of the expositional strategy is not disguised by a factitious though equally aesthetic motivation. It is dissimulated in a mode that wholly transcends the aesthetic, namely, the quasi-mimetic (or "realistic"). What characterizes this second mode of motivation is that it accounts for one or more of the three aspects of informational disposition not in terms of artistic or rhetorical exigencies, real or pretended, but of various patterns located in the fictive world itself—such as contiguity in time or space, the logic of events, relations between characters, psychological traits, etc.

The most prevalent pattern by which the introduction of material into the work is realistically motivated consists in one character being made to convey to another—usually at the latter's request—some information that to the reader is expositional. In the *Odyssey,* for instance, this pattern constantly recurs. Telemachus's journey is a quasi-mimetic framework that subsumes a variety of minor expositional motivations. Wherever the youngster lands, he naturally inquires after his father: "'I have come here to plead with you in the hope that you will tell me the truth about my father's unhappy end, if by any chance you witnessed it yourself'" (p. 43); and again, with regard to Agamemnon's history, "'How did imperial Agamemnon meet his end? Where was Menelaus, and by what cunning snare did that false man Aegisthus contrive to kill a man far braver than himself?'" (p. 47). Alcinous, intrigued by his guest's appearance and conduct, can also be made to ask the stranger to unfold his past adventures, even to the point of specifying the subjects he would like the prospective narrator to dwell upon:

> "And now I call upon you for a true account of your wanderings. To what parts of the inhabited world did they take you? What lovely cities did you see; what people in them? . . . Explain to us also what secret sorrow makes you weep as you listen to the tragic story of the Argives and the fall of Troy. . . . Perhaps one of your kinsmen by marriage fell before Ilium. . . ? Or perhaps it was a comrade?" (P. 116)

In C. P. Snow's *The Corridors of Power,* the narrator, Lewis Eliot, is made to impart his antecedents in the course of a grueling security investigation he is put through; and so are most suspects in detective stories. The quarrel between Face and Subtle opening Ben Jonson's *The Alchemist* realistically motivates the dialogic recriminations that give the reader a good idea of the nature of the criminal set-up in Lovewit's house.

The realistically motivated communication of exposition may take a written as well as oral form. Soon after the beginning of Richardson's *Clarissa,* the heroine is made to comply with Miss Howe's urgent request to write to her "the whole of [her] story from the time that Mr. Lovelace was first introduced into [her] family; and particularly an account of all that passed between him and [her] sister; about which there are different reports; some people scrupling not to insinuate that the younger sister has stolen a lover from the elder." This is just another variation on the principle of (quasi-mimetic) frame within (rhetorical) frame, each with its own speaker and addressee. But the basic quasi-mimetic pattern may even undergo a more radical, asymmetrical change with the disappearance of the internal audience. In a stream of consciousness novel, for instance, most of the expositional information must emerge not under the guise of dialogue scenes but through the quasi-mimetic process of association taking place in the privacy of the mind. Critical overemphasis of the revolutionary nature of the modern novel sometimes tends to blur the continuity of narrative art by indiscriminately taking its new motivational tactics for strategic innovations. A functionally oriented review of historical developments in terms of shifts from one dominant mode of motivation to another or from one device or variation or degree of consistency to another within the same basic mode (to be later exemplified in miniature by the development of Henry James's art) may serve to redress a considerably disturbed balance in our view of aesthetic ends in relation to quasi-mimetic means. What largely marks the modern novel is the invention of new or the radicalization of old quasi-mimetic frameworks—whether Joyce's or Proust's psychological or Ford's and Conrad's "impressionistic" modes of progression—rather than new aesthetic and rhetorical motivations. As far as the latter alone are concerned, there is little difference between the permanent ambiguation of the final horrors experienced by Abraham about to sacrifice Isaac, James's Milly Theale with her face to the wall, and Conrad's Kurtz in the heart of darkness; or between the gradated disclosure of Leopold Bloom's sexual and his Homeric prototype's social aberrations.

In spite of their diversity, all these patterns of motivation have a common denominator that is peculiar to the purely realistic mode of introducing motifs. In all of them the expositional material stands at one further remove from the narrator (or author) than in the case of corresponding aesthetic motivations; it is conveyed to the reader not directly, by a narrator who openly shows himself aware of the duty of providing the necessary antecedents, but obliquely, through the mediation of the characters framed within their fictive world. The reader gathers the required information by eavesdropping, as it were, on the dramatis personae.[5] The dynamics of the reading-process is effected and propelled under the guise of the dynamics of the action. And the dissimulation accordingly consists in the exposition being formally integrated as part of the represented events and only indirectly as the premises to a textual proposition. It may be conventional or new, a mere means or an artistic ideal per se, consistent or local, plausible or weak, or even deliberately tenuous. But behind every quasi-mimetic motivation there is an aesthetic motivation—of the kind we have been dealing with throughout—though not vice versa.[6]

One often discovers, moreover, that where the motivation for the introduction of expositional matter is realistic, those for location and form concur with it, all three mutually reinforcing one another. In the detective story, for example, the investigation forms an overall motivational framework for all three aspects in that its inevitable exigencies realistically motivate (1) the dramatized emergence of expositional material throughout; (2) the indispensable retardatory structure consisting in the delay of the true exposition to the last chapter; and (3) the tantalizing distribution and ordering of disconnected expositional (and other) clues throughout the body of the work and their orderly concentration at the end. The artist pulling the strings of hypothesis-construction is thus concealed by a facade of *vraisemblance.* In the *Odyssey,* the complication of the initial outside views and the intermediate scenic views through the concentrated and conspicuously delayed intercalation of Odysseus's wanderings is accounted for by another tight complex of motivations; the hero has for the first time been urged to tell the whole story of his adventures, of which the rest of the informants we have met so far are ignorant. On the other hand, while employing much the same quasi-mimetic pattern for inserting and locating Booth's tale in *Amelia,* Fielding manages, by appropriately adjusting the circumstances of the narration and the relations between secondary narrator and internal audience, freely to segment this expositional block.

But the text does not necessarily have to limit itself to a single mode of motivation (though, I shall argue later, some works consistently do so). Even a glance at the list of local expositions distributed along the *Odyssey,* for example, will reveal the flexibility with which Homer turns from one mode to another, according to the varying artistic needs I have analyzed: e.g., the preliminary block or the interpolated retrospect about Odysseus's scar as opposed to the numerous dialogue scenes in books 1–4. Even the presentation of a single piece or block may be motivationally mixed. In this regard, a few comparisons between the old novel and the new, with its authorial distancing and internalized or unreliable focuses of narration, will prove generally suggestive. The ostensibly metonymic progression, usually disguising subtle metaphoric links, informs both Balzac's external and (microcosmically) the stream-of-consciousness's internal landscaping. But in the former the quasi-mimetic logic of development motivates at most the form and local ordering of the information conveyed—say, the concentric portrayal of the pension—while in the latter, the framework of the workings of a given mind also makes it possible to cover its very selection ("introduction") and its overall ordering.

No less common: equally aware of the drawbacks of the natural order of presentation from the viewpoint of narrative interest, both Trollope and Graves in *I, Claudius* feel obliged to account for their recourse to it. But while Trollope tries to justify the preliminary location and concentrated form of his exposition, as well as its very introduction and its specificity, on purely aesthetic grounds, Graves motivates the same presentational choices realistically too, in terms of the dramatized characteristics and qualifications of Claudius, the narrator-agent. In fact, it is Graves's ambition to present a panoramic picture of Roman society that dictates the recourse to chronological sequence, the long stretches of preliminary exposition, and the avoidance of such distracting interests as sustained curiosity and suspense. But instead of openly adducing these artistic exigencies to explain his strategy, Graves throws the blame, so to speak, on the shoulders of his narrator. As a professional historian, Claudius is obviously conscious of the need for exposition; what is more, he looks down on the slipshod narrative techniques of irresponsible artists, preferring "the thorough Roman method, which misses nothing, to that of Homer and the Greeks generally, who love to jump into the middle of things and then work backwards and forwards as they feel inclined"; he is intent on incorporating introductory "genealogies and family histories," however tedious to the reader; and he naturally disparages such cheap artistic effects as curiosity, suspense, and surprise. Having been delegated to the dramatized narrator, these aesthetic motivations assume a quasi-mimetic appearance absent in Trollope, for *Graves's* aesthetic motivations are in this way realistically dissimulated as *Claudius's* aesthetic motivations. The complex of realistic motivations centering in Claudius is particularly effective in that it dovetails into the overall aesthetic aims of the novel, lending it an air of historical authenticity while at the same time throwing a good-humoured ironic light on the long-winded, slightly pompous narrator.

In *The Devils,* Dostoyevsky covers the same presentational choices by the dramatized narrator's plea of inexperience in literary composition (and in *A Raw Youth,* also by his professed contempt for "literary graces"): "Before describing the extraordinary events which took place so recently in our town . . . I find it necessary, since I am not a skilled writer, to go back a little and begin with certain biographical details concerning our talented and greatly esteemed Stepan Trofimovich Verkhovensky. I hope these details will serve as an introduction to the social and political chronicle of our town." The strength of his apology—like that of the excuse offered by the old professor of languages in Conrad's *Under Western Eyes* for his failure to provide proper transitions between the various parts of the novel—"lies not in its art, but in its artlessness."[7] In *The Catcher in the Rye,* on the other hand, essentially the same quasi-mimetic motivation, carried to an extreme, is exploited for diametrically opposed ends. While in *I, Claudius* and *The Devils* it is the narrators' awareness of the need for exposition (manifested in their overt aesthetic motivations) that enables the authors to justify realistically its preliminary location and concentrated form, here Holden Caulfield's naiveté, leading to a categorical denial of the existence of expositional exigencies, makes not only for a stronger realistic dissimulation of the expositional material he unconsciously communicates but mainly for its temporary suppression, delay, and distribution. And again, what is so striking about this motivation is its psychological appropriateness as well as compositional efficacy.

III

The foregoing account of modes of motivation and illustration of (mostly local) motivational devices have, I believe, sufficiently paved the way for an analysis of the most comprehensive principle (or framework) motivating the selection, combination, and distribution of elements in the narrative text, namely, point of view.

Of the various aspects of point of view, the three that most directly relate to the problem of temporal structure and its motivation are the narrator's "privilege" or range of knowledge; the use he makes of his privilege; and the question of his self-consciousness—not in Booth's sense of awareness of writing a literary work and discussion of writing chores but simply in the sense of awareness of facing an audience or reader.[8] For it is impossible to account fully for such choices as expositional delay, distribution, and order of presentation without investigating (1) whether the narrator is aware of addressing an audience, external or internal, who must be provided with the necessary antecedents if it is to make anything of the story and whose response to the story will largely turn on the expositional procedure employed; (2) what the narrator himself knows at the start of the telling and the range of information to which he has access throughout; and (3) whether he fully shares his information with the reader. Other facets of the problem of narrative perspective—reliability, for instance—will be shown to be ancillary to these in the framework of the present study.

Both in point of informational privilege and self-consciousness, the author must be sharply distinguished from the narrator. The author or (in Wayne Booth's suggestive phrase) "implied author"—the omnipotent artistic figure behind the work, incessantly selecting, combining, and distributing information, and pulling various strings with a view to manipulating the reader into the desired responses—is the creator of the art of the work as well as its meaning, of its rhetoric as well as its normative groundwork and thematic pattern. As such, he is by definition acutely self-conscious throughout. Within the limits of the microcosm he has himself created, moreover, the author is invariably, divinely omniscient; the common phrase "the omniscient author" forms, as a matter of fact, a self-implicative attribution, in which the modifier is logically redundant.

The reader, however, does not as a rule come into direct contact with the implied author himself. Instead of addressing us in person, the author interposes another figure between himself and the reader, namely, the narrator—the person or persona that actually does the telling. And the two are not necessarily interchangeable, although in some cases they virtually merge into each other. For the author is under no obligation to delegate to his deputy the whole complex of godlike privileges and artistic attributes by which he is characterized, or even a single one of them. He may indeed choose to create the narrator in his own image by investing him with full omniscience, self-consciousness, and reliability—as Homer, Fielding, or George Eliot generally do for their own artistic purposes. But he also may, and in many instances he does, break the identity to a greater or lesser extent by depriving his narrator of one or more of these attributes, thus retiring to his position behind the scenes. Significantly, this is true even of omniscient narration. The authors of *Vanity Fair, The Brothers Karamazov, Don Quixote,* or "The Overcoat"—to cite a few notable examples—partly divest their narrators of reliability, though leaving them as variously omniscient as George Eliot's. In *Don Quixote,* for example, the author (who also acts as editor or primary narrator) is not content with making his characters impugn the veracity of Cid Hamet Benengeli, the Moorish historian from whose manuscript the bulk of the story is "translated," but goes out of his way to do so himself both with reference to particular episodes and to the infidel narrator's procedure as a whole:

> [Don Quixote] relaps'd into melancholick Doubts and Anxieties, when he consider'd that the Author had given himself the Title of *Cid,* and consequently must be a *Moor.* A Nation from whom no Truth could be expected, they all being given to impose on others with Lies and fabulous Stories, to falsify and counterfeit, and very fond of their own Chimera's [sic].
>
> I must only acquaint the Reader, that if any Objection is to be made as to the Veracity of this [History], 'tis only that the Author is an Arabian, and those of that Country are not a little addicted to Lying: But yet, if we consider that they are our Enemies, we shou'd sooner imagine, that the Author has rather suppress'd the Truth, than added to the real Worth of our Knight; and I am the more inclinable to think so, because 'tis plain, that where he ought to have enlarg'd on his Praises, he maliciously chooses to be silent; a Proceeding unworthy of an Historian, who ought to be exact, sincere, and impartial.[9]

It thus emerges that the almost axiomatic presupposition of novel criticism since Lubbock that the omniscient narrator coincides with the author at all points or rather *is* the author—a presupposition that accounts for the prevalent tendency to use the two terms interchangeably[10]—fails to stand up to the facts; the omniscient narrator is as much a creation of the author's as are dramatized narrators that are obviously distant from him. The eponymous narrators in *Barry Lyndon* or *Tristram Shandy*, for instance, have only been placed at one further remove from their authors, being self-conscious but restricted as well as unreliable; while in Gogol's "A Diary of a Madman" or James's "The Diary of a Man of Fifty" they are wholly unselfconscious into the bargain. Whatever logic or theology may lead us to expect, there are no package-deals in narration.

As part of his general self-consciousness, the implied author is of course fully aware of the inevitability of his expositional duties and also of the beginning as, both logically and chronologically, the natural place for concentrating the premises; and owing to his unqualified omniscience and omnipotence, there is nothing to keep him from acting upon this awareness, if he wishes to do so, by resorting to preliminary exposition. But since different artistic goals, as I have demonstrated, dictate different narrative strategies and expositional modes, and since it is not usually the author who addresses us in person, he must in each case account for his presentational techniques in terms of the point of view actually employed in the work. Once we come to consider the problems of temporal structure in these terms, we realize that the author cannot but motivate his expositional choices, whatever they are, through the postulation of a certain kind of narrator, the "concrete deputy or delegate, [the] convenient substitute or apologist for the creative power otherwise so veiled and disembodied."[11] For it is evident that the particular manner in which the communication of information is effected inextricably depends in each instance on the attributes, privileges, or limitations of the narrator, the channel through which the information is actually transmitted. This point has, in fact, already been touched on in the foregoing section. But there I confined myself to indicating the interrelationship between expositional motivation and such accidental or idiosyncratic traits of the narrator's as Claudius's historical training or Holden's adolescence and naiveté; here I wish to deal with such fundamental and inescapable motivational factors as self-consciousness or range of knowledge.

IV

The type of narrator that most closely approximates the implied author is the omniscient. Like the author, into whom he in some cases fully merges, the all-knowing narrator is, and often presents himself openly as, an artistic figure with superhuman powers. Though he may pretend (as Thackeray's and Fielding's do) to descend into the fictive arena and rub shoulders with the characters, he essentially stands above the world which he sometimes professes to have created and over which he has complete control owing to his godlike privileges of unhampered vision, penetration to the innermost recesses of his agents' minds, free movement in time and space, and knowledge of past and future. But in his role as quasi-maker or maker's duplicate, the omniscient narrator is characterized not only by omnipotence and omnipresence but also by his intense awareness of facing an audience. As Thackeray puts it in the preface to *Pendennis,* the "perpetual speaker" is in such "constant communication with the reader" that the process of narration may be described as "a sort of confidential talk between writer and reader." In modern times, this self-consciousness is seldom openly avowed; but the flagrantly intrusive omniscient narrators of the eighteenth- and nineteenth-century novel devote considerable energy to striking up an acquaintance with the reader, to characterizing themselves and him or themselves in relation to him, to praising and flattering or rebuking and calumniating him, to preaching or poking fun at him, to anticipating his every wish, or to taking pride in having frustrated his expectation.

Qua self-conscious artistic figure, the omniscient narrator is thus by nature as aware as the author himself of the need for exposition and of the natural place for imparting it; and since, unlike an equally self-conscious but humanly restricted narrator, he is also by definition possessed of all the relevant information from the very start, there is no realistic obstacle to keep the author from making him proceed in accordance with this consciousness. Consequently, whenever the omniscient narrator starts his sujet by giving the reader a concentrated exposition *ab ovo,* thus combining all three aspects of straightforward temporal communication, he does no more than might be expected of him. And irrespective of whether he sets forth his reasons for doing so in such preambles as cited in a previous section, or whether he refers to them in such chapter headings as "The birth, parentage, and education of Mr. Jonathan Wild the Great" (*Jonathan Wild,* chap. 3), or "The Old Pyncheon Family" (*The House of the Seven Gables,* chap. 1); or whether he simply goes through his preliminary summary as a matter of course, the motivation for this procedure is *purely aesthetic:* the artist's deputy knows but too well that if he is to launch us successfully into his unique fictive world, he must ensure our acquaintance with it.

The point is, of course, that omniscient narrators more often than not fail to act upon this inherent awareness in that they delay the exposition as a whole or at least some parts of it to later stages—so often indeed that nowadays it is chronological progression (*pace* the Russian Formalists with their a priori view of the sujet) that may be said to carry a peculiar power of perceptual defamiliarization.

This goes to show again that omniscient narration by no means forms a homogeneous category. Different narrators, though possessing omniscience as a common denominator, may radically differ in other, and equally important, respects. Reliability is only one of these; what is even more significant in the present context is the possible disparity in their readiness to share their unlimited knowledge with the reader. Both Fielding and Trollope, for example, almost invariably postulate obtrusively omniscient, highly self-conscious, and fully reliable narrators, who are practically identical with their implied authors. But what a chasm separates these narrators in all that concerns the question of the proper use to be made of their omniscience:

> It is an observation sometimes made, that to indicate our idea of a simple fellow, we say, he is easily to be seen through: nor do I believe it a more improper denotation of a simple book. Instead of applying this to any particular performance, we chuse rather to remark the contrary in this history, where the scene opens itself by small degrees; and he is a sagacious reader who can see two chapters before him.
>
> For this reason, we have not hitherto hinted a matter which now seems necessary to be explained; since it may be wondered at, first, that Joseph made such extraordinary haste out of town, which hath been already shown; and secondly, which will be now shown, that, instead of proceeding to the habitation of his father and mother, or to his beloved sister Pamela, he chose rather to set out full speed to the Lady Booby's country-seat. . . .
>
> Be it known, then, that in the same parish where this seat stood there lived a young girl whom Joseph (though the best of sons and brothers) longed more impatiently to see than his parents or his sister. (*Joseph Andrews*, bk. 1, chap. 11—aptly entitled "Of Several New Matters Not Expected")

> To bring our favourites out of their present anguish and distress, and to land them at last on the shore of happiness, seems a very hard task, a task indeed so hard that we do not undertake to execute it. In regard to Sophia, it is more than probable that we shall somewhere or other provide a good husband for her in the end, either Blifil, or my lord, or somebody else, but as to poor Jones, such are the calamities in which he is at present involved . . . that we almost despair of bringing him to any good, and if our reader delights in seeing executions, I think he ought not to lose any time in taking a first row in Tyburn. (*Tom Jones*, 17.1)

But let the gentle-hearted reader be under no apprehension whatsoever. It is not destined that Eleanor shall marry Mr. Slope or Bertie Stanhope. And here perhaps it may be allowed to the novelist to explain his views on a very important point in the art of telling tales. He ventures to reprobate that system which goes so far to violate all proper confidence between the author and his readers by maintaining nearly to the end of the third volume a mystery as to the fate of their favourite personage. Nay, more, and worse than this is too frequently done. Have not often the profoundest efforts of genius been used to baffle the aspirations of the reader, to raise false hopes and false fears, and to give rise to expectations which are never to be realised? . . . And is there not a species of deceit in this to which the honesty of the present age should lend no countenance?

And what can be the worth of that solicitude which a peep into the third volume can utterly dissipate? What the value of these literary charms which are absolutely destroyed by their enjoyment? When we have once learnt what was that picture before which was hung Mrs. Ratcliffe's [sic] solemn curtain, we feel no further interest about either the frame or the veil. They are to us merely a receptacle for old bones. . . .

And then how grievous a thing it is to have the pleasure of your novel destroyed by the ill-considered triumph of a previous reader. "Oh, you needn't be alarmed for Augusta, of course she accepts Gustavus in the end." "How very ill-natured you are, Susan," says Kitty with tears in her eyes: "I don't care a bit about it now." Dear Kitty, if you will read my book, you may defy the ill-nature of your sister. There shall be no secret that she can tell you. Nay, take the third volume if you please— learn from the last pages all the results of our troubled story, and the story shall have lost none of its interest, if indeed there be any interest in it to lose.

Our doctrine is that the author and the reader should move along together in full confidence with each other. Let the personages of the drama undergo ever so complete a comedy of errors among themselves, but let the spectator never mistake the Syracusan for the Ephesian; otherwise he is one of the dupes, and the part of a dupe is never dignified. (*Barchester Towers,* chap. 15)

The dichotomy of omniscience versus restrictedness, exclusively relating as it does to the narrator's potential range of knowledge, is obviously inadequate for describing the diametric opposition between the two kinds of narrator and narrative technique adumbrated in these statements. This blanket-distinction must be complemented by a more specific differentiation, on another axis altogether, which will account for the opposition in terms of the two narrators' actual practice of communication: Trollope's narrator is omnicommunicative as well as omniscient, while Fielding's is deliberately suppressive.[12]

To put it differently: the act of narrative communication presupposes a complex of four basic components or participants, namely, the author who creates the story, the narrator who tells it, the audience or reader who receives it, and the fictive agents who enact it.[13] As regards informational privilege, therefore, point of view involves a set of no less than six closely connected relationships, some of which may occasionally overlap, as when the narrator is practically identical with the author or when he is himself one of the agents. Of these six fundamental relationships, that between the author and the characters alone always remains constant in its informational inequality; while the five others—between author and narrator, author and reader, narrator and reader, narrator and characters, and reader and characters—are flexibly variable.[14]

Thus Fielding and Trollope are wholly agreed as to the proper relations to be postulated between author and narrator on the one hand and between both of these and the dramatis personae on the other—the first kind being in each case characterized by perfect informational (and normative) parity, the second by radical imparity. It is only in their conception of the relations between the author's plenipotentiary and the reader—and consequently between the reader and the characters—with regard to informational privilege in general and expositional privilege in particular that these two novelists (and for that matter any omnicommunicative and deliberately suppressive omniscient narrators) are so violently opposed. In previous chapters I have already demonstrated the correlations between given effects and hierarchies of value on the one hand and overall orders of presentation and expositional modes on the other. I shall now proceed to argue that in order to describe adequately the disparities in narrative strategy between different works and writers, another related factor must be taken into account, namely, the nature and attributes of the narrator and his relations with the other three basic components of point of view. In the present case of Fielding and Trollope, I intend to show, part of the artistic goals aimed at by each dictate the postulation of an omniscient narrator as a conventional (ultimately quasi-mimetic, though by no means "realistic" in the sense of "verisimilar") motivation of the unlimited range of knowledge that he must be assumed to possess in order to achieve them; while the radically different strategy of communication—the order and modes of presentation—must in each case be accounted for in purely artistic terms, that is, in terms of some other or related effects that the omniscient narrator desires to produce and that call for different relations between him and the reader as far as informational privilege is concerned. In short, both in Trollope and in Fielding, the narrator's unlimited principles of selection—on the axis of delegated power—are quasi-mimetically motivated, whereas his principles of combination, distribution, and ordering—on the axis of actual communication—only aesthetically.

Fielding would no doubt be inclined to dismiss Trollope and his books as "simple"; Trollope in effect accuses Fielding of "deceit." Such an exchange of compliments would not in itself lead us very far, but it may offer a convenient starting-point for the comparison of their narrative strategies in that it raises the question of how each of them conceives of the reader—the person who, after all, is most likely to suffer from authorial simplicity or deceitfulness. It is, I shall argue, the differences in the reader envisaged that entail the disparities not only in temporal structure but in point of view as well.

The idea behind James's pregnant aphorism that the novelist makes his reader very much as he makes his characters has been rediscovered and developed in recent criticism. Walker Gibson, for instance, claims:

> Every time we open the pages of another piece of writing, we are embarked on a new adventure in which we become a new person—a person as controlled and definable and as remote from the chaotic self of daily life as the lover in the sonnet. . . . Subject to the degree of literary sensibility, we are recreated by the language. We assume, for the sake of the experience, that set of attitudes and qualities which the language asks us to assume, and, if we cannot assume them, we throw the book away.
>
> I am arguing, then, that there are two readers distinguishable in every literary experience. First, there is the "real" individual . . . whose personality is as complex and ultimately inexpressible as any dead poet's. Second, there is the fictitious reader—I shall call him the "mock reader"—whose mask and costume the individual takes on in order to experience the language. The mock reader is an artifact, controlled, simplified, abstracted out of the chaos of day-to-day sensation.[15]

The best way of putting it is that the "mock reader"—or in Rebecca Price Parkin's even more appropriate phrase, the "implied audience"[16]—created by the work ultimately forms an embodiment of its norms and interests, just like the implied author, to whom he indeed stands in the same relationship as the "real" reader does to the "real," biographical author. And as such an embodiment, he may evidently vary from one work to another. What is so striking about the reader Fielding envisages is, first, that—again precisely like Fielding's implied author—he is not only implied by the work's structure and narrative strategy (what Gibson probably means by the rather vague or poetry-oriented phrase "recreated by the language") but is also overtly evoked in the narrator's commentary. And, second, that whatever change the other attributes of this implied reader may undergo from novel to novel in line with the variations of the implied authors,[17] at least one central trait remains constant—his partiality for such narrative interests as curiosity, suspense, and surprise and, in general, for all the dynamic effects that similarly turn on chronological deformations and the suppression, delay, and distribution of information.

Fielding's narrators, for instance, largely create or mold their implied reader by constantly heightening his consciousness of the withholding as opposed to the timely communication of information. They often preface the disclosure of a piece of news, especially a secret (expositional or non-expositional), with a remark in which the point or benefit of the disclosure is explained (e.g., *Tom Jones,* 8.3; 9.7; *Joseph Andrews,* 1.15) or in which its previous suppression is commented on (*Tom Jones,* 10.6), accounted for (*Tom Jones,* 5.6), or simply apologized for (*Tom Jones,* 8.9; *Amelia,* 11.3). They likewise refer time and again to the reader's curiosity (or suspense)—asking him to "suspend" it for a while and promising to allay it in due course (*Tom Jones,* 2.6; *Amelia,* 8.9); announcing their intention to proceed at once to ease or indulge his curiosity, which "must be now awake and hungry" (*Tom Jones,* 2.8; 15.1; *Joseph Andrews,* 2.1; *Amelia,* 4.8; 12.9); characterizing the reader as "curious" or "impatient" (*Tom Jones,* 2.9; *Joseph Andrews,* 4.9); and even going so far as to declare outright that "our most favourite readers . . . are the most curious" (*Amelia,* 12.5).

But Fielding's overt rhetoric, though it effectively canalizes the reader's expectations into the desired grooves and heightens his readiness to indulge in inferential activity, only serves to reinforce the staple means by which narrative interest is engendered, molded, and sustained, namely, the handling of the plot itself, which involves a constant suppression of information through temporal displacement. Some of the temporary gaps thus created are conspicuously manipulated in the interests of curiosity, while others are almost imperceptibly opened so as to redouble the surprising effect of their ultimate filling in; and there is also an abundance of devices particularly designed to stimulate suspense, such as ominous anticipatory hints and retardatory structure.

Fielding's recourse to this narrative strategy is decisively to be explained in terms of his theory of fiction and his view of himself as the founder of a new species of writing. Fielding sees himself as innovator not so much in the invention of new literary interests as in the manner of achieving those that writers of all ages have pursued. The thorough discussion of the effect of surprise (*Tom Jones,* 8.1) may serve as an example. His conclusion that "every writer may be permitted to deal as much in the wonderful as he pleases; nay, the more he can surprise the reader, if he thus keeps within the rules of credibility, the more he will engage his attention and the more he will charm him" was anticipated by Aristotle by a good two thousand years and had become by his own time something of a critical truism. Where he breaks fresh ground is in his insistence on credibility, in his definition of it, and above all in the means he devises for reconciling it with a narrative strategy that largely consists in piling surprise on surprise.

Like that of most of his contemporaries,[18] Fielding's "realism" takes the form of a violent break with the tradition of the romance in all that concerns the incorporation of supernatural or otherwise inherently improbable subject-matter. Fielding repeatedly argues that the introduction of miracles and supernatural agents was perfectly natural in ancient times, when "poetical fables were articles of faith" and "deities were always ready at the writer's elbow to execute any of his purposes, and the more extraordinary the intervention was, the greater was the surprise and delight of the credulous reader"; similarly, the historian not only may but must "record matters as he finds them, though they may be of so extraordinary a nature as will require no small degree of historical faith to swallow them." But for the modern novelist, he insists, the improbable should be out of bounds, even by way of paralogism: "As we have no public notoriety, no concurrent testimony, no records to support and corroborate what we deliver, it becomes us not only to keep within the limits of possibility but of probability too." So far he is in essential agreement with Richardson or Trollope, but from now on their ways part, for Fielding has no intention of giving up or even playing down the interest of surprise. The comic epic in prose, like the Aristotelian pattern of epic upon which it is manifestly modeled, turns to no small extent on surprising reversals and recognitions: besides offering comic and seriocomic entertainment throughout, these compositional resources also afford a neat closure to the work. As I pointed out in the previous chapter, moreover, surprise rather than curiosity has often been the favorite effect of writers who, like Fielding, have wished to avoid riveting the reader's mind on the last chapter but instead to leave it free to dwell on each stage of the fictive journey.[19] So, having rejected the possibility of manipulating the reader's surprise through the free extension of the principles of selection, he hit upon the idea of producing it, within the prescribed limits of realistic subject-matter, through the principles of combination, mainly the modes of informational distribution.

It is accordingly no wonder that in all three of Fielding's novels proper the happy resolution of the imbroglio in the fictive world is brought about by the unexpected coming to light of hitherto suppressed information that to the reader is expositional, namely, the revelation that Mrs. Harris's will has been forged by Amelia's sister; and the discovery of the parentage of Tom Jones and Joseph Andrews in full-scale recognition scenes, the former being especially remarkable in that it also satisfies our long-aroused curiosity and dispels the steadily mounting suspense. In the instance of Tom's delivery, Fielding even goes out of his way to impress on the reader the novelty of his procedure. Having warned us that Tom will as likely as not be hanged, he goes on to promise that

> notwithstanding any affection which we may be supposed to have for this rogue, whom we have unfortunately made our hero, we will lend him none of that supernatural assistance with which we are entrusted upon condition that we use it only on very important occasions. If he doth not, therefore, find some natural means of fairly extricating himself from all his distresses, we will do no violence to the truth and dignity of history for his sake; for we had rather relate that he was hanged at Tyburn (which may very probably be the case) than forfeit our integrity, or shock the faith of our reader" (17.1).

The distributive art characterizing a large number of his scenes, moreover, reflects in miniature the dynamic structure of the plot as a whole. A case in point is the occasion on which the dumbfounded Tom discovers Square hiding in Molly's closet, "in a posture (for the place would not near admit his standing upright) as ridiculous as can possibly be conceived" (5.5). In retrospect we realize that this small-scale recognition scene closely resembles the major one that is still to come, since the impact of the delightful surprise itself and also of the concomitant thematic point (the deflation of the philosopher's as well as Molly's pretensions and the similar unmasking of Blifil) and generic twist (the sudden reversal of fortunes) is redoubled in both owing to the temporary suppression and ambiguation of chronologically anterior events.

Given the interests of Fielding's implied reader and the implied author's views of his craft, it thus emerges that the postulation of a narrator who is not omnicommunicative is inescapably dictated as the only means of effecting the necessary chronological dislocations. Basically, however, there are two possible ways of accounting for the lack of a fullness of communication on the part of the narrator: the quasi-mimetic motivation, in terms of the narrator's own human limitations of knowledge and insight, and the purely aesthetic, in terms of the superhumanly omniscient narrator's deliberately pursued artistic aims. And of the two Fielding significantly resorts and adheres to the second in all of his novels. His reasons for thus employing an omniscient narrator are not all directly related to the question of temporal ordering. (One must not lose sight of the consideration that a restricted narrator, by definition as humanly fallible as any other fictive agent, could hardly be invested with the authority necessary for devising and making the reader accept the running choric commentary—on the conduct of the characters, on human nature, on literary problems, and occasionally on cabbages and kings—that is indispensable to the work. This overt rhetoric, which even the late James cannot but warmly praise as an embodiment of Fielding's "fine old moralism, fine old humour and fine old style, which somehow really enlarge, make every one and every thing important,"[20] had to come from a reliable source, of infinite knowledge and wisdom.) But there is no doubt that this compositional choice is designed to reinforce and control the dynamics of the reading-process in the way most congenial to Fielding. Let me illustrate its effects in a descending order of specificity.

Ian Watt has noted Fielding's custom of presenting events so "as to deflect our attention from the events themselves to the way that Fielding is handling them," and his use of devices that "compromise the narrative's general air of literal authenticity by suggesting the manipulated sequences of literature rather than the ordinary processes of life" and thus make up "an intellectual and literary structure which has a considerable degree of autonomy."[21] Had Watt's tone been descriptive instead of prescriptive, had he not in effect blamed Fielding for not being Richardson, these remarks might have afforded an even better formulation of one of Fielding's hallmarks—the tendency to direct the limelight on his artifice, contrivance, and compositional ingenuity, which contemporary readers were quick to appreciate. One prime manifestation of this fondness for calling attention to the game of art consists in the postulation of an omniscient but suppressive narrator, whose temporal manipulations are naturally much more conspicuous—being motivated in purely "artificial," aesthetic terms—than any restricted narrator's could be. Fielding's *personae,* moreover, constantly take care to highlight their suppressiveness—and thus to intensify the effect of the gaps—by flaunting their omniscience in the reader's face. With regard to the central expositional ambiguity in *Tom Jones,* the parentage of the foundling, the narrator addresses us as follows:

> Though I called him poor Partridge in the last paragraph, I would have the reader rather impute that epithet to the compassion of my temper than conceive it to be any declaration of his innocence [of fathering Tom]. Whether he was innocent or not will perhaps appear hereafter; but if the historic Muse has entrusted me with any secrets, I will by no means be guilty of discovering them till she shall give me leave.
>
> Here, therefore, the reader must suspend his curiosity. (2.6)

The same applies to such tantalizing displays of foreknowledge as "something whispers me in the ear that [Tom] doth not yet know the worst of his fortune, and that a more shocking piece of news than any he hath yet heard remains for him in the unopened leaves of fate" (17.1).

Strangely enough, however, devices of this kind, while heightening our curiosity and suspense, also have at the same time a reassuring effect. By drawing attention to his superior knowledge and his preference for holding all the trumps in his hand, the narrator leaves no doubt in our mind that the situation is under perfect control from start to finish, thereby giving our anxiety for the protagonist the desired comic flavor and keeping it at the desired comic pitch. The closer the novel draws to an end, for example, the surer we become that the still undivulged secret of Tom's birth is going to play a decisive role in the resolution of the increasingly thickening imbroglio; and that, however serious Tom's plight may appear, the omnipotent narrator, replacing the supernatural agents of earlier fiction, will play Providence in the end ("Let us try what by these [natural] means may be done for poor Jones"; 17.1).

The first book of *Joseph Andrews* gives us an even more impressive measure of the indispensability of the narrator's informational privilege for the control of generic tone. The excerpt from chapter 11 with which I started this section coincides with a decisive generic shift within the novel—from the burlesque tone of the opening to the comic epic proper. What crystallizes the burlesque of the London scenes is the "motivelessness" of Joseph's defense of his virtue against Lady Booby's onslaught, and the parodistic analogy with Richardson's paragon is fully articulated in the young man's pietistic letter to his sister Pamela in chapter 10. In the next chapter, however, having stated his doctrine of opening the scene by small degrees, the narrator springs on us the disclosure that Joseph has been in love for years with a beautiful girl, this naturalistic explanation retrospectively "redeeming" the hero's common humanity, qualifying him for his new task, and in general paving the way for the future operation of comic probability. Whether this shift of the generic gears was part of Fielding's original plan or whether it resulted from a sudden change of mind marking the stage at which Fielding found himself at last, is for our purposes beside the point. The point consists in the extent to which the shift (reminiscent of Gogol's three-phase strategy in *Dead Souls*) hinges on a carefully timed expositional manipulation, which in turn requires a narrator who is in full command of his materials throughout.

Furthermore: the narrator's omniscience enables him not only to control the effects of his suppressions but also to impart to the reader at will such privileged information as no restricted narrator could have access to. For the most part, he indeed prefers to promote various ends by keeping us in ignorance of some facts possessed by one or more of the dramatis personae as well as by himself; but his unlimited range of information makes it possible for him to transpose perspectives whenever it suits his purposes to place the reader on a level of awareness higher than that of his characters. This is often done, for instance, to create and sustain dramatic irony. It is by keeping us informed of the characters' secret thoughts, true intentions, or even simply their identities, that he puts us in a position to enjoy in his company the series of comic misunderstandings and complications marking the occasion on which Blifil makes his unwelcome addresses to Sophia (6.7), or the uproarious fun of the slapstick scene that starts with Beau Didapper's stealing at night into Slipslop's bedroom under the impression that it is Fanny's and ends with the naked Adams engaging in a ferocious mock-heroic battle with Slipslop, having mistaken the rough-bearded virago for the would-be rapist and the soft-skinned gallant for the damsel in distress (4.14).

The same potentialities of conveying to the reader otherwise inaccessible information are exploited for more serious purposes too, particularly the control of our response to the characters' moral nature. Thus, by introducing the reader into the minds of both Tom and Blifil, the narrator ensures that we should not for a moment be in danger of falling into the same errors of judgment as Allworthy—even though his other goals dictate our being kept in as much ignorance as Allworthy of the clinching proof of Blifil's villainy. His omniscience, then, often enables him to eat his cake and have it too. Finally, to mention what is perhaps the most striking local instance of the manifold use of omniscience in this work, when the gossips of the neighborhood begin to whisper that the father of the foundling is none other than Allworthy himself and that he has "spirited [Jenny] away with a design too black to be mentioned," Fielding is confronted by a tricky problem. He must at all costs prevent the reader from entertaining this suspicion, for by throwing the moral stature of his fallible but not too fallible paragon in doubt, he is liable to undermine the normative groundwork of the novel; and yet he must delay the true account of Tom's birth if he is to keep his secret hidden. Here again it is due to the narrator's omniscience (this time, his undoubted knowledge of past and future rather than his powers of penetration into the minds of his characters) that he can have it both ways. For while it enables him to reinforce the effect of the expositional gap concerning Tom's parentage through the deliberately mystifying comment on poor Partridge, whom he could so easily exculpate from guilt at once, it also enables him to do the opposite with regard to Allworthy. To leave the latter's integrity unquestioned, he does not have to disambiguate the whole sequence by divulging the identity of Tom's true father. All he has to do is to put his authority behind the "very early intimation that Mr. Allworthy was, and will hereafter appear to be, absolutely innocent of any criminal intention whatever [in sending Jenny away]. He had indeed committed no other than an error in politics by tempering justice with mercy" (1.9).

The relationships established in Fielding's novels between author, narrator, audience, and agents in point of informational privilege and expositional privilege in particular[22] are thus to be explained in terms of the variety of effects he aims at producing through his manipulations of chronology and perspectival discrepancies. The narrator's claim (appropriately made soon after Squire Western bursts upon the London scene, just in time to save his daughter from being raped by his lordship) that "we dearly love to oblige [the reader] whenever it is in our power" is, when one compares his "power" with his habitual practice of communication, mockingly ironic; while the ensuing declaration that "it is not our custom to unfold at any time more than is necessary for the occasion" (15.6) may be viewed either as an understatement or, given his peculiar conception of what is "necessary," as an affirmation of the literal truth. For one of the laws regulating life in the new province of writing which Fielding sees himself as having founded consists in the reader (the "subject") being placed in an essentially inferior position in relation to the narrator. And having constituted himself absolute master of the situation, the narrator is able to take advantage of his superiority with the greatest flexibility, transposing privileges and discrepancies from one segment and sometimes one phrase to another according to his varying needs. He may use his power in order to raise what Trollope calls false fears and false alarms, and yet subtly to allay them at the same time. He may open temporary gaps at any point, stress their temporary nature, challenge the reader to fill them in by his own ingenuity, and yet remain confident that "the reader, without being a conjurer, cannot possibly guess, till we have given him . . . hints" (*Joseph Andrews,* 1.10)—the more so since his hints are, as I shall soon indicate, not only few and insubstantial but sometimes even misleading as well. In fact, he likes to play the conjurer himself—and it is generally in order to be able to pull informational rabbits out of his hat and enhance the impact of his exquisitely timed surprises, unmaskings, and denouements that he prevents the reader from peeping behind the scenes. And finally, he may also partly or temporarily abandon his suppressive procedure, taking the reader into his confidence in order to achieve ends that can be encompassed in no other way. The narrator's assumption of an Olympian vantage-point is, in short, Fielding's main device for controlling the reader's reactions and keeping him variously entertained; and he accordingly expects the implied audience cheerfully to accept the prescribed rules of the game, since (as he points out in another context) he is an enlightened tyrant: "I am, indeed, set over them for their good only, and was created for their use and not they for mine" (2.1).

If Fielding's *personae* are classic examples of the suppressive omniscient narrator, Trollope's are the quintessential manifestation of the omnicommunicative. I have already shown how Trollope's insistence on the primacy of character over plot—curiously enough, also in the name of "realism"—presupposes a hierarchy of literary value in which the complex of narrative interests is demoted to the lowest rank; how his views of fiction imply a reader—created in his own image and naturally honored with the title "real novel reader"—who, far from "curious" or "sagacious," is characterized by his impatience with plot contrivances and his corresponding partiality for the "lucid" delineation of psychological conflicts; and how the interests of his implied reader call for "straightforward, simple, plain story-telling," notably for the adherence to chronology and hence preliminary and concentrated exposition. It now remains to be shown that it is the opposition in some of the main desired effects between Trollope and Fielding (or for that matter between Trollope and the author of the *Odyssey* or *Bleak House*) that accounts not only for the radical disparity in their habitual orders of presentation and expositional procedures but also for the related difference in point of view within the omniscient mode.

In the light of Trollope's aims, the postulation of either a deliberately suppressive or even a humanly restricted narrator—in other words, the postulation of any point of view, whether omniscient or not, that for some reason involves a plunge *in medias res* or any other form of informational delay and distribution—is a procedure fraught with risks, most of them gratuitous at best. As Trollope has it, to leave the reader in the dark (at any point, but especially at the beginning) as to the secret motives and activities of the dramatis personae, let alone consistently to play on his curiosity, is to risk his mind wandering away from what cannot but be the primary focus of interest; to leave him in doubt, even temporarily, about the probability of their conduct or the validity of the causal reconstitution during the opening scenes—till the narrator either sees fit to divulge the necessary explanation or finally manages to discover it himself—is to risk a possibly irredeemable impression of a lack of verisimilitude (hence, for instance, "I cannot bring in my doctor speaking his mind freely among the bigwigs till I have explained that it is in accordance with his usual character to do so"); and to juggle with the reader's sympathies, even unintentionally, by leaving him to form his own impression of a character from the initially dramatized events or by conveying only part of the expositional material and subsequently modifying or, even worse, altogether uprooting the false impression through surprising disclosures is to risk in addition an indelible primacy effect (in such a case, the reader would be sure to "begin to masticate the real kernel of [the] story with infinite prejudices" against the not unworthy Mary Lovelace).

To Trollope's mind, therefore, narration that is not omnicommunicative—whether omniscient or restricted, whether intentionally or involuntarily suppressive, whether aesthetically or realistically motivated, though of course the more deliberately pursued it is the worse its effects and the sharper the displeasure of "real" novel readers—should be categorically avoided; it is at best attended by serious dangers and can offer no commensurate compensations in return, the pleasures it may give being inherently equivocal if not worthless. But if restricted narration almost inevitably incurs these drawbacks, however freely communicative the narrator, the omnicommunicative omniscient mode not only precludes them but has a number of interrelated positive virtues as well.

One of these is that it immediately establishes between narrator and reader the only kind of relationship that Trollope views (even apart from its salutary effects) as honest and honorable. The narrator does not exploit his delegated or self-constituted superiority in order to turn the reader into the dupe of his tricks ("and the part of a dupe is never dignified") but lets him know from the very beginning, through the exhaustive preliminary exposition, that they are to "move along in full confidence with each other." Such a relationship can of course be postulated in restricted narration too, when the narrator does his best to share with us all the information he himself possesses or possessed at every stage of the action. But the higher the narrator's initially fixed vantage-point, the greater the confidence inspired by his abstention from making use of his advantage over the reader—both because the egalitarian gesture is more impressive and because the information conveyed is as a rule incomparably more complete and reliable.

This gesture of abstention yields in turn the further gain of increased reliability. Like Fielding, Trollope habitually postulates an omniscient narrator not only because his goals cannot be achieved unless the reader has access to a wide range of privileged information but also because we naturally tend to trust (and fictional theory, even to overtrust) in the norms and value-judgments of a divinely endowed guide until he proves to be unreliable. When he shows himself to be all-telling as well as all-knowing, however, our sense of his reliability is reinforced. Not fearing verbal traps and compositional trickery, the reader neither pursues the whole work in a spirit of suspicion nor suspends belief in the narrator's word—his information, his commentary, his presentation and valuation of character and event—but is more ready than ever to accept it at face value.

Last, the preclusion or drastic playing down of expositional gaps by the communication of the detailed and authoritative opening account impresses on the reader from the outset that his position with regard to the narrator on the one hand and the fictive characters on the other is to be radically different from that imposed on him by Fielding or in restricted narration. There, due either to the suppressiveness or the limitations of the narrator, we often find ourselves as baffled and mystified as the characters themselves. In Trollope's novels, however, the narrator extricates or exempts us from this human predicament by sharing with us from beginning to end the privileges of omniscience.

With Fielding, it is the narrator alone that is aware of everything all along, while both the dramatis personae and the reader are to a smaller or greater extent afflicted by ignorance: the former, owing to their human limitations, personal and universal; the latter, owing to the narrator's tendency to keep his own counsel. In each of his novels there are a number of agents who hold an advantage over the reader in that they possess some piece of information that is denied to us: in *Tom Jones,* for example, Bridget Allworthy, Jenny, Dowling, and Blifil know the secret of Tom's parentage at an early stage of the action, whereas we as well as the other characters are kept in the dark almost to the end. In this case we are reduced to experiencing the same emotions of curiosity, suspense, and surprise as those of the agents who are equally ignorant; indeed, their dramatized reactions repeatedly reflect our own. On other occasions, the reader is temporarily placed on a higher level of awareness than one or more characters by the disclosure of some privileged information. It is, in short, through the manipulation and shifting of various perspectival discrepancies or combinations of discrepancies—between narrator and reader or character or both, between reader and character as well as between character and character—that Fielding produces a great many of his effects.

On the other hand, by permanently elevating the reader to his own level of awareness from the beginning and unreservedly sharing with him the privileges of omniscience, Trollope's narrator shares with him his overwhelming advantage over the characters. Communication can of course never be complete, for, owing to the unavoidable selectivity of the literary text, the whole of anything can never be told.[23] But by this rigorous abstention from withholding information through chronological displacements, the narrator ensures that we shall be at every point in possession of all the material that is necessary for such a full comprehension of the present state of affairs as none of the agents can even dream of attaining to. There is thus not a wide variety of discrepancies in awareness but only a single basic discrepancy—between the coalition of author, narrator, and reader on the one hand and the dramatis personae on the other, between those who, in Berowne's words, "Like a demigod . . . sit . . . in the sky, / And wretched fools' secrets heedfully o'ereye" (*Love's Labour's Lost,* 4.3. 79–80) and the "wretched fools" who enact their drama below.[24] And while depriving the reader of what Trollope considers the lower sources of interest, the poetics of lucidity places him, by the same stroke, on an Olympian vantage-point whose occupation is not only flattering and enjoyable in itself but also ideal for the unhampered observation of the fictive arena as a whole, especially the interplay of character. The unenlightened agents, suffering from the defects of vision inherent in the sublunary state of nature, may make false valuations of one another and misjudge one another's (and their own) motives and intentions: Eleanor Bold may be suspected by her family of being partial to Slope; the Peacockes may pass in the eyes of their environment for a married couple; Lady Mason's innocence may be insisted on by Sir Peregrine Orme. But the reader—always in the know because always in the narrator's confidence, his vision sharpened and adjusted at the very start and kept clear throughout by constant injections of privileged fact and commentary—is aware of the truth from beginning to end, and can often, as I have argued, predict future developments as well as see the present in the round. It is accordingly the characters alone, for the most part, that are devoured by curiosity, agitated by suspense and overwhelmed by surprise; while the reader, tranquilly watching them from his coign of vantage and never in danger of mistaking the Syracusan for the Ephesian,[25] is supremely equipped to condone or condemn their lapses, to chuckle or grieve at their antics and fallibility, and above all to appreciate the clash between character and character and the tangle of motive within each throughout the essentially human comedy of errors.

Thus, though Trollope's poetics is in many respects diametrically opposed to Fielding's, the postulation of an omniscient narrator is equally indispensable to both. It is this opposition in desired effects, however, that accounts for the pronounced disparities in the privileged narrators' strategy of communication, as manifested in their different handling of the fabula, and particularly of its expositional section, which is of prime importance in both. Fielding cannot create his implied reader, mold his expectations, and control his reactions without employing an openly suppressive narrator; Trollope cannot do so without joining forces with the reader against the characters. Consequently, Fielding may exploit to the full the potentialities of the verbal medium, especially its linearity and irreversibility, for safeguarding his informational advantage over the reader; it is no accident that, in the quotation from *Joseph Andrews,* the narrator describes his superiority in terms of the continuum of the text, not of events—"he is a sagacious reader who can see *two chapters* before him [my emphasis]." But Trollope deliberately waives this advantage, at times even forgoing the natural gains in suspense that derive from a perfectly straightforward handling of the fabula. While Fielding elaborately shrouds Tom's birth in mystery, Trollope loses no time in giving us a circumstantial account of Mary Thorne's, even before anyone in the world of the novel can suspect that it is to become an issue; while Fielding does not conceal his satisfaction at having managed to spring a surprise on the reader, Trollope in *Orley Farm* anxiously hopes that Lady Mason's abruptly avowed guilt has long ago been detected by us; and while Fielding draws out our suspense as to Tom Jones's ultimate fate to the last possible moment, Trollope takes the first opportunity of reassuring us as to Eleanor

Bold's. In this Trollope simply practices, and as usual carries to an extreme, the doctrine he preaches whenever he reveals to us another of the secrets of *The Eustace Diamonds* (while almost the whole of London, including the police, is still in the dark): "The chronicler . . . scorns to keep from his reader any secret that is known to himself" (chap. 42).

V

Between the two poles of Trollope's ideal of perfect confidence between omniscient narrator and reader and Fielding's ideal of the reader's unconditional surrender to his mentor's superior knowledge, there stand the relations characterizing the detective story. On the one hand this genre necessarily presupposes, like Fielding, a narrator who is not omnicommunicative (he does not necessarily have to be omniscient but he often is), since its effect turns on the creation of temporary gaps and multiple hypotheses; on the other hand it postulates, like Trollope, a peculiar form of confidence between reader and narrator (or author), that is, the convention of fair play.

This narrative mode obviously cannot consist in full communication; but nor can it in arbitrary suppressiveness. Rather, its hallmark is sharply and functionally circumscribed suppression. Here the problem of the narrator's inherent or potential range of knowledge in relation to those of the reader and the characters is of minor importance compared with the communicative rule that the reader's informational privilege must be equal throughout to that of one of the characters, namely, the investigator. For regardless of whether the narrator postulated is omniscient or restricted like ourselves and whether the indispensable chronological deformations are aesthetically or realistically motivated, the author must somehow see to it that we are provided with all the information required to beat the detective to the solution. The starting-point for the race must be identical—a state of ignorance due to which the author and some of the agents, notably the culprit, hold an advantage over both the reader and the detective. The latter endeavor throughout to close this informational discrepancy by rearranging the numerous clues that crop up during the investigation: the question is only which of them will manage to climb to the author's Olympian vantage-point first.

The overall aims of the detective story, therefore, while leaving the channel of information itself at the author's discretion, dictate a narrative strategy that combines in a way several of the features characterizing the strategies of Trollope and Fielding. What I believe of particular significance is that the detective genre, though diametrically opposed to Trollope's novels rather than to Fielding's as regards its implied hierarchy of interest, curiously resembles the former at least as much as the latter as regards the reader's position vis-à-vis the author. Like Fielding, this genre postulates a contest of wits between omniscient narrator (or, when the narrator is restricted, author) and reader, and the techniques of expositional distribution are accordingly similar in some respects; but like Trollope, it encourages the reader to rely on the narrator's imparting to him *all* the relevant information by a certain point. Unlike Fielding, it does not arbitrarily withhold the information and abruptly spring it on us; and unlike Trollope, the information it communicates is not preliminary but delayed, not concentrated but distributed, not direct and authoritative but dissimulated and ambiguous.

As the whole generic effect of the detective story turns on the adherence to the convention of fair play, and as the whole of the reader's effort may be frustrated, and his only pleasure spoiled, by the suppression of vital clues, it is *here* that such an abuse of confidence may indeed—while it may not in Fielding, who postulates quite another kind of relationship between reader and narrator—be denounced as a "species of deceit." Walter Allen's indignation at Charles Reade's suppressiveness—"one can only stare goggle-eyed at the effrontery of a novelist who can baldly . . . write, 'He drew George aside, and made him a secret communication,' the secret of which, of considerable interest to the plot, is not to be revealed until several hundred pages later"[26]—is understandable but not wholly justifiable by the internal premises of the work; and one suspects it rather derives from displeasure at the narrator's clumsiness than from the suppression itself—why else does he not make the same strictures upon Fielding's equally obtrusive devices? On the other hand, it is not at all surprising that Poe should closely scrutinize Dickens's *Barnaby Rudge*—which is in effect a detective story or, in Poe's own words, a novel with a "*thesis* . . . based upon curiosity"—for possible betrayals of confidence on the part of the omniscient narrator:

> The design of *mystery* . . . being once determined upon by an author, it becomes imperative, first, that no undue or inartistical means be employed to conceal the secret of his plot; and, secondly, that the secret be well kept. Now, when at page 16, we read that "the body of *poor Mr. Rudge, the steward, was found*" months after the outrage, etc., we see that Mr. Dickens has been guilty of no misdemeanor against Art in stating what was not the fact; since the falsehood is put into the mouth of Solomon Daisy, and given merely as the impression of this individual and of the public. The writer has not asserted it in his own person, but ingeniously conveyed an idea (false in itself, yet a belief in which is necessary for the effect of the tale) by the mouth of one of his characters. The case is different, however, when Mrs. Rudge is repeatedly

denominated "the widow." It is the author who, himself, frequently so terms her. This is disingenuous and inartistic: accidentally so, of course.[27]

To subject Fielding to such scrutiny, however, is to do him great injustice. Not only is his spectrum of interests (indeed like Dickens's) wider and more various than that postulated in the detective story, but his main narrative effect is also different, as can be structurally inferred from the predominance of surprise over curiosity in his novels. He may encourage the reader to exert his sagacity, but he clearly indicates that he has no intention of providing him with the material necessary for filling in the temporary gaps, fathoming the mysteries, or anticipating the surprises. On the contrary, he delights in misdirecting his reader even by way of overt authorial commentary, a trick to which no self-respecting mystery writer would stoop. Thus, he blandly comments that

> notwithstanding the positiveness of Mrs. Partridge . . . there is a possibility that the schoolmaster [Partridge] was entirely innocent; for though it appeared clear on comparing the time when Jenny departed from Little Baddington with that of her delivery that she had there conceived this infant, yet it by no means followed of necessity that Partridge must have been its father; for, to omit other particulars, there was in the same house a lad near eighteen, between whom and Jenny there had subsisted sufficient intimacy to found a reasonable suspicion. (*Tom Jones,* 2.6)

He is not to be trusted even when explicitly professing to have disclosed to the reader all the information relating to a certain character or event. He takes pride in having given us "the fruits of a very painful inquiry, which for [our] satisfaction [he has] made into" the history of Mrs. Waters, but he has of course omitted to tell us that this lady is none other than Jenny Jones (9.7). And finally, even the most sagacious reader cannot possibly penetrate the secret of Tom's birth for the simple reason that the narrator has already referred to Tom, on his own authority, as Jenny's "child" (1.9), while the father turns out to be a character who has not even been mentioned in the novel previous to the resolution.

CHAPTER NINE

EXPOSITIONAL MOTIVATION, TEMPORAL STRUCTURE, AND POINT OF VIEW (2): RESTRICTED AND SELF-RESTRICTED NARRATION

> The sense of a system saves the painter from
> the baseness of the *arbitrary* stroke, the
> touch without its reason.
>
> Henry James, Preface to *The Tragic Muse*

The suppressiveness of the omniscient narrator may take different forms, according to the ends it is designed to serve. It may be tacit or obtrusive; wholly unshackled or rigorously circumscribed; consistent and sustained throughout the work, as in the mystery story, or intermittent and momentary, as in Thackeray, or both, as in Fielding; it may make for a heightened manipulation of gaps or for their concealment, for prospection or for retrospection; and the control obtained over the reader may be exploited for the promotion of any or all of the artistic goals analyzed throughout this study.

It is important to realize, at any rate, that the unfairness that Trollope and many subsequent readers found fundamentally to inhere in this narrative mode primarily derives from the purely aesthetic motivation in terms of which the delay and distribution of information practiced by the kinds of omniscient narrator mentioned so far is to be accounted for. The narrator who actually shows himself to be freely omniscient in his principles of selection can obviously devise realistic motivations for the communication of expositional or other material; but he can adduce none for its suppression, whatever form it may take. He cannot, and indeed does not, expect his pleas of ignorance to be taken seriously. In *Pendennis,* for example, the narrator's playful claim that "as Pen himself never had any accurate notion of the manner in which he spent his money . . . it is, of course, impossible for me to give any accurate account of his involvements" (chap. 19) is flatly contradicted not only by his habitual omniscient practice in this novel but, more significantly still, by his boast that "novelists are supposed to know everything, even the secrets of female hearts, which the owners themselves do not perhaps know" (chap. 23). In fact, such evasions may fulfill various functions—from the production of a humorous effect to the insistence on a permanent gap (e.g., the ambiguity of Becky Sharp's "guilt"); but whatever their effect, it largely turns on the very baselessness of the narrator's plea of ignorance—on its not being taken at face value.

It is because the omniscient narrator so obviously knows everything that the purely aesthetic logic underlying his deformations has often been considered inadequate and the whole procedure condemned as an abuse, or at least a misuse, of informational privilege. Complaints of this kind have been directed not only against such rank offenders as Reade but even against the incomparably less obtrusive practice of Jane Austen:

> One objection to this selective dipping into what mind best serves our immediate purposes is that it suggests mere trickery. . . . If Jane Austen can tell us what Mrs. Weston is thinking, why not what Frank Churchill and Jane Fairfax are thinking? Obviously because she chooses to build a mystery, and to do so she must refuse, arbitrarily and obtrusively, to grant the privilege of an inside view to characters whose minds would reveal too much. But is not the mystery purchased at the price of shaking the reader's faith in Jane Austen's integrity? If she simply withholds until later what she might as well relate now—if her procedure is not dictated by the very nature of her materials—why should we take her seriously?[1]

As I argued, such strictures are not always justified; but the point is that the presuppositions on which they are grounded have influenced the compositional choices of many writers. Some of these have resorted to the omnicommunicative mode; while the majority have only been impelled to devise such superior procedures of accounting for the artful ordering as will appear not arbitrary but "dictated by the very nature of [the] materials"—in short, to different varieties of realistic motivation.

The strongest realistic motivation for deviations from the fabula is to be found in the narrative form that is characterized by an unselfconscious as well as restricted narrator, namely, the diary. Nobody can blame the diarist for withholding expositional material since he is generally unaware of the existence of any prospective reader and does not regard what he is writing as a story intended for publication. On the contrary, what often induces the narrator to be absolutely frank with himself is the reassuring consideration that nobody else is ever going to violate the privacy of his writings. In other words, the implied author's choice of this confessionlike form is aesthetically motivated by his desire for authenticity or psychological immediacy; but if it were not for the quasi-mimetic reassurance of privacy, he could not with any show of probability make the narrator lay bare his innermost thoughts.

At any rate, since the diarist is his own audience as well as his own chronicler, he evidently does not feel called upon to start by imparting to *himself* the antecedents to his story;[2] and since his range of information is also necessarily restricted, he would often be unable to do so with any approach to thoroughness and authoritativeness even if he wished it. Owing to this combination of realistic premises, the self-conscious author finds himself here in a position diametrically opposed to that of the author who postulates an omniscient narrator: the suppression, delay, and distribution of exposition is not only perfectly natural but almost inescapable in the very nature of the case, while it is its communication at the proper chronological point that becomes the problem. And this may prove a liability as well as an asset.

In "The Diary of a Man of Fifty," for instance, James can accordingly manipulate gaps to his heart's content. Due to the narrator's unselfconsciousness, his expositional relations with the Italian countess can be made to emerge gradually, side by side with the development of the strikingly analogical story of the young Englishman whom he wishes to rescue from her daughter's clutches; and due to the narrator's limitations of knowledge and self-knowledge James can perpetuate the tantalizing ambiguity as to what really happened thirty years before by showing how the general's confidence in his own version of the affair with the mother is badly shaken through his contact with the daughter. On the other hand, whenever the diary-form requires the introduction of preliminary and concentrated exposition, the author is generally forced to fall back on fairly complicated devices involving aesthetic motivation. The most common of these consists in turning the journal of the unselfconscious narrator into an inset, framed by some fictitious editor's prefatory account. This additional narrator, being intensely conscious of presenting a story to the public, can be made to carry out the expositional chore as a matter of course, sometimes even overscrupulously. In James's "The Landscape Painter," the editor informs the reader in the frame about his friend Mr. Locksley, so that when he proceeds to put before us a hundred pages from Locksley's diary, we are already in a position to understand what is happening. The aesthetic motivation for both the communication of exposition and its location thus relates exclusively to the superadded narrator, who stands to Locksley's story in point of function and to Locksley himself in point of self-consciousness as the prologue does to the body of the play and to the dramatis personae.

Between the two extremes—the diary, with its powerful quasi-mimetic motivations for chronological dislocations and informational suppressions, and the omniscient mode as practiced by Fielding or Dickens, with its purely aesthetic motivations—there stand two highly important narrative complexes that by their very nature partake of both kinds of motivation. I refer, first, to self-conscious restricted narration; and second, to the late James's habitual procedure—later popularized by Lubbock and other exponents of the modern theory of the novel—consisting in the narrator's representation of the whole action as it is filtered through the eyes of some reflector or vessel of consciousness.

These two types of narration (and the relations between them) have proved a constant source of confusion, largely due to the failure to distinguish between narrative range of potentialities and actual communicative choice and, on the side of commission, to automatic linkages of what are in fact distinct and variable narrative features. To start with restricted narration, the myth of "first-person" as opposed to "third-person" narrator is still flourishing,[3] though invalid on any conceivable ground. First, if this distinction turns on the narrator's pronominal reference to himself-as-narrator, then Fielding's omniscient persona in *Tom Jones* or James's in *The Ambassadors* are as much of "first-person" narrators as Tristram Shandy or Serenus Zeitblom in *Dr. Faustus;* and what is perhaps less obvious, so is the teller of Hemingway's "The Killers" or Joyce's *Portrait* (or any other "impersonal" tale), for though he does not actually refer to himself as "I," there is nothing to prevent him from intruding in this way. Second, if the distinction turns on the narrator's pronominal reference to himself-as-agent, then it rests on still another confusion of potentiality and choice and a limited view of narrative options. For this criterion would force us to classify Xenophon's *Anabasis* (say) as a third-person narrative, since Xenophon consistently refers to himself as "he" in his capacity as agent and as "I" only in his capacity as (restricted) narrator. And again, this trick of double reference could theoretically be adopted by any narrator-agent—this presumably leading to a complete mergence of the restricted into the omniscient mode on grounds so negligible (the pose of objectivity) as to have no effect whatever on the narrator's privilege or reliability or informational distribution.

The weaknesses of the distinction in terms of "person" bring out all the more forcefully the advantages of isolating inherent and relational features of narration instead of classifying narrators *in toto,* and of viewing each (actual or possible) narrator as a variable, ad hoc rather than as a mutually implicative and hence predictable complex of features. Thus, once the restricted narrator (whatever his form of reference) is invested with self-consciousness, he shares no less fundamental features with the omniscient mode than with some of his equally restricted counterparts. And this has decisive implications for temporal strategy and its motivation. What such narrators as Zeitblom, Xenophon, James's governess, or Doctor Shepherd in Agatha Christie's *The Murder of Roger Ackroyd* have in common with the diarist is mainly their limited range of knowledge, enabling the author again to motivate the play of *permanent* gaps in purely realistic terms. But on the other hand, the realistic camouflage of informational delay and *temporary* ambiguity is here considerably attenuated in comparison with the diarist's case, though still possibly not completely destroyed as in that of the freely communicative omniscient narrator. For owing to his quasi-authorial awareness of the audience, such a narrator-agent can easily be made to perform (like Xenophon) and only with difficulty to evade (like Doctor Shepherd) the task of imparting to the reader at once all the antecedents known to him prior to the start of the action proper; it is precisely for this reason that one should avoid the common tendency of lumping him together, under the terminological umbrella of "first-person" narrative, with such wholly unselfconscious informants as the modern interior monologist, whether Molly Bloom in *Ulysses* or Faulkner's trio in *The Sound and the Fury*. [4] And owing to the temporal distance usually separating here the mind that creates from the man who suffers—the subject from the object, in James's terms, or the narrating self from the experiencing self, in Stanzel's[5]—this narrative technique also involves undiarylike tensions between the teller's knowledge after the fact and his actual practice of communication. Not being omniscient, the narrating self can hardly be blamed for not being omnicommunicative, but he definitely can for not being (like Graves's Claudius) as fully communicative as he could. Since the discrepancy between him and the author on the axis of delegated power can in itself account for the narrator's principles of selection only, the realistic appearance of his temporary, combinational suppressions is necessarily weakened; he could easily rearrange his "story-stuff" in retrospect into the proper chronological order so as to give us at an early stage the benefit of the discoveries that he himself, owing to his human and personal limitations, made much later.

This is in fact done in *Pickwick Papers,* where the old man starts his tale about the queer client by declaring that "it matters little . . . where, or how, I picked up this brief history. If I were to relate it in the order in which it reached me, I should commence in the middle, and when I had arrived at the conclusion, go back for a beginning" (chap. 21). But most self-conscious restricted narratives, like their omniscient counterparts and for similar reasons, choose to refrain from overall chronological reshufflings. Many of them combine the perspectives of the experiencing and the narrating self—either simultaneously and sporadically (as in *A Raw Youth,* where Dostoyevsky exploits Dolgoruky-the-agent's ignorance for sustaining the mystery and Dolgoruky-the-narrator's frequent anticipations for creating suspense or preventing "muddles") or sequentially and more or less systematically (as in *The Devils,* where in part 2 the narrator suddenly announces that "having described our enigmatic situation during the eight days we knew nothing, I shall go on to describe the subsequent events of my chronicle, writing, as it were, with full knowledge and describing everything as it became known afterwards"). Others are even more extreme in maintaining the informational discrepancy between the two perspectives and hence the temporal tensions between the reconstituted order of occurrence and the presented order of discovery—whether the Watson tradition of the detective story, in the interests of the game of art, or the modern Ford-Conrad impressionist novel, in the name of faithfulness to life. In this framework, such shifts as that apologized for by Nick Carraway ("[Gatsby] told me all this very much later, but I've put it down here with the idea of exploding those first wild rumours about his antecedents"; *The Great Gatsby,* chap. 6) are the exception rather than the rule.

All self-conscious restricted narration that resorts to deliberate suppressiveness must, then, either pay for its aesthetic gains an omniscientlike price in weakened realistic motivation, or go on to devise some new motivation for its temporal ordering in addition to that of restrictedness. Such compensation for the loss of unselfconsciousness may take two forms. The first consists in the author's investing his narrator with special or distancing traits, as in the already-mentioned case of *The Catcher in the Rye* as opposed to *I, Claudius*—lack of experience, absent-mindedness, literary aspirations, defiance of convention, or even (as with Dr. Shepherd) interested withholding and ambiguation. The second consists in the narrating self's superimposing once for all the realistic motivation of the experiencing self's restrictedness on his own aesthetic motivation for suppressiveness, in terms of a systematic adherence to the "order of discovery." And in this the self-restricted restricted mode strikingly comes to resemble in structure and effect the self-restricted omniscient mode as established by Henry James.

It is with regard to the latter technique that the critical fog shrouding the question of omniscience has most thickened. This technique—currently designated as the "dramatic" or "objective" or "figural"—is usually described as a drastic deviation from the omniscient. Wellek and Warren, for instance, in their well-known chapter on the nature of fiction, characterize the modern objective mode as follows:

> Its essentials are the voluntary absence from the novel of the "omniscient novelist" and, instead, the presence of a controlled "point of view."[6]

Leon Edel, listing the innovations introduced into the art of fiction by such modern novelists as Dorothy Richardson and James Joyce, claims:

> This was a distinct departure from the way in which the conventional novels unrolled themselves in majestic leisure with the author constantly telling the story and omniscient to the extent of knowing everything about his characters.[7]

Such descriptions of the Jamesian and post-Jamesian novel clearly confuse what the narrator knows and what he chooses to divulge. They are ultimately grounded on such curious presuppositions as that a narrator cannot but tell all that he knows, or, to put it the other way round, that when he fails to communicate something, it necessarily follows that he does not know it; and that he cannot choose to convey some of his information implicitly, let alone suppress it altogether. And these descriptions also fail to take into account that omniscience, being a superhuman privilege, is logically not a quantitative but a qualitative and indivisible attribute; if a narrator authoritatively shows himself to be able to penetrate the mind of one of his characters and report all his secret activities—something none of us can do in everyday life—he has thus decisively established his ability to do so in regard to the others as well. As Thackeray's narrator comments, "If a few pages back, the present writer claimed the privilege of peeping into Miss Amelia Sedley's bedroom, and understanding with the omniscience of the novelist all the gentle pains and passions which were tossing upon that innocent pillow, why should he not declare himself to be Rebecca's confidant too, master of her secrets, and seal-keeper of that young woman's conscience?" (*Vanity Fair,* chap. 15).

Why not, indeed? The answer is provided by none other than Henry James himself, in an invaluable aside of the narrator's in *The Tragic Muse:*

> That mystery [the reason for Miriam's repeated visits to Nick's studio] would be cleared up only if it were open to us to regard this young lady through some other medium than the minds of her friends. We have chosen, as it happens, for some of the advantages it carries with it, the indirect vision [through the eyes of Nick and Peter]; and it fails as yet to tell us . . . why a young person crowned with success should have taken it into her head that there was something for her in so blighted a spot." (Chap. 25).

As is the case with Fielding, James's narrator thus flaunts his omniscience in the reader's face (and again, with a view to drawing attention to a central gap). He impresses on the reader that he could easily clear up the mystery by entering Miriam's mind, just as he constantly goes behind the two alternately postulated centres of consciousness, if the artistic advantages of the indirect presentation did not determine him against this course. There is nothing to keep him from declaring himself to be Miriam's confidant too, master of her secrets, and seal-keeper of that young woman's consciousness, except his own free choice. If, therefore, "We have no direct exhibition of [her mind] whatever, [if] . . . we get at it all inferentially and inductively, seeing it only through a more or less bewildered interpretation of it by others,"[8] it is not because the narrator is restricted but because he is self-restricted. It is not, then, the omniscience of James's or Joyce's narrators that is "selective," as Norman Friedman suggests in his essay,[9] but their communicativeness.

This type of narrator being omniscient, his chronological manipulations are of course aesthetically motivated. But what renders this deliberately suppressive mode more acceptable to James (and later moderns) than Fielding's or even Jane Austen's is the consistency dictated by the partial realistic motivation that is superimposed on the aesthetic. James's attacks on "the mere muffled majesty of irresponsible 'authorship'" (p. 328) are directed, in fact, not against omniscient narrative as such—as Scholes and Kellog, for instance, maintain[10]—but only against what he considers its irresponsible manifestations: against presentational choices on the omniscient narrator's part that cannot otherwise be accounted for except in bald aesthetic terms. Such narrative procedures as Fielding's are in his opinion arbitrary to the point of unfairness; when the narrator's constant shifts of point of view indicate that his principles of selection are actually limited in no way, he has no right to exploit his superior position by keeping back from us whatever he likes simply because it happens to suit his artistic purposes that we should not know it for the time being or at all. It is, in short, the lack of system in the narrator's suppressiveness that lays bare its purely aesthetic function and stamps it as arbitrary ("majestic"[11]).

When the omniscient narrator, on the other hand, consistently restricts himself as well as the reader to the perspective of one or more of his figures, "the sense of a system saves the painter from the baseness of the *arbitrary* stroke, the touch without its reason" (p. 89); and the more consistent this self-imposed limitation, the more strongly does the sense of a system prevail and reconcile us to the informational gaps. The narrator's self-restriction is aesthetically motivated (to an even greater extent than the narrating self's in the inherently restricted mode, who cannot be held responsible for all permanent gaps) in that it is artificial. But once we accept the system as a basic artistic premise, it readily provides an overall realistic justification within the fictive world for all subsequent presentational choices—for the principles of selection and those of combination, for what is communicated and what is not communicated and the order in which things are communicated, for ambiguities and discontinuities on all levels, for possible violations of chronology and the delay and distribution of information. For while the narrator himself is both self-conscious and omniscient, the postulated vessel of consciousness is neither. He goes about his daily business, not even suspecting that he is made a show of (to adapt Hawthorne's description of Trollope's characters), just like the diarist; but he is even less self-conscious, if possible, than the latter, who is at least aware of himself as chronicler of a sequence of events. And he naturally suffers from all the limitations and defects of vision—both those inherent in the human condition, transcended by the omniscient narrator alone, and those varying from one individual to another—characterizing the narrator-agent or any other agent. Therefore, by interposing between himself and the reader a center of consciousness that is by definition unaware of expositional exigencies and has a limited access to information throughout, the narrator may retain (as I shall show) some of the advantages of the omniscient mode and at the same time reap some of the fruits of restricted narration. It is true that when his plan calls for preliminary exposition he is confronted by the same difficulties as the author of the diary (though his form enables him to solve them with greater ease, e.g., by communicating the introductory account prior to the postulation of the vessel, as is done by Balzac in *Père Goriot* or by Jane Austen in *Persuasion*). But when the narrator's design necessitates dislocations of order and coherence, the system simply plays into his hands. For he can easily avoid orderly exposition, he can manipulate gaps, temporary and permanent, and he can in general carry out his presentational choices and play of hypotheses in at least as realistic a guise as if his task were delegated altogether to a humanly limited agent.[12]

II

This method of accounting for the disposition as well as the selection of materials, besides being to James's mind (like omnicommunicative narration to Trollope's) a virtue in itself, also carries with it or paves the way for a complex of interrelated advantages. Some of these primarily adhere to the quasi-mimetic mode in which the method motivates the introduction of expositional and other materials, and others to the systematic manner in which it justifies the selection, distribution, and ordering of these materials. I propose to analyze these advantages in some detail for more than one reason: their importance for the understanding of Jamesian poetics and its influence; their representative value within the framework of the modern novel; and most general, their power of illustrating my recurrent theme of the functional interaction of point of view with other compositional principles in the interests of formal cohesion, semantic patterning, and rhetorical control.

James objects to the purely aesthetic motivation of informational introduction just as he does to that of suppression, though on somewhat different grounds. This is implied, for instance, in his already cited strictures upon "the custom of the seated mass of explanation after the fact, the inserted block of merely referential narrative, which flourishes so, to the shame of the modern impatience, on the serried page of Balzac, but which seems to appal our actual, our general weaker, digestion." The attack is mainly directed against the indisputable fact that the aesthetically motivated "insertion" of exposition, whether preliminary or delayed, generally involves its presentation in a concentrated form, in the form of a block or series of blocks of summary addressed directly by the narrator to the reader. As both the form and the introductory mode of the expositional material lay bare its "merely referential," purely informational function, its assimilation is rendered excessively irritating and arduous. To be forced to digest a mass of antecedents is unpleasant enough, even when its intercalation is realistically motivated; but to have it thrust down one's throat for no other purpose than the purely expositional is even worse. The reader, therefore, must be (as James puts it in a wholly different context) "skillfully and successfully drugged" (p. 34)—must be made unaware of being provided with exposition or interscenic summary; and the best way of drugging him is to dramatize or frame the insertion of the antecedents in terms of the occurrences taking place in the fictive world.

Moreover, by making his (usually omniscient) narrator introduce merely referential blocks of summary, Balzac, in James's opinion, sins against the very nature of art, which is differentiated from life by its incessant striving for tight integration and "economy," or what I call multifunctionality: "Life being all inclusion and confusion, and art being all discrimination and selection, the latter, in search of the hard latent *value* with which alone it is concerned, sniffs around the mass as instinctively and unerringly as a dog suspicious of a buried bone. . . . The artist finds in *his* tiny nugget, washed free of awkward accretions and hammered into a sacred hardness, the very stuff for a clear affirmation, the happiest chance for the indestructible" (p. 120). As it forms a "seated mass of explanation after the fact," the expositional material in Balzac is insufficiently integrated with the bulk of the work. Instead of being woven into the fabric of the action proper through realistic motivation, it is made to stand out as something sharply distinct from it in texture and function: not fully dramatized but drastically telescoped and expository ("foreshortened"), not causally dynamic but static, not related to the action as part to whole but as premises to a proposition. James conceives of the novel as "a living thing, all one and continuous, like any other organism, and in proportion as it lives will it be found . . . that in each of the parts there is something of each of the other parts. The critic who over the close texture of a finished work shall pretend to trace a geography of items will mark some frontiers as artificial . . . as any that have been known to history";[13] it is therefore understandable that he should object to the artist marking these artificial frontiers himself, sometimes even by way of explicit indication of the point where the exposition gives way to the action proper. To his mind the author must avoid such aesthetically motivated delimitations and instead hammer his material into a sacred hardness by incorporating the exposition in the discriminated occasions themselves; instead of being presented as immutably past ("after the fact"), the events anterior to the beginning of the fictive present must be quasi-mimetically synthesized with the developing action. When, for example, in the course of a scenic occasion one character unbosoms himself to another (even to such *ficelles* as Mrs. Tristram in *The American* or Maria Gostrey in *The Ambassadors*, often introduced to motivate precisely this compositional exigency) or is made to recall his history in the privacy of his mind, the past is felt to be not an explanation after the fact but part and parcel of the fictive present in that its communication has been dramatized.

James's ideal, in short, is the "self-expository thing," where the necessary antecedents emerge "dramatically and *actionally*," in and through "the unfolding of the action itself—the action of which my story essentially consists and which of itself involves and achieves all presentation and explanation."[14] This tight integrative mode makes not only for heightened interest in the expositional material, for its distribution and for the dissimulation of its nature, but also for economical representation. The reason he objects to such summaries as those directly communicated to us by Balzac's omniscient narrators is not that, due to his anti-intrusive bias, he wishes to refine the narrator out of existence—this is another of the many critical distortions of his doctrine—but that he finds them weak, lacking in vividness, and worst of all, artistically wasteful. Being concentrated, they mostly lack the twists, readjustments, and very gradualness of distribution that ensure perceptual potency and accuracy: "A character is interesting as it comes out, and by the process and duration of that emergence; just as a procession is effective by the way it unrolls, turning to a mere mob if all of it passes at once" (pp. 127–28). And besides being "a figure of attestation at once too gross and too bloodless," the "poor author's cold affirmation or thin guarantee" (p. 301) also limits the functionality of the foreshortened material, since it can play no role outside the rhetorical sphere inhabited by author and reader alone, to the exclusion of the dramatis personae. It has no effect whatever on the dynamics of the action and the characters figuring in it but only on the reader's response to them, whereas realistically motivated exposition can easily be made to affect both agent and reader. James would accordingly dismiss as ridiculous prescriptions of the kind made by Gustav Freytag: "The exposition should be kept free from anything distracting; its task, to prepare for the action, it best accomplishes if it so proceeds that the first short introductory chord is followed by a well-executed scene which by a quick transition is connected with the following scene containing the exciting force."[15] By the very nature of art, he would affirm, an account introduced for purely referential purposes (and thus scrupulously "kept free from anything distracting") is necessarily inferior to an indirectly relayed, multifunctional exposition—one whose communication is invested with actional or propulsive value, one in which a character reveals himself both to us and to an internal, preferably dramatized auditor, or one in which the conveyed facts are richly charged and colored by their refraction through a character's consciousness. For while in the first case exposition suffers from the dead weight of the narrator's "platitude of statement," in the second it partakes of "the rich density of a wedding-cake" (pp. 137, 88).

One fascinating manifestation of this urge to "dramatise, dramatise!" is the way James combines the retardatory structure of *The Ambassadors* with a device strongly reminiscent of Balzac's concentric circles. In James, however, the device is not used by way of authorial summary but embodied in actional terms. Up to the point where Strether decides to side actively with Madame de Vionnet, he is mainly engaged in an expositional reconstruction of her character. Everything obviously depends on this. But he is not allowed to arrive at what seems to him a direct apprehension of her character before having undergone a process that may be conceived of as successively traversing three major concentric circles (with the Countess's character as center), each composed in turn of another three concentric circles (with the innermost one serving as core, theme, or concentrated note). The novel starts with the widest circumference, namely Europe, the component rings giving the hero a sense of a progressively purer distillation of the essence of the old world: Chester, London, Paris. The last stage leads him straight into the next major circle, in which he is concerned with the inquiry into Chad's personality and the nature of *his* involvement; and the retardatory structure sees to it that Strether should first come into contact with Chad's milieu, next with the strayed lamb himself, and last of all with the two candidates for his virtuous attachment. The scene at Gloriani's links this intermediate phase with the final one, composed of the three encounters with the Countess de Vionnet, which affords Strether an increasingly direct view of what he takes to be her nature—the order of perception being house, dress and appearance, and finally, character-in-action.

As in Balzac, the various concentric circles enveloping the heroine are related both metonymically or synecdochically and analogically; and this is partly perceived by the hero himself who repeatedly invests the rings confronting him at the moment with the attributes of those he has already left behind in his gap-filling movement towards the heart of the matter. His delight with Europe affects his judgment of Chad's milieu, which seems to concentrate most European amenities; this milieu in turn leads him to revaluate Chad himself, who has become part of it; and Chad's transformation conditions his attitude to the Countess, the cause whom he gradually comes to view in terms of her beneficial effects. Predictably, this cumulative centripetal process of discovery culminates in Strether's conception of the Countess as the embodiment of Europe as a whole.

In his insistence on the need for interweaving the exposition with the action proper so tightly as to make them indistinguishable, James is again a true and tremendously influential precursor of the modern novel. In the old novel—in Cervantes or Fielding or Trollope or Dostoyevsky—what makes the ubiquitous blocks of summary communicated by the narrator stand out as texturally and functionally separate segments is the large disparity between their time-ratio and that of the discriminated occasions. In many modern novels, in contrast, the expositional material has no distinctive time-ratio of its own since (unlike the "Time Passes" section in Woolf's *To the Lighthouse*) its unfolding has been made part of the overall progression in the fictive present; it is the scenic norm alone that prevails from beginning to end, embracing the whole narrative material, so that it is no wonder some critics question the applicability of the term "exposition" to any part of a work of this kind.[16] And it cannot even be claimed that this synthesis is made possible owing to the relative meagerness of the exposition incorporated in the modern novel. On the contrary, in a stream of consciousness novel such as *Ulysses* or in such "impressionistic" novels as Conrad's *Chance,* Ford's *The Good Soldier,* or Fitzgerald's *The Great Gatsby,* the material relating to the expositional past (a whole lifetime) occupies the bulk of the work.

Consequently, we must further refine the distinction between representational and represented time in order to describe adequately the time values of those works—particularly but not exclusively modern ones—where the emergence of the exposition as a whole, or parts of it (as in the *Odyssey* or *Pride and Prejudice*), is realistically motivated. What I previously called "represented time" is, in fact, sujet time; and it may radically diverge from the fabula time of the same scene or narrative. What realistic motivation of expositional insertion does is to replace the fabula time of the material by a much shorter sujet time by dramatizing and framing its communication in terms of the events taking place in the fictive present. In the aesthetically motivated opening of *Père Goriot* or *The Brothers Karamazov,* fabula and sujet time are identical, with the result that the ratio between representational and represented sujet time differs greatly from the scenic norm. In contrast, the essentially similar fabula time of *Ulysses* or *Mrs. Dalloway*—several decades—is compressed into a single day of sujet time through the newly promoted overall quasi-mimetic pattern of mental association; the decade of Odysseus's wanderings is telescoped into the single sujet night that it takes him to narrate his tale to the Phaeacians; and the same is true of Marlow's "deformed" evocation of Kurtz.

This modern radicalization of basic quasi-mimetic patterns, both as an end in itself and as a framework for realizing equally basic literary strategies and functions, is reflected in the career of James himself, who groped his way towards it during a long period of experimentation. Tracing his development from the sixties and seventies through the middle period to the late works, we discover that the evolution of his expositional techniques involves a steady shift from purely aesthetic to realistic motivation and an increasingly economical use of his materials. In the early stories, the antecedents largely constitute a "seated mass of explanation after the fact." Not even the most perfunctory attempt is made to dissimulate the stark referentiality of these summaries and retrospects. In some stories of this period James even explicitly indicates their purely aesthetic motivation—especially when he plunges *in medias res*. In "The Story of a Masterpiece" (1868), the narrator declares after the opening scene that "I may as well take advantage of the moment rapidly to make plain to the reader the events to which the above conversation refers"; he proceeds to hark back till he reaches the previously established beginning of the action proper, and then calls attention again to the referential function of the retrospect by commenting that "the reader has now an adequate conception of the feelings with which these two old friends have found themselves face to face."[17]

By the time James wrote *Roderick Hudson* (1875) he was already aware of the necessity of effecting a more natural transition between action and antecedents, but the solutions he devised were often clumsy since he had not yet learnt to do away with the "artificial frontiers" separating past from present through consistent realistic motivation. When Rowland Mallet's cousin Cecilia threatens to invite the plainest girl in town to pester him, Rowland imperturbably replies that he will give even such a visitor his most respectful attention. The narrator thereupon cuts in with the observation that "this little profession of ideal chivalry . . . was not quite so fanciful on Mallet's lips as it would have been on those of many another man; as a rapid glance at his antecedents may help to make the reader perceive." The plain girl, of whom we do not even catch a glimpse in the sequel, is obviously a mere pretext for intercalated retrospection, and a lame one at that. In the same work, however, some important expositional material concerning Roderick Hudson naturally emerges during the conversation of the cousins. And in James's next novel, *The American* (1875-76), the modes of motivation are somewhat differently mixed; the authorial block-description of Newman with which the novel opens is soon followed, for instance, by the sudden encounter between the hero and his old friend Tristram, during which the two tell each other about their respective adventures since their last meeting.

As James's art developed, however, he not only took care to avoid the overtly aesthetic mode by "dramatizing" the insertion of antecedent matter through dialogue scenes or the inner play of association,[18] but he always kept in view his ideal of economy and endeavored to render the unfolding of the narrative past as actionally and thematically meaningful as possible. In *The American* and *Roderick Hudson,* the dialogues of Newman and Tristram or Mallet and Cecilia are still mainly referential, since the relations between the speakers later prove to be of negligible importance; in book 1 of *The Awkward Age* (1899), however, the exposition scenes are multifunctional. The exchange between Mr. Longdon and Vanderbank enlightens the reader (as to the circle of Buckingham Crescent) and at the same time contributes to the progression of the relations between these two central agents, who discover that they have taken to each other at once. And the results of this encounter continue to manifest themselves to the very end of the novel.

III

To the advantages that accrue to the novelist, according to Jamesian poetics, from the superiority of realistic over aesthetic motivation, one must add those that adhere to the consistent motivation of presentational choices in terms of the perceptions of a single character. What I have so far explained is why James (locally) refrains from addressing the exposition straight to the reader, preferring to relay it through the mediation of the represented agents; it now remains to discover why he (architectonically) chooses to relate its emergence almost exclusively to the activities of one of the agents—the vessel of consciousness.

The gain that on the face of it appears to be least connected with the question of informational disposition is that of unity. To James's mind, the narrator who exploits his omniscience to jump from the mind of one character to another's gratuitously smashes the unity of his work, thus incurring "that dreariest displeasure it is open to experiments in this general order to inflict, the sense of any hanging-together precluded as by the very terms of the case" (p. 16). Disregarding (in theory) the alternative principles of unity open to the artist, James doggedly maintains that, if the author is to avoid giving birth to "large loose baggy monsters, with their queer elements of the accidental and the arbitrary" (p. 84), he must strenuously refrain from breaking the compositional line or chain which concatenates the various episodes and characters:[19] "Stick to it—don't shift—and don't shift from it *arbitrarily*—how otherwise do you get your unity of subject or keep up your reader's sense of it? . . . Go behind her [the heroine and vessel]—miles and miles; don't go behind the others, or the subject—i.e., the unity of impression—goes to smash."[20] When a single channel of information is employed throughout, moreover, a story that is poor in other respects may still be saved, for in this case "faults may show, faults may disfigure, and yet not upset the work. It remains in equilibrium by having found its centre, the point of command of all the rest. From this centre the subject has been treated, from this centre the interest has spread, and so, whatever else it may do or may not do, the thing has acknowledged a principle of composition and contrives at least to hang together" (p. 15). For the conviction that the novel cannot get "any *objective* unity from any other source" the late James was ready to "go to the stake and burn with slow fire . . . —the slowest that will burn at all."[21]

It is no accident, moreover, that in his many references to the vessel of consciousness as a unifying principle James frequently shifts his emphasis back and forth from compositional to thematic unity, or from unity of "treatment" to that of "subject." For while making for compositional tightness, the use of a single channel of information also directs the reader's attention to the reflector as the focus of interest as well as narration: "From this centre the subject has been treated, from this centre the interest has spread." When we try to account in aesthetic terms for the realistically motivated principles of selection, combination, and distribution of materials, asking ourselves why the omniscient narrator has so consistently chosen to restrict himself to presenting only those things that the vessel observes and in the order in which they impinge on his consciousness, the explanation that most naturally comes to mind is that of all the dramatis personae, "he was to be the lighted figure, the others . . . were to be the obscured . . . The interest of everything is all that it is *his* vision, *his* conception, *his* interpretation: at the window of his wide . . . consciousness we are seated, from that admirable position we 'assist'. He therefore supremely matters; all the rest matters only as he feels it, treats it, meets it" (p. 37). And as I pointed out in reference to Balzac's Rastignac, the more pronounced the consequent chronological deformations and gaps and the more the reader is left in complete or partial ignorance together with him, the more conspicuous both his position as protagonist and that of his mind as dramatic arena. The fact that all presentational choices are related, in quasi-mimetic terms, to the vessel's consciousness forms, then, a vital compositional indicator as well as a compositional measure since it reveals that this mind is not merely a chain on which the various episodes are strung but also the center round which the tale is built; the center of interest is located neither in the occurrences themselves nor in the predicaments of the other characters but primarily in the reflector's reactions to them or the process by which he comes to realize their true significance. Therefore, any other means of motivation, whether aesthetic or realistic, would distribute interest as well as weaken

unity: "the beauty of the constructional game was to preserve in everything its especial value for him" (p. 16).

By realistically accounting for his (usually deformed) temporal ordering, James thus focuses our attention on the protagonist's ordeal. But it is
not every character that is worthy of being postulated as center.[22] If
compositional unity alone were in question, the vessel's nature and qualifications would be of little account; but since a great deal more is at stake,
it must be selected with care:

> The agents in any drama, are interesting only in proportion as they
> feel their respective situations. . . . But there are degrees of feeling—the
> muffled, the faint, the just sufficient, the barely intelligent . . . and the
> acute, the intense, the complete, in a word—the power to be finely
> aware and richly responsible. It is those moved in this latter fashion who
> "get most" out of all that happens to them and who in so doing enable
> us, as readers of their record, as participators by a fond attention, also
> to get most. Their being finely aware—as Hamlet and Lear, say, are fine-
> ly aware—*makes* absolutely the intensity of their adventure, gives the
> maximum of sense to what befalls them. We care, our curiosity and our
> sympathy care, comparatively little for what happens to the stupid, the
> coarse and the blind; care for it, and for the effects of it, at most as
> helping to precipitate what happens to the more deeply wondering, to
> the really sentient. (P. 62)

Here again the two aspects of the problem—the vessel's double role as both
dramatic or thematic center and exclusive channel of information—are so
closely related in James's mind that he unconsciously shifts from one to
the other. What he emphasizes in the opening and concluding part of this
quotation is that since the vessel's mind forms the dramatic arena, the
whole interest of the story and the reader's involvement in it depend on its
intrinsic attractiveness, namely, its degree of consciousness. To offer as
reflector and dramatic center so limited, vulgar, and provincial a consciousness as that of Emma Bovary—"A pretty young woman who lives,
socially and morally speaking, in a hole, and who is ignorant, foolish,
flimsy"—is to leave the very core of the novel hollow, since the "dignity
of its substance is the dignity of Madame Bovary herself as a vessel of
experience."[23] Whereas by making the registering mind acute, imaginative,
morally and psychologically sensitive, "one made its own movement—or
rather, its movement in the particular connexion—interesting; this movement being really quite the stuff of one's thesis" (p. 16). Of course, no
story can do without its fools and its blind. But they are interesting only
as fermenting agents or as foils, having their "subordinate, comparative,
illustrative human value"; therefore it is only as mirrored in the tormented
mind of the sentient center that "the gross fools, the headlong fools, the

fatal fools play their part for us—they have much less to show us in themselves" (pp. 62, 66–67, 129–30).

Toward the middle of the excerpt, however, when James dwells on the
issue of "getting most" out of the drama, emphasis shifts to the vessel's
role as channel of information. Qua refracting and coloring medium, the
quality of his mind determines the intelligibility of the action as well as
its interest: "This means, exactly, that the person capable of feeling in the
given case more than another of what is to be felt for it, and so serving in
the highest degree to *record* it dramatically and objectively, is the only
sort of person on whom we can count not to betray, to cheapen or . . .
give away, the value and beauty of the thing. By so much as the affair
matters *for* some such individual, by so much do we get the best there is of
it, and by so much as it falls within the scope of a denser and duller, a
more vulgar and more shallow capacity, do we get a picture dim and
meagre" (p. 67). The stupid and the blind are simply incapable of projecting for us their imbroglio in all its complexity, since they can make but
little of their own situation, not to speak of that of the other characters,
"each with his or her axe to grind, his or her situation to treat, his or her
coherency not to fail of" (p. 317). There are too little given to introspec-
tion to know themselves and analyze their own feelings and reactions, too
little curious to pursue the truth, too little imaginative to penetrate the
thoughts and motives of others; and therefore they cannot but blur and
vulgarize anything they touch. Madame Arnoux, in *L'Education senti-
mentale* is, for instance, Flaubert's "one marked attempt . . . to represent
beauty otherwise than for the senses, beauty of character and life; and
what becomes of the attempt is a matter highly significant": her figure
falls short of real distinction precisely because it is registered through the
mean consciousness of Frédéric Moreau.[24] On the other hand, James's
Fleda Vetches, Merton Denshers, or Lambert Strethers have minds so fine
that little is lost upon them; and they have such a passion for knowledge
and self-knowledge and such a horror of acting basely that they exercise
their perspicacity even amidst their worst predicaments—following every
clue that comes their way, weighing the moral implications of every act
or thought, and at each point considering most of the relevant factors,
since one of their notable endowments is that they can "commune with
the unseen," that is, enter into the thoughts of others to a startling extent
and imaginatively participate in occasions at which they cannot physically
"assist." Their polished minds are in consequence eminently equipped,
"like a set and lighted scene, to hold the play" (p. 16).

It is, in fact, only the postulation of this kind of reflector that enables
James to dispense with what he regards as the vicious practice of arbitrarily
omniscient narration. Fielding's apology for one of his appearances, by
way of chorus, on the stage—"This, as I could not prevail on any of my

actors to speak, I was obliged to declare myself" (*Tom Jones,* 3.7)—is of course not entirely spoken in jest. For the shifts of point of view as well as the recourse to authorial commentary typical of most unrestricted narration are, among other things, dictated by the need to illuminate the various aspects of the action; it often happens that the narrator must not only be invested with superhuman, quasi-divine powers but must constantly be made to bring them to bear on the fictive world because none of the agents, all belonging in varying degrees to the category of the stupid and the blind, is able ("could be prevailed on") to project the whole drama for our benefit, to interpret it and comment on it, either as narrator or as vessel. To endow the compositional center with "intelligent consciousness, consciousness of the whole, or of something ominously like it" (p. 128) is, on the other hand, to retain many of the advantages of the unselfrestricted omniscient mode and enjoy all those of restricted and self-restricted narration without incurring their respective drawbacks, due to the superior realistic motivation of the principles of selection and combination: "More or less of the treasure is stored safe from the moment such a quality of inward life is distilled, or in other words from the moment so fine an interpretation and criticism as that of Fleda Vetch's . . . is applied without waste to the surrounding tangle" (pp. 128–29).

But can these polished mirrors be made to replace the unrestrictedly omniscient narrator altogether as channel of information? Can they be postulated as all-conscious, infallible, and hence wholly reliable? James does not explicitly make the comparison, but his comments on the limits of human awareness are noteworthy in this context:

If persons either tragically or comically embroiled with life allow us the comic or tragic value of their embroilment in proportion as their struggle is a measured and directed one, it is strangely true, none the less, that beyond a certain point they are spoiled for us by this carrying of a due light. They may carry too much of it for our credence, for our compassion, for our derision. They may be shown as knowing too much and feeling too much—not certainly for their remaining remarkable, but for their remaining "natural" and typical, for their having the needful communities with our own precious liability to fall into traps and be bewildered. It seems probable that if we were never bewildered there would never be a story to tell about us; we should partake of the superior nature of the all-knowing immortals whose annals are dreadfully dull so long as flurried humans are not, for the positive relief of bored Olympians, mixed up with them. Therefore it is that the wary reader warns the novelist against making his characters too *interpretative* of the muddle of fate, or in other words too divinely, too priggishly clever. (Pp. 63–64)

A narrator's omniscience is an established convention, and as such it is not amenable to the usual canons of probability. Not being one of the fictive agents, such a narrator may safely share the infallible awareness of the all-knowing immortals, in terms of whose superior nature alone his super-human attributes can indeed be conceived of at all. His unlimited knowl-edge, in short, is by definition motivated in terms that are quasi-mimetic (godlike) but flagrantly lacking in verisimilitude. As the vessel, on the other hand, is "one of us," his powers of penetration must be rendered credible.

First, they must not exceed the limits of his own nature and qualifica-tions, as dramatized in the work. Indeed, many specific choices that seem to have nothing to do with the exigencies of temporal ordering, point of view or James's wish to shun the muffled majesty of irresponsible author-ship, are actually explainable in terms of the motivation of the reflector's uncommon perspicacity. Why is the little protagonist of *What Maisie Knew* not a boy but a girl? One would hardly think of raising the question did not James provide us with the answer: "I at once recognised, that my little vessel of consciousness . . . couldn't be with verisimilitude a rude little boy; since, beyond the fact that little boys are never so 'present', the sensibility of the female young is indubitably, for early youth, the greater, and my plan would call, on the part of my protagonist, for 'no end' of sensibility" (pp. 143-44).[25]

Second, the vessel's perceptual powers must also conform to the limits of human knowledge in general. He must partake of the human state of bewilderment or else he is liable to be dismissed as superhuman—which, applied to him, would be not a descriptive but a pejorative epithet. James does not demand such realism merely for realism's sake. It is with great reluctance that he restrains the urge to make his reflectors flood every-thing with light; and if he does so this is only because precisely here the vessel's function as channel of information clashes with his second role, the role never fulfilled by the detached omniscient narrator—that of dramatic center or protagonist. The desire for intelligibility must to some extent give way to the consideration that the reader's whole response to the vessel's ordeal as well as the possibility of the vessel's undergoing an ordeal at all decidedly turn on his "having the needful communities with our own precious liability to fall into traps and be bewildered." True, "We care, our curiosity and sympathy care, comparatively little for what hap-pens to the stupid, the coarse and the blind" (p. 62), while the reflector's "passion for intelligence is . . . precisely his highest value for our curiosity and our sympathy" (p. 69); but our sympathy and hence our interest be-gin to drop as soon as the protagonist's intelligence is shown to differ from ours in kind. Consequently, though James often stretches the limits of credibility beyond the point Trollope would be prepared to allow, they are in essential agreement that the reader's involvement depends on his being convinced that not gods or demons but "men and women with flesh and blood, creatures with whom we can sympathise, are struggling amidst their woes."

The desired mixture of intelligence and bewilderment may vary with the particular needs of each story. When the work aims at producing a sustained comic or ironic response, as in "Pandora," "In the Cage," or *What Maisie Knew,* the vessel's fallibility is only too apparent, and the main problem is how to invest him with a sufficient degree of consciousness without transgressing the bounds of probability. Much more often, the reverse is true. James's vessels may thus be located at any point along the scale—later more densely populated by modern fiction—that ranges from what he called the "inconscient" (e.g., Faulkner's Benjy) to the "conscient" (e.g., Beckett's supersubtle fry); but most of them belong to that part of the scale ascending from the "semi-conscient" in the direction of the never-reached pole of the fully conscient.

To gather up the threads: it is this sophisticated compositional strategy that enables James to achieve such a rich variety of effects through his realistically motivated disposition of materials—in fact, to reconcile after his own fashion the Fieldingesque partiality for narrative interest with the Trollopian preoccupation with psychological drama. On the one hand, in spite of his contempt for the intelligence of the contemporary reading-public, James (like many subsequent modern novelists, such as Joyce, Faulkner, or Nabokov) envisages a reader who is characterized by curiosity, ingenuity, and readiness to take an active part in the process of literary communication by exercising his wits or pitting them against the narrator's or the author's; a reader, in short, who would be inclined to regard Trollope's ideal of unambiguous "lucidity" or "straightforward story-telling" as a threat to his pleasure and an insult to his intelligence. Thus, the following quotation—in which James commends the device of heightening interest through a deliberate retardatory manipulation of expositional hypotheses and criticizes the opposite procedure—indicates his conception of the relations between author (or omniscient narrator) and reader to correspond to Fielding's doctrine of "opening by small degrees":

> I think [he writes to Mrs. Humphrey Ward] your material suffers a little from the fact that the reader feels you approach your subject too immediately, show him its elements, the cards in your hand, too bang off in the first page—so that a wait to begin to guess *what and whom the thing is going to be about* doesn't impose itself: the antechamber or two and the crooked corridor before he is already in the Presence."[26]

Or, as he bluntly tells Paul Bourget: "Your excess of anticipatory analysis undermines too often the reader's curiosity."[27] Elsewhere he directly and eloquently relates his conception of the "cunning" reader to his fondness for the whole complex of narrative interests, when he says that his supernatural tales may serve to exemplify

> that love of "a story as a story" which had from far back beset and beguiled their author. To this passion, the vital flame at the heart of any sincere attempt to lay a scene and launch a drama, he flatters himself he has never been false; and he will indeed have done his duty but little by it if he has failed to let it, whether robustly or quite insidiously, fire his fancy or rule his scheme. He has consistently felt it (the appeal to wonder and terror and curiosity and pity and the delight of fine recognitions, as well as the joy, perhaps sharper still, of the mystified state) the very source of wise counsel and the very law of charming effect. He has revelled in the creation of alarm and suspense and surprise and relief, in all the arts that practise, with a scruple for nothing but a lapse of application, on the credulous soul of the candid or, immeasurably better, on the seasoned spirit of the cunning reader. He has built, rejoicingly, on the blest faculty of wonder just named, in the latent eagerness of which the novelist so finds, throughout, his best warrant that he can but pin his faith and attach his car to it, rest in fine his monstrous weight and his queer case on it, as on a strange passion planted in the heart of man for his benefit, a mysterious provision made for him in the scheme of nature. (Pp. 252-53)

This firm belief in the indispensability of narrative interest naturally entails a narrative mode that is far from omnicommunicative. Unlike Homer or Fielding, however, James effects the necessary chronological "crookedness" simply by adhering to his reflectors' angle of vision. Once this center is postulated, the narrator does not have to suppress information in order to create gaps; he can scrupulously report all that passes through the vessel's mind and yet produce the desired curiosity, surprise, and suspense. For the vessel being unselfconscious, the need for exposition does not of course occur to him at all (even in the improbable case that he possesses all of it right from the beginning); and being limited and bewildered, he cannot but lack information, or true information, himself. Maisie's "infant mind would at best leave great gaps and voids," since a great deal of what she saw "she either wouldn't understand at all or would quite misunderstand" (p. 145). And what is true of Maisie is also true of more polished mirrors, whose imbroglios often derive precisely from their lack of knowledge or self-knowledge or both—in short, of what is to us expositional material. Newman, for example, is "engaged with forces, with difficulties and dangers that [he] but half understands" (p. 37); Isabel Archer neither fathoms Osmond's true character nor knows about his past relations with Madame Merle; and Strether is in the dark as to the real state of affairs in Paris. The self-restricted narrator "cannot," therefore, convey to us the facts they are ignorant of, cannot communicate the information except in the order in which they gather it, cannot but leave the various gaps open unless, and until, they have filled them in for themselves, usually at the end or climax of their quest. In the meantime, the motivated temporal deformations ensure our sharing in varying degrees their dramatized curiosity, wonder, mystification, suspense, and surprise throughout the tortuous route leading them to enlightenment.

On the other hand, even Trollope could hardly accuse James of sacrificing or subordinating the portrayal of character and psychology to the manipulation of narrative dynamics. Having expressed his gratitude for the "strange passion planted in the heart of man for [the novelist's] benefit," he goes on to say that he considers it "the beginning and the end of his affair—thanks to the innumerable ways in which that chord may vibrate." His own ideal is to make narrative interest "vibrate as finely as possible"—to refine and enrich it and at the same time not simply reconcile but interrelate it with the postulated psychological focus. It will vibrate most finely not when the deformed sequence of motifs creating and sustaining it is communicated straight from omniscient narrator to reader but when refracted through an observing mind: "We but too probably break down, I have ever reasoned, when we attempt the prodigy, the appeal to mystification, in itself; with its 'objective' side too emphasised the report (it is ten to one) will practically run thin. We want it clear, goodness knows, but we also want it thick, and we get the thickness in the human consciousness that entertains and records, that amplifies and interprets it" (p. 256). The "human emotion and the human attestation" positively heighten as well as thicken "our thrill and our suspense" (p. 257), because these emotions are not externally but internally dramatized, because we share them with the struggling vessel. Unlike the detective story, human and psychological problems are not sacrificed on the altar of narrative interest, but both intensify and are in turn intensified by it; the hero, frequently an investigator, is not the most emotionally detached of all the dramatis personae but, on the contrary, the most involved—since, as with Hyacinth Robinson, he may be aware of its "mattering to his very life what he does make of things" (p. 69). The manipulation of chronology, far from distracting our attention from the vessel's inner conflict, focuses it on his ordeal. For the principles of selection and combination being realistically determined by his perceptions, the delay and distribution of the necessary antecedents have significant psychological implications: the opening and play of gaps is decisively conditioned by, and in turn concretely dramatizes and illuminates, the quality of his mind, his blind spots, his bewilderment and rationalizations, just as his insights and discoveries directly derive from, and in turn define and establish, the powers of his consciousness.

Frequently, the reflector's attempts to fill in the gaps, to solve some secret or fathom some ambiguity, constitute his very adventure: Strether's inquiry, or the constant prying of the dramatized narrator in *The Sacred Fount* into the amatory relationships of his friends. More ironic, the hero of "The Beast in the Jungle" goes through life avoiding normal human relationships since he is obsessed by the thought of being destined for "some rare distinction, some incalculable violence or unprecedented stroke": "Like the blinded seeker in the old-fashioned game he 'burns' on occasion, as with the sense of the hidden thing near—only to deviate again however into the chill. . . . Such a course of existence naturally involves a climax—the final flash of light under which he reads his lifelong riddle and sees his conviction proved. He has indeed been marked and indeed suffered his fortune—which is precisely to have been the man in the world to whom nothing whatever was to happen. My picture leaves him overwhelmed—at last he has understood" (p. 247). In such "mysteries"—and the same is basically true of Dostoyevsky's psychological thrillers, Faulkner's straight (*Knight's Gambit*) and less orthodox (*Intruder in the Dust, Absalom, Absalom!*) crime stories, the progressive biographical reconstruction in Nabokov's *The Secret Life of Sebastian Knight,* or Joseph K.'s search for his own elusive guilt—the differences between James's complex effects and those characterizing the detective story are thrown into particularly high relief against the background of the conspicuously similar distributive choices. The retardatory framework of the investigation is retained (and even reinforced by the "language of quest" and by figurative and situational allusions to the crooked corridor). But what was in the detective story an intellectual puzzle is here transformed— as it already was in *Oedipus Rex*—into a process of vision, gradual enlightenment, or self-discovery; the clues consist in thematically charged human phenomena; the inquirer's success or failure in spotting and interpreting them depends on his nature, illustrates his predicament, or reflects his development. His curiosity is sometimes shown to be obsessive, his suspense to consist in conflicting pulls of the mind, and his surprise to constitute a retrospective insight. The roles of Holmes and Watson may be reversed (as with Strether and Maria Gostrey); the denouement of overall disambiguation in which the detective story invariably culminates may never come; and when it does, it is not a clever solution but mainly a painful recognition or self-recognition, an attainment of knowledge after a long quest.

This narrative mode, finally, also makes for a tight and flexible control over the reader's distance. Many novelists betray the concern that, when elevated to the narrator's Olympian vantage-point, the reader may forget that omniscience is by no means man's natural state and consequently look down from his godlike altitude on the characters below, who in their ignorance make much ado about nothing, commit flagrant errors of judgment, and in general behave in an ill-considered and downright foolish way. Where he aims (as Shakespeare often does in his comedies) at no more than comic pleasure pure and simple, the author may of course wish to promote precisely this attitude of simple irony through the manipulation of informational discrepancies. However, when his design is to place the predicament of his misguided agents in the proper human perspective so as to produce a more just, balanced, and sympathetic response to their ordeal, he may have considerable trouble in decreasing the distance that attends his strategy of communication. To prevent the characters appearing much more stupid or blind than they actually are, the narrator is sometimes even reduced to warning us against a smug, unwarrantably ironic attitude by way of overt commentary reminding us of our unnatural superiority. Thus, as one might well expect, Trollope is repeatedly forced to counteract the effects of his communicativeness by such admonitions as: "It is to be hoped that the reader, to whom every tittle of this story has been told without reserve, and every secret unfolded, will remember that others were not treated with so much open candour. The reader knows much more of Lizzie Eustace than did her cousin Frank" (*The Eustace Diamonds*, chap. 56). And Fielding, who also treats the reader to different varieties of privileged knowledge, is even more peremptory when commenting on Allworthy's ill-founded appreciation of Thwackum's virtues: "The reader is greatly mistaken if he conceives that Thwackum appeared to Mr. Allworthy in the same light as he doth to him in this history; and he is as much deceived if he imagines that the most intimate acquaintance which he himself could have had with that divine would have informed him of those things which we, from our inspiration, are enabled to open and discover. Of readers who from such conceits as these condemn the wisdom or penetration of Mr. Allworthy, I shall not scruple to say that they make a very bad and ungrateful use of that knowledge which we have communicated to them" (3.5). The reader, then, is explicitly warned to be on his guard against jumping to extreme conclusions on the evidence of the agent's beclouded vision, for their state of bewilderment is essentially human, while his exemption from it is not. However sensitive or clear-eyed, they cannot—certainly not at once and sometimes not ever—arrive at the information that he has so effortlessly come by straight from the beginning, through the omniscient narrator's anticipatory expositional histories or authoritative character-sketches; and he would fare no better if he were in their shoes.

This does not mean of course that omnicommunicative or freely omniscient narration cannot manipulate the reader's response with great success (and the *Odyssey* exemplifies the consummate art that such a narrative mode may involve). The point is rather that the technique of consistently limited communication avoids this difficulty by definition. Its control strategy not only substitutes dramatized, built-in rhetoric for such overt commentary as Trollope's or Fielding's but, what is equally important, manages effectively to enlist our sympathy for the misguided hero by way of actual demonstration, as it were.

All other things being equal, restricting the reader to the vessels' vision throughout, so that he perceives the action and receives the information from within, makes for greater involvement than an outside view or the narrator's "word of honour": "Their emotions, their stirred intelligence, their moral consciousness become thus, by sufficiently charmed perusal, our own very adventure" (p. 70). The precise degree of our involvement may vary from one work and even from one stage to another. But in James, distance is frequently minimized owing to the operation of a complex of variable, mutually reinforcing factors—all of them closely related to his perspectival technique and one to his consistently quasi-mimetic motivation of presentational choices.

First, the step-by-step notation of the workings of the vessel's mind tends to promote involvement in that it ensures the reader's "[getting] into the skin of the creature" (p. 37). The closer the notation, the greater our sympathy, for we are proportionately immersed in the atmosphere of the protagonist's consciousness, put in a position to learn the idiom of his mind, and specifically shown the determinants of his actions, bewilderments, first impressions, and errors of judgment as they evolve in the process of cerebration. We accordingly come to be convinced that, given the particular vessel in the particular conditions, things could simply not turn out otherwise.

Second, the effectiveness of these inside views is heightened in direct proportion to the reflector's lucidity and sentience. The more polished the mirror of his mind, the more he can surprise us by feats of penetration we ourselves would be incapable of, the more he towers above his environment (the analogized "fools") in insight and moral delicacy—the more clearly do his mistakes appear in their true light, as lapses inevitably conditioned by circumstance and passion ("these persons are, so far as their other passions permit, intense *perceivers*"; p. 71).

These two devices, moreover, beautifully dovetail into and are further reinforced by James's quasi-mimetically motivated principles of informational distribution. The temporally and perspectivally deformed presentation sustains two processes of discovery, each differing in principle from the fabulaic sequence (which each attempts to reconstruct). And because we are never placed on a vantage-point as in Trollope but are fettered to the vessel's consciousness throughout, so that we start by knowing even less than he and in the sequel receive only such information as he himself gathers at every point, any sense of superiority on the reader's part is effectively precluded. The narrator does not have to intrude upon the story in order to defend his characters by reminding the reader of his own fallibility in everyday life. The system of presentation itself serves to put us in our place by driving home to us in the most concrete, drastic, and sometimes painful manner that, when we share the limitations of the human predicament in general and those in which the vessel is enveloped in particular, we can often do no better than he and are all liable to the same human errors.

In *The Ambassadors* James even goes so far as to exploit his motivated presentation (or rather suppression) of expositional material about Strether and Maria in order to lure the reader into a mistake about their relationship that the vessel is evidently never in danger of committing. But his usual procedure essentially resembles that of Balzac in *Père Goriot,* where the erroneous primacy effect designed to extenuate our condemnation of Rastignac's conduct is produced precisely by communicating to us at the start the same partial information about the boarding-house vis-à-vis the great world that the hero starts with.[28] In some instances, accordingly, the reader's enlightenment coincides in varying degrees with that of the vessel; in others, they both fail to disambiguate the truth. In "The Lesson of the Master," for example, neither reader nor protagonist conclusively reconstitute St. George's motives to the end of the action; and this permanent gap gives rise throughout to mutually exclusive hypotheses or multiple systems of gap-filling, whose recurrent exploitation and many-sided development into a major compositional principle is one of James's original contributions to the art of fiction. The sustained clash of hypotheses not only promotes interest and heightens attention to verbal and situational ambiguities but also relates the control strategy to the probability-register and the normative groundwork of the narrative. For the double manipulation of such permanent gaps (both actionally in the fictive world and rhetorically in the reader's mind) contributes to the dramatization of one of James's (and later, Conrad's) recurrent themes—none other than the limitations of human knowledge and the consequent difficulty, sometimes the impossibility, of penetrating appearances so as to reach the bare reality they envelop.[29]

I have suggested that this concurrent propulsion of two (or more) processes of discovery and impression-formation originates in Jane Austen, and that the development of her art may be traced in terms of the increasingly tightened correspondence between the two crooked corridors. But so too—roughly—may the later and more radical development of fiction, largely due to the influence of Henry James. While Jane Austen still adheres to the dynamics of anticipatory caution, with its perceptual discrepancy in the reader's favor, modern fiction has no hesitation in resorting to the two other, potentially more egalitarian control strategies as well. While Jane Austen's poetics still involves at least one perspective with superhuman powers of insight—the omniscient narrator's—such novels as *The Good Soldier* not only minimize and ambiguate the powers of the narrating self but in a sense deliberately raise doubts even about the author's. And while Jane Austen still concentrates on temporary gaps, the modern novel has turned the unresolved clash of hypotheses into an equally integral part of the writer's repertoire. One impressive measure of this development is its recent penetration (in the name of "realism") into popular literature, the natural preserve of the strictly temporary ambiguity: Julian Symons's detective story *The Colour of Murder* leaves the identity of the murderer open; Charles McCarry's spy story *The Miernik Dossier* refuses to decide for us whether the hero was a spy; and Nicolas Freeling's thriller *The Dresden Green* actually contains two alternative endings, just like John Fowles's contemporaneous but more canonical *The French Lieutenant's Woman.*

IV

Finally, I want to emphasize that disparities in the local or overall motivation of presentational choices, just like the disparities in the presentational choices themselves, must not be automatically invested with normative significance. James and his followers err in categorically demoting purely aesthetic motivation, since each motivational mode may equally vary in its suitability and effectiveness. Richard Sheridan's *The Critic* contains a wonderful parody of the implausible and cumbersome realistic motivations vitiating Elizabethan and later drama. Puff's play-within-a-play (2.2) opens with two sentinels fast asleep on the eve of battle, the author explaining that, since the two generals are soon to come to that very spot to convey the exposition and since " 'it is not to be supposed they would open their lips, if these fellows were watching them; so, egad, I must either have sent them off their posts, or set them asleep.' " The great men thereupon appear and the ensuing expositional exchange is extremely amusing; one of the speakers is made to pose to the other a series of questions the answers to which he cannot but be well aware of beforehand, as is indeed demonstrated by his constant punctuation of his friend's replies with such exclamations as "I know it well." The audience is consequently provoked into puzzled or jeering commentary that is countered by the author's explanations:

> *Dangle.* Mr. Puff, as he knows all this, why does Sir Walter go on telling him?
>
> *Puff.* But the audience are not supposed to know anything of the matter, are they?
>
> *Sneer.* True; but I think you manage ill: for there certainly appears to be no reason why Sir Walter should be so communicative.
>
> *Puff.* 'Fore Gad, now, that is one of the most ungrateful observations I ever heard!—for the less inducement he has to tell all this, the more, I think, you ought to be obliged to him; for I'm sure you'd know nothing of the matter without it. . . .
>
> *Puff.* Here, now you see, Sir Christopher did not in effect ask any one question for his own information.
>
> *Sneer.* No, indeed: his has been a most disinterested curiosity.

The recourse to such awkward pretexts, resulting in the sacrifice of verisimilitude on the altar of realistic motivation, is not confined to Elizabethan drama. It also vitiates not a few novels, old and new. In *Guy Mannering,* Scott commits the absurdity of making Colonel Mannering address a letter to his best friend to "remind" him of "the odd and wayward fates of my youth, and the misfortunes of my manhood" (chap. 12). In *Lafcadio's Adventures,* André Gide makes the taciturn Lafcadio step out of character by having him inform his half-brother of his antecedents. Interestingly enough, Gide is driven to anticipate the reader's objections to the psychological improbability of this "quasi-mimetic" disclosure by "laying bare the device," that is, making the speaker himself comment on the oddity of his own behaviour: "'M. de Baraglioul, I have hitherto allowed no one to pry in the smallest degree into my life. . . . But to-day is a red-letter day; for once in my life I will give myself a holiday. Put your questions—I undertake to answer them all'" (bk. 2. chap. 6). Whereas Evelyn Waugh, who in *Decline and Fall* has almost every character confide his career to Paul Pennyfeather at their first meeting, finds it necessary to lay bare the addressee's role so as to disarm criticism. The absurdity of the gratuitous outpourings is enhanced by Paul's receiving them only under pressure or protest ("I don't in the least want to know anything about you; d'you hear?"); and when finally approached by the Minister of Transportation himself, the hero is made to wonder at his strange fate: "Why was it . . . that everyone he met seemed to specialise in this form of autobiography? He supposed he must have a sympathetic air" (pt. 1. chap. 7; pt. 2. chap. 3).

And in many similar instances of volunteered information, disinterested curiosity, and various kinds of abrupt lapses of knowledge or memory, an aesthetically motivated exposition, either by way of prologue or authorial summary, would be more economical and would spare the author some quite unnecessary compositional acrobatics.

James's compositional ideal, however, particularly lends itself to normative conclusions because with him, as I have shown, realistic motivation does not form simply a dramatized mode of conveying information but, in combination with his techniques of point of view, is exploited for achieving a rich variety of artistic effects. By dramatizing the emergence of exposition, he makes the same material simultaneously operate on different levels and in different ways, both in the actional framework of the fictive world and in the rhetorical framework consisting in the text-mediated relationship between implied author and reader. For the realistically motivated disclosure of exposition at the same time propels the fictive action forward and affects the fate of the agents, on the one hand, and is used to manipulate narrative interest, consolidate structure, focus attention, delineate character, control distance, and develop theme on the other. And since the multifunctionality of materials is indeed a central distinctive feature of literary art as opposed to other kinds of verbal communication—irrespective of the term employed to denote this concept, whether the old-fashioned "economy" and "complexity" or the more modern "semantic density"—it is small wonder that so many moderns have been tempted to erect the Jamesian principles into a universally binding model of composition. But this temptation must be withstood. The Jamesian model, where motivation systematically serves to propel and dissimulate the (aesthetic) dynamics of response and hypothesis-making in terms of the (realistic) vessel-centered dynamics of the action, is inherently superior neither in theory nor in practice to other models—where the divergence between the two dynamics may be dictated by different views or exigencies and compensated for by a wealth or intensity of aesthetic motivation. Narrative strategies opposed to the Jamesian can be shown to yield in their own way as multifunctional results as his (as demonstrated in my analysis of Balzac's aesthetically motivated, preliminary and concentrated exposition or of the flexible techniques of the *Odyssey*); while many modern imitations of the Jamesian model have resulted in pitiful failure. Each case must be judged on its own merits, even if we are agreed on our basic criteria of evaluation.

NOTES

CHAPTER ONE

1. V. Sackville-West, *The Edwardians* (New York, 1930), p. 1.

2. Thus Malcolm Cowley claims that all Faulkner's "books in the Yoknapatawpha saga are parts of the same living pattern. It is this pattern, and not the printed volumes in which part of it is recorded, that is Faulkner's real achievement. Its existence helps to explain one feature of his work: that each novel, each long or short story, seems to reveal more than it states explicitly and to have a bigger subject than itself" (*The Portable Faulkner* [New York, 1954], pp. 7-8).

3. See Ernest Schanzer, *The Problem Plays of Shakespeare* (London, 1966), chap. 2.

4. Cowley, ed., *The Portable Faulkner*, pp. 7-8.

5. Ibid., p. 8. Cowley, significantly enough, adds in the same sentence that these inconsistencies are "afterthoughts rather than oversights."

6. On taking leave of Archdeacon Grantley in the last but one chapter of *The Warden*, for instance, Trollope regrets "that he is represented in these pages as worse than he is" and twice repeats the explanation that in this novel "we have had to do with his foibles, and not with his virtues." What Trollope does here, in fact, is to account and lay the ground for the different presentation of the Archdeacon in *Barchester Towers*.

7. Anthony Trollope, *An Autobiography* (1883; reprint ed., London, 1961), p. 275.

8. Ibid., pp. 159, 309-10.

9. Percy Lubbock, *The Craft of Fiction* (New York, 1963; first published 1921), p. 210. Cf. Felicien Marceau, *Balzac and His World*, trans. Derek Coltman (London, 1967), pp. 3-6.

10. Gustav Freytag, *Technique of the Drama*, trans. Elias J. MacEwan (Chicago, 1908; first published 1863), pp. 114-15.

11. See, for example, pp. 119-21; note particularly that Freytag's definition of the function of the exposition ("its task, to prepare for the action," p. 120) largely overlaps with that of the introduction (pp. 115, 117-18).

12. To cite a single example: Vladimir Nabokov claims that in Gogol's *The Government Inspector* "there is no so-called 'exposition.' Thunderbolts do not lose time explaining meteorological conditions" (*Nikolai Gogol* [New York, 1961], p. 42). This statement is also based on the preconception that exposition must necessarily be preliminary. The exposition in this play is only delayed and distributed, but it is clearly there.

13. Robin H. Farquhar, "Dramatic Structure in the Novels of Ernest Hemingway," *Modern Fiction Studies* 14 (1968): 272, 282.

14. Ibid., p. 272.

15. See especially Boris Tomashevsky's "Thématique," in *Théorie de la littérature*, ed. Tzvetan Todorov (Paris, 1965), pp. 240-42; part of this essay has been reprinted in *Russian Formalist Criticism: Four Essays*, ed. Lee T. Lemon and Marion J. Reis (Lincoln, 1965). Strangely enough, Tomashevsky himself gives but an indifferent account of exposition, neither fully exploiting the terms he himself suggests nor taking into account the complex of time-problems involved (e.g., the fictive present).

Historically, as I have argued elsewhere, the distinction between *fabula* and *sujet* is already implicit in the Aristotelian view of "whole" as against "mythos" ("Elements of Tragedy and the Concept of Plot in Tragedy: On the Methodology of Constituting a Generic Whole," *Hasifrut* 4 [1973]: 23-69); and it was later formulated in the prevalent Renaissance and Neo-classical opposition of the "natural order" (employed by historians) and the "artificial order" (distinctive of literary art). There is no doubt that in the hands of the Russian Formalists some of the practical implications of this fundamental distinction were brought out more impressively than ever before; and that is why I am using *fabula* and *sujet* here rather than the more ancient terminology or, as is the fashion nowadays, some new terminology of my own. But I should perhaps warn the reader that in view of various theoretical and methodological weaknesses from which I believe the Formalist position(s) on this issue suffer, my account of these terms significantly diverges from theirs at a number of points. I should be held responsible only for the distinctions as explicitly defined in this chapter and further developed and demonstrated throughout the argument.

16. This conception of "motif" must be sharply distinguished from that of many folklorists and literary critics, who refer by this term to a recurrent, and sometimes migratory, thematic unit, often reducible to smaller units (e.g., the victory of the Cinderella or the son's quest for his father). As used here, *motif* primarily designates an irreducible narrative unit, which may or may not recur. Cf. Tomashevsky, "Thématique," pp. 268-69.

17. *The Notebooks of Henry James,* ed. F. O. Matthiessen and Kenneth B. Murdock (New York, 1961), p. 231. For another striking example, see p. 55.

18. Henry James, *The Art of the Novel,* ed. R. P. Blackmur (New York, 1962), pp. 320-21. See also below, Chapter 4, n. 6.

19. E. M. Forster, *Aspects of the Novel* (Harmondsworth, 1962; first published 1927), pp. 35, 93.

20. Aristotle, *Poetics,* 1452a20-22; trans. S. H. Butcher.

21. Nor is it a story, though clearly a narrative; Forster's categories also cover less ground than the other pair.

22. Todorov, ed., *Théorie de la littérature,* p. 267. At this point my definition of fabula again diverges from Tomashevsky's. I see no reason for postulating causality as a necessary condition for fabula. This additional condition seems to me gratuitous, since the distinction between fabula and sujet is designed to differentiate not between linkages but between the logical-chronological sequence in which the motifs might have been arranged and the order in which they are actually presented to the reader. In this context, the additive series of motifs is as much of a fabula as the causal, for the chronological framework common to both renders them equally amenable to the artistic deformation distinctive of the sujet. I see no justification, therefore, for Tomashevsky's lumping together purely descriptive books and episodic narratives as works equally devoid of a fabula. At any rate, while Tomashevsky would hold that story can never be equated with fabula, I content myself with indicating that the two concepts fail to overlap in many cases, namely, whenever the sujet is causally concatenated as a whole or even in parts; the process of abstraction producing the story will then be markedly more drastic than that producing the fabula since it will necessarily involve the elimination of the causal links too.

23. Similarly, for example, what R. S. Crane actually does in "The Concept of Plot and the Plot of *Tom Jones*" (*Critics and Criticism,* ed. R. S. Crane [Chicago, 1952], pp. 616 ff.), is first to reconstitute the plot-type fabula of this novel and then to consider the function of its deformation into a plot-type sujet. The use of suchlike terms would spare the reader some quite unnecessary confusion.

24. As will be argued in Chapter 9, however, a triad and not merely a pair of terms is required in order to describe adequately the various aspects of these time-ratios. See especially p. 288.

25. See Bernard Weinberg's "Castelvetro's Theory of Poetics," in Crane, ed., *Critics and Criticism,* p. 365.

26. *Essays of John Dryden,* ed. W. P. Ker, 2 vols. (New York, 1961), 1:131.

27. See, for example, Günter Müller's "Aufbauformen des Romans," in *Zur Poetik des Romans,* ed. Volker Klotz (Darmstadt, 1965), pp. 285-86.

28. A. A. Mendilow, *Time and the Novel* (London, 1952), p. 65.

29. Ibid., pp. 65, 71. See also Müller, "Aufbauformen des Romans," p. 285.

30. Cf. Fielding's shrewd observation in *Jonathan Wild* that the principal difference between the stage of the world and that of Drury Lane is that "on the former, the hero or great man is always behind the curtain, and seldom or never appears or doth anything in his own person," whereas "on the latter, the hero or chief figure is almost continually before your eyes, whilst the under-actors are not seen above once in an evening" (3.11). On the set of significance-determining factors and possible clashes between these indicators, see my "Faulkner's *Light in August* and the Poetics of the Modern Novel," *Hasifrut* 2 (1970), especially pp. 499-508.

31. Henry James, "The Art of Fiction" (1884), in *The Future of the Novel,* ed. Leon Edel (New York, 1956), p. 16; James, *The Art of the Novel,* pp. 56-57.

32. Edel, ed., *The Future of the Novel,* p. 23; James, *The Art of the Novel,* p. 57. But see also Chapter 7, section IV, above.

33. The reader may of course find this contextually determined scale false or stereotyped or trivial—that is, not compatible with what he or any other reader holds intrinsically significant in life or art or both. But this is already a question of evaluation, which should not affect the interpretative procedure leading him to the normative conclusion.

34. James shrewdly describes "a discriminated occasion" or "scene" as "copious, comprehensive, and accordingly never short, but with its office as definite as that of the hammer on the gong of the clock, the office of expressing *all that is in* the hour" (*The Art of the Novel,* p. 323).

35. Anthony Trollope, *Is He Popenjoy?*, chap. 1.

36. Mendilow, *Time and the Novel,* pp. 96-97. On the vexed question of presentness in German scholarship see, for instance, Käte Hamburger, *Die Logik der Dichtung* (Stuttgart, 1957); Franz Stanzel, "Episches Praeteritum, erlebte Rede, historisches Praesens," in Klotz, ed., *Zur Poetik des Romans,* pp. 319-38; Roy Pascal, "Tense and Novel," *Modern Language Review* 57 (1962): 1-11.

37. The point that most troubles me, however, in Mendilow's statement that "everything that antedates that point, as for instance exposition, is felt as a fictive past" is how to interpret the words "for instance." What else can antedate the fictive present—even according to Mendilow's conception of it—besides exposition? Is this a mere slip of the pen or does it suggest that had Mendilow offered a formal definition of exposition we would have found ourselves disagreeing even more than it seems to me we do?

38. It is often difficult to arrive at an exact computation of time-ratios. But even a rough calculation in the present instance will prove suggestive. Suppose the representational or reading time of each of the segments is one minute. It will not be unreasonable to assume that the fictive period covered by the first segment is no less than forty years, while that covered by the second is at most an hour. The first time-ratio would then be 1:21.024.000; the second, only 1:60. It is obvious that no variation in the speed of reading or in the calculation of the represented periods can seriously affect the size of this disparity.

39. Again, the scenic norm can be determined only contextually. Therefore, for instance, James's assertion that a scene is by definition "copious, comprehensive, and accordingly never short" (*The Art of the Novel,* p. 323) is indeed valid for his own scenic norm and for that of most modern authors, but does not apply to the scenic norm of biblical narrative.

40. Honoré de Balzac, *La Cousine Bette* (Verviers, n.d.), p. 109.

41. Charles Reade, *It Is Never Too Late to Mend* (London and Glasgow, n.d.), p. 6; Anthony Trollope, *Barchester Towers* (New York, 1963), p. 23.

42. Isaac Bashevis Singer, *Short Friday and Other Stories* (New York, 1965), pp. 10, 23, 33.

43. For interesting examples of problematic authorial delimitations see *Père Goriot* (Chapter 7, n. 35, below) and *La Cousine Bette.*

44. Phyllis Bentley, for instance, frequently confuses scene with summary as a result of her awareness of only one criterion that distinguishes them. She claims: "'There drove up a coach'—we are being told of a specific action at a specific time in a specific place; that is a scene" (*Some Observations on the Art of Narrative* [London, 1946], p. 19). According to her, then, the only *differentia specifica* of a scene is its "specificity" (what I call "concreteness"). This single criterion, however, is, by itself, inadequate for distinguishing "scene" from "summary," as can be concluded even from an examination of Bentley's own examples. She maintains, for instance, that the sentence "Elizabeth passed the chief of the night in her sister's room" (p. 9) is definitely not a scene but a summary. But according to her own criterion, she should have pronounced this to be a scene, for here too the reader is "being told of a specific [i.e., nonrecurrent] action at a specific time in a specific place." It is, in fact, summary not because of its lack of concreteness but of specificity (in my sense of the words), which is revealed by the striking disparity between its representational time (only a sentence) and its represented time (a whole night). In other words, a scene must be both specific and concrete. A narrative passage that lacks either of these defining properties is summary. Most expositional summaries, however, lack both in varying degrees.

CHAPTER TWO

1. Trans. James Harry and Sarah Catron Smith, in *The Great Critics,* ed. James Harry Smith and Edd Winfield Parks (New York, 1951), p. 119.

2. Rodney Delasanta, *The Epic Voice* (The Hague, 1967), pp. 45-46.

3. The notoriously eclectic Horace probably derived this idea, as he did others, from the *Poetics* (1459^a22-37; 1451^a24-30).

4. In this, too, Horace follows in the footsteps of Aristotle, who requires a causal concatenation of "beginning, middle and end" (1459^a19-21).

5. H. T. Swedenberg in *The Theory of the Epic in England: 1650-1800* (Berkley and Los Angeles, 1944) cites, for example, the eighteenth-century critic J. Trapp: "Homer first gave the beautiful example in his *Odyssée*. For his *Iliad* opens at the beginning" (p. 229; see also pp. 225, 230). Such claims as W. J. Woodhouse's that "in the Iliad, all the events are narrated in their proper sequence" (*The Composition of Homer's Odyssey* [Oxford, 1930], p. 13) instructively explain part of the mistake in terms of the size of the conceptual units employed; an "event" (or "episode" or "scene") may be composed of (and reduced to) a variety of temporally heterogeneous motifs. On scenic synthesis of discontinuous fabulaic motifs, see also pp. 20 and 288 above.

6. For some prescriptive statements on this see pp. 29-30 of his book.

7. For some quotations see Swedenberg, *The Theory of the Epic*, pp. 227-28, 233, 235.

8. See Bernard Weinberg's monumental study, *A History of Literary Criticism in the Italian Renaissance* (Chicago, 1961).

9. *The Poetical Works of Edmund Spenser*, ed. J. C. Smith and E. de Selincourt (London, 1935), p. 408.

10. E.g., James Beattie, "On Poetry and Music as they affect the mind," in *Essays* (Edinburgh, 1776), p. 423. Gibbon's reference to the chronological order as the "natural historical order" (quoted in Swedenberg, *The Theory of the Epic*, p. 235) shows to what an extent the terms were considered synonymous.

11. *The Oxford Book of Eighteenth-Century Verse*, ed. David Nichol Smith (Oxford, 1936), p. 548.

12. *David Copperfield* opens with the narrator's announcement that "to begin my life with the beginning of my life, I record that I was born (as I have been informed and believe) on a Friday, at twelve o'clock at night."

13. J. D. Salinger, *The Catcher in the Rye* (Harmondsworth, 1960), p. 5.

14. Hugh Blair, *Lectures on Rhetoric and Belles Lettres* (1783), quoted in Swedenberg, *The Theory of the Epic*, p. 225.

15. Quoted in ibid., p. 233.

16. *History of the Peloponnesian War*, trans. Rex Werner (Harmondsworth, 1962), p. 24.

17. Ibid., p. 25.

18. For example, R. J. Renier in *History: Its Purpose and Method* (London, 1961): "*Chronology*, which takes charge of the very framework of narrative, the time element, deserves place of honour. It arranges the significant events which took place in the past in their time order" (p. 112); Langlois and Seignobos impress upon aspiring historians that "chronological order should be followed as far as possible because this is the order in which we know that the facts occurred, and by which we are guided in seeking for causes and effects" (*Introduction to the Study of History*, trans. G. G. Berry [New York, 1906], p. 249). Of especial interest is Morton White's equation of "chronicle" with E. M. Forster's "story" and his definition of "history" as a narrative arranged in "story" order but causally concatenated as well. "The chronicler is likely to tell us: 'The King of England died, and then the Queen of England died, and then the Prince of England died, and then the Princess of England died. And here endeth our chronicle.' But a corresponding history is likely to read: 'The King of England died, so the Queen of England died of grief. And because he worried so much about the Queen's death, the Prince of England committed suicide; and therefore the Princess of England died later of loneliness. And so endeth our lugubrious history.'" "The Logic of Historical Narration," in *Philosophy and History*, ed. Sidney Hook (New York, 1963), p. 6.

19. Swedenberg, *The Theory of the Epic*, p. 236.

20. Robert Graves, *I, Claudius* (New York, n.d.; first published 1934), p. 35.

21. Ibid., pp. 20, 35.

22. Robert Graves, *Claudius the God* (Harmondsworth, 1962; first published 1934), p. 9. However, the extreme views professed by this narrator are to be sharply distinguished from those of the implied author. The latter is, qua literary artist, keenly interested in precisely the artistic effects spurned by his agent. He has in fact postulated as narrator a professional historian with fairly representative views on his craft in order to achieve (or "motivate") a variety of rhetorical ends,

such as an impression of historical authenticity. To the relations between Claudius and his creator I shall revert in Chapter 8.

23. *Johnson: Prose and Poetry*, ed. Mona Wilson (London, 1950), p. 864.

24. See C. S. Lewis, *An Experiment in Criticism* (Cambridge, 1961), pp. 10 ff.

25. See, however, Wayne C. Booth's stimulating analysis of literary interests in *The Rhetoric of Fiction* (Chicago, 1961), pp. 124 ff.

26. Wilson, ed., *Johnson: Prose and Poetry*, pp. 881, 503.

27. Henry James, *The Art of the Novel*, ed. R. P. Blackmur (New York, 1962), pp. 252-53.

28. Ibid., p. 253.

29. This view of the literary work was first outlined in an essay on which I collaborated with Menakhem Perry, "The King through Ironic Eyes: The Narrator's Devices in the Biblical Story of David and Bathsheba and Two Exursuses on the Theory of the Narrative Text," *Hasifrut* 1 (1968): 263-92. I am responsible, however, for the later development of the theory in the present book, based on the relation of gaps to chronology and the view of exposition as the basis of the narrative structure of probabilities. For a general theoretical account of the problem of divergent or conflicting literary hypotheses in relation to the chronological gaps that produce them, see my "Delicate Balance in the Story of the Rape of Dinah: Biblical Narrative and the Rhetoric of the Narrative Text," *Hasifrut* 4 (1973): 221-27.

To prevent possible misunderstandings, it may be well to note at once that the present conception of gap—or for that matter the earlier, 1968 view—has little to do with Roman Ingarden's notion of *Unbestimmtheitstellen* ("indeterminacies") or *Lücken* ("lacunae" or "gaps"), first presented in *Das literarische Kunstwerk* (1931; especially chap. 7) and recently taken up by Wolfgang Iser, especially in *The Implied Reader* (Baltimore, 1974). Briefly, Ingarden's indeterminacies, whatever the fictive object they relate to—character or event, space or time—are neither dynamic nor systematic nor even usually felt as gaps. For they are (1) the inevitable result of the selectivity of literary art, which by definition cannot compete with the fullness and many-sidedness of life, rather than of deliberate artistic manipulations (combinational and distributive as well as selective) of narrative material; (2) local, isolated, and heterogeneous rather than structurally and functionally interrelated; (3) static features (or more precisely, nonfeatures) rather than developmental and even sequentially specifiable and determinable configurations; (4) wholly unnoticed by the reader or, when noticed, freely or even subjectively filled out rather than perceptibly foregrounded or temporarily camouflaged at will, in line with the author's overall strategy and precisely in order to obtain tight control of the reading-process; (5) irrelevant or at best incidental rather than compositionally, semantically, and rhetorically crucial. Wolfgang Iser's variously designated "gaps," while endowed with a far more active (though still subjectively variable) role, are no less removed from mine, since they are not even necessarily referential, let alone chronological, but may relate to any number of levels or frameworks other than the represented reality. They may, for instance, consist in the "space" between "two contrasting sides" of an object (p. 48); in Fielding's "vacant spaces of time," left totally unrepresented (p. 51); in the typographical space between chapters (pp. 40-41); in "empty spaces" between different styles (p. 226); in "blanks" of judgement (pp. 112-13); in a "gap" between the "familiar repertoire in the novel and one's own observation of it" (p. 33), between "imagination and reality" (p. 96), between "the characters' actions and the narrator's comments" (p. 108), between "monologue and overall situation" (p. 208), between unrelated themes (p. 210), or between heading and text (p. 214). His gaps are, in short, whatever the text has left unsaid or unconnected and invites each reader to complete in his own way. There is no need here to go into the question whether such heterogeneous phenomena may be profitably yoked together under this heading. For my present purposes it is sufficient to indicate in advance the magnitude of the conceptual disparity behind the unfortunate terminological similarity.

30. On the problem of mutually exclusive ambiguity and gap-filling in this paradigmatic Jamesian tale, see Perry and Sternberg, "The King through Ironic Eyes," pp. 283-88.

31. Most expositional gaps are temporary. But even those that ultimately prove to be permanent (e.g., Iago's motives, which form an essential part of the premises that directly lead to the catastrophe) function as temporary ones as long as the reader has not reached the last page of the work; it is the reader's belief in their temporariness that constantly impels him forward in the hope of finding them fully and authoritatively filled in. And vice versa: even gaps that ultimately prove to be temporary operate as permanent ones, in all that concerns the construction and clash of hypotheses, as long as they have not been explicitly filled in.

CHAPTER THREE

1. P. 171 in E. V. Rieu's translation (New York, 1944). Subsequent references to this translation will be incorporated in the text.

2. Howard W. Clarke, *The Art of the "Odyssey"* (Englewood Cliffs, N.J., 1967), p. 6. For even sharper strictures see W. J. Woodhouse, *The Composition of Homer's "Odyssey"* (Oxford, 1930), pp. 23 ff.

3. Cf. Wayne C. Booth, *The Rhetoric of Fiction* (Chicago, 1961), p. 5.

4. But the former mode of manipulating response is not wholly abandoned. Mentor thus discloses a new attractive quality of Odysseus's when he refers to him as "the admirable king . . . who ruled like a loving father" (p. 35).

5. Charles Rowan Beye, *The "Iliad," the "Odyssey," and the Epic Tradition* (London, 1968), pp. 178–79.

6. But even the ultimate complication of our response to the Suitors is never allowed to involve a division of our sympathies, being indulged in merely owing to Homer's distaste for black-and-white portraiture. The complexity of Odysseus's own character as it later unfolds sufficiently endangers the equilibrium of our sentiments towards him.

7. This is further corroborated by the different tenor given to the gods' decision in the "second" assembly scene (book 5).

8. See, for instance, S. E. Basset, "The Suitors of Penelope," *Transactions of the American Philological Association* 49 (1918): 46–47; S. E. Basset, *The Poetry of Homer* (Berkeley, 1938), p. 187; H. D. F. Kitto, *Poiesis* (Berkeley and Los Angeles, 1966), pp. 127–28.

9. One of the rare exceptions strikingly illustrates in miniature Homer's overall method. At the start of the assembly scene, there is a reference to an Ithacan whose son was "killed by the savage Cyclops in his cavern home when he made the last of his meals off Odysseus's men" (p. 30). This is another stage in the (typically tripartite) process by which Homer progressively excites our interest in the battle against the Cyclops through a piecemeal, increasingly specific distribution of expositional material relating to this gap. Poseidon's inveterate hostility toward Odysseus was first obscurely touched on (p. 19); later we were allowed to gather that the reason for Poseidon's enmity is Odysseus's blinding of his son the Cyclops (p. 20); and now Homer pricks our curiosity afresh, in order to prevent it from sinking into inertia.

10. Beye, *Epic Tradition*, p. 171; see also Clarke, *The Art of the "Odyssey,"* p. 36.

11. G. S. Kirk, in *The Songs of Homer* (Cambridge, 1962), indeed goes so far as to dismiss the "rambling and repetitious reminiscences and the wordy conversations" of books 3–4 as little better than padding; Telemachus "discovers little about his father, and apart from the subsidiary theme of his education and development the so-called Telemachy contributes little to the main plot of the poem" (pp. 358–59).

12. See Rodney Delasanta, *The Epic Voice* (The Hague, 1967), pp. 57–58; Beye, *Epic Tradition*, p. 161; Woodhouse, *The Composition of Homer's "Odyssey,"* p. 247; Basset, *The Poetry of Homer*, p. 196.

13. *On the Sublime*, trans. Thomas R. R. Stebbing (London, 1867), pp. 33–36.

14. *Poetics*, 1460^{a}18–26; trans. S. H. Butcher.

15. Predictably, Menelaus's imagery (like that of the omen) recurs later. After the slaughter of the Suitors, Odysseus looks "like a lion when he comes from feeding on some farmer's bullock, with the blood dripping from his breast and jaws on either side, a fearsome spectacle" (p. 287; see also pp. 70, 89, 291). Note how the last part of this simile links it up, by way of figurative montage, with the portent of the eagles.

16. "Yes, if only Odysseus, as he then was, could get among these Suitors, there'd be a quick death and a sorry wedding for them all" (p. 25).

17. The recurrence of this very number later on affords another retrospective confirmation of my argument that the reader is expected to regard the ambush mainly as a threat to Odysseus's life; in Penelope's dream, the eagle-Oydsseus breaks the necks of her "flock of twenty geese" (p. 257).

18. Beye, *Epic Tradition*, p. 159.

19. See Auerbach's widely anthologised essay "Odysseus's Scar," in *Mimesis: The Representation of Reality in Western Literature*, trans. Willard Trask (New York, 1957; originally published 1946), pp. 2–3.

20. Ibid., p. 2.

21. See Denys Page, *The Homeric Odyssey* (Oxford, 1955), pp. 64 ff.

22. Page's dismissal of the second assembly scene as "a pale and uninteresting image of the one which begins the *Odyssey*, [introduced] for no visible purpose but to go over much the same ground again" (p. 70) is, then, another instance of Homer's art of repetition being taken for artless repetitiousness.

23. To which C. S. Lewis reduces this epic in *A Preface to "Paradise Lost"* (London, 1960; first published 1942), p. 28.

24. This task once accomplished, however, Homer at once proceeds to increase our suspense again. He introduces a new line of suspense, carefully played down before and saved especially for the new stage, namely, the consequences of the Suitors' destruction. The new danger is obliquely suggested through the otherwise inexplicable introduction of Theoclymenus (whose role is dismissed by Page as "wonderfully unimportant," p. 84); having killed a nobleman in Argos, he has been so relentlessly pursued by his kinsmen that "to avoid the certainty of death . . . [he] ran away and embraced [his] new identity as a wanderer" (p. 202). In the light of this internal norm—again one established through a concrete expositional precedent—can Odysseus slaughter the young nobility of Ithaca and other states without incurring a civil war? This line of suspense is further developed, side by side with the others, till we find our worst fears realized in the outbreak of the insurrection in the last book.

CHAPTER FOUR

1. *The Ulysses Theme* (Oxford, 1963), p. 13.

2. For a strained argument to the contrary, see George deF. Lord, "The *Odyssey* and the Western World," *Sewanee Review* 62 (1954): 406-27.

3. Robert Scholes and Robert Kellog, *The Nature of Narrative* (New York, 1968), p. 164.

4. Ed. Carl I. Hovland (New Haven, 1957). Some of these findings have recently been put to excellent use by M. Perry, in a Hebrew study of H. N. Bialik's "inverted poem" (see "Thematic Structures in Bialik's Poetry: The Inverted Poem and Related Kinds," *Hasifrut* 1 [1969/70]: 74, n. 129). But whether such experiments do more than confirm what oft was thought and (in art) e'er so better expressed, is still an open question.

5. Quite literally; for a close analysis of the biblical use of the control strategy that is to be illustrated in this chapter through Homer, see my "Delicate Balance in the Story of the Rape of Dinah: Biblical Narrative and the Rhetoric of the Narrative Text," *Hasifrut* 4 (1973): 193-231.

6. There is varied evidence that these potentialities, which I have been developing as a theoretical and interpretative tool for reconstructing the choices made by the implied author, may even be actually considered, experimented with, and intentionally exploited by the biographical author during the process of composition. For instance: the distribution, fragmentation, and deformed ordering of the antecedents of such Jamesian characters as Strether or Mrs. Newsome in *The Ambassadors* become doubly revealing in view of the fact that the scenario to this novel does contain concentrated, orderly expositional accounts of both (*The Notebooks of Henry James*, ed. F. O. Matthiessen and Kenneth B. Murdock [New York, 1961], pp. 382 ff., 379 ff.); James deliberately avoided making use of the character-sketches ready to his hand. This scenario being in fact a foreshortened fabula, the temporal and other presentational discrepancies between it and the finished product go to show that the concept of preexistent fabula, though indeed primarily a theoretical or reconstitutive rather than genetic model, may actually serve as "raw material" and starting point for the process of artistic manipulation. Distributive choices must not, at any rate, be confused with such authorial changes of mind (or heart) as Thackeray's about Rawdon Crawley or Trollope's, in *Orley Farm*, about Lady Mason.

7. *Light in August* (Harmondsworth, 1967), pp. 25-26.

8. On the role this strategy plays in the novel's overall shifting of focus, see my "Faulkner's *Light in August* and the Poetics of the Modern Novel," *Hasifrut* 2 (1970): 498-537, especially 501-4. For an interesting analysis of the shaping of response in Faulkner's best-known short story, see M. Perry, "O Rose, Thou Art Sick!," *Siman Kria* 3-4 (1974): 423-58.

9. Odysseus's maternal grandfather was Autolycus, "the most accomplished thief and liar of

his day" (pp. 253–54). So, as Stanford comments (p. 12), Odysseus was doomed to Autolycan cleverness at his birth.

10. W. B. Stanford makes the same point about the *Iliad:* "One is intended . . . to see him as a man consciously controlling his unusual versatility and flexibility in an uneasy environment, moving with alert circumspection among people of different heredity and outlook" (p. 14).

11. The Homeric techniques devised for the control of distance in books 5–12 are remarkably similar to those employed in books 1–4 for the manipulation of suspense, particularly in the subtle shifting, balancing, and counterbalancing of the reader's emotions (sympathy and antipathy in place of hope and fear) through either a continual harping on or gradual disclosure, development, and patterning of various expositional motifs. It is such correspondences that reveal an artist's figure in the carpet.

12. Note, for instance, the specification of the beauties of Calypso's island (p. 75) and Alcinous's palace (pp. 95–97).

13. Rodney Delasanta notes the rarity of epic simile in Odysseus's tale (*The Epic Voice* [The Hague, 1967], pp. 50–51).

14. E.g., ibid., pp. 52 ff.

15. Homer even informs us that the Phaeacians had once formed part (as "neighbours to the Cyclopes"; p. 86) of the eerie world evoked by Odysseus.

16. In tracing the movement of the text, one discovers that the claim made by Scholes and Kellog that the "very recurring epithets of formulaic narrative are signs of flatness in characterization" (p. 164) is baseless. The epithets attached to Odysseus's name, far from being lifeless formulas, functionally vary at each stage so as to dovetail into the overall control strategy. In the primacy-effect phase, books 1–4, it is Penelope rather than Odysseus who receives such Autolycan epithets as "clever," "prudent," or "shrewd," while he himself is constantly honored with "dauntless," "gallant," "indomitable," "stalwart," or "admirable king." Throughout books 5–8, where the epic unfolds for the first time the apparent polarity of Odysseus's heroic nature, it employs two opposed sets of epithets—sometimes designating him by a purely heroic formula (including "the heroic Odysseus" or "Odysseus, the royal sacker of cities") and sometimes by an Autolycan (e.g., "the nimble-witted Odysseus"). At the present stage, finally, when the epic is intent on showing how in Odysseus the heroic and Autolycan talents are welded into a unique, indissoluble unity, the polar sets of epithets are also generally fused into the compound formula "Royal son of Laertes, Odysseus of the nimble wits" (e.g., pp. 142, 146, 147, 154). See also Chapter 7, n. 49, below.

17. Still, it is thoroughly typical of Homer's method that he should further delay, but not suppress altogether, the trickiest piece of information. The real normative dynamite, the revelation that Odysseus was none too eager to join the expedition against Troy, is appropriately sprung as late as the final book; they had to spend a full month at Ithaca, Agamemnon recalls, "so hard did we find it to win over the man who now is styled the Sacker of Cities" (p. 301).

CHAPTER FIVE

1. Jane Austen, *Pride and Prejudice* (London and Glasgow, 1958), pp. 229–42.

2. Like most of the devices analyzed throughout the chapter, this structural metaphor of the "winding" route and the surprising "turn" is an integral feature of Jane Austen's poetics (and later reappears in an even more elaborate form as part of Henry James's principle of "the crooked corridor"). It is worked into each of her six major novels—in situational and, less often, figurative terms—covertly operating as an encapsulated embodiment of the overall actional movement (past, present, and future), as an externalized equivalent of psychological processes, and as a warning-signal designed to foreshadow surprises and thus put the reader on his guard against the protagonist's fanciful impressions. Catherine Morland, her imagination inflamed by Gothic fiction, thus expects "every bend in the road" to Northanger Abbey to reveal all kinds of thrilling curiosities, only to discover that the abbey has been thoroughly renovated; with regard to the similarly inspired horrors she soon comes to imagine about her host, the General, the same moral (and warning) is implicitly pointed through the "winding path" in his park and the "winding staircase" in the house itself; the villain, like the house, has been modernized. Finally, when the heroine is ignominiously driven out of the house by the General and all is apparently lost, the ultimate happy

ending (the last dramatic twist) is cunningly foreshadowed by the description that on her way home Catherine passes "a turning" that leads to her lover's parsonage (*Northanger Abbey,* chaps. 20, 22, 23, 29). The surprising twists and painful turns of Emma Woodhouse's way to enlightenment about her matchmaking plans for Harriet Smith are metonymically objectified in reference to two of the matrimonial candidates; while she is walking with Harriet down Vicarage Lane, "the lane made a slight bend; and when the bend was passed, Mr. Elton was immediately in sight" (*Emma,* chap. 10) and it is indeed predictable that her plans concerning the vicar should soon take "a perverse turn" (chap. 15)—just as we are reassured that Robert Martin's chances of marrying Harriet are not so desperate in spite of Emma's objections when she visits the neighborhood of his farm, again in Harriet's company, and the river is described as "making a close and handsome curve around it" (chap. 42). But perhaps the finest handling of this signal occurs in chapters 9-10 of *Mansfield Park,* where six young people (composing three triangles of established lovers, would-be lovers, and future lovers) are described as symmetrically "winding in and out" of "very serpentine" and "circuitous" paths.

3. Mark Schorer, "Fiction and the 'Matrix of Analogy,'" *Kenyon Review* 11 (1949): 540; David Lodge, *Language of Fiction* (London, 1966), pp. 94 ff.

4. The potentially opposed semantic connotations of "know," "be acquainted with," or "character," as well as their situational equivalents, are often played off against each other in Jane Austen's novels, in the interests of contrastive characterization or self-characterization, thematic structuring, and rhetorical adjustment. Take for instance the following exchange about John Willoughby, the (recently introduced) attractive villain of *Sense and Sensibility:*

"You [Sir John Middleton] know him then", said Mrs. Dashwood.

"Know him! To be sure I do. Why, he is down here every year."

"And what sort of a young man is he?"

"As good a kind of fellow as ever lived, I assure you. A very decent shot, and there is not a bolder rider in England."

"And is *that* all you can say for him?" cried Marianne indignantly. "But what are his manners on more intimate acquaintance? What his pursuits, his talents and genius?"

Sir John was rather puzzled.

"Upon my soul," said he, "I do not know much about him as to all *that.* But he is a pleasant, good humoured fellow, and has got the nicest little black bitch of a pointer I ever saw" (chap. 9).

5. Marvin Mudrick, *Jane Austen: Irony as Defense and Discovery* (Princeton, 1952), p. 95.

6. Henry James, *The Art of the Novel,* ed. R. P. Blackmur (New York, 1962), p. 62.

7. Including even such a paragon as Mr. Knightley, whose change of attitude towards Frank Churchill is finally given the amusing form of a miniature tripartite inversion, in a passage where the paratactic structure of the (progressively longer) coupled sentences actually highlights at each stage the link between subjective, "interested" cause and evaluative effect: "He [Mr. Knightley] had found her [Emma] agitated and low. Frank Churchill was a villain. He heard her declare that she had never loved him. Frank Churchill's character was not desperate. She was his own Emma, by hand and word, when they returned into the house; and if he could have thought of Frank Churchill then, he might have deemed him a very good sort of fellow" (*Emma,* chap. 49).

8. She herself has twice told Collins it was "impossible" for her to accept his proposal (pp. 107, 109).

9. In *Emma,* interestingly enough, the author insinuates from the start suggestive points of unflattering and seemingly incongruous similarity between the heroine and her father—in his way as comically unique as Mrs. Bennet—with his "habits of gentle selfishness, and of never being able to suppose that other people could feel differently from himself" and his unfitness "for any acquaintance but such as would visit him on his own terms" (chaps. 1, 3). And again, note the structural and functional correspondence between this particular principle of collocating the large compositional units of character or event and Jane Austen's manipulation of the verbal microcosm by way of yoking together several incongruous words or phrases and reinforcing their semantic incongruity by placing them in equivalent syntactic positions within the same sentence: "Lady Lucas was inquiring . . . after the welfare and poultry of her eldest daughter" (*Pride and Prejudice,* chap. 39); "He had made his fortune, bought his house and obtained his wife" (*Emma,* chap. 2).

10. In the framework of Jane Austen's work as a whole, it emerges that such words as "perverse," "inexplicable," "inconsistent," and above all "unaccountable" invariably play an important role in the control strategy (and in the unfolding structure of probabilities in general) as charged psychological and normative indicators of the protagonist's prejudices, ready-made labels, and blind spots—especially vis-à-vis complexity of character. Elizabeth Bennet thus joins the company of a great many Austenian figures: the innocent Catherine Morland, who looks upon the General's conduct as "inexplicable" and "most unaccountable! How were people at that rate to be understood?" (*Northanger Abbey*, chap. 26); the romantic Marianne Dashwood, who cannot view the undemonstrative behaviour of her sister as otherwise than "strange," "unaccountable," "most unaccountably" cold, as well as the unimaginative Sir John Middleton, who considers the faithlessness of "such a good-natured fellow" as Willoughby "an unaccountable business," and the grasping John Dashwood, who in view of Brandon's generosity comes to be convinced that "there is a vast deal of inconsistency in almost every human character" (*Sense and Sensibility*, chaps. 8, 16, 32, 41); or Emma Woodhouse, amazed at the "perverse turn" brought about by Mr. Elton's "inconstancy" and "unsteadiness of character" (*Emma*, chap. 15), shocked by the "unequal, inconsistent, incongruous" nature of human affairs (chap. 47), and finally "perfectly satisfied, unaccountable as it was, that Robert Martin had thoroughly supplanted Mr. Knightley" in her friend's affection (chap. 55).

11. Reuben A. Brower, *The Fields of Light* (New York, 1962), p. 164 ff.

12. In all that concerns informational distribution and the dynamics of control, Jane Austen's six major novels fall into two unequal groups. The larger group includes *Sense and Sensibility*, *Northanger Abbey* and *Emma*, where the reader's position vis-à-vis the heroine basically corresponds to the *Pride and Prejudice* pattern. Fanny Price in *Mansfield Park* and Anne Elliot in *Persuasion*, on the other hand, are sharply (and favorably) contrasted with their respective human environments in that both share from the start the reader's early suspicions of the artful villain as well as the reader's approving view of the hero. Fanny's rejection of Henry Crawford on moral grounds is thus triumphantly vindicated toward the end of the novel. And having been informed of Mr. Elliot's heartlessness, Anne can justifiably claim: "I have heard nothing which really surprises me. I know those who would be shocked by such a representation of Mr. Elliot, who would have difficulty in believing it, but I have never been satisfied. I have always wanted some other motive for his conduct than appeared" (*Persuasion*, chap. 21).

13. Elsewhere, in an analysis of the various methods of "constituting a generic whole," such as tragic plot, I have defined this difference in terms of a distinction between "thematic" and "structural" logic: "Elements of Tragedy and the Concept of Plot in Tragedy: On the Methodology of Constituting a Generic Whole," *Hasifrut* 4 (1973): 23–69.

14. For an account of Henry James's interrelated principles of temporal structure, referential ambiguation, and point of view, see Chapter 9 below. For a closer view of the correspondence between his novelistic practice and Jane Austen's, see my analysis of *The Ambassadors* in "Expositional Modes and Order of Presentation in Fiction" (Ph.D. diss., Jerusalem, 1971), pp. 299–431.

15. Wayne C. Booth, *The Rhetoric of Fiction* (Chicago, 1961), p. 255.

16. W. J. Harvey, "The Plot of *Emma*," *Essays in Criticism* 17 (1967): 57.

CHAPTER SIX

1. Henry Fielding, *Joseph Andrews* (London, 1960), p. 203 [bk. 3, chap. 10].

2. Toward the end of the fourth chapter of *Dead Souls*, on the other hand, Gogol interpolates an elaborate comic simile in order to impede the representation of the drubbing Chichikov is about to get from Nozdrev.

3. Viktor Shklovsky's suggestive comments on the subject in *Theorie der Prosa* (trans. Giselda Drohla [Frankfurt am Main, 1966; first published 1925]) are, typically, theoretically indiscriminate. His "staircase-like construction" includes verbal repetition, synonymic repetition, tautological correspondence, and the formulaic structure of adventure stories. But he leaves unexplained the distinctive features of this construction—the common denominator justifying the subsumption of such heterogeneous phenomena under a single theoretical heading—beyond the general claim that art aims at decelerating, complicating, and thus sharpening perception. Actually, the centrality and

multifariousness of the principle of retardation in temporal art is even greater than Shklovsky seems to think, but the constant that informs all its different manifestations is the (multifunctional) rivalry or clash between different expectations or interests.

4. See, for instance, John Butt and Kathleen Tillotson, *Dickens at Work* (London, 1957); and Kathleen Tillotson's *Novels of the Eighteen-Forties* (Oxford, 1954), pp. 21-47.

5. With the possible exception of the text's permanent gaps, which are left open in the fabula as well as in the sujet.

6. William M. Thackeray, *The History of Pendennis* (London, 1885), p. 66.

7. Charles Rowan Beye, *The "Iliad," the "Odyssey," and the Epic Tradition* (London, 1968), pp. 89-90.

8. Significantly, classical catalogues were considered a thing apart from standard narrative because they could be transposed from one context to another; and this particular catalogue was frequently omitted from manuscripts by later copyists.

9. Henry Fielding, *Amelia,* ed. A. R. Humphreys, 2 vols. (London, 1962), 1:294 [6.9].

10. Quoted in *Henry Fielding: The Critical Heritage,* ed. Ronald Paulson and Thomas Lockwood (London, 1969), p. 268. Cf. Chapter 3, n. 11, above.

11. *Tom Jones* (New York, 1963), p. 440 [10.1].

12. *Poetics,* Chap. 8; 1451ᵃ30-36 (trans. S. H. Butcher).

13. Even in the case of Mrs. Bennet's narrative, the elements that directly contribute to the propulsion of the action are outnumbered by those that fail to do so, however remotely.

14. For an excellent analysis of Fielding's interpolated tales along similar lines see Sheldon Sacks, *Fiction and the Shape of Belief* (Berkeley and Los Angeles, 1967), pp. 193 ff.

15. Ibid., pp. 199-200.

16. Henry James, *The Art of the Novel,* ed. R. P. Blackmur (New York, 1962), p. 132.

17. From the viewpoint of reducing retardatory effect this digression, then, enjoys the benefit of preclusion of suspense that is usually peculiar to preliminary exposition, while at the same time retaining the "anticipatory" advantages typical of perceptibly delayed exposition.

18. This phrase is used by Bertil Romberg in *Studies in the Narrative Technique of the First-Person Novel* (Stockholm, 1962) to denote the situation in which a story is narrated, as distinguished from the action projected by this narrative.

19. For a similar thematic and normative use of interposed argument see Tom Jones's remonstrance with the old man (pp. 406-8 [8.15]).

20. Other common variations on these devices are the narrator's temporary refusal to go on with his tale (e.g., Odysseus waiting for a bribe from the tense Phaeacians, and Scheherazade, with even better reason) or the auditor's refusal to go on listening (e.g., the indignant expostulations of suspects punctuating the detective's reconstruction of the crime).

21. The only exception to this rule may occur when the narrator is a fictive character who is engaged in *writing* down his history. In this case, quasi-mimetic interruptions, to which he is as liable as an oral narrator in an inset epic situation, may indeed influence the narrator's segmentation of his text. In this way Richardson manages to spread the record of Clarissa's expositional adventures (addressed to Miss Howe) over a number of letters. He simply makes the heroine account for her repeatedly breaking up the textual continuity of her narrative in terms of external exigencies, e.g., "I must break off here. But will continue the subject the very first opportunity."

22. Cf. Philip Stevick, "The Theory of Fictional Chapters," in *The Theory of the Novel,* ed. Philip Stevick (New York, 1968), pp. 179-82. The body of the essay, particularly the discussion of Fielding, is rather disappointing in view of the promising title.

23. Edwin Muir, *The Structure of the Novel* (London, 1960; first published 1928), p. 71. Muir's whole chapter on "Time and Space" has significant implications for the study of retardatory structure. But this kind of structure is not peculiar to the "dramatic novel" as Muir suggests. It equally characterizes the "novel of action," which also postulates a definite end resulting from a conflict. On the other hand, the "novel of character"—with its densely populated canvas, multiplicity of relationships and conflicts, and more relaxed pace—differs from the two other categories in the more limited span and the reduced intensity of its retardatory arches.

24. *Barchester Towers* (New York, 1963), p. 300 [chap. 30].

25. For useful historical surveys of these genres see Fredson Thayer Bowers, *Elizabethan Revenge Tragedy: 1587-1642* (Gloucester, Mass., 1959); A. E. Murch, *The Development of the*

Detective Story (London, 1968); and Julian Symons, *Bloody Murder* (Harmondsworth, 1974).

26. Conan Doyle's attempt in *A Study in Scarlet,* for instance, to hold up the continuity of the action by intercalating a lengthy expositional account of some of the characters is not exactly successful.

27. I have said "two or three" because the third gap is distinctly expositional only when the murder is chronologically anterior to the beginning of the sujet; and because emphasis, and hence interest, may not be equally distributed among the three: some detective stories turn on an ingenious method of murder, others on the emergence of a surprising motive, and still others on the guilt of a person who is above or below suspicion.

28. Ellery Queen, *Halfway House* (New York, 1962), p. 217.

29. As Edgar Allan Poe excellently puts it: "The design of *mystery* . . . being once determined upon by an author, it becomes imperative, first, that no undue or inartistical means be employed to conceal the secret of the plot; and, secondly, that the secret be well kept. . . . A failure to preserve it until the proper moment of *denouement,* throws all into confusion, so far as regards the *effect* intended. If the mystery leak out, against the author's will, his purposes are immediately at odds and ends; for he proceeds upon the supposition that certain impressions *do* exist, which do *not* exist, in the mind of his readers." "Charles Dickens," in *The Works of Edgar Allan Poe* (New York, n.d.), 7:36.

30. The implications of these functional and presentational features for the generic point of view, with its distinctive perspectival latitude and constraints, will be pursued in Chapter 8 below.

31. The convention of a clearing-up chapter with all its paraphernalia was created as early as Dickens's *Bleak House* (1852-53). See Murch, *The Development of the Detective Story,* p. 96.

CHAPTER SEVEN

1. Anthony Trollope, *An Autobiography* (London, 1961; first published 1883), p. 85.

2. His closest approach to a definition comes in a comment on Thackeray's style: "The realistic must not be true,—but just so far removed from truth as to suit the erroneous idea of truth which the reader may be supposed to entertain" (Anthony Trollope, *Thackeray* [Detroit, 1968; first published 1879], p. 185).

3. Anthony Trollope, *Barchester Towers* (New York, 1963), p. 181 [chap. 20]; Trollope, *Autobiography,* pp. 85, 212.

4. For an account of the lively wrangling over the plot-character crux during the Victorian era, see Richard Stang, *The Theory of the Novel in England: 1850-1870* (London, 1959), pp. 127-32; and Kenneth Graham, *English Criticism of the Novel: 1865-1900* (London, 1966), pp. 97 ff.

5. In *Framley Parsonage,* for example, "the real plot consists at last simply of a girl refusing to marry the man she loves till the man's friends agreed to accept her lovingly" (*Autobiography,* p. 123); and even more clearly: "I have composed better stories—that is, have created better plots" (p. 150).

6. In a letter to his publisher about *John Caldigate,* Trollope objects: "I have never found myself able to effect changes in the plot of a story. Small as the links are, one little thing hinges on another to such an extent that any change sets the whole narrative wrong" (quoted in Michael Sadleir, *Trollope: A Commentary* [London, 1933], pp. 349-50).

7. The advance layouts for his novels (appended to Sadleir, *Trollope,* pp. 422-24) indeed consist of little more than thumbnail sketches of the characters.

8. From the preface to the 1861 edition of *The Woman in White:* "The primary object of a work of fiction should be to tell a story; and I have never believed that the novelist who properly performed this first condition of his art, was in danger, on that account, of neglecting the delineation of character—for this plain reason, that the effect produced by any narrative of events is essentially dependent, not on the events themselves, but on the human interest which is directly connected with them. It may be possible in novel-writing to present characters successfully without telling a story; but it is not possible to tell a story successfully without presenting characters . . . as recognisable realities."

9. Wilkie Collins, *The Moonstone,* intro. T. S. Eliot (London, 1961), p. x.

10. Edmund Crispin, ed., *Best Detective Stories* (London, 1959), introduction, pp. 10, 11.

11. Trollope, *Thackeray,* p. 190.

12. It is this last source of pleasure that Dryden, the first pluralist in the history of literary criticism, has in mind when defending the intricacy of English plots against the cavils of admirers of the French simplicity of construction: "You will find it infinitely pleasing to be led in a labyrinth of design, where you see some of your way before you, yet discern not the end till you arrive at it" ("An Essay of Dramatic Poesy," in *Essays of John Dryden,* ed. W. P. Ker [New York, 1961], p. 73).

13. Trollope erects "lucidity" or "intelligibility" into a major evaluative criterion, doggedly asserting that a book "intended to recreate should be easily understood—for which purpose lucid narration is essential" (*Thackeray,* p. 184). But his conception of lucidity, however odd to modern novelists and even common readers, is directly related to the kind of reader he had in mind. To be lucid—in structure and characterization as well as style, which is his immediate concern in the following excerpt—is to be "intelligible without trouble. . . . It is not sufficient that there be a meaning which may be hammered out of the sentence, but that the language should be so pellucid that the meaning should be rendered without an effort to the reader;—and not only some proportion of meaning, but the very sense, no more and no less, which the writer has intended to put into his words. . . . In matters recondite the recipient will search to see that he misses nothing, and that he takes nothing away too much. The novelist cannot expect that any such search will be made" (pp. 201-2). One of his highest commendations of Thackeray, for instance, is that "the language is always lucid. The reader, without labour, knows what he means" (p. 210). Whereas George Eliot's *Daniel Deronda* does not come up to the required standard since it contains "sentences which I have found myself compelled to read three times before I have been able to take home to myself all that the writer has intended" (p. 212). Trollope's theory of fiction thus accounts, among the rest, for his remarkably nonmetaphoric style.

14. Henry James, "Anthony Trollope," in *The Future of the Novel,* ed. Leon Edel (New York, 1956), pp. 259-60.

15. "Our history is destined in this chapter to go backwards and forwards in a very irresolute manner seemingly, and having conducted our story to to-morrow presently, we shall immediately again have occasion to step back to yesterday, so that the whole of the tale may get a hearing" (*Vanity Fair,* chap. 25). On Thackeray's handling of time see John A. Lester, Jr., "Thackeray's Narrative Technique," *PMLA* 69 (1954): 393 ff.

16. The classic description of the "novel of character"—a somewhat misleading denomination—is in Edwin Muir, *The Structure of the Novel* (London, 1960; first published 1928), pp. 23 ff.

17. These effects must have operated much more powerfully on those contemporary readers who encountered the novel in its original serial form.

18. It is in these terms that we can account for the difference between the surprise ending in the detective story, toward which we impatiently strive throughout the reading-process, and that in a picaresque, panoramic novel like Smollet's *Roderick Random,* which, though equally produced by the prior suppression of exposition, is surprising in a more startling way—being totally unprepared for and contrived merely in order to provide a happy resolution. In *Tom Jones,* which partakes of the nature of both, the ending functionally comes in between these extremes.

19. With Thackeray, as with Trollope, the playing down of this class of interests correlates with a notoriously desultory process of composition.

20. Henry James, *The Art of the Novel,* ed. R. P. Blackmur (New York, 1962), p. 321. See also his *French Poets and Novelists* (New York, 1964; first published 1878), pp. 76, 93.

21. *Père Goriot and Eugénie Grandet,* trans. E. K. Brown, Dorothea Walter, and John Watkins (New York, 1950), p. 4.

22. Henry James, *Notes on Novelists* (New York, 1914), pp. 113-14.

23. James, *French Poets and Novelists,* p. 78.

24. James, *Notes on Novelists,* pp. 138, 141.

25. Ibid., p. 109; Edel, ed., *The Future of the Novel,* p. 102.

26. See his withering criticism of H. G. Wells and Arnold Bennet's allegedly pointless "density of illustration" in "The New Novel" (*Notes on Novelists,* pp. 318 ff.). Virginia Woolf is similarly severe on these materialists in her "Modern Fiction" and "Mr. Bennet and Mrs. Brown."

27. Edel, ed., *The Future of the Novel,* p. 111.

28. James, *Notes on Novelists,* p. 119.

29. Roman Jakobson views this mode of development as a distinctive mark of realistic fiction. See "Two Aspects of Language and Two Types of Aphasic Disturbances," in Roman Jakobson and Morris Halle, *Fundamentals of Language* (The Hague, 1956), p. 78.

30. For a good compilation of quotations on the subject see Felicien Marceau, *Balzac and His World,* trans. Derek Coltman (London, 1967), pp. 371 ff.

31. To elevate the complementary relations that this essentially artistic device postulates to "demonic unities" (Erich Auerbach, *Mimesis: The Representation of Reality in Western Literature,* trans. Willard Trask [New York, 1957], pp. 416 ff.) is, I think, to take the name of the devil in vain.

32. James, *The Art of the Novel,* pp. 175–76.

33. Cf. Thackeray's presentation of Sir Francis Clavering: "To the dragoons . . . the Baronet made no overtures: it was unluckily his own regiment: he had left it on bad terms with some officers of the corps—an ugly business about a horse bargain—a disputed play account at blind-hookey—a white feather—who need ask?" And having thus gone out of his way to damn the Baronet, the omniscient narrator evades the necessity of telling us which of the proposed hypotheses is the true one (a disclosure that would compel him to forgo the effect of the others) not by pleading ignorance but under the equally transparent pretext of "Who need ask?—it is not our business to inquire too closely into the bygones of our characters, except in so far as their previous history appertains to the development of this present story" (*Pendennis,* p. 236). It is no accident that all three novelists (or for that matter, Shakespeare in his handling of Iago's motives) apply this permanent-gapping device to the evocation of evil or the characterization of sinister figures. Evil being, alas, infinitely more suggestive than good, to abstain from specifying the goodness of a character is to leave it colorless and insubstantial. And indeed, the past of Victorine, say, or Madame Couture, is duly specified.

34. See, for example, Albert Prioult's "Introduction" to *Père Goriot: La Comédie humaine* (Paris, 1948), 5:344–45.

35. James, *The Art of the Novel,* p. 37. Rastignac's postulation as dramatic and compositional center also accounts for the curious fact that the narrator announces "the end of the exposition" (p. 93) at a point where a few important scenic occasions have already taken place. For Balzac, the end of the exposition simply coincides with the hero's discovery of the truth about Goriot's antecedents, i.e., with the end of the first stage of his initiation, just as the end of the whole novel coincides with the uprooting of his last illusions about society. The similarity between this view and Freytag's theory of dramatic structure is fairly close.

36. Edel, ed., *The Future of the Novel,* p. 107. For an amusing illustration of the "realist's" interest in phenomena for their own sake, see Roman Jakobson, "Du Réalisme artistique," in *Théorie de la littérature,* ed. Tzvetan Todorov (Paris, 1965), p. 106.

37. Percy Lubock, *The Craft of Fiction* (New York, 1963; first published 1921), pp. 211–12.

38. "The moving accident, the rare conjunction, whatever it be, doesn't make the story—in the sense that the story is our excitement, our thrill and our suspense; the human emotion and the human attestation, the clustering human conditions we expect presented, only make it. The extraordinary is most extraordinary in that it happens to you and me (ibid., p. 257).

39. Nikolai Gogol, *The Diary of a Madman and Other Stories,* trans. Andrew R. MacAndrew (New York, 1960), pp. 29–30.

40. W. K. Wimsatt, *The Verbal Icon* (Lexington, Ky., 1954), pp. 69 ff.

41. *Johnson: Prose and Poetry,* ed. Mona Wilson (London, 1950), pp. 491, 492.

42. Ibid., p. 491.

43. Which is more specific in the original, with its topical allusions.

44. Balzac thus practices here what he preaches about the artist's duty to avoid springing surprises of this kind unless the reader is first given a fair chance of fathoming the mystery. See his strictures on Cooper, quoted in Maurice Bardèche, *Balzac, Romancier* (Geneva, 1967), p. 533.

45. Or, in terms of one of the wider concentric rings, the dresses of the women, which are described as "out of style; dyed and re-dyed" (p. 12).

46. But Balzac takes advantage of the list to smuggle in two other clues ("laws" and "prisons") and terminally recollocate "hotels" and "prisons."

47. This metaphorical collocation, it emerges in retrospect, also prefigures the "handy-dandy"

theme of the novel: in the corrupt society of Paris the judge is indeed often no better than a criminal. See section VII of this chapter.

48. As can be inferred from his avant-propos to the *Comédie humaine* (1842), Balzac was obsessed with the correspondence between the human and animal order; but one should be thankful that his practice is subtler than his theory. *Père Goriot* (1834) was dedicated to Geoffroy Saint-Hilaire, the biologist whose theses he publicly adopted eight years later.

49. In "Les Métaphores animales dans *Le Père Goriot*" (*L'Année Balzacienne*, 1963, 91–105), Léon-François Hoffman, treating the whole animal imagery as if it were simultaneously present, analyzes its overall statistical distribution among the different characters rather than its actual distribution along the textual sequence. The interpretative, semantic consequences of this typical hindsight fallacy—this time on the verbal level (as with Odysseus's progressive epithets) as well as the referential (as with Odysseus's traits)—are particularly instructive. It leads to the distortion of some crucial points that turn either on developments in the reader's knowledge (e.g., to the view of high society, on numerical grounds, as favorably contrasted with the pension) or on developments in the represented action (e.g., to the view of Rastignac as just another animal rather than an initially nonbestial being gradually invested with animal features). One can hardly exaggerate the need for using statistics in literary studies according to dynamic (or distributive) as well as static (or distributional) criteria.

50. Rastignac's postulation as the focus of the narration throughout the action proper retrospectively illuminates the principles of selection operating in the exposition, which indeed contains little information Rastignac could not have been aware of at the time. See also n. 35 above.

51. One measure of his deterioration is that from the moment he makes up his mind to crash into society he is recurrently projected in terms of animal imagery—e.g., eel (p. 131), horse (p. 143), snake (p. 225)—significantly absent from his expositional presentation.

52. That is why Balzac must keep Rastignac at the pension to the end and is driven to invent ingenious pretexts to explain why the squeamish youth does not leave it in the days of his prosperity (e.g., pp. 156–57).

53. James, "The Art of Fiction," in Edel, ed., *The Future of the Novel*, p. 17.

CHAPTER EIGHT

1. See Chapter 2, n. 29 above. The analysis and classifications here follow the lines proposed in my "Delicate Balance in the Story of the Rape of Dinah: Biblical Narrative and the Rhetoric of the Narrative Text," *Hasifrut* 4 (1973), where temporal ordering is placed within an outlined framework of literary rhetoric.

2. Shipley's *Dictionary of World Literature* (Paterson, N.J., 1962).

3. The term *motivation* is used in a sense similar to this by the Russian Formalists (see especially Tomashevsky in *Russian Formalist Criticism: Four Essays*, ed. Lee T. Lemon and Marion J. Reis [Lincoln, 1965], pp. 78 ff.). The notion itself originates in the neglected Art-Nature distinction of the *Poetics* and is often alluded to (e.g., as "dissimulation") in James's critical writings.

4. Nikolai Gogol, *Dead Souls*, trans. Bernard Guilbert Guerney (New York, 1948), p. 273.

5. The "realistic" motivation, accordingly, does not necessarily have to be strictly verisimilar but only quasi-mimetic in the sense I have defined. For instance, the emergence of exposition concerning Odysseus in and through the divine assembly scenes on Olympus is no less realistically motivated than the emergence of similar material through the Ithacan assembly or Telemachus's exchanges with his various hosts.

6. That the realistic motivation is designed to disguise rather than replace the aesthetic becomes conspicuous whenever the narrator chooses to lay bare the artistic function underlying the quasi-mimetic device. This may be done in the bluntest manner, as when Trollope indicates the expositional function of Lady de Guest's letter to John Eames by the prefatory comment that "the nature of some of the barriers [to Eames's marriage] may possibly be made intelligible to my readers by the following letter" (*The Last Chronicle of Barset*, chap. 15); or more subtly, as when Fielding's discussions of the artistic ends achieved through his practice of chapter division highlight the segmental functions of his two complementary but quasi-mimetic segmental devices.

7. Joseph Conrad, *Under Western Eyes,* opening of part 2. In fact, the aesthetic motivation underlying this procedure is Conrad's wish to direct the reader to integrate the novel in spatial as well as linear terms. Joyce's *A Portrait of An Artist As a Young Man* and Faulkner's *The Unvanquished* are constructed on the same principle, but minus the quasi-mimetic motivation.

8. As can be seen from Booth's examples (*The Rhetoric of Fiction* [Chicago, 1961], p. 155), the two denotations of the term by no means necessarily overlap. Thus, unlike Booth, I consider Huckleberry Finn and the barber in Ring Lardner's "Haircut" to be self-conscious narrators in that they are respectively conscious of an external and an internal audience.

9. Miguel de Cervantes, *Don Quixote,* trans. Peter Motteux (New York, 1950), pp. 460, 54–55.

10. This confusion vitiates, for example, Norman Friedman's "Point of View in Fiction: The Development of a Critical Concept," *PMLA* 70 (1955): 1160–84. Even Booth categorically lays down that "the omniscient narrator [to whom he has significantly referred as "author" three lines above] is obviously not bewildered" (p. 45).

11. Henry James, *The Art of the Novel,* ed. R. P. Blackmur (New York, 1962), p. 327. Or from the reader's viewpoint: the narrator is reconstructed and characterized in terms of the presentational modes employed.

12. This distinction between two kinds of narrator was first suggested, in another context, in M. Perry and M. Sternberg, "The King through Ironic Eyes," *Hasifrut* 1 (1968): 288 ff.

13. Robert Scholes and Robert Kellog (*The Nature of Narrative* [New York, 1968], pp. 240–41) claim that the quality of irony is built into the narrative form owing to the different viewpoints it necessarily involves. As I try to show, however, it is preferable to conceive of these "viewpoints" as necessary components of the overall point of view in the text. Cf. also Booth, pp. 155–59.

14. Drama involves and poetry often involves only three components (no distinct narrator and no characters, respectively) and hence only three relationships; therefore, they are by nature considerably less amenable to complex manipulations of informational discrepancies than narrative, which may of course also introduce secondary or even tertiary narrators and audiences by framing techniques corresponding to the play-within-a-play.

15. Walker Gibson, "Authors, Speakers, Readers, and Mock Readers," *College English* 11 (1950): 265–66. Wolfgang Iser's more recent *The Implied Reader* (Baltimore, 1974) has many interesting things to say on the problem, but I find some of his views of reader and reading-process basically unacceptable—such as the very introduction of "first" and "second" reading as a dimension of the reading-process and the realization of the time sequence (e.g., pp. 280–81) rather than (as I see it) as a hopelessly subjective factor that is quite incidental to literary theory and interpretation.

16. Rebecca Price Parkins, "Alexander Pope's Use of the Implied Dramatic Speaker," *College English* 10 (1949): 137.

17. For an excellent discussion of Fielding's different projections of his personality see Booth, *The Rhetoric of Fiction,* pp. 71–73.

18. For some representative excerpts concerning the pros and cons of this issue see George L. Barnett's anthology *Eighteenth-Century British Novelists on the Novel* (New York, 1968), pp. 22, 41, 72–73, 99–100, 112, 165–66, 171.

19. Cf. R. S. Crane, "The Concept of Plot and the Plot of *Tom Jones,*" in *Critics and Criticism,* ed. R. S. Crane (Chicago, 1952), pp. 643–45.

20. James, *The Art of the Novel,* p. 68.

21. Ian Watt, *The Rise of the Novel* (Harmondsworth, 1963), pp. 264, 289.

22. But these relations may vary in other respects, notably normative attitude.

23. Owing to doctrinal disparities or historical changes in hierarchies of value and interest, this sometimes leads to readers finding gaps or being accused of inventing pseudo-gaps where none have been intended by the text. A notorious case in point is the kind of questions raised by A. C. Bradley in the appendices to *Shakespearean Tragedy,* which the New Critics furiously attacked as a portrait-gallery view of Shakespeare's characters and which their successors treat much more sympathetically.

24. I discount of course the discrepancies in knowledge between different characters, without which few dramatic actions could exist.

25. As Trollope's allusion to *The Comedy of Errors* suggests, this is usually the auditor's posi-

tion in Shakespeare's comedies too. For a discussion of Shakespeare's exploitation of different levels of awareness, see Bertrand Evans, *Shakespeare's Comedies* (Oxford, 1960).

26. Walter Allen, *The English Novel* (Harmondsworth, 1960), pp. 213-14.

27. "Charles Dickens," in *The Works of Edgar Allan Poe* (New York, n.d.), 7:36. Interestingly enough, Poe goes on to say that it was precisely the omniscient narrator's evident reluctance to state Rudge's death on his own authority that immediately led him to the conclusion that the steward, far from murdered, is himself the murderer (pp. 37 ff.).

CHAPTER NINE

1. Wayne C. Booth, *The Rhetoric of Fiction* (Chicago, 1961), p. 254.

2. Or in a related modern form of unselfconscious narrative: why should the dying Malone decide "to remind [him]self briefly of [his] present state before embarking on [his] stories"? (Samuel Beckett, *Malone Dies*, in *Three Novels* [New York, 1965], p. 182).

3. Even in such serious recent studies as Wolfgang Iser's *The Implied Reader* (Baltimore, 1974) and Boris Uspensky's *A Poetics of Composition* (Berkeley and Los Angeles, 1973).

4. On Molly Bloom, see Franz Stanzel, *Narrative Situations in the Novel*, trans. James P. Pusack (Bloomington, 1971), p. 137; on Faulkner's trio, see Iser, *The Implied Reader*, p. 135.

5. James, *The Art of the Novel*, p. 321; Stanzel, *Narrative Situations in the Novel*, p. 61.

6. René Wellek and Austin Warren, *Theory of Literature* (New York, 1956), p. 213. For some further discussion see M. Perry and M. Sternberg, "The King through Ironic Eyes," *Hasifrut* 1 (1968): 288 ff.

7. Leon Edel, *The Modern Psychological Novel* (New York, 1964), pp. 14-15.

8. James, *The Art of the Novel*, p. 89. All future references, in this chapter, to the collection of prefaces will be incorporated in the text.

9. Norman Friedman, "Point of View in Fiction: The Development of a Critical Concept," *PMLA* 70 (1955): 1177-78.

10. Robert Scholes and Robert Kellog, *The Nature of Narrative* (New York, 1968), pp. 272, 273.

11. Cf. Fielding's own metaphor of enlightened tyrant and subjects.

12. "At least," because the vessel of consciousness and the narrator-agent, though equally restricted, may be opposed in self-consciousness. It is this motivational factor that should warn us against confusing the vessel (including Joyce's or Faulkner's directly "quoted" interior monologists) with the standard narrator, whether omniscient or restricted. To describe him as "narrator"—as Booth doctrinally does, in his reaction to classifications of point of view according to "person"—is to rectify a typological limitation at the cost not only of a semantic wrenching but the blurring of a vital distinction. James himself distinguishes the vessel from the narrator proper by referring to him as "non-narrator" (*The Notebooks of Henry James*, ed. F. O. Matthiessen and Kenneth B. Murdock [New York, 1961], p. 308).

13. Henry James, "The Art of Fiction" in *The Future of the Novel*, ed. Leon Edel (New York, 1956), p. 15.

14. *The Notebooks of Henry James*, pp. 295, 349, 375.

15. Gustav Freytag, *Technique of the Drama*, trans. Elias J. MacEwan (Chicago, 1908; first published 1863), p. 120.

16. See, for example, A. A. Mendilow, *Time and the Novel* (London, 1952), p. 106.

17. *The Complete Tales of Henry James*, ed. Leon Edel, 12 vols. (London, 1963), 1:272-79.

18. It is thus natural that a host of memories, composing a "little retrospect," should crowd in upon the narrator in "Louisa Pallant" (1888) once he spots an old flame of his (*The Notebooks of Henry James*, p. 74 n.).

19. *The Notebooks of Henry James*, p. 236; James, *The Art of the Novel*, p. 137.

20. *The Letters of Henry James*, ed. Percy Lubbock, 2 vols. (London, 1920), 1:330.

21. Ibid., p. 326.

22. For a fine discussion of the Jamesian vessel, from a somewhat different viewpoint, see Dorothea Krook, *The Ordeal of Consciousness in Henry James* (Cambridge, 1962), pp. 15 ff., 399 ff.

23. "Gustave Flaubert," in Edel, ed., *The Future of the Novel,* pp. 138, 137.

24. Ibid., pp. 142, 143.

25. James ruefully avows that he sometimes transgressed the bounds of probability in this regard. The telegraphist in *In the Cage,* for instance, "is, for verisimilitude . . . too ardent a focus of divination"; and he was driven to this excess only because otherwise "the phenomena detailed would have lacked their principle of cohesion" (p. 157).

26. *Letters,* 1:330.

27. Ibid., p. 296.

28. The close connection between the exigencies of rhetorical control and the recourse to that particular variety of the realistically deformed order of presentation that I called "order of discovery" is pointed out in Part 5 of Stevenson's *The Master of Ballantrae,* where the narrator motivates his sudden departure from his usual procedure of retrospective (and hence essentially chronological) narration: "Where [the Master] went, or what he did, we never concerned ourselves to ask until next day. If we had done so, and by any chance found out, it might have changed all. But as all we did was done in ignorance, and should be so judged, I shall so narrate these passages as they appeared to us in the moment of their birth, and reserve all that I since discovered for the time of its discovery. For I have now come to one of the dark parts of my narrative, and must engage the reader's indulgence for my patron." The implications of this comment obviously apply to omniscient as well as restricted narration.

29. The principles of Jamesian poetics traced throughout this chapter are illustrated in action in my "Expositional Modes and Order of Presentation in Fiction" (Ph.D. diss., Jerusalem, 1971), pp. 299-431.

INDEX